Patagonian Prehistory

Patagonian Prehistory

Human Ecology and Cultural Evolution in the Land of Giants

RAVEN GARVEY

THE UNIVERSITY OF UTAH PRESS
Salt Lake City

The Defiance House Man colophon is a registered trademark
of the University of Utah Press. It is based upon a four-foot-tall,
Ancient Puebloan pictograph (late PIII) near Glen Canyon, Utah.

Library of Congress Cataloging-in-Publication Data

Names: Garvey, Raven, author.
Title: Patagonian prehistory : human ecology and cultural evolution in the land of giants / by Raven
    Garvey.
Description: Salt Lake City : University of Utah Press, [2021] | Includesbibliographical references and
    index.
Identifiers: LCCN 2020042475 | ISBN 9781647690267 (cloth)
Subjects: LCSH: Hunting and gathering societies—Patagonia (Argentina and Chile) | Human ecology—
    Patagonia (Argentina and Chile) | Social evolution. | Excavations (Archaeology)—Patagonia
    (Argentina and Chile) | Paleo-Indians—Patagonia (Argentina and Chile) | Patagonia (Argentina and
    Chile)—Antiquities.
Classification: LCC F2821.1.P29 G37 2021 | DDC 982/.7—DC23
LC record available at https://lccn.loc.gov/2020042475

Errata and further information on this and other titles available at UofUpress.com.

To B. T. Garvey, Jr. (1948–2017),
my original giant.

∾

Contents

Figures

Tables

Preface

Patagonia's centrality to hunter-gatherer theory is clear to anyone who has ever worked there. Archaeological research in the region contributes significantly to our understanding of major issues in anthropology and archaeology, including large-scale human migrations, the limits of our adaptive flexibility, and origins of food production. In fact, it is a region *without which* our understanding of these issues is detrimentally incomplete. Still, relative to regions historically at the heart of transformative research on Holocene foragers—places like Australia and western North America, which have inspired some of the most profound contributions to hunter-gatherer theory—Patagonia's importance has been underappreciated on the world stage. This book aims to reposition Patagonia as an essential testing ground for pivotal hypotheses relating to hunter-gatherers, human ecology, and cultural evolution.

Patagonia is so large and diverse a place, both ecologically and culturally, that any summary of its prehistory necessarily ignores a lot of excellent and interesting work. This might be particularly true in the present case. What's presented is a critical synthesis of Patagonian prehistory—from initial colonization to European contact—but, rather than attempting a comprehensive summary of the last 13,000+ years, this book focuses on three key periods to articulate the region's archaeological record with longstanding debates in the field. Intervening periods are certainly also relevant to anthropological theory and, in fact, there is a growing recognition among archaeologists that many archaeological phenomena are best understood in light of the adaptations, cultural manifestations, and landscape modifications

that preceded them (Laland and O'Brien 2010; Zeder 2015). I have attended to this as feasible but, still, much of the time between focal periods is given short shrift. My hope is that what is lost in scope is gained in depth.

This book takes distinct theoretical and methodological approaches to Patagonian records and historical debates. Notably, I have drawn data from the region's extensive literature—including my own research there over the last 15 years—and analyzed them from a Darwinian perspective. Chapter 3 provides a detailed account of this perspective but, in brief, *Darwinian* refers here to theories that explain large-scale phenomena (e.g., cultural change) in terms of processes acting at the scale of individual people (Bettinger et al. 2015:187). In the decades since its introduction, this perspective has afforded compelling, instructive and, sometimes, refreshingly counterintuitive explanations of archaeological data. This book combines classic and innovative Darwinian social science approaches to provide an alternative view of Patagonian prehistory and to generate novel hypotheses whose implications extend well beyond southern South America.

This book is also distinct in its attempt to blend two often-separated Darwinian theories, one that focuses on individuals' cost-benefit decision-making and another that centers on systems of cultural inheritance. The first is a powerful means of identifying *motivations* for behavioral and cultural change and the second, of understanding the *mechanisms* of change. Many anthropologists inclined towards evolutionary approaches elect one or the other of these, but it is my belief (and my training) that foraging theory and cultural transmission are not only compatible but, in fact, mutually essential to our understanding of human behaviors and cultural expressions, past and present.

It is probably clear that I had theoretically-oriented archaeologists in mind when I wrote this book. However, they are not the only intended audience, and I have assumed no prior familiarity with the particular theories that guide my work. There is much here for scholars more generally interested in South American and world prehistory, hunter-gatherers, and cross-cultural comparison, for graduate and advanced undergraduate students of anthropology and archaeology, and for interested members of the general public. Patagonia is undeniably captivating and inspiring, and a corner of the Holocene hunter-gatherer world whose archaeological record we cannot afford to ignore.

Acknowledgments

Many people contributed in important ways to this book's development. Here at the start, special recognition is due the five who read and provided extensive feedback on the entire draft manuscript. For their heroic efforts, I thank (alphabetically) Bob Bettinger, Bob Kelly, Francisco Mena, James O'Connell, and John Speth. Their insights, suggestions, criticisms, and self-described "musings" helped me think through thorny issues, clarify particular arguments, and avoid foolish errors. They also inspired me to think about where next to take some of the ideas introduced here. I am incredibly grateful for their careful attention and advice. This book is far the better for it.

From my very first days as his student, Bob Bettinger has been unfailingly generous with his time and guidance. He has helped me become a better thinker, writer, and anthropologist, and—in ways both direct and subtle—he has contributed to the ideas presented here. Others of the UC Davis faculty certainly also influenced my thinking, Bruce Winterhalder, Pete Richerson, and Richard McElreath in particular. It was an exciting time to be at UC Davis (2005–2012), as the confluence of two Darwinian approaches—human behavioral ecology and cultural transmission/dual inheritance theory—bubbled furiously with ideas and activity. I had the great fortune of overlapping with some truly gifted archaeologists as well—Trine Johansen, Loukas Barton, Shannon Tushingham, and Chris Morgan—who encouraged me, challenged me, and helped to me see things in new ways. Their imprint is evident here, too.

Likewise, I am hugely grateful to my Patagonian colleagues for all of the many ways they have contributed to this book and my scholarship more generally. For their support, collaboration, and friendship, I owe special thanks to Ramiro Barberena, Francisco Mena, Carina Llano, Víctor Dúran, Valeria Cortegoso, César Méndez, and Amalia Nuevo Delaunay.

Bob Kelly may be largely unaware of a second way in which he influenced this book's development: It was in the context of a 2015 symposium in his honor (80th Annual Meeting of the Society for American Archaeology, San Francisco) that I first presented the germ of the "clothing hypothesis" that features prominently in this book (preliminarily published in a resulting volume [Garvey 2018b]). Bob was the session discussant and his reaction to my paper encouraged me to develop the hypothesis further.

I will forever be indebted to my R guru, Andy Marshall, for sacrificing his own research time and energy to provide absolutely indispensable help in producing the data figures. Truly, there might not have *been* any figures without him. UMMAA Illustrator John Klausmeyer talked me down from the ledge each time I fought with my vector graphics program. He also supplied the base map I used throughout the book, created Figure 4.3, and provided timely advice and moral support. UM undergraduate Emily Wolfe produced Figure 4.2 (thanks, Emily!). UMMAA Editor Elizabeth Knoll provided helpful feedback and skilled technical editing before the manuscript went out for review. Many thanks to UM undergraduate Robert Snell for his unwavering enthusiasm as he compiled data on protohistoric and historic clothing, and graduate student Jenny Larios for all of her help combing the Patagonian literature for radiocarbon dates. Thanks to Kriszti Fehervary, my writing companion during the "big push" summer, and to my colleagues in West Hall for their support and engagement with my scholarship. I thank the University of Utah Press's staff for deftly shepherding this manuscript through the production process, and Reba Rauch in particular for all of her help, advice, and patience.

My fieldwork and analyses have been funded by grants and fellowship from the National Science Foundation, Fulbright Scholar Program, University of Michigan (College of Literature, Science, and the Arts; Office of Research; and ADVANCE program), Consejo Nacional de Investigaciones Científicas y Técnicas, and University of California, Davis (Department of Anthropology, Office of Graduate Studies, Consortium for Women and Research, Hemispheric Institute for the Americas, and Institute of Government Affairs). The University of Michigan Office of Research and College of Literature, Science, and the Arts awarded a generous publication subvention to offset this book's production costs.

My kin have been so tremendously supportive and patient through this process. To Julie, Bart, Connell, Trine, Phil, Brenda, Sara, Will, Nick, and Ali, my deepest gratitude. Nearly-three-year-old Lex has kept me, in turns, grounded and distracted—both very helpful in their way. Finally, none of this would have been possible without the encouragement and support of my amazing husband, Andy Marshall (*terima kasih banyak, suamiku*).

Patagonian Prehistory

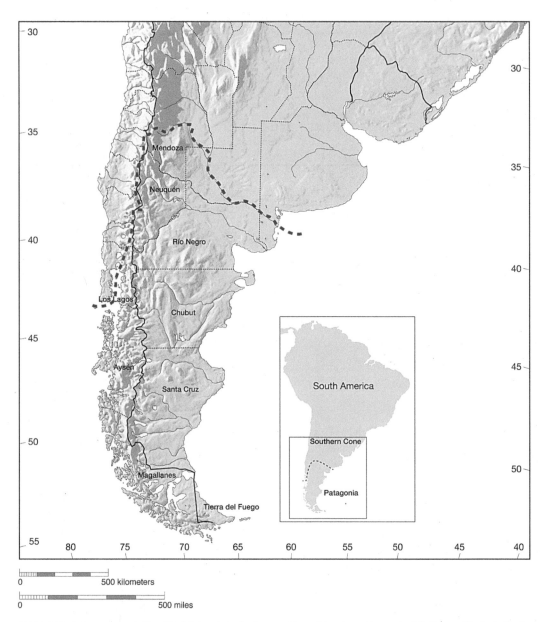

FIGURE 1.1. Patagonia as defined in this book, including southern Mendoza, Neuquén, Río Negro, Chubut, Santa Cruz, and Tierra del Fuego Provinces in Argentina, and southern Los Lagos, Aysén, and Magallanes Regions of Chile. Please see Chapter 2 for more details.

1

Patagonian Giants

This wonderful relationship in the same continent between the dead and the living, will, I do not doubt, hereafter throw more light on the appearance of organic beings on our earth, and their disappearance from it, than any other class of facts.

—Charles Darwin (1839:173)

The diversity of life in Patagonia's rugged outback has intrigued evolution-minded scientists since the early 1800s. Among them, giants: Charles Darwin and George Gaylord Simpson observed things during Patagonian expeditions that inspired some of their most profound contributions to evolutionary theory. It is that kind of place.

Patagonia is a land of paradoxes. Rubbed raw by the wind and seemingly barren, it harbors a curious—if cryptic—abundance of life. It constitutes the southern extreme of the so-called *Southern Cone* of South America, the relatively narrow, tapering projection of land between 34° and 55° southern latitude (Figure 1.1). Its ~1,000,000 km² (~620,000 mi²) are tremendously diverse, with a steep and tortuous Pacific coastline, a glacier-honed stretch of the Southern Andes Cordillera, dense rainforests, windswept moors, scrubby plateaus, desertic steppes, and an Atlantic coastal plain. Patagonia is temporally diverse, too. It is a highly dynamic landscape, with glaciers that grow and subside, coastlines that expand and contract with changes in global sea level, and rivers whose channels meander, changing course over time. Volcanoes erupt, faults slip, earth flows, tsunamis break. These dynamics affected prehistoric peoples' use of the landscape. Likewise, the changing landscape shapes our archaeological understanding of Patagonia's human past.

Patagonia is multidimensionally heterogeneous and, as we will see, culturally diverse, too.

Nevertheless, *Patagonia* is a meaningful unit of cultural analysis, in part because it is one of relatively few world regions where people neither engaged in food production to any significant degree nor developed pronounced sociopolitical hierarchies, living instead as relatively egalitarian, committed hunter-gatherers until the nineteenth century. This despite the fact that Patagonian groups lived in the shadow of the largest precolumbian agrarian state in the New World—perhaps in the *entire* world at that time—the Inca Empire. It is also the farthest place to which people traveled from eastern Siberia during New World colonization at the end of the last Ice Age. For these reasons, and because it is generally considered marginal for human habitation, studying the human past in Patagonia can help us better understand human adaptive capacities and the ways ecological, demographic, and social factors interact to influence cultural evolution.

Giants in Patagonia

Patagonia's diversity captivated a young Charles Darwin on his maiden voyage as a naturalist. As the HMS *Beagle* sailed around southernmost South America, making stops along the way, Darwin collected and wrote extensively about a wide variety of insects, marine invertebrates, birds, and mammals, noting the ways each seemed suited to its particular habitat. In fact, though, some remarkable *similarities* between "the dead and the living"—the fossil and extant forms of related creatures referred to in this chapter's epigraph—may have been the germ of his theory of evolution by natural selection.

The first of these similarities struck Darwin in 1832 near the start of his South American tour, while the *Beagle* was anchored off Bahía Blanca, 643.7 km (400 mi) southwest of Buenos Aires, Argentina. It was there he unearthed fossils of extinct ground sloths (*Megatherium*), giant armadillos (glyptodonts), and a camel-like ungulate (*Macrauchenia*), which not only intrigued him in their novelty (most were previously unknown to science), but also struck him as startlingly familiar. They resembled the living tree sloths, armadillos, and guanaco he encountered day to day at his ports of call (Darwin 1839; Quammen 2009).

A few months later, another encounter, this time off the northeast coast of Patagonia, made a similar impression on Darwin. By chance he observed a distinct variety of the ostrich-like ratites (*Rhea* spp.) he had seen farther north. He noted that the two forms, now known as the greater or American rhea (*Rhea americana*) and the lesser or Darwin's rhea (*Rhea pennata*), were very similar but for their different average sizes and the fact that they had distinct geographic ranges (Darwin 1839; Quammen 2009).

At first Darwin's Patagonian observations and his Bahía Blanca fossil finds only intrigued him; he seems not to have had any real inkling of evolutionary mechanisms at that point. But these ideas fermented as the *Beagle* continued south, through the Strait of Magellan and up the west coast of South America, eventually arriving at the Galápagos Islands where he met the famous finches with their finely tuned beaks. Certainly his Galápagos observations were influential, too, but the diversity and distribution, both temporal (e.g., extinct versus extant forms of armadillos) and spatial (e.g., *Rhea* distributions), and striking similarities between far-flung Patagonian species contributed significantly to his understanding of "descent with modification," eventually laid out in *On the Origin of Species by Means of Natural Selection* (Darwin 1859; Quammen 2009).

On the Origin of Species was an immediate success, and Darwin's general theory of evolution was accepted within his lifetime. His argument for its primary mechanism—natural selection—was not, however. Resistance to natural selection was primarily due to its anti-progressivism, the idea that evolution is not "goal oriented" or directed toward the perfection of a structure or species. It also struck some as implausible that so "weak" a force, so relatively slow or subtle a process, could account for the tremendous diversity of life on Earth. Gregor Mendel, whose now famous experiments with pea plants demonstrated selection at work, was a contemporary of Darwin's, but his writings remained obscure until the early 1900s. As it was, then, skepticism regarding evolution by natural selection persisted into the 1920s and 1930s, when a group of statistically adept biologists and geneticists including R. A. Fisher, J. B. S. Haldane, and Sewall Wright united Darwin's theory of evolution and principles of genetic inheritance in a mathematical framework, demonstrating how natural selection can carry an advantageous variant through a population over time. There remained a rift, though, between microevolution as studied by biologists and geneticists and macroevolution as studied by paleontologists, most of whom did not accept that microscale mechanisms (e.g., natural selection) could account for large-scale phenomena (e.g., speciation).

Between 1930 and 1934, almost exactly 100 years after Darwin's voyage aboard the *Beagle*, another evolutionary giant, George Gaylord Simpson, made two paleontological expeditions to Patagonia that contributed to the bridging of the rift between micro- and macroevolution. In Patagonia, Simpson made careful observations of the diversity and distribution of extinct mammals and hypothesized their intercontinental migrations (Olson 1991). These observations, his meticulous taxonomic analyses, and his mathematical proclivities led Simpson to accept what other paleontologists of the time would not: that the same microevolutionary mechanism observed by laboratory geneticists could explain macroevolutionary trends observed in the paleontological record. Simpson's seminal contribution to the so-called modern evolutionary synthesis (*sensu* Huxley 1942) begun by the likes of Fisher, Haldane, and Wright was a book called *Tempo and Mode in Evolution* (Simpson 1944), which demonstrated that models of evolution by natural selection accurately predict the nondirectional, irregular branching patterns seen in the fossil record.

In this book, I use principles and methods developed by Darwin, Simpson, and the "modern synthesists" to understand the ecology and cultural evolution of another class of giant—the "Patagones." This is what Ferdinand Magellan and his men called the "race of giants" they claimed to have encountered in 1520, likely in Aónikenk (southern Tehuelche) territory (Fondebrider 2003). As described by crew member Antonio Pigafetta, these people were twice the size of Magellan's mostly Spanish crew, and Magellan himself referred to them as "Patagão" (or Patagón or Patagoni; Figure 1.2). The word's etymology is disputed, but it was long thought to derive from *pata*, Spanish for leg or foot, so *Patagón* might mean "big foot/long legs" and, by extension, *Patagonia*, the "land of giants." As it happens, Magellan might have been referring, instead, to an obscure literary figure (Doura 2011; Munday 1619) but Patagón nonetheless became synonymous with "giant" and the lore of Patagonian behemoths persisted for centuries. Reliable documentation of Aónikenk height is hard to come by but, by some accounts, they were indeed taller than the average European of the time (Fondebrider 2003), perhaps six feet on average, which, while certainly tall by sixteenth-century standards was only half the height sometimes claimed.

Incidentally, it is hard to grow a big body if calories and nutrients are in short supply (de Onis and Blössner 2003), even when one is genetically predisposed, so it seems the story of Patagonian giants is at odds with the notion that Patagonia is a windswept wasteland—another Patagonian paradox, and precisely the sort of problem that the Darwinian/New Synthesis paradigm is designed to address, at the intersection of ecology, demography, and culture.

Cultural Diversity Across Space and Through Time

Patagonia is sometimes perceived as a land forgotten by time, and the Patagones—the Tehuelche (Aónikenk, Gununa'Kena, and Mecharnúekenk), Selk'nam (Ona), Manek'enk (Haush), Yámana (Yaghan), and Káwesqar (Alacaluf)—little changed from their colonizing ancestors of the last Ice Age (Salemme and Miotti 2008). Darwin's own reaction to a group of Yámana seems to reflect this sentiment: "The astonishment which I felt on first seeing a party of Fuegians on a wild and broken shore will never be forgotten by me, for the reflection at once rushed into my mind—such were our ancestors" (Darwin 1871:405). Perhaps if Darwin had observed artifacts in the Bahía Blanca stratigraphic profiles, he would have appreciated that Patagonian cultures had changed at least as much and likely much more than the armadillos and sloths.

Despite his current stature as an observant and thoughtful scientist, Darwin was a product of his time, and his perception was a common one in the 1830s. In fact, even into the early decades of the twentieth century the predominant belief among anthropologists was that "savages" like the Yámana were "unevolved" cultural laggards but that, given enough time and sufficient impetus, they, too, would inevitably progress towards a higher state of being (i.e., "civilization"). It really was not until the 1920s and 1930s that archaeologists came to appreciate Native Americans' developmental past and to see change-through-time as a valid topic of study (Bettinger et al. 2015). Even then, though, the tendency was to assume a level of cultural constancy that made ethnographic records a reliable source of information for interpreting archaeological records through homology or analogy. Since then, many hands have been wrung over the "tyranny of the ethnographic record" (Wobst 1978), and most of us now use analogy more responsibly than during the heyday of the direct historical approach (*sensu* Strong 1929). So, while this chapter's epigraph might seem to subtly endorse freewheeling use of ethnographic

FIGURE 1.2. Historical (1764) drawing of the "Patagones" as they were perceived by Europeans. (Original housed at the Museo Histórico Nacional de Argentina; image in the public domain and obtained through Wikimedia Commons on June 14, 2018; file name "Habits of the Patagoniansin—Patagón—1764.JPG")

analogy, in fact I meant it only to highlight Patagonian's centrality to the development of Darwin's evolutionary insights.

It is nonetheless true that I believe, as Darwin did, that comparisons through time and across space can teach us much about the processes that shaped particular cultural expressions and that led to global patterns of cultural similarity and difference. Rather than basing our inferences of past behaviors strictly on ethnographic accounts, however, I believe archaeologists should aim to identify behavioral diversity unique to the prehistoric past—that is, diversity without ethnographic analog. To do this, we must identify and analyze potential *sources* of prehistoric diversity; understanding causal relationships and mechanisms of change will help us interpret archaeological records in their own terms. These relationships and mechanisms are environmental, demographic, and cultural. Many such causal relationships and mechanisms of change have been modeled and rigorously tested in laboratories and at field sites, both by anthropologists and in other disciplines. The effects of some sources of diversity, then, can be predicted with reasonable confidence, at least to a first approximation (Garvey 2018b).

But cultural diversity is also a product of less predictable interactions among variables and of stochastic events, which is what makes comparison such a valuable tool in archaeology. As we will see in the coming chapters, environmental variables sometimes accurately predict basic elements of behavior (e.g., relative mobility); challenges posed and opportunities presented by the environment certainly influence adaptive aspects of culture. However, if, through cross cultural comparison, we find a striking contrast in, say, technological complexity between groups living in very similar environments, we probably need a more nuanced hypothesis (Chapter 3). For this, we can draw on the modern evolutionary synthesis and more recent applications of modern synthetic ideas to human behavior and cultural evolution (e.g., Boyd and Richerson 1985; Cavalli-Sforza and Feldman 1981; Richerson and Boyd 2005). This approach, recall, is based on formal

(mathematical) modeling, which allows us to approach even nuanced causal relationships in a principled way, identifying variables we think might be relevant and explicitly modeling their effects. That is, we can predict *what, theoretically, should be* under the specified circumstances and compare these predictions to our empirical data (*what, actually*), and in this way iteratively refine our understanding of the past.

Modeling and cross-cultural comparison are indispensable to the observational sciences (e.g., archaeology, paleontology, astronomy). Ours is not an experimental science (e.g., evolutionary biology, genetics, experimental psychology), and we can neither induce cultural evolution under controlled conditions nor replay (pre)history to observe cause and effect in real time. Yet, as Simpson demonstrated during the modern evolutionary synthesis, well-conceived models and comparative analyses are analogous tools in the observational scientist's kit. Moreover, archaeology, like paleontology, deals in real-world, long-run outcomes of evolutionary processes that can differ from laboratory-based, short-term ones, and understanding these is equally central to a robust evolutionary theory. So, just as Darwin was inspired by the "intoxicating array of foreign cultures and ecosystems" he encountered in his travels (Yannielli 2013:417), this book is likewise animated by comparison, and for similar reasons: I believe cultural comparisons across space and through time, and of empirical data to modeled expectations, are our best means of identifying causal relationships and mechanisms of change. Ultimately, comparison will help us better understand cultural evolution and cultural diversity, past and present.

Charting Our Course

This book's approach to Patagonian prehistory is broadly chronological, exploring three important periods between the Pleistocene colonization and the ethnographic present. Each chapter unpacks an intriguing, and often controversial, aspect of Patagonian prehistory and relates it to longstanding questions in anthropology and archaeology. As the following chapters attest, studies of human ecology and cultural evolution in Patagonia have global-scale implications because they can help us identify causal relationships and mechanisms of change that are relevant to those broader spatial and temporal scales.

To realize this potential, we need detailed information about Patagonia's physical environment. *Chapter 2: Environment and Ecology* provides data related to past and present Patagonian climates, physical geography, and resources, all with an eye towards their effects on the density and distribution of human populations. The discussion transcends "supply side" economics (e.g., availability of calories and nutrients) to include the "demand side," or the energetic constraints imposed by Patagonia's challenging environment (e.g., extremes of altitude and temperature, which can increase basal metabolism). A general theme running through the chapter is the paradox I mentioned above: Patagonia is often described as a harsh environment, marginal for human habitation (e.g., Salemme and Miotti 2008; Saxon 1976), yet several lines of evidence suggest this may not have been true prehistorically. Among these lines of evidence is a database of nearly 2,000 Patagonian radiocarbon dates, presented in Chapter 2's final section, which indicate denser and more sustained human occupations than might be expected if Patagonia were truly marginal.

This "productivity paradox," if you will, is less puzzling when assessed using evolutionary principles and methods. *Chapter 3: The Evolutionary Perspective* attends to three basic questions: (1) What is an evolutionary perspective? (2) How can an evolutionary perspective help us understand prehistory? and (3) Which specific models are most useful for addressing questions about Patagonian prehistory posed in this book? The brief answer to the first question, amplified in Chapter 3, is that an evolutionary perspective sees "macro-level phenomena [e.g., cultural change] as the cumulative consequence of explicitly defined processes [e.g., natural selection, biased transmission] . . . acting on a micro level, specifically on reproductive individuals"

(Bettinger et al. 2015:187). That is, as Simpson argued for the paleontological record, the same mechanisms hypothesized to govern cultural change on short timescales (e.g., learning biases) can explain patterns we see in the archaeological record. However, as Simpson also argued, to make use of this fact—to advance our understanding of Patagonian prehistory specifically, and cultural evolution more generally—we must first formalize our expectations about human behaviors and cultural change under specific circumstances (i.e., define appropriate models). One benefit to this approach is that it helps us distill the unnumbered complexities of reality to a tractable number of abstractions and to, thereby, identify variables central to a particular outcome (Friedman 1953:36). In the final section of Chapter 3, I describe how, specifically, each of three different classes of model used in this book—macroecological, microeconomic, and co-evolutionary—reduces complexities and identifies central variables. To illustrate how these models can work in tandem to help us understand Patagonia prehistory, I offer a comparison of contemporaneous hunter-gatherers of the Subantarctic (coastal southern Patagonia) and Subarctic (coastal Alaska), demonstrating that ecological constraints on and/or cultural attitudes towards group size and connectivity, culturally mediated differences in fertility, and feedback between demographic variables and technological innovation led to more and less favorable conditions for cumulative cultural evolution among the Alaskan and Patagonian groups, respectively.

Factors central to the initial "peopling" of Patagonia, the topic of *Chapter 4: Explorers of an Empty Landscape*, include a highly variable late Pleistocene environment, a diverse and unfamiliar landscape, and probably a relatively small founding population. What's more, the initial colonists may have lacked the benefit of ecological knowledge accumulated over generations. A fair bit of what any of us knows is learned from conspecifics, such as parents, peers, roommates, and role models, who teach us what is good (and safe) to eat and where to find it, and how to avoid environmental pitfalls (unsafe exposure to the elements, dangerous animals or situations). Chapter 4 considers what learning a whole new world might have been like for groups of uniformly uninitiated colonists.

As it turns out, environmental savvy is, in part, a function of colonization speed. We do not yet have a firm handle on how quickly people moved from eastern Siberia to Tierra del Fuego, or, for that matter, whether Patagonia was truly among the last places colonized or just the farthest from the starting line. We can, though, use multiple lines of evidence, some of them unconventional, to triangulate on a most likely scenario. For example, we can model the material signature of a rapid migration favoring trial-and-error learning, and potential losses of particular technologies under a slow migration model. While many of these lines of evidence are currently circumstantial, firm paleoenvironmental data make clear that the environment to which the earliest Patagonians adapted demanded much.

In stark contrast to the tenacity and ingenuity of the initial colonizers, the human subjects of Chapter 5 seem (at first) halfhearted and dimwitted, unwilling or unable to adapt to climate change; *Chapter 5: The Mysterious Middle Holocene* explores a possible *de*colonization event. Climate scientists have shown that the middle Holocene (between 9,000 and 4,500 years ago) was a time of pronounced heat and aridity in many parts of the world. Indigenous populations living in areas affected by this climatic trend likely experienced changes in the availability of their key resources, and it has long been tacitly assumed that any decrease in precipitation, increase in heat (affecting evaporation), or resource fluctuation in already "marginal" regions would make them virtually uninhabitable. In arid northern Patagonia, for example, an apparent occupational hiatus coincident with the middle Holocene droughts has historically been interpreted as regional abandonment or population decline; causality has not been thoroughly explored because the decrease in sites is contemporaneous with climatic change. Similar phenomena in other parts of the world (e.g., the Great Basin of North America,

southern Africa) remain controversial for this same reason. Occupational hiatuses at scales detectable in the archaeological record have profound implications for our understanding of human adaptive capabilities, but we must first determine whether the scarcity of middle Holocene-aged sites in these regions is truly due to abandonment or, alternatively, to climatically induced adaptive reorganizations that produced more cryptic and difficult to detect archaeological records. This chapter presents data that challenge the notion that vast portions of Patagonia were abandoned during the middle Holocene and considers whether parts of Patagonia are truly marginal habitats for humans.

In another bald juxtaposition, it was during the middle Holocene that many other world regions saw the dawn of plant and animal domestication and, ultimately, sociopolitical complexity. This includes groups living just to the north of Patagonia. Among them, the ancestors of the Inca, who ultimately formed the largest agrarian state in the precolumbian New World. The transition from foraging to farming is one of the most enduringly contentious topics in archaeology. In recent decades this, too, has been approached from an evolutionary perspective, which has provided compelling insights. Similar evolutionary models and arguments can be used to explore the flip side of the coin: groups that did *not* transition to farming.

Northern Patagonians lived side by side with agriculturalists for at least 2,000 years, yet almost without exception, prehistoric Patagonians remained foragers until European contact. For obvious reasons, most studies of the transition to food production examine details of the "revolution" in a particular region or compare disparate regions to understand the precipitating events in each. There is much to be learned, however, from areas where farming was not invented or adopted, and this is the subject of *Chapter 6: Foragers in a Land of Farmers*.

Patagonians might have remained foragers for any of several reasons. Perhaps it was a matter of simple economics: foraging was so beneficial, or farming so costly, that the choice was simple. There is evidence to suggest that both were true to some extent, though not enough in either regard to close the case. It might, instead, owe to a more complex, but still fundamentally economic decision: irrespective of their relative profitability, foraging and farming are distinct peaks on the adaptive landscape. Each requires a very different technology, schedule, risk-management strategy, and view of property ownership. Perhaps in prehistoric Patagonia the valley between the two peaks was so low that moving from one to the other was prohibitively difficult or risky. Whatever the reason initially, assuming the particular challenges could eventually have been met, foraging might nonetheless have persisted as social and physical climates changed. In the final decades before European contact, for example, living in the shadow of the Inca empire might well have been an impetus to deliberately resist farming—perhaps foragers are simply harder to dominate and assimilate. Resolution of the issue will require more data than we currently have, and likely more modeling and theory-building, as well, but the discussion in Chapter 6 raises important questions and makes

clear that, while Patagonian groups at contact seem to have been relatively simple compared to their contemporaries to the north and elsewhere in the world, Patagonian prehistory is every bit as complex as that of other regions.

Nonetheless, archaeological interpretations—of sparse records, apparent occupational gaps, and the lack of farming, for example—have historically been colored by the outward severity of the landscape, alternative causes left unexplored when archaeological evidence aligns with preconceptions of hardship and fragility. The preceding chapters build to the realization, presented in the concluding chapter, *Chapter 7: The "K" in Patagonia?*, that Patagonia's carrying capacity (K) is likely higher than previously believed, and the prehistoric inhabitants much more resilient. Chapter 7 closes with an invitation to Patagonia, the *fin del mundo*, an unmatched yet understudied testing ground for some of the most important anthropological and archaeological hypotheses relating to human adaptive capacities and cultural evolutionary trajectories.

2

Environment and Ecology

[I]n few parts of the world is the climate of the region and its life so determined by a single meteorological element, as is the climate of Patagonia by the constancy and strength of the wind.

—Fritz Prohaska (1976:14)

Patagonia's intense and ever-present winds undoubtedly influenced prehistoric behaviors. The "westerlies" likely had direct effects on practical matters such as site placement and hunting logistics. Protected areas for encampment may have been at a premium, and hunting strategies were possibly designed with an eye towards simultaneously avoiding detection, which favors a downwind position, and maximizing projectile efficiency by firing with the wind (i.e., from upwind). Perhaps the westerlies even colored social relationships and cultural norms, air currents carrying sounds, smoke, and smells as they do. The west winds had (and still have) indirect effects, too, including wind chill and impenetrable seasonal cloudiness, which shapes the distribution and density of plants and animals. People surely responded to the winds, temperature, and clouds—and all of their downstream effects—through behavioral adaptations and cultural innovations.

On the face of it, the assertion that environmental factors influenced prehistoric Patagonians' behavior and culture is uncontroversial; all organisms, from fruit flies to first-world urbanites, are affected by the environment on one level or another. Just below the surface, though, are important and enduring questions related to human-environment interactions. Namely, given all of our cultural trappings, our instruments and institutions, to what extent are humans subject to nature's influence? Does culture

free us from the struggles of survival that other animals face?

Through much of anthropology's history, the answer has been, "it depends [on a group's level of cultural sophistication]," and often it is assumed that the relationship between sophistication and environmental susceptibility is strongly negative: the more sociopolitically complex and materially replete the group, the freer from environmental concerns. This was certainly a common view during the late nineteenth century, when foragers were viewed as "savages" wholly at the whims of nature, their every action governed by environmental constraints on basic needs (Bettinger et al. 2015; Hobbes 1962; Kelly 1995, 2013; Powell 1888). Even after a tectonic shift in thinking during the 1960s to the hunter-gatherers-as-lay-ecologists perspective, which saw foragers instead as skillfully and perpetually adapted to local environmental conditions (Bettinger et al. 2015; Garvey and Bettinger 2014; Lee and DeVore 1968), the assumption remained that hunter-gatherers are (were) more closely linked to the environment than food producers.

The result has been a sliding scale in the study of cultures and, especially, cultural change: Environmental factors are given more or less weight depending on both the subject of study (hunter-gatherers versus food producers) and the prevailing paradigm (Bettinger et al. 2015; Garvey and Bettinger 2014). The "progressive social evolutionary theory" of the late nineteenth and early twentieth centuries, for example, saw the environment as proximately influential, but ultimately unimportant; cultural change was inevitable and, given enough time, all hunter-gatherers (the presumed basal state) would achieve statehood and civilization (the presumed pinnacle). The environment was simply seen as an accelerant (or deterrent), with culture changing fastest where conditions challenged people sufficiently to innovate. Beginning in the first decades of the twentieth century, there was a shift in North American anthropology and archaeology away from the progressivist diagnosis of cultural stages (e.g., savagery, barbarism, and civilization *sensu* Morgan 1877) towards the identification of cultural change on much smaller temporal and spatial scales. This paradigm of "normativism" was not particularly concerned with the environment and its effects, tending to explain change in terms of diffusion and cultural contact. About mid-century, the pendulum swung again, away from "historical particularism" where cultures were understood purely in their own terms, toward attempts to identify "covering laws" and causal mechanisms. Among processualists, the environment was often seen as a singular causal mechanism whose effects are direct and unambiguous: a *prime mover* (Bettinger et al. 2015).

The modern evolutionary perspective that guides this book is rather more neutral on both counts. Hunter-gatherers, to the extent that such a category is meaningful at all (Morgan et al. 2017), cannot be understood in purely environmental terms any more than agriculturalists can, and the environment is important to the extent that it is important. That is, the environment certainly *can* be a prime mover in the evolution of culture among those who hunt, gather, tend livestock, and farm, just as it can be relatively unimportant (Chapter 3). One goal of this book's evolutionary approach is to calibrate the importance of the environment relative to other variables (e.g., social, demographic), and to identify interactions among variables that might amplify or attenuate potential outcomes. Ultimately, the environment is a single factor

among many, and one that is often poorly defined, at that. Its weight should be estimated empirically and through modeling.

This is not to downplay the importance of environmental factors in archaeological analyses. Indeed, ecology bulks large in this book's approach to Patagonian prehistory and I devote a fair bit of the next chapter to simple ecological relationships that seem to account for a portion of worldwide cultural variation. Nonetheless, human culture is one of the most complex traits ever to have evolved and, as with any complex phenomenon, it is reasonable to think—in fact we should *expect*—that cultural outcomes are most often the results of interactions among environmental, cultural, and demographic factors.

This chapter explores aspects of Patagonia's physical environment and ecological relationships that may have influenced human behavior and cultural development over the course of prehistory. Whether the physical environment is identified as a major force of cultural change or simply a backdrop for human behavior, ecological relationships are a good place to start when trying to understand cultural evolution in Patagonia.

Patagonia: Definition and General Characteristics

Patagonia is the southern extreme of the so-called Southern Cone of South America, the relatively narrow, tapering projection of land south of the Tropic of Capricorn (Figure 2.1). It is bounded by the Pacific Ocean to the west and the Atlantic to the east; its southernmost headland, Cape Horn on Hornos Island, projects into Drake Passage. There is some disagreement, though, about the region's northeastern boundary. Geologically, the line is often drawn at the Huincul Dorsal, a transversal interplate deformation north of Río Limay, where Río Negro and Neuquén Provinces meet (39° S; Coronato et al. 2008; Ramos et al. 2004). A more common, political division defines the northern limit of Patagonia at *ríos* Colorado and Barrancas, rivers that, together, form the natural boundary between Neuquén and Mendoza Provinces.

Acknowledging the logic of these divisions, I believe there is an argument to be made for the inclusion of not only Neuquén Province but southern Mendoza Province as well. This more inclusive definition roughly approximates the so-called Arid Diagonal, a band of maximum aridity created by the boundary between the two primary South American weather systems (the South Pacific High and Atlantic Anticyclone; Bruinard and Osuna 1982) and, farther south, by the Andes orographic barrier (see below). Because it is within the Arid Diagonal, southern Mendoza is more ecologically similar to the Patagonian steppes than to the adjacent Pampas grasslands; semiarid conditions and steppic vegetation characteristic of Argentine Patagonia continue north of the Barrancas and Colorado rivers (Neuquén Province) to roughly 34° S (Roig 1998). Moreover, central Mendoza Province may mark the boundary between groups that routinely engaged in farming during the late Holocene (the Huarpes, to the north) and those that did not (the Puelche/Pehuenche, to the south; Gil et al. 2011; see also Chapter 6). Because the near-exclusive commitment to hunting and gathering is one of Patagonia's defining cultural features, I have adopted the more liberal northern boundary for this book, including Neuquén and southern Mendoza Provinces.

Patagonia's northwestern boundary is also reported differently in different sources. Many Chilean geographers include only Aysén and Magallanes administrative regions (excluding the Chilean Antarctic). Others also include coastal Los Lagos region to Reloncaví Sound (41° S), exclusive of Chiloé Island (Figure 2.1; Coronato et al. 2008). This alternative delineation may be culturally justified since Chiloé Island was occupied protohistorically by farming groups (Cuncos, Huilliche; Alcamán 1997), whereas the continental coast from approximately 42° S to the islands in northern Golfo de Penas was hunting-gathering Chono (Alcamán 1997) territory. Granting that boundaries recognized prehistorically may not align perfectly (or at all) with those identified today by geologists, ecologists, and anthropologists, and that social boundaries can be quite fluid, I again prefer the definition that attends to the distribution of late prehistoric/protohistoric hunter-gatherers relative to food producers. I also note here that, while I do not consider it part of Patagonia, the Puerto Montt area, just north of Reloncaví Sound, features prominently in Chapter 4. This is the location of the famous early site at Monte Verde, with whose (widely accepted) initial occupation (ca. 14,500 cal BP[1]) all early sites in Patagonia—and the New World, for that matter—must be reconciled.

As defined here, then, Patagonia is an elongated diamond shape. The northeastern boundary runs northwest by southeast, from the headwaters of the Río Diamante (~34° S), southeast to that river's eventual emptying into the Atlantic (via the ríos Desaguadero and Colorado) at roughly 39° S. The northwestern boundary is formed by the Andes (and the modern political boundary between Argentina and Chile), from Río Diamante south to San Carlos de Bariloche, where it runs out to sea south of Chiloé Island. The remaining boundaries are formed naturally by the Pacific and Atlantic oceans (Figure 2.1).

At its widest, Patagonia is about 1400 km (870 mi) west to east, and in that relatively short distance spans several dramatically different environmental zones, including the steep and convoluted Pacific Coast, Andes Cordillera, dense forests, arid steppe, Atlantic Coast, and a total

---

1. A word about radiocarbon dates and the radiocarbon database compiled for this book: I calibrated all dates using Calib version 7.1 (Stuvier et al. 2020), the SHcal13 calibration curve for South American dates (Hogg et al. 2013), and the IntCal13 curve for North American dates (Reimer et al. 2013). The calibrated age of each sample is estimated as the median of the calibrated age range at two standard deviations. The radiocarbon database was compiled primarily by Jennifer Larios (University of Michgan), who combed the region's Spanish- and English-language literature for reported dates. She and I then identified and removed duplicate dates and any that lacked sufficient information to be useful in this context (e.g., no reported standard deviation). We also added locational data—latitude and longitude derived or estimated from publications. Locational data may be imprecise in some instances, but this does not likely affect associated analyses in this book, which are at a relatively gross level.

FIGURE 2.1. Map of Patagonia indicating the northeastern and northwestern boundaries (red dashed line), associated provinces (Argentina) and administrative regions (Chile), and geographic landmarks mentioned in the text.

relief of nearly 5,200 m (~17,000 ft). While the general cross section of environmental zones does not change significantly from north to south (Figure 2.2), temperature and precipitation regimes do, in part because Patagonia also spans nearly 20° of latitude, roughly equivalent to the distance between Las Vegas, Nevada, and Kodiak Island, Alaska. Temperature and precipitation data are described in more detail in the following climate overview.

Geometric Properties and Cultural Complexity

A final point related to general features of the Patagonian subcontinent, namely its shape, orientation, and size: Patagonia is an elongated diamond, as described above, and its major axis is aligned essentially north-south. In contrast, corresponding New World latitudes north of the equator form an east-west-oriented rectangle

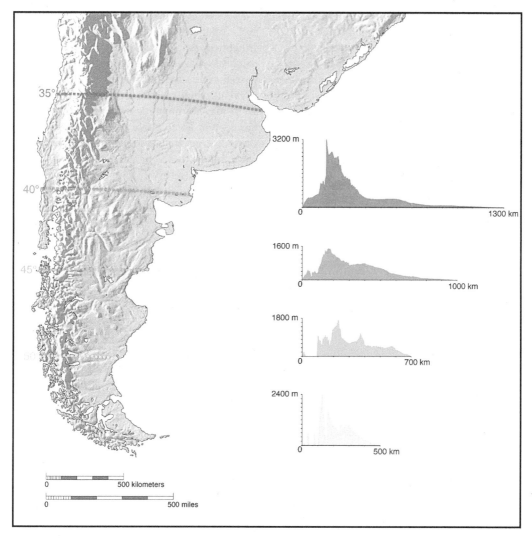

FIGURE 2.2. Elevational profiles at four latitudes across Patagonia.

more than four times wider (coast to coast) than Patagonia is at its widest (Figure 2.3). Patagonian human ecology and cultural evolutionary trajectories may have been influenced by these geometric properties (cf. Diamond 1997). Chapters 3 and 7 explore this idea in more detail but, in brief, even if Patagonian populations had been as dense as those in parts of the corresponding North American "rectangle" (e.g., California, the northwest coast of North America)—and, as best we can tell, they were not—Patagonia's size, shape, and orientation may have affected rates of cultural change in the region. That is, the narrow, north-south configuration may have limited the number of people experiencing similar environmental conditions (the number of minds at work on common problems) and the relevance of particular adaptations to people spread along the major axis. Any such "geometric isolation" effect may have been exacerbated by pronounced environmental heterogeneity. The following section (Climate Overview) describes conditions that produce a mosaic of vastly different environment types in Patagonia's

relatively small area. Dramatic differences between resource zones may have further limited
information relevance across habitats, resulting
in disproportionately large cultural differences
among groups relative to the physical distances
between them. So, it is possible that the subcontinent's geometry and stark environmental heterogeneity led to small "effective populations"
or groups of interacting individuals, the size of
which are a function of both absolute population size and intergroup connectivity (Henrich
2004). Effective population size is a potentially
important factor in cultural evolution, and empirical studies demonstrate links between small
effective populations and relatively slow rates of
cultural change, low overall cultural complexity,
and even maladaptive losses of culture (Collard
et al. 2013; Henrich 2004; Kobayashi and Aoki
2012; Powell et al. 2009; Premo and Kuhn 2010;
Shennan 2001). Indeed, some Patagonian groups
of the ethnographic period appear to have had
less complex material culture than their ecological counterparts in North America (fewer tools,
fewer parts per tool). This was certainly the case
with the Yámana (Yaghan) of Tierra del Fuego
relative to the Unangan (Aleut) of Alaska's Aleutian Islands, a comparison I draw at length in
Chapter 3.

In contrast to this hypothesis of environ-
mentally imposed insularity, a very different
phenomenon might account for the relatively
low levels of technological complexity observed
in Patagonia. As described in the Major Environmental Zones section below, parts of Patagonia are characterized by patchy resource distributions (e.g., the steppe), which might have
required groups to range across large areas and,
potentially, multiple environment types. This
response may have favored generalized subsistence strategies and technologies that would
work across large areas, and perhaps wide, well-
maintained social networks. A generalist strategy and the "Swiss Army knife" toolkits often
associated with high mobility and broad diets
(e.g., Kelly 1988; Kelly and Todd 1988) could
likewise account for instances of relatively low
material cultural complexity, regardless of cultural connectivity.

Of course, both insular local specialists and
well-connected regional generalists could have
inhabited Patagonia simultaneously. Groups
might also have switched strategies, from isolated
to well-connected and vice versa, over the course
of prehistory. Moreover, local specialists need not
be insular nor must regional generalists be well-
connected. Fortunately, these behaviors likely
have distinct archaeological signatures despite
the common outcome predicted in both original scenarios (relatively low cultural complexity).
Insularity, for example, is more likely to produce
a landscape-level pattern indicative of local spe-
cializations, and possibly group-specific design
elements, even within particular environment
types. Regional generalists' large and interconnected ranges, on the other hand, might have had
a homogenizing effect on material culture both
through the generality of toolkits and sharing of
design elements across broad swaths of land.

Determining whether such archaeological
patterns in fact owe to features of the landscape
or distributions of resources rather than to purely social or historical factors is another matter
altogether. But, as I argue in the next chapter
and elsewhere throughout the book, isolating
the contributions of environmental factors is
one of the best ways to tease out features that
are largely cultural. Later chapters in this book
explore examples of technological complexity in
prehistoric Patagonia and case-specific hypotheses related to environment, ecology, demography, and culture.

Climate Overview

Any overview of Patagonia's climate must begin
with a discussion of the wind. Patagonian winds
are formidable, as this chapter's epigraph so poi-
gnantly describes. Westerly surface winds originate over the Pacific and, unobstructed by other
landmasses, reach southern South America in
full force (Coronato et al. 2008). They are intense
year-round, though there is some seasonal ebb
and flow. Wind speeds are generally higher in
summer. In winter, they are notably less intense
in the interior (Prohaska 1976). In northern
Tierra del Fuego, winds over 60 kmh (~37 mph)

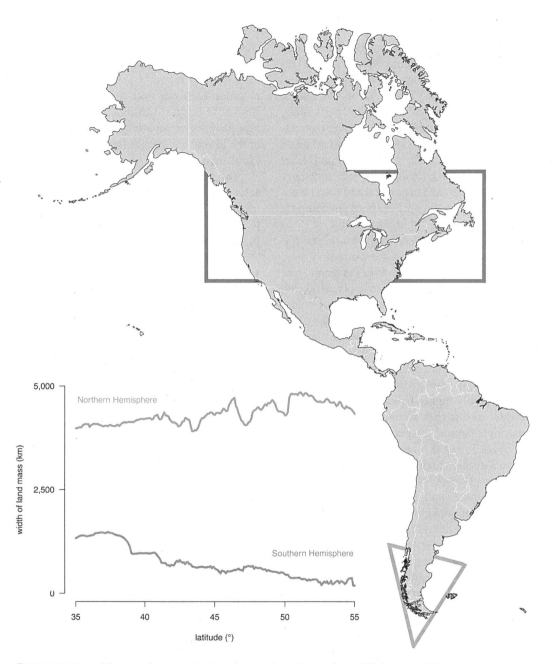

FIGURE 2.3. Map of the Americas showing the shape, orientation, and size of Patagonia relative to corresponding latitudes in North America. Patagonia is an elongated diamond, its major axis aligned essentially north-south. Corresponding North American latitudes are an east-west-oriented rectangle more than four times wider (coast to coast) than Patagonia is at its widest. The inset shows the respective widths of the North (blue) and South American (orange) landmasses. Plotted data depict the land width (in kilometers) in 0.1° increments, excluding inland water bodies.

blow 200 or more days per year, and gusts can reach 150 kmh (~93 mph; Borrazzo 2013; Vilas et al. 1999). Farther north, in Chubut and Santa Cruz Provinces, Argentina, Borrazzo (2016) recorded 80 kmh (50 mph) sustained winds and 100 kmh (62 mph) gusts. Across Patagonia, wind direction is highly consistent, particularly along the west coast before currents are redirected by the Andes; winds along the coast originate from the west at least 75% of the time (Miller 1976:125). So, while strong, the winds' constancy may have facilitated behavioral and cultural adaptations that might not have been possible were they not only high but highly variable.

The westerlies affect temperature, precipitation patterns, and insolation, and they are a major determiner of climate in Patagonia, particularly south of 40° S. For example, wind chill makes mean annual temperatures feel colder by 4.2°C, which is particularly significant given the limited use of clothing and impermanence of shelters described among Patagonian groups at the time of European contact (Chapter 3). Interestingly, though, because wind speeds are generally higher in summer, wind chill is greater during that season, which reduces the perceived annual temperature range (Coronato 1993). In Punta Arenas, Chile, for example, annual average highs (9.4°C) and lows (3.0°C) differ by just over 6°C, and the perceived difference is smaller still due to wind chill. Like the constancy of the winds themselves, relatively invariant temperatures in parts of Patagonia may have permitted particular adaptations to the cold that may not have been possible otherwise.

Annual temperature ranges increase from south to north, as do mean annual temperatures. For example, the annual mean in Ushuaia, Argentina (54° S) is 5.8°C, with an average range of 1.3–9.6°C. The annual mean in central Mendoza Province, Argentina (34° S) is 15.3°C, and the average range is 8.3–23.3°C. Mean thermal amplitude is as low as 4°C in the south and as great as 15°C in the north (Coronato et al. 2008:21).

Cloud cover and insolation follow similar south-north gradients. On account of the summer winds, southern Patagonia is cloudier in summer—average monthly cloud cover in Tierra del Fuego, for example, exceeds 80%—and intense cloudiness typically persists from October to March. Summer cloudiness decreases to the north, and in southern Mendoza cloudiness is low year-round. Correspondingly, solar radiation increases from south to north; there is a single hour of sunshine near the Strait of Magellan during an average June, which is one of the lowest one-month averages in the world (Tuhkanen 1992).

The westerlies also govern precipitation across much of Patagonia. More precisely, it is the westerlies' behavior at the Andes orographic barrier. Here, storm tracks are forced to rise abruptly, releasing the majority of their moisture on the western slopes of the mountains (Garreaud 2009). The air that reaches the eastern slopes is considerably drier, and adiabatic warming and surface winds further dry the air, leading to a nearly 70-fold difference in annual precipitation between the wettest (~7,000 mm/year) and driest (~100 mm/year) parts of Patagonia (Austin and Sala 2002; McEwan et al. 1997). The precipitation gradient is so steep in places that average annual precipitation can change from 4,000 to 200 mm per year in less than 200 km, west to east (Ariztegui et al. 2008:241). The result is a cross section of dramatically different environment types, from lush rainforests and temperate forests on the western slopes of the Andes to deserts and semideserts on the eastern steppe, in a relatively short distance. This hydrologic skew plays out in the runoff system, as well: because river discharge is governed by rainfall and snowmelt, and the eastern slopes experience less of both, aridity in the rain shadow is exacerbated by lower stream volume. This is particularly true on the steppe, where precipitation is especially low, evaporation relatively high, and organisms heavily reliant on allochthonous water (e.g., water from the Andes; Coronato et al. 2008:51).

The landscape-level differences between Patagonia's wet, forested west and dry, sparsely vegetated east are stark. Within ecoregions, though, conditions are not uniform. At a local level, day length, aspect, wind exposure, the mountains' height and prominence, coastline geometry, and a host of other factors create microclimates that, together, form a complex mosaic of habitats that differ significantly in the density and distribution of available resources. The following section describes Patagonian ecoregions, available resources and their ecology, dynamic aspects of the landscape and climate, and our understanding of human density and distribution in light of these things.

Major Environmental Zones

Patagonian physiography is both diverse and complex, with several major environmental zones overlapping in places. Each zone presents particular benefits and challenges to human occupation. Distinctions between them, however, are not as tidy as the following descriptions might suggest. In Chilean Patagonia, for example, mountains descend rapidly to the ocean (montane and coastal environments converge), while dense forests cover both the Pacific archipelagos and lower elevations of the Andes (forest, coastal, and montane environments converge). To the south, forests and moorlands are so intricately interdigitated in some places that attempting to define their respective boundaries is impossible. Moreover, the Patagonian landscape is highly dynamic: boundaries between environment types shift on timescales relevant to human occupation. The following descriptions of Patagonia's major environmental zones provide approximate modern boundaries and general conditions, which are relevant to interpretations of human population density and dispersion, broad-scale behavioral and cultural adaptations, and other coarse-grained analyses.

West Coast

Patagonia's west coast extends from Reloncaví Sound to the Strait of Magellan and includes both the continental coast of Chile and adjacent archipelagos (Figure 2.4).

Environment and Resources

The exceedingly rugged west coast poses significant challenges to human habitation but offers a bounty of marine resources in return. The archipelagos present a complex maze of tortuous straits separating thickly forested islands, most with undergrowth so dense their interiors are impenetrable. The topographical relief is extreme, with some islands rising abruptly from sea level to peaks as high as 1,600 m (Figure 2.5). In fact, the islands are an extension of Chile's Coast Range, each one a former mountain peak, the valleys between them shaped by glacial erosion and then drowned as sea levels rose in the early Holocene (Silva and Vargas 2014). The adjacent continental coasts of Aysén and Magallanes administrative regions are similarly convoluted, deeply incised by fjords, and currently flanked on the east by the extensive Patagonian Ice Fields, among the largest expanses of extrapolar ice in the world (Figures 2.4 and 2.6).

The coastal climate is governed in large part by the Southeast Pacific Subtropical Anticyclone (SPSA), a quasi-stationary high-pressure atmospheric system centered on the west coast of South America's Southern Cone. The anticyclone draws moisture-laden marine air to the west coast and, when SPSA weather systems rise towards the Patagonian Andes, they release their moisture (Ancapichún and Garcés-Vargas 2015). As a result, the archipelagos, continental coast, and western mountain slopes receive a tremendous amount of precipitation—between 4,000 and 7,000 mm in an average year (approximately 13 to 22 ft), the amount generally decreasing from northwest to southeast (McEwan et al. 1997). In Patagonia, the SPSA is most intense during summer, though precipitation is relatively evenly distributed throughout the year. The anticyclone is subject to both seasonal and longer-term fluctuations, and the interannual cycle is responsible for El Niño Southern Oscillations, well known for their effects on both climate and marine productivity (Ancapichún and Garcés-Vargas 2015). SPSA storm tracks are also characterized by high winds; wind speed, intensity, and frequency are determined in part by seasonal, interannual, and decadal cycles. Strong gusts and high, sustained westerly winds are common, as are violent storms and turbulent seas (McCulloch et al. 2005). Nonetheless,

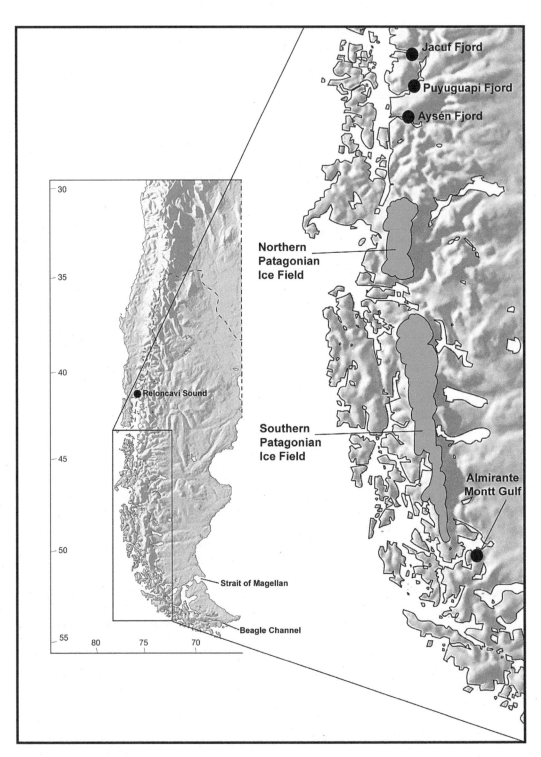

FIGURE 2.4. Map of the Chilean Patagonian Inland Sea and adjacent mainland. Jacuf, Puyuguapi, and Aysén Fjord heads and Almirante Montt Gulf have been identified as currently hypoxic "dead zones" (Silva and Vargas 2014).

FIGURE 2.5. View of the Chilean Patagonian Inland Sea, west of Coyhaique. Photograph taken by the author, 2014.

regional temperatures, while cold, are moderated by the marine effect (annual average of 6°C, or 43°F, near the Strait of Magellan), and wind chill is such that temperature varies little throughout the year (McCulloch et al. 2005).

Additionally, the SPSA is a major forcing mechanism of the Humboldt current, one of the most biologically productive ocean currents in the world (Chavez et al. 2008). SPSA-induced surface winds increase marine upwelling along most of the western Patagonian coast and north to Peru, bringing cold, nutrient-rich deep water to the surface. The replenishment of nutrients at the ocean's surface stimulates the growth of primary biomass, which in turn feeds an enormous abundance of marine life (Chavez et al. 2008). Today, the Humboldt current supports some of the world's largest commercial fisheries. Prehistorically, it may have been a draw for marine- and littoral-adapted foragers. In addition to fish, marine mammals, and shellfish, the rocky coast and islets host seabirds, including gulls, terns, auks, and albatross, which may have been sought for their meat, eggs, and feathers.

To access the bounty of the outer islands, prehistoric people would have had to brave the rough seas and high winds generated by the SPSA. However, the Chilean Patagonian Inland Sea—the straits, interior channels, and fjords of western Patagonia—may have provided easier access to marine resources (Figure 2.4). Fjords in particular offer calm, relatively protected waters. Their hydrology is complex, though, and some fjords are hypoxic or even anoxic, which can create biotic "dead zones" (Silva and Vargas 2014). This is primarily due to the seasonal (summer) injection of cold, fresh glacial meltwater, which results in a stratified water column at

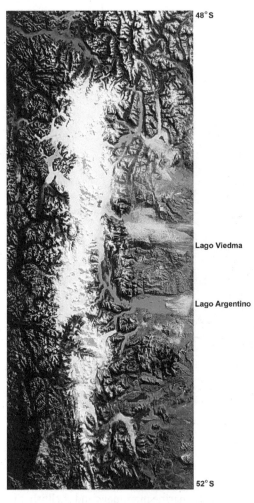

48°S

Lago Viedma

Lago Argentino

52°S

FIGURE 2.6. Satellite image of the Southern Patagonian Ice Field. Image credit: NASA, 2017 (image in the public domain: https://landsat.visibleearth.nasa.gov /view.php?id=90464)

of 90 locations across the Chilean Patagonian Inland Sea, Silva and Vargas (2014) identified four currently hypoxic zones, including three fjord heads (Jacaf, Puyuguapi, and Aysén; Figure 2.4) and the Almirante Montt Gulf farther south. Similar adverse conditions may have affected marine taxa in these and other locations in the prehistoric past, since factors influencing dissolved oxygen content are variable at seasonal and other timescales. So, while protected and potentially productive, the Inland Sea may have had dead zones that affected foraging behaviors and site placement.

Human Use

Our understanding of the prehistoric use of the western archipelagos and adjacent coast is currently limited. The same high winds, rough seas, and dense forests that likely affected prehistoric use of the region make surveying the area tremendously challenging. Given the ~40 m rise in global sea level since the end of the last glacial period (Lambeck et al. 2014), it is also possible that any evidence of human occupation of these areas is now under water. Moreover, annual melting of the snow pack brings large amounts of sediment down from the mountains, so even higher-elevation sites that were not submerged may have been deeply buried or washed away, particularly along rivers. It might also be true that coastal toolkits were largely organic (wood and bone abound, but high-quality stone is harder to come by) and these would have deteriorated in the region's acidic soils. Reyes and colleagues (2015) surveyed parts of coastal Aysén and report that the area appears to have been initially occupied during the middle Holocene, but that most of the dated components postdate circa 2000 cal BP. They note that it is currently unclear whether this reflects the true settlement history or some combination of postdepositional biases.

fjord heads (estuaries where rivers and streams enter the ocean) and, secondarily, diminished dissolved oxygen due to limited vertical mixing. Higher concentrations of particulate organic matter introduced by mountain runoff further decrease dissolved oxygen at fjord heads because oxygen is consumed in organic matter decomposition (Silva and Vargas 2014). In some places, the problem is exacerbated by submerged terminal moraines and sills that can restrict the flow of oxygenated ocean currents into the fjords (Dowdeswell and Vásquez 2013). In a survey

Western Temperate Rainforests

Due in part to the abundant rainfall associated with the SPSA and Andes orographic barrier, much of western Patagonia is densely forested

FIGURE 2.7. Valdivian temperate rainforest, southern Chile. Photo credit: Juan Vilata/Shutterstock.

(Figure 2.7). In fact, the area is so humid it is classified as rainforest. The Valdivian and Magellanic forests are, together, the second largest temperate rainforests in the world and similar in many respects to the larger Pacific temperate rainforest of western North America (northern California to Prince William Sound, Alaska; Tecklin et al. 2010).

Environment and Resources

The Valdivian temperate rainforest extends from 36° to 47° S (Tecklin et al. 2010). Though forest composition varies with elevation, latitude, and local precipitation, the Nothofagaceae (southern beeches; *Nothofagus obliqua, N. Dombeyi, Lophozonia alpina*) are everywhere dominant; bamboo (*Chusquea quila*) is abundant at lower elevations, as are evergreen conifers (*pehuén; Araucaria araucana*) at higher elevations in northern Patagonia. Farther south, there are high-elevation stands of (endangered) *alerce (Fitzroya cupressoides)*, an immense and long-lived species

similar to bristlecone pine (*Pinus*, subsection *Balfourianae*; Figure 2.8; Tecklin et al. 2010). The oldest living specimen currently known is more than 3,600 years old (Lara and Villalba 1993), and the existing dendrochronological sequence goes back approximately 5,600 years (Wolodarsky-Franke and Lara 2005). To this point, the sequence has been used primarily for climatic reconstructions (Aravena 2007), but there may be potential for archaeological dating, though wood preservation in sites may be poor.

The dense Magellanic temperate/subpolar rainforest, which extends south of 47° S to Cape Horn, is characterized by slow-growing canopy and understory trees, most prolific among them the evergreen *guindo* (*Nothofagus betuloides*). Deciduous beeches *lenga* (*N. pumilio*) and *ñire* (*N. antarctica*) increase to the east (Young 1972). Both rainfall and temperature are generally lower in the Magellanic than in the more northern Valdivian rainforest, and the plant species composition is correspondingly restricted (Hogan 2014a).

FIGURE 2.8. A giant alerce larch (*Fitzroya cupressoides*). Photo credit: Charles Lewis/Shutterstock.

The Magellanic forest is interdigitated with boggy moorlands characterized by poorly drained soils, which, combined with low temperatures and high precipitation and winds, impede forest growth (Figure 2.9; McEwan et al. 1997). These shrub-dominated tundras are estimated to cover more than four million hectares (McCulloch et al. 2005). While much of this ecoregion remains poorly known, in part because it is highly fragmented and accessible only by sea, the moorlands of southernmost Patagonia may hold exciting secrets for archaeologists, since bogs generally offer better preservation than other types of open-air settings.

The rainforests extend from the crest of the Andes (or the ice fields, where present; see Figure 2.4) clear to the western and southern coasts and archipelagos. In a sense, then, a host of marine and littoral resources (fish, sea mammals, seabirds, and shellfish) are available from the westernmost forests. Farther inland, the forested west hosts a range of fauna including *huemul* (*Hippocamelus bisulcus*; Figure 2.10), *pudú* (*Pudu puda*), puma (*Felis concolor*), river otter (*Lontra provocax*), smaller rodents (rats and mice), and a wide variety of birds (e.g., condor, woodpeckers, finches; Hogan 2014a, 2014b; Tecklin et al. 2010). Guanaco (*Lama guanicoe*) and *vizcacha* (*Lagidium viscacia*) are present, but rare.

Beeches in the Nothofagaceae family, which includes species common in the Valdivian and Magellanic rainforests (*Nothofagus* spp. and *Lophozonia* spp.), have pulsed fruiting events (González et al. 2002). During these "mast events," which happen approximately every four to six years, coincident with heavier-than-usual rains, communities produce abnormally large seed crops. Several species in the northern Valdivian rainforest, including *raulí* (*Lophozonia alpina*; distribution 35°–42° S) and *haulo* (*L. glauca*; 34°–37° S), have edible nuts that were harvested traditionally (Food and Agriculture Organization of the United Nations 2018). Beechnuts are rich in fat and, if these resources were use prehistorically, mast year bumper crops could have been an important—if unpredictable—source of this and other key nutrients.

I found no reference to human consumption of other Patagonian beech species' seeds, traditionally or prehistorically. This, of course, does not necessarily mean they were not eaten, only that the practice is not widely recognized. If in fact the nuts of southern beeches were not eaten south of the haulo and raulí distributions (~42° S), it may owe to differences in seed morphology or other physical limitations on the profitability of the nuts as a resource (e.g., substantial competition from rodents and birds). It is also possible that the social and material culture associated with tree nut harvesting and processing were constrained to northern Patagonian latitudes. We know, for example, that the piñon-like nuts of the evergreen conifer *pehuén* (*Araucaria araucana*; Figure 2.11), whose distribution is roughly coincident with those of haulo and raulí (37°–40° S; IUCN 2017), was a staple among the precolumbian Pehuenche people. The pehuén was so central to their diet, in fact,

FIGURE 2.9. Magellanic temperate forest interdigitated with moorlands. Photo credit: Galyna Andrushko/ Shutterstock.

FIGURE 2.10. Huemul deer (*Hippocamelus bisulcus*). Photograph taken by the author, 2015.

that the group is named for it (from Mapudu-ngun, the Mapuche language: *pehuén*, "piñon" and *che*, "people"; Cooper 1963). The apparent disuse of tree nuts farther south might simply reflect use that was more casual, unobserved by ethnographers and missionaries, or that left no obvious archaeological trace. However, it might also be that the social and technological adjustments associated with tree-nut centered subsistence were substantial, limiting the spread of the practice. One source (Stuart 2009), referencing an article on the Museum of Patagonia's website (itself unavailable at the time of this writing), describes traditional pehuén use in this way:

> Collection of piñones takes place from March to May. The seed pods are knocked down with long poles or by climbing the tree clad in protective leather. The Pehu-enches of the Chilean side of the Andes wait until the ripe piñones fall spontaneously; believing that to do otherwise is offensive to the spirit owners of the araucarias [pehuén trees]. The piñones can be eaten raw (if very ripe), toasted or boiled. Various types of flour for bread can be made, using a flat milling stone.... To keep piñones they are threaded into long chains called MENKEŇ and allowed to dry. The storage pits DOLLINKO have a drainage system that allows storage of 400 to 500 kg of clean piñones for 3 or 4 years. They put hot stones in the pit and above them the piñones topped with a lattice of canes and covered with earth (Stuart's translation).

So, while consumption of pehuén (and other Patagonian nuts) need not be labor intensive, at a certain level of use, this resource is quite costly to harvest, cook, grind, and store. The autumn harvest likely created scheduling conflicts with other resources, and reliance on stored nuts for overwintering may have required substantial changes to mobility. These costs could well have impeded the spread of intensive nut harvesting.

Whether the nuts of pulsed-fruiting species were consumed prehistorically, mast events

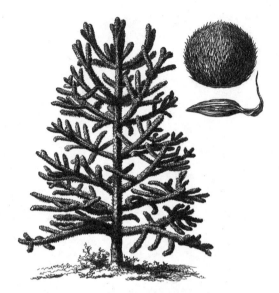

FIGURE 2.11. Edible nuts of pehuén (*Araucaria araucana*) from the Meyers Konversations-Lexikon, 1897. Image credit: Hein Nouwens / Shutterstock.

would have affected prehistoric foraging behavior: masts temporarily change forest ecology, aggregating large numbers of seed-eaters whose own populations then increase as a result of the bumper crop (Ostfeld and Keesing 2000). People might have been drawn to the abundance of rodents and birds, which are more profitable resources when aggregated than they are when dispersed (i.e., in non-mast years). This is particularly true for groups that use traps and snares because foraging time (setting and checking traps) is minimal and much of it can be embedded in other activities. Of course, this practice, too, would leave little archaeological evidence. If people were living in the forest or at the forest margin (see below) they may well have exploited a wide variety of plant and animal resources, some of which we may not be able to see archaeologically.

Human Use

As is true of the west coast, we know little about prehistoric use of the western temperate rainforests, and for many of the same reasons. The region is difficult to access and, in places, impossible to traverse. For example, Young (1972:310) describes the area near Isla Wellington (~50° S) in the Magellanic Rainforest: "The dense forest is developed mainly on unconsolidated talus derived from the steep slopes. . . . The floor of the dense forest is often covered to a depth of 2–3 m by a layer of undecomposed tree trunks and branches. Travel here is difficult and hazardous." Soils are acidic, biasing against preservation of perishable materials, and the highly dynamic landscape may have destroyed or deeply buried other kinds of evidence that may have existed. The probability of finding archaeological sites in this region is low on account of both. However, forests—particularly the forest-steppe ecotone (see below)—might have been quite attractive to prehistoric humans. With important exceptions, archaeological data from Patagonian forests remain relatively few, but forest resources should be part of the calculus when we consider the profitability and attractiveness of a place, especially when seeking to answer questions about the initial colonization of the subcontinent and region (Chapter 4). Of course, *when* these plant communities developed is highly relevant, a topic considered in more detail in the section on dynamics, below.

Mountains: The Southern Andes

Mountains dominate the Patagonian landform, particularly in the far south where they extend nearly coast to coast. Farther north, they occupy roughly half of the subcontinent, from the Pacific Ocean to the eastern steppes. Patagonia's mountains are part of the Southern Andes orographic region, which comprises three main mountain chains (north to south): the Chilean Coast, Patagonian, and Fuegian Ranges. North of Reloncaví Sound, the Chilean Coast Range extends most of the length of the Chilean coast; south of the Sound, it runs into the Pacific Ocean. Many of western Patagonia's islands are, in fact, partially submerged mountain peaks, as described above. The Patagonian Range likewise runs north-south, from roughly 40° S to the Strait of Magellan, and has distinctive glacial features: deep and steep-sided valleys, extensive

moraines, and extant glaciers, including those of the vast Patagonian Ice Fields (Figure 2.12). South of the Strait of Magellan, the Fuegian Range runs west-east and, like the southern Coast range, it is partially submerged, forming mountainous archipelagos including the Isla Grande de Tierra del Fuego (Silva and Vargas 2014).

Environment and Resources

Though rugged, the Southern Andes are generally lower in elevation than the Central and Northern Andes, the crest averaging approximately 2,000–2,500 masl; their average height decreases from north to south (Stewart et al. 2020). Important peaks include (from north to south) Cerro el Sosneado (5,169 m; Mendoza Province, Argentina, near 34°45'), Volcán Domuyo (4,709 m; Neuquén Province, Argentina, near 36°45'), Volcán Lanín (3,747 m; Chile-Argentina border near 39°38' S), Cerro Tronador (3,491 m; Chile-Argentina border near 41° S), Monte San Valentín/San Clemente (4,058 m; Chile, ~46°35' S), Monte San Lorenzo/Cochrane (3,706 m; Chile-Argentina border near 47°35' S), and Monte Fitzroy/Cerro Chaltén (3,405 m; Chile-Argentina border near 49°16' S). These are perennially snow-capped and the permanent snow line in the Southern Andes ranges from roughly 3,600 m at 36° S to just 700 m in Tierra del Fuego (Hogan 2014a).

Despite their lower elevation, the mountains strongly affect Patagonian weather patterns and vegetation, creating a pronounced precipitation gradient and, therefore, a rapid change from rainforest to desert as one moves west to east, as described in previous sections. Conditions also change rapidly with elevation, largely due to the adiabatic lapse rate (a dry-air temperature decrease of roughly 3°C per 1,000 ft [~305 m] increase in elevation; Danielson et al. 2003). Atmospheric pressure decreases with altitude, and reduced pressure amplifies the effects of climatic variables, including low temperatures, solar radiation, wind, and aridity. This affects the type and distribution of plants and animals at altitude and, as a result, the attractiveness of

FIGURE 2.12. The Southern Andes. Photograph taken by the author, 2015.

such landscapes to people (Stewart et al. 2020). In many places, steep terrain, near-complete runoff, poor soil development, high winds, and solar radiation select for low-lying, slow-growing plants. For all but a few months of the year, the entire ground surface is snow-covered, which deters herbivores, and biomass edible to humans is relatively low, patchy, and highly seasonal. The lack of vegetation, combined with a low winter snow line, restricts human use of the Southern Andes to a small portion of the year.

Even when weather conditions are favorable for human use of the Andes, low atmospheric pressure reduces the amount of available oxygen, which can, in turn, cause headaches, nausea, disorientation, dizziness, sleeplessness, and fatigue that can persist for days or months when the unacclimatized ascend to elevations above 2,500 m (Aldenderfer 1998). Moreover, hypoxia severely limits human work capacity, measured as maximum amount of oxygen used by working muscles (VO$_2$max). Studies among modern populations indicate a 9–24% reduction in VO$_2$max when unacclimatized individuals were tested at altitude, and a loss of approximately 11% of aerobic capacity with each 1,000 m of elevation beyond 1,500 m (Frisancho and Greksa 1989). The effect is compounded when exertion is increased, as when carrying a load, which dramatically increases the maximum oxygen uptake required simply to walk. The average person at sea level walking, unladen, on even terrain works at 30%–40% VO$_2$max; carrying a load can increase work effort to 70% or more (Ward et al. 1989). Slope and uneven terrain further increase work effort and decrease walking speeds. A 10% slope on even terrain decreases the average unladen adult's walking pace (5.5 kmh) by up to 20%. A 20% grade cuts walking speed in half (Aldenderfer 1998; Lee

1979; Silberbaur 1981). Hypoxia becomes less a concern as average elevation decreases from north to south in Patagonia, but steep and uneven terrain, low snow lines (permanent and seasonal), low temperatures, and high winds likely presented challenges for prehistoric use of the Southern Andes.

In spite of these challenges, there are several features that might have attracted prehistoric populations to upland environments. Among them are caves and rock shelters, which provide protection from the wind and rain and have interior temperatures that are both naturally more moderate and easier to control artificially than other settings. Many of Patagonia's natural caves and shelters have extensive records of human occupation, and many local chronologies are based on cave records. These records are, therefore, invaluable, but it is worth bearing in mind that caves and rock shelters are special places on the landscape. Caves are always rare relative to open-air settings and, in most places, they are also rare in an absolute sense. Even when they appear to have been used in the same way as open-air sites (e.g., as residential locations), a region's cave record is unlikely to accurately represent the full suite of behaviors performed in that region, and might offer only an incomplete or skewed view of a region's prehistory. However, when interpreted in conjunction with open-air sites, scatters, and isolates, caves and rock shelters contribute to a clearer picture of regional prehistory (Garvey and Bettinger 2018). Moreover, since large parts of Patagonia are erosional landscapes, open-air sites frequently lack well-preserved stratigraphy, making stratified deposits in caves and natural shelters essential for calibrating and contextualizing other finds through dated sequences of artifacts and materials not often preserved in open-air settings. We will revisit this topic in Chapter 5.

While caves and shelters are relatively rare on the landscape, boulders and cobbles are abundant, making it possible to construct shelters and windbreaks. These artificial shelters provided protection from the elements, particularly the wind, and afforded efficient use of fuel (which is limited in some areas), better

containment of heat generated by both fire and human bodies, and absorption of solar radiation by the rocks themselves. Much of the surface geology in the Southern Andes is basaltic (Aguirre 1985). Basalt has a high energy density (specific heat multiplied by density), so it absorbs and retains heat well (Robertson 1988). A structure made of basalt would have absorbed solar radiation and provided a warmer living area.

Just as caves offer respite from harsh conditions in the mountain biome and beyond, so, too, do other features of the montane landscape. Mountain valleys, for example, are generally more protected, provide more reliable access to water, and host a wider variety of plants and animals than some adjacent ecoregions (e.g., the steppe; see below). Interior valleys would have been particularly desirable, since they are less exposed to the high winds and storms that buffet west-facing slopes and valleys. The added protection comes at a price, however: the farther into the montane landscape one moves, the more costly and/or limited one's options for subsequent moves, which is worth bearing in mind as we interpret the use of mountain environments.

The Southern Andes are also dotted with verdant *vegas* or *mallines* and rich lacustrine zones around glacial lakes. Vegas/mallines are meadows or marshes that develop in glacial depressions and valleys flat enough for streams to slow and water to accumulate. Many of the plants available here have edible seeds and roots (e.g., rushes [Juncaceae], sedges [Cypereceae], grasses [Poaceae]), and prey species, including guanaco, are drawn to these oases because they provide both water and forage where it is otherwise unavailable or sparse (Utrilla et al. 2005). Lacustrine zones form around extant glacial lakes, as in the Lakes District south of 39° S. These zones host flora similar to that of vegas/mallines and, as perennial sources of fresh water, attract diverse and abundant waterfowl.

The Southern Andes are rugged, and average conditions there are harsh, but the ecoregion is certainly not homogenous. Indeed, it presents a tremendously complex array of microclimates governed by geographic position, slope, aspect, and many other variables. Some of these micro-climates were surely more amenable to human habitation than the average location on the coast or steppe, for example, so the mountains may not have been merely a place to which people made pilgrimages for lithic raw materials (see the section on resources, below) or a marginal habitat, moved to only when populations else-where became uncomfortable large (e.g., Neme and Gil 2008a). The mountains may instead have been an attractive, protected, bountiful place where resources were abundant, if patchily distributed in time and space.

Human Use

The mountains appear to have been sparsely inhabited in the past, as they are today. One or more of several factors could account for this. It may be that the relatively low density and patchy spatiotemporal distribution of resourc-es result in a relatively low carrying capacity in the ecoregion (Chapter 7). As mentioned, life in the mountains requires greater work effort, and there are mobility and opportunity costs associated with committed use of mountain en-vironments, particularly ones from which other environments are difficult to reach. The appar-ently low density of sites in the mountains might also owe to issues of visibility: the Andes are highly dynamic, with known glaciations, annual snowmelt and associated flooding, volcanic and seismic events, landslides, and routine erosion. These phenomena negatively affect the archae-ological record and limit our understanding of how this ecoregion was used prehistorically.

The Eastern Temperate Forest and Forest-Steppe Ecotone

East of the Andean crest, the mountains descend to the iconic Patagonian steppe, and the vegeta-tion changes rapidly from moist forest to arid shrub grassland. The eastern Andean slopes, which are generally drier than the western, are nonetheless forested. Correspondingly, while the western forests are predominantly ever-green, the east side is dominated by deciduous

species. These comprise a narrow band of tem-perate forest that runs virtually the entire length of Patagonia, from 40° S to Tierra del Fuego.

Environment and Resources

Patagonia's temperate forests are characterized by the Southern beeches lenga (*Nothofagus pu-milio*) and ñire (*N. antarctica*) above 1,700 m in the north and above 400 m in the south. This vegetation community is interdigitated at high-er elevations with high Andean tundra domi-nated by *murtilla* (*Empetrum rubrum*; a shrub-by plant with edible fruits); the forest-tundra boundary fluctuates with large-scale climate changes. *Coigüe* (*N. dombeyi*) is most abundant between 1,500 and 1,200 m, and *ciprés cordil-lerano* (*Austrocedrus chilensis*) dominates low-elevation dry forests. Continuing downslope, the forest transitions to shrubs and xerophytic taxa characteristic of the steppe (Coronato et al. 2008).

Like the forest-tundra boundary, location of the transition from temperate deciduous forest to Patagonian steppe is also impermanent. Pol-len and charcoal from lake deposits indicate that this boundary is sensitive to both environmental change on short timescales and anthropic dis-turbance (Iglesias and Whitlock 2014; Iglesias et al. 2014). In northern Patagonia, for example, early European explorers and missionaries re-ported indigenous groups' controlled use of fire to clear patches of forest and facilitate guana-co and rhea hunting (Cox 1963; Musters 1871). The charcoal record might, therefore, help us track placement of the forest-steppe boundary through time (Méndez, de Porras, Maldona-do, Reyes, Delaunay, García 2016), which will, in turn, help us better understand local prehis-toric adaptations.

The location of the forest's edge likely had important implications for prehistoric settle-ment since humans, like many species, often prefer such boundary zones (ecotones), which provide access to resources from both adjoining environment types, as well as some that are ex-clusive to the "edge" environment. The eastern temperate forest offers a variety of resources,

FIGURE 2.13. Ñandú/choique (*Rhea pennata*). Photograph taken by the author, 2009.

including tree nuts, succulent fruits, mush-rooms, solitary cervids (huemul and pudú), and small game, as well as wood for fuel, tools, and shelters. However, dense vegetation and rugged topography in the eastern forests impede mo-bility (Scheinsohn et al. 2009). Meanwhile, the adjacent steppe is much easier to move through, and hosts large herds of guanaco and flocks of flightless *ñandú/choique* (*Rhea pennata*; Fig-ure 2.13). Yet, on the flip side, protection from the western winds and water availability are gen-erally reduced on the steppe. Living at the forest-steppe boundary would have allowed people to maximize the benefits and sidestep some of the costs associated with each environment type.

Human Use

Ecological models predict high carrying capac-ities for hunter-gatherers in temperate forests (Tallavaara et al. 2018; see Chapter 3). Howev-er—granting that the eastern forests and the forest-steppe ecotone have not been explored as extensively as the adjacent steppe—relatively low site densities are reported for this Patago-nian ecoregion (forest-steppe: 0.36 sites/km², compared to 0.53/km² on the steppe; Méndez and Reyes 2008). Nonetheless, there is some ev-idence of early Holocene occupation in north-ern Patagonia. Three forest-steppe ecotone sites near the headwaters of Río Limay (between Neuquén and Río Negro Provinces, Argentina; see Figure 2.1)—Cueva Traful (ca. 10,800 cal BP; Crivelli Montero et al. 1993); Cueva Cuyín Man-zano (ca. 11,400 cal BP; Ceballos 1982); and El Trebol (Hajduk et al. 2004)—indicate what has been described as an ephemeral human pres-ence during the early Holocene (Borrero 2008), with deposits dominated by unretouched flakes, abundant fox remains, and small amounts of guanaco. Still, evidence of human occupation before about 3500 cal BP remains sparse (Barberena, Prates, and de Porras 2015; Méndez, Reyes, Delaunay, Velásquez, Trejo, Hormazábal, Solari, and Stern 2016) and site frequencies relatively low until about 2000 cal BP (Borrero 2008; Iglesias and Whitlock 2014). Méndez and Reyes (2008) suggest that prehistoric use of the forest in the Cisnes River basin (Aysén, Chile) may have been in response to a period of increased aridity on the steppe, which likely affected the distribution of resources. Indeed, several scholars have argued that the resource structure in Patagonian forests was not conducive to long-term human habitation (e.g., Mena 1995). Small and/or solitary forest species are generally less profitable than the larger and more gregarious camelids and rhea of the steppe, and forests therefore might have been marginal for human habitation, used only occasionally and opportunistically by steppe-dwellers (Borrero 2004; Méndez, Reyes, Delaunay, Velásquez, Trejo, Hormazábal, Solari, and Stern 2016). Lithic evidence currently supports this complementary use of the forest/forest-steppe by people of the steppe in the Cisnes River watershed (~44° S; Méndez and Reyes 2008).

Méndez, Reyes, Delaunay, Velásquez, Trejo, Hormazábal, Solari, and Stern (2016) believe that low site densities in these habitats probably owe primarily to low-intensity occupation, but they also note that our understanding of prehistoric forest and forest-steppe habitation may be colored by preservation. At Las Quemas rock shelter, for example (~44°38' S in the forest-steppe ecotone), bones are completely absent from all excavated levels, probably on account of acidic soils (Méndez and Reyes 2008). If the same destructive agents have been active throughout the Holocene, we would expect a sparse early record even if forest occupation intensity were constant through time. Moreover, if prehistoric forest-dwellers relied on organic technologies as we might expect, both tools and people will be underrepresented in the record. It remains unclear whether the sparse record prior to ~2000 cal BP accurately reflects prehistoric forest use.

Steppe

The Patagonian steppe accounts for the majority of the Patagonian landmass: nearly 75% of Patagonia's one million square kilometers between the Andes and the Atlantic Ocean. This vast area is correspondingly central to our understanding of Patagonian prehistory.

Environment and Resources

Much of the steppe is a true desert (semidesert in northern Neuquén and southern Mendoza), receiving an average of 200 mm of precipitation per year (Figure 2.14; Coronato et al. 2008). Some areas get as little as 100 mm/year, and aridity across the ecoregion is exacerbated by strong westerly winds and rapid evaporation, leaving parts of the steppe barren, with little more than exposed rock on the surface (Coronato et al. 2011). As a result, much life on the steppe is dependent on allochthonous water, originating in the Andes as rain or meltwater and flowing east across the steppe to the Atlantic Ocean (Coronato et al. 2008). The region's major rivers—the Negro, Chubut, Deseado, Chico-Chalía, Santa Cruz, Gallegos, and Chico de Gallegos—appear to have been established by the end of the Pleistocene, and have probably always been a focal point of human activity in the ecoregion (Borrero 2015). Other sources of inland water include glacial lakes, particularly at the foot of the Andes near 40° S, and seasonal marshes that form in shallow depressions.

The steppe is configured in a series of terraces that rise from near sea level along the Atlantic coast to 1,500 m on the highest plateaus. These terraces are less regular in places, including south of Río Negro where basaltic lava flows and massifs sprawl and rise, respectively, between the Lakes District and the coast (Coronato et al. 2008). The steppe is predominantly a shrub-grassland, characterized by low-growth shrubs—*neneo* (*Mulinum spinosum*), *calafate* (*Berberis heterophylla*), *molle* (*Schinus* sp.), and various *jarillas* (*Larrea* spp.)—and hardy tussock grasses with tough, sharp above-ground parts (e.g., *Festucia pallescens, F. gracillima,*

FIGURE 2.14. The Patagonian steppe. Photograph taken by the author, 2009.

Stipa speciosa; Green and Ferreyra 2011). In fact, the plant community in the driest parts of the steppe, the Patagonian phytogeographic province, is characterized by "diverse adaptations to moisture deficit and winds ... such as thorns, hairs and protective waxes" (Coronato et al. 2008:40). Better-watered regions, including riparian and lacustrine zones, have plants that are less armored, including *Stipa, Festuca, Poa, Carex, Potentilla, Eleocharis,* and *Taraxacum.* Only about 5% of the region is riparian or lacustrine, and these patches are thought to contribute significantly to the browse available to herbivores (Utrilla et al. 2006).

Guanaco thrive on the steppe because they are opportunistic feeders able to digest the stout grasses and shrubs that characterize the ecoregion (see below). Ñandú/choique (*Rhea pennata*) are also abundant, as are hare-like *mara* (*Dolichotis patagonum*), and armadillos *pichi*

(*Zaedyus pichiy*) and *peludo* (*Chaetophractus villusus*). Other relatively small-bodied potential human prey are opossum (*Lestodelphys halli*), weasel (*Lyncodon patagonicus*), dwarf cavy (*Microcavia australis*), and *tuco-tuco* (*Ctenomys* spp.). Nonhuman terrestrial predators are red and grey foxes (*Lycalopex culpaeus* and *L. gymnocerus,* respectively), puma (*Felis concolor*), and the pampas cat (*Lynchailurus pajeros*) (Díaz and Webb 2020). Birds are fairly diverse in the Patagonian desert, with more than 450 species (World Bird Database 2018); tinamous (*Eudromia elegans, Tinamotis engoufi*) are particularly common, as are insectivorous ovenbirds (e.g., Geositta spp., Upcertia spp.). Birds of prey include the buzzard eagle (*Geranoaetus melanoleucus*), hawk (*Buteo polyosoma*), falcon (*Falco peregrinus*), and burrowing owls (*Athene cunicularia*). The rivers and lakes are naturally poor in fish, but perch (*Perca* spp.) and catfish

(Siluriformes) are noteworthy exceptions (Díaz and Webb 2020).

Clearly, the steppe offers a wide variety of resources despite the withering aridity. However, only a small fraction is recurrently identified in the region's archaeological records, and within that fraction guanaco frequently dominates. Surprisingly, this is even true of late Pleistocene sites despite the presence of megafauna, as at Cerro Tres Tetas (Central Plateau, Deseado Basin, ca. 13,400 cal BP; Paunero 1993–1994) and Cueva de las Manos, approximately 100 km to the west (ca. 10,500 cal BP; Gradín et al. 1976; see also Chapter 4). Likewise, guanaco remain prevalent even as diets appear to broaden in the later Holocene with the incorporation of small mammals (in Patagonia, armadillo, skunk, tucotuco), birds, and plants (Borrero 2008). For these reasons, I give guanaco special attention below.

Rhea reach a sometimes-distant second place in archaeofaunal assemblages across the steppe subregion. Relative to guanaco, rhea are smaller on average, but their meat is typically fattier, which may have made these large, flightless birds particularly attractive to prehistoric hunters. Among ethnographic groups, their intra-osseous grease and eggs were prized as well (Cooper 1963), perhaps for the same reason (fat), and Rhea feathers likely had many prehistoric uses.

There is little archaeological evidence of fishing, and the contact-period Tehuelche reportedly avoided fish (Coan 1880; Cooper 1963; D'Orbigny 1835–1847), though they used a wide variety of plant foods, including roots, "wild potatoes," seeds, dandelions, berries, and legumes (Cooper 1963). These and other plants were likely consumed in the more distant past, too, but with few exceptions (see Chapter 6 and citations therein), we know very little about prehistoric plant use in the region. Across the steppe, plants with underground storage organs (tubers, corms, bulbs, rhizomes), and/or edible fruits, seeds, shoots, leaves, and (cactus) pads are (and were) available—abundant, even, especially in riparian and lacustrine zones—but they are either missing from archaeological records (i.e., not eaten or not preserved) or they have

gone unrecognized. In some areas, prehistoric milling equipment suggests plant processing, and plant residues have even been extracted from some objects, providing rare direct evidence of plant species attended to in the past (e.g., maize and *Prosopis* spp. in Neuquén; Lema et al. 2012). Importantly, though, partially-hollowed logs were sometimes used as mortars in protohistoric/historic northern Patagonia, which raises the possibility that even significant plant processing could go undetected by traditional archaeological methods. A recent attempt to tease meat and wild plant consumption from stable isotope signals in human tissues (bones and teeth) could help us approximate the plant portion of prehistoric diets going forward (Bernal et al. 2016; see Chapter 6), and systematic incorporation of plant macrofossil and pollen analyses in our project methodologies may be instructive regarding the diversity (richness and evenness) of prehistoric plant use.

Clearly, broadening our understanding of prehistoric plant use in Patagonia will provide a more complete picture of prehistoric subsistence. Moreover, and perhaps more importantly, plant use data could fundamentally change our approach to Patagonian prehistory. Evidence suggests the acquisition of carbohydrates—namely plant foods, traditionally gathered by women—is a primary driver of settlement decisions at all but the highest latitudes where plants are truly in short supply (Binford 2001; Hawkes 1996; O'Connell and Allen 2012; Zeanah 2004). Historically, archaeological analyses in Patagonia and elsewhere have centered on "traditionally male" datasets, particularly large-bodied prey and projectile weaponry. We know, though, that guanaco, perhaps the most important meat source in prehistoric Patagonia's interior (e.g., De Nigris and Mengoni Goñalons 2002; see below), are very lean and that lean meat cannot sustainably make up more than ~30% of human dietary intake due to our nutrient physiology (Speth and Spielmann 1983). It is, therefore, highly likely that plants played a much more important dietary role than is currently appreciated. Accordingly, studies of the timing and distribution of available plant resources, their prehistoric use, and the effects of gendered foraging on subsistence and settlement decisions will be key going forward.

Human Use

Despite the diversity of plant and animal resources found on the steppe, the ecoregion is widely considered marginal for human habitation relative to neighboring ones (e.g., the pampas, Atlantic coast). Nonetheless, some very early sites (certainly the earliest in Patagonia) are found on the steppe. In particular, two Patagonian subregions—the central plateau of the Deseado Basin (Santa Cruz, Argentina) and the Pali Aike volcanic field (Isla Grande de Tierra del Fuego)—appear to have been colonized early and occupied more or less continuously into the early Holocene. I discuss this earliest period in detail in Chapter 4, but it is worth mentioning here that these two subregions offer reasonable access to both food resources and quality tool stone (Borrero 2015; Cattáneo 2006; Charlin 2009; Hermo 2009; Martin and Borrero 2017), for which these locations might have been preferred by early explorers. They are also characterized by relatively high frequencies of rock shelters (Borrero 2015; Miotti 1998), which provide some of the only natural shelter from the unrelenting westerlies.

The steppe record is, in fact, primarily a cave record; much of what we know about prehistoric use of the steppe is through cave sites (Borrero 2015). It is certainly plausible that caves were preferred and that open-air locations were considered less desirable. But if caves were inhabited to the exclusion of all other landforms (i.e., if caves were a population-limiting resource), Patagonia could only have supported a vanishingly small population relative to its land area. We know, though, that shelters and windbreaks were sometimes constructed. Contact-period Tehuelche, for example, used a form of skin lean-to, described by Cooper (1963:110–111): "the windbreak consisted of guanaco hides sewn together and painted red and attached to a few poles stuck in the ground in a curve or semicircle and inclined toward the center . . . it thus formed a fencing without a roof, but in bad weather could be nearly closed over." Intensive survey of open-air locations across the steppe might reveal a surprising intensity of use, as it did in far northern Patagonia (southern Mendoza Province; Garvey and Bettinger 2018). Neme and Gil (2008a) have argued that, in northern Patagonia, the arid plains east of the Andes were avoided prior to about 2000 cal BP, when human populations outgrew preferred habitats in the foothills. When the cave record is augmented with data from regional surface surveys, however, it appears that the plains were occupied fairly early and relatively continuously throughout the Holocene (Garvey and Bettinger 2018; see Chapter 5).

East Coast

Relative to the jagged and densely forested west coast, Patagonia's eastern shore may have been more amenable to human habitation. Although the resource base is not quite as rich as the Humboldt-fed bounty of the west, the east coast offers a wide variety of resources, due in part to that coastline's heterogeneity.

Environment and Resources

The north coast of Santa Cruz (Golfo San Jorge area, between ~46° S and 48° S) exemplifies the subregion's diversity. It is characterized by large sand and pebble beaches, extensive intertidal zones, sedimentary spits, and rocky outcrops. In some places, the steppic mesas extend clear to the sea (Cruz and Caracotche 2008; Figure 2.15). The diversity of environment types provides habitat for a range of fauna, including shorebirds and aquatic birds such as cormorants (*Phalacrocorax* sp.) and penguins (*Sphenicus* sp.), which would have been sought for meat and eggs and perhaps feathers and skins as well. Other important resources are fish, shellfish, and pinnipeds, including sea lions (*Otaria byronia*) and fur seals (*Arctocephalus australis*). Plants with parts edible to humans include *algarrobo* (*Prosopis* sp.) and *chañar* (*Geoffroea decorticans*).

The east coast as we know it today is a fairly young ecosystem, and it is hard to overstate how dramatically Patagonia's Atlantic coast has changed since the last glacial period. Prior to a

FIGURE 2.15. Patagonia's Atlantic coast, Valdez Peninsula. Photo credit: Iakov Filimonov/Shutterstock.

~140 m rise in global sea levels, triggered by glacial retreat, Patagonia was roughly half again as large as it is currently (Ponce et al. 2011). When the first people arrived during the late Pleistocene, a vast portion of now-submerged Atlantic continental shelf was exposed and available for human habitation (Figure 2.16). We do not know much about prehistoric use of the Atlantic coast prior to about 8000 cal BP, but sedimentological studies of the drowned landscape indicate a similar variety of habitats to today's, including sand and pebble beaches, rocky outcrops that may have hosted sea lion rookeries and penguin breeding grounds, major river deltas that would have provided access to both fresh water and marine resources, and muddy substrates ideal for shellfish (Ponce et al. 2011).

Human Use

Archaeologically, we know more about the east coast than the west. Nonetheless, our understanding of prehistoric use of the Atlantic coast

is limited relative to the adjacent steppe, even for the period following sea level stabilization. For example, there was not a single radiocarbon date recorded for coastal Río Negro Province prior to 2003, when the entire ~350 km coastline was systematically surveyed as part of a major research initiative (Favier Dubois et al. 2006). This effort led to the discovery of a large number of previously unknown sites, many of which are shell middens. Data from the middens suggest that the hunter-gatherers who frequented the coast may have done so seasonally to supplement their use of other environment types throughout the year. The middens are generally shallow (<30 cm) and indicate selective harvesting of shellfish of particular sizes and species (primarily mussels, *Mytilus edulis* and *Aulacomya atra*), pinniped hunting (*Otaria flavescens* and *Arctocephalus australis*, the latter not presently found in Río Negro), and use of shorebirds and crabs. Remains also include terrestrial species (e.g., guanaco, armadillo), which suggests to Favier Dubois and colleagues (2006) that people in

FIGURE 2.16. Satellite image of Patagonia. The Argentine Continental Shelf (ACS) is clearly visible off the current east coast of Patagonia. At the height of the Last Glacial Maximum, sea levels were 120–140 m lower than present, and nearly 600,000 km² of the ACS was exposed dry land available for human habitation.

the area did not have a true marine adaptation. Radiocarbon dates are still relatively few, but dated sites suggest that people frequented the coast of Río Negro by at least 4000 cal BP. Local sea levels reached their maximum during the middle Holocene, circa 8,000 to 7,000 years ago (Favier Dubois et al. 2006).

Farther south, in Chubut Province, the record has been interpreted as one of year-round coastal occupation, despite extensive use of terrestrial foods (Gómez-Otero 2006). The highest density of sites in coastal Chubut Province is at the mouth of the Río Chubut. This is also the location of some of the oldest recorded coastal sites in Patagonia (ca. 8200 cal BP). Archaeofaunal data indicate considerable dietary variation between sites and through time, including both marine (pinnipeds, mollusks) and terrestrial resources (guanaco, rhea, armadillo, rodents, plants). Stable isotope studies of human remains suggest greater reliance on terrestrial resources on average, though some individuals' profiles indicate half or more of the diet comprised marine resources.

Still farther south, in the Golfo San Jorge area (southern Chubut and northern Santa Cruz Provinces), use of the coast likewise appears to have been year-round rather than seasonal.

Arrigoni and colleagues (2006) argue that Golfo sites' inhabitants exploited both terrestrial and marine resources but, while marine resources are common in these assemblages, they appear to have been procured without the development of specialized technologies.

These studies highlight one of the enduring questions regarding prehistoric use of the Atlantic coast: Were coastal resources supplemental to a predominantly terrestrial lifeway, or do archaeological patterns instead reflect a fully-developed coastal adaptation, occasionally augmented with terrestrial resources. Of course, this could have varied through time and across space, groups more or less dependent on coastal resources according to environmental and cultural circumstances. It is nonetheless significant that the records in all three locations described above—which, together, account for a significant stretch of Patagonia's Atlantic coast—indicate the continued importance of terrestrial resources throughout the Holocene, even after sea levels stabilized. If only early records (ca. 8000–7000 cal BP) showed a mix of terrestrial and coastal resources, we might hypothesize that rapidly rising seas encroached on the territories of long-established terrestrial hunter-gatherers, who then made opportunistic use of coastal resources but never fully committed to their exploitation. Persistence of the pattern (mixed resource use and lack of specialized coast-resource tools) into the later Holocene suggests a more interesting story that on-going work on Patagonia's east coast will surely help to tell.

Tierra del Fuego

Tierra del Fuego is composed of the Isla Grande (Big Island) and adjacent archipelago, and the subregion is similar in many ways to the west coast and steppe, described above. Nonetheless, important differences warrant this separate section.

Environment and Resources

In a sense, Tierra del Fuego is Patagonia in miniature, with virtually all of the ecoregions represented in a relatively small area (ca. 50,000 km², one-twentieth of Patagonia's total area). From west to east, Tierra del Fuego grades from temperate rainforest interdigitated with moorlands, into deciduous forest, followed by grasslands and steppe desert. The Southern Andes, oriented north-south along much of Patagonia, shift to an east-west orientation south of 52° S. The mountains also decrease in height and continuity, lessening the rain shadow effect such that deciduous forests and grasslands extend to the Atlantic coast above this latitude, rather than transitioning to arid steppe as they do farther north (Coronato et al. 2008:20). As the southernmost tip of Patagonia, Fuegian habitats are also among the coldest and windiest, and the outer seas around Cape Horn are notoriously treacherous. The strong currents, high winds, large waves, and icebergs make it one of the world's most difficult stretches to navigate (Chichester 1966). Even in the more protected Beagle Channel area, annual average temperatures are low (~6°C) and the windchill is significant. Daylight hours are highly variable throughout the year, with about 17 per day in austral summer and only seven per day in winter (Hernández et al. 1997).

Forest composition is generally similar to that described in previous sections, dominated by southern beeches (e.g., *Nothofagus betuloides* and *N. pumilio*), *canelo* (*Drymys winteri*), and cypress (*Pilgerodendron uviferum*). The understory is dense with *calafate* or barberry (*Berberis microphylla*). Terrestrial fauna is fairly limited and, on Isla Grande de Tierra del Fuego, includes huemul and guanaco, *culpeo* fox (*Lycalopex culpaeus*), river otter (*Lontra provocax*), and a selection of rodents and birds.

Tierra del Fuego marks the confluence of distinct ocean currents—the Cape Horn and Malvinas/Falklands currents—which do not stimulate the same level of marine productivity as the Humboldt does along Patagonia's west coast (Campagna et al. 2005). Marine resources are nonetheless abundant. Mussels were of primary importance among the contact-period Yámana, for example, as were seals and a variety of near-shore fishes (Cooper 1946). Notably, while whale meat was prized among the Yámana, whales "were not hunted in the usual sense of the word," but were dispatched if beached or wounded and run into shallow waters by marine predators (Oswalt 1973:102).

A beached whale is, in a sense, a pulsed resource event similar to a beech mast (see the discussion of temperate forests, above). Pulsed events temporarily change local ecology and attract large numbers of opportunistic feeders, some of which may themselves have been attractive to human foragers. However, unlike beech masts, which happen semiregularly (every four to six years), there is very little predictability in the timing and location of cetacean stranding ("beaching"). The unanticipated windfall nonetheless drew large groups of contact-period Yámana, and this was one of very few occasions on which large groups assembled (Cooper 1946)—a fact relevant to theories of material cultural change in this region (Chapter 3).

Also worth a brief mention in this discussion of Fuegian marine resources is the potential proliferation of *Alexandrium catenella*, a toxin-producing dinoflagellate alga that can contaminate shellfish and cause paralytic shellfish poisoning (PSP) in humans (Paredes et al. 2014). As the name suggests, PSP is a paralytic reaction to *A. catenella* toxins ingested via shellfish that can result in sudden death if the breathing muscles are affected. *A. catenella* concentrations are generally low in western Patagonia but can proliferate seasonally and interannually given particular sea temperatures and nitrogen levels. A recent study by Paredes and colleagues (2014) detected three regions of particularly high toxicity: near Última Esperanza, at the western end of the Strait of Magellan, and along the Beagle Channel. It is not clear the extent to which this might have posed a risk to prehistoric people, but it is a point for consideration.

Human Use

Borromei and Quattrocchio (2008) use prehistoric fire frequency data to argue for an early initial human occupation of Tierra del Fuego. Their data—charcoal particles in pollen

sequences collected near Bahía Inútil (western Isla Grande)—show increased burning at approximately 16,000 cal BP, which they suggest is more likely due to human activity than to lightning strikes or volcanic eruptions. This early date is not generally accepted, however, and archaeological evidence currently indicates the region was initially occupied circa 12,500 cal BP (Tres Arroyos 1 site; Massone 2004) before postglacial sea levels rose sufficiently to cut Tierra del Fuego off from mainland Patagonia (ca. 10,000 cal BP; Ponce et al. 2011). Interestingly, evidence of human activity during the early Holocene is quite limited. It appears that initial colonization was followed by a gap of several thousand years, after which the archaeological signal is not only strong but suggests rapid development of a maritime lifeway in the Beagle Channel area around 7500 cal BP (Salemme and Santiago 2017).

Key Patagonian Resources

To this point, we have explored Patagonia's major ecoregions and some of the known or hypothesized ecological relationships between prehistoric humans and key resources within these regions. Later chapters examine other such relationships in detail (e.g., with marine resources in Chapter 3, Pleistocene megafauna in Chapter 4, and plants in Chapter 6). One resource in particular, guanaco, appears to have been a preferred hunting target throughout prehistory and across much of Patagonia, and it is worth devoting a bit of space to their general features and habits here at the start. This is followed by a brief discussion of a similarly important mineral resource: obsidian.

Guanaco

Guanaco (*Lama guanicoe*) is the only wild member of the camelid genus *Lama*, which also contains domesticated llama (*L. glama*). *Lama* and closely associated genus *Vicugna* (wild vicuña, *V. vicugna*, and domesticated alpaca, *V. pacos*) are the only extant New World members of the Camelidae (camel) family, though several other

FIGURE 2.17. Guanaco (*Lama guanicoe*). Photograph taken by the author, 2010.

genera were present when humans first colonized the Americas (Chapter 4).

Distribution and Habits

Guanaco have a wide geographic distribution (approximately 8° S to 53° S) spanning multiple environment types, "from sea level to 4,250 masl . . . [including] deserts, semideserts, scrub, grassland zones, savannas, bushy zones, high-altitude pampas, plateaus, foothills, and mountains" (Figure 2.17; Bonavia and Monge 2008:25–26). Modern overhunting, habitat destruction, and competition from introduced domesticates (e.g., sheep) have reduced populations to potentially as low as 5% of their numbers at European contact, estimated to have been in the tens of millions (Bonavia and Monge 2008:30).

Guanaco are able to persist in such varied environments because they are dietarily and socially flexible. Studies of modern guanaco populations' feeding habits in various microenvironments throughout their present range indicate that they are drought-tolerant generalists, able

to subsist on a wide range of plant types and parts (Raedeke and Simonetti 1988:200). For example, microhistological analyses of guanaco feces in Neuquén Province indicate that the individuals in this area subsist primarily on forbs (Bahamonde et al. 1986), while a similar study shows that their conspecifics in the Atacama Desert of northern Chile focus on lichens and shrubs (Raedeke and Simonetti 1988). Moreover, individual guanaco exhibit considerable dietary flexibility, changing diets seasonally, annually, and situationally, as when competitors are introduced.

Guanacos' chambered stomachs allow them to extract adequate nutrients from the medium- to low-quality foods they consume, many of which are avoided by other animals because they are low in nutrients and hard to digest (Bonavia and Monge 2008:20). Water from the foods they eat is often sufficient, though they certainly also drink and have even been observed consuming briny water from tidal pools (Bonavia and Monge 2008:26). In brief, their metabolism is extremely energy- and water-efficient, and guanaco can go extended periods without food or water (Bonavia and Monge 2008).

Guanaco populations have been observed practicing what Baker (1978) refers to as "facultative migration": whereas some species' migrations are obligate, facultative migrators move only sometimes, in response to local environmental conditions (Bonavia and Monge 2008). In one Chilean population, for example, the guanacos' facultative responses in particularly harsh winters involved summering in grassy lowland meadows, moving towards more protected Andean foothills during the cold season, and returning to the meadows in the spring (Ortega and Franklin 1995). The home ranges of groups that migrate facultatively are rarely more than 50 km in maximum dimension (Borrero 1990) and all guanaco—migratory or not—are territorial (Borrero 1990, 1997; Franklin 1982; Garrido et al. 1981), which makes their location on the landscape fairly predictable.

Guanaco are gregarious, but their social groups fission and fuse seasonally over the course of a year. In the Chilean population cited above, two kinds of aggregations are common during the summer reproductive season: family groups, consisting of a single adult male and several females with their young, and all-male groups, containing both adult and subadult males. In winter, the Chilean guanaco live in mixed groups, with both sexes and all ages represented. In spring, males tend to forage alone (Ortega and Franklin 1995). Social group size ranges from around 30 animals in spring mixed groups to 15 or fewer in other group types throughout the annual cycle (Ortega and Franklin 1995). Population densities also vary seasonally, averaging five individuals per hectare (Borrero 1990; Franklin 1982). Gestation averages 11 months and births typically occur between December and March. Survivorship is relatively high (30%), and more deaths owe to starvation than to predation (Bonavia and Monge 2008).

Profitability

The guanaco is currently the largest terrestrial mammal in southern South America. The average adult weighs between 100 and 120 kg (De Nigris 2004), though there is a north-south clinal size difference: guanaco are smallest in the northern part of their range and largest in Tierra del Fuego (L'Heureux and Cornaglia Fernández 2015). If body size can be taken as a proxy for caloric yield (Broughton 1994; Broughton et al. 2011; Winterhalder 1981), guanaco has been the highest-ranking terrestrial resource in southern South America (i.e., the animal with the highest post-encounter return rate; see Chapter 3) since the terminal Pleistocene/early Holocene when the last of the megafauna became extinct (see Chapter 4). It is worth restating, however, that they are quite lean—guanaco muscle tissues contain less than 1% fat (Mengoni Goñalons 1996)—and marrow extraction and bone grease rendering were probably important subsistence activities (De Nigris and Mengoni Goñalons 2002).

Borrero (1990) created a meat utility index for guanaco using data derived from a single butchering event (Bridges 1951; Gusinde 1982). He found the guanaco meat utility index to be significantly correlated with that of caribou ($r = 0.71$; $p < 0.05$) and, therefore, calculated a standardized meat plus marrow index for guanaco using marrow distributions in caribou (Borrero 1990). Neme and Gil (2002) combined Borrero's utility index with Elkin's (1995) bone density calculations (Table 2.1). These data provide a useful frame of reference for interpreting skeletal element representation in the region's archaeofaunal records, and for understanding human foraging in Patagonia more generally.

Obsidian

In parts of the world where it is available, volcanic glass was a preferred material among stone tool users. This is partly because obsidian flakes and tools can have incredibly sharp edges that, while brittle, may be superior for certain tasks. Obsidian's amorphous crystalline structure also makes it ideal for controlled knapping (i.e., producing desired forms) and resharpening. Moreover, volcanic glass has properties of high archaeological value, including distinguishable

TABLE 2.1. *Lama guanicoe* standardized meat utility, standardized meat plus marrow index, and bone density measures (from Neme and Gil 2002). For each anatomical element, standardized scores are presented as a percentage of the highest utility element.

element	meat utility	meat + marrow index	bone density
cranium	20.8	8.29	n.d.
mandible	5.7	8.62	n.d.
atlas	8.8	7.39	0.82
axis	8.8	7.39	0.67
cervical	51.3	39.43	0.56
thoracic	22.1	17.41	0.64
lumbar	44.9	34.61	0.42
pelvis	40.2	36.23	0.35
ribs	100	76.16	0.71
sternum	8.5	7.16	0.2
scapula	38.4	33.78	0.6
proximal humerus	23.8	40.33	0.42
distal humerus	23.8	39.31	0.79
proximal radio-ulna	7.8	38.79	0.81
distal radio-ulna	7.8	55.73	0.72
carpals	1.3	1.73	0.71
proximal metacarpals	1.3	47.49	0.98
distal metacarpals	1.3	51.56	0.87
proximal femur	83.2	88	0.62
distal femur	83.2	100	0.48
proximal tibia	21.3	49.07	0.55
distal tibia	21.3	86.11	0.82
astragalus	1.7	2.03	0.79
calcaneus	1.7	17.26	0.85
proximal metatarsals	1.7	68.92	0.93
distal metatarsals	1.7	76.69	0.73
1st phalange	2.1	24.2	0.95
2nd phalange	2.1	18.28	0.56
3rd phalange	2.1	2.3	n.d.

Data from Borrero 1990; Elkin 1995; Neme and Gil 2002. N.d. = no data

chemical variability and the potential for direct estimation of obsidian artifacts' ages.

Patagonian obsidian sources are chemically distinct, and obsidian artifacts can confidently be assigned to known sources in many cases (Stern 2018). In recent decades, there has been a concerted effort to characterize the region's sources using trace element analyses, including X-ray fluorescence spectrometry (XRF), instrumental neutron activation analysis (INAA), and inductively coupled plasma mass spectrometry (ICP-MS; Barberena et al. 2011; Cortegoso et al. 2016; Cortegoso et al. 2014; Cortegoso et al. 2012; De Francesco et al. 2017; De Francesco et al. 2006; Durán et al. 2012; Durán et al. 2004; Fernández et al. 2017; Giesso et al. 2011; Salgán et al. 2015; Seelenfreund et al. 1996; Stern 2018). These studies have identified a number of archaeologically important obsidian sources in Patagonia as well as several others whose prehistoric use was more limited. Comprehensive descriptions of these sources' chemical signatures,

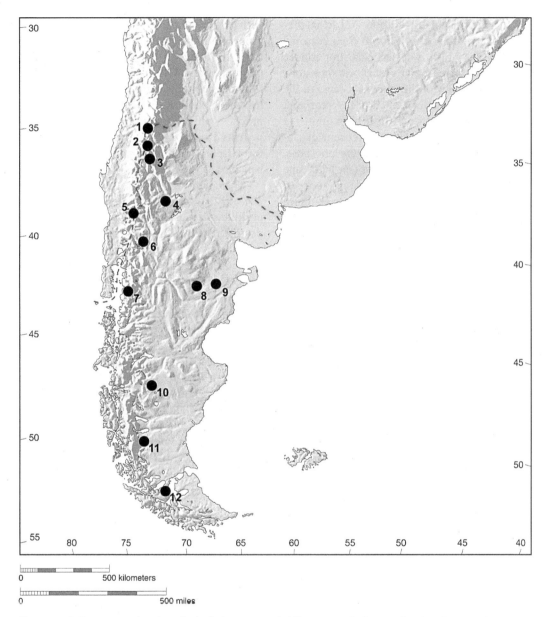

FIGURE 2.18. Documented, archaeologically important obsidian sources in Patagonia: 1. Las Cargas; 2. Laguna del Maule; 3. Cerro Huenul; 4. Portada Covunco; 5. Nevados de Sollipulli; 6. Cerro de la Planicies/Lago Lolog; 7. Chaitén; 8. Sacanana; 9. Telsen/Sierra Negra; 10. Pampa del Asador; 11. Cordillera baguales; 12. Seno Otway (after Stern 2018).

knapping-related properties, and archaeological distributions can be found in the primary sources cited above. Here, I provide a brief overview.

Figure 2.18 indicates the approximate locations of Patagonia's major obsidian sources, some of which have not yet been pinpointed, though distributions of nodules in drainages and archaeological "distance-decay curves" indicate their likely location. Sources differ in color, "purity" (namely, inclusions), and suitability for knapping, areal distribution, and actual prehistoric use. They also differ in their seasonal accessibility, which is of particular importance to our understanding of prehistoric tool stone economics. Many of the sources located in the Andes are inaccessible much of the year and, prehistorically, access may have been limited at larger timescales, too, due to Holocene glaciations, volcanic and tectonic activity, landslides, and flooding along access routes (see landscape dynamics, below). Extra-Andean sources, though, would have been accessible year-round and from year to year, largely without interruption (Barberena et al. 2011; Cortegoso et al. 2016; Durán et al. 2012; Fernández et al. 2017; Giesso et al. 2011; Salgán et al. 2015).

Even when not seasonally constrained, obsidians are both more geographically restricted and less common than other kinds of stone (Stern 2018). In many parts of Patagonia, surface geology is dominated by nonvitreous volcanic materials, including basalts, andesites, and dacites, many of which are suitable for the production of tools but tend to be of lower quality than obsidian. Bedrock is exposed or thinly buried in some areas, making these volcanic rocks ubiquitous on the ground surface, in river and arroyo channels, and in glacial moraines. Obsidians, on the other hand, tend to occur in discrete and relatively small pockets (cf. Barberena et al. 2019), creating an interesting economic problem. If we assume people selected tool stone according to tradeoffs between quality and accessibility, material type frequencies in archaeological records can tell us something about tool use. A simple model of stone procurement predicts that, at a certain intensity of tool use, having the most effective tool for a task—the one that increases overall return rates—outweighs the costs of procuring high-quality raw materials (Garvey 2015a). That is, there is a critical level of tool use beyond which it makes sense to incur the upfront costs of pursuing spatially and sometimes seasonally restricted obsidians, despite the immediate availability of serviceable but inferior local stone. For any given archaeological site, we could calculate costs associated with (direct) obsidian procurement and use the proportion of obsidian relative to other stone types to interpret, say, hunting intensity at a particular time. Of course, this should be carefully considered in light of the zooarchaeological record and our understanding of hunting practices and trade relationships. Still, costs and benefits associated with stone procurement can form the basis of novel hypotheses of prehistoric behavior.

Geochemical data have allowed us to track not only spatial distributions of Patagonian obsidians, but also temporal ones. One way to do this is to identify the chemical signatures of archaeological obsidians found in stratified deposits, match these to sources, and track the frequencies of particular material types through time. In most cases, this will provide a reliable estimate of obsidian source use through time, though stratigraphic mixing, unconformities, or other disturbances can complicate this type of analysis. Meanwhile, another property of volcanic glass—the fact that it absorbs ambient moisture at knowable rates—allows us to estimate the ages of obsidian artifacts themselves. This can reduce problems caused by stratigraphic disturbance, potentially even helping to identify such problems in the first place (Garvey and Bettinger 2018).

Despite obsidian's abundance in Patagonian archaeological assemblages (i.e., its frequent use among prehistoric people, particularly in central and northern Patagonia), obsidian hydration has not been used extensively as a dating technique. This is partly because most research in the region has centered on stratified sites that can be dated by other means (e.g., radiocarbon). Historical debates regarding the accuracy of obsidian hydration dating (e.g., Anovitz et al. 1999; Ridings 1996; Rogers 2006) may have further discouraged exploration of the technique's efficacy in Patagonia. Recent research, however, shows that appropriately calibrated hydration measurements predict radiocarbon dates with reasonable accuracy, and hydration data can now reliably be used to estimate the ages of obsidian artifacts from two of northern Patagonia's sources, Las Cargas and Laguna del Maule (Garvey 2012a, 2012b; Garvey et al. 2016).

Obsidian hydration dating (OHD) is particularly useful in the analysis of surface assemblages. When these lack time-marker artifacts (e.g., projectile points or ceramic styles of known age) but contain obsidian, OHD is sometimes the only means of obtaining an age estimate. OHD can also help clarify whether a surface assemblage represents a single occupation or multiple, conflated ones (i.e., a palimpsest). Moreover, OHD can be used in buried contexts as an economical means of identifying stratigraphic anomalies that may not be detectable in radiocarbon trends, partly because many OHD estimates can be obtained for the price of a single radiocarbon date (at the time of this writing, the ratio is between twenty- and thirty-to-one).

A final point worth mentioning is the double-edged sword of obsidian's high visibility, both on the landscape and in the literature. Obsidian is easy to spot and identify; its reflectiveness makes it stand out in both surface and buried contexts. On account of its ultra-fine grain (an amorphous crystalline structure, in fact), evidence of human manipulation (flaking) is readily recognizable. Lastly, many sites where obsidian is found are located some distance from the source, which increases the likelihood of cultural attribution of even "questionable" pieces. Conversely, other material types may be less visible and less readily identifiable as cultural, particularly those that are local, coarse-grained, or both (Garvey and Mena 2016). Obsidian seems to have been a preferred material in prehistoric Patagonia, but the degree of preference might in some cases be inflated by the relative *invisibility* of other stone types.

Landscape Dynamics

The Patagonian landscape has changed dramatically in the millennia since initial colonization. Most significant among the changes are the retreat of major glaciers following the Last Glacial Maximum (LGM) and the resultant reduction of Patagonia's land area by a third due to global sea level rise. Change occurred (and continues to occur) on other geographic and temporal scales, too, and all of these dynamics affected prehistoric peoples' use of the landscape. Results of these processes now affect our access to Patagonia's human past.

Glaciers

Of all prehistoric landscape modeling agents in Patagonia, Coronato and colleagues (2008) identify Pliocene-Quaternary glaciations as the most significant. Throwing their tremendous weight around, glaciers carved cirques, horns, and arêtes into the very mountains. They deposited massive moraines and huge erratics, some of which people later used as shelters. The till they left behind is unproductive and difficult to traverse. However, large glacial lakes, numbering more than 50 south of 39° S, may have been focal points of human activity.

At the height of the last glacial age, virtually all of Chilean Patagonia was covered in ice (McEwan et al. 1997); the Patagonian Ice Sheet, of which the current Northern and Southern Patagonian Ice Fields (Figure 2.4) are remnants, covered the western Andes and west coast ecoregion south of Puerto Montt. This has significant implications for the initial peopling of Patagonia. For example, the oldest accepted New World site—Monte Verde, located near Puerto Montt—was in a periglacial environment circa 14,500 cal BP, and movement south may not have been possible at that time. Argentine Patagonia, therefore, was not likely colonized from Chilean Patagonia, and people may have been unable to cross the Southern Andes prior to circa 11,000 cal BP on account of the Patagonian Ice Sheet (Salemme and Miotti 2008:43). It is also worth bearing in mind the destructive power of glaciers—both direct and indirect, as described below—and the fact that deglaciation was a protracted process that continued well into the Holocene. Furthermore, while glacial readvances subsequent to the LGM were less significant, they had similar effects, proportional to the magnitude of glacier growth.

Sea Levels

Arguably, glacial retreat following the LGM had more widespread and profound effects on the Patagonian landscape than did the glaciers themselves. Global sea level rise was particularly transformational. At the height of the LGM, when sea levels were 120 to 140 m below their current position, nearly 600,000 km^2 of the Argentine Continental Shelf (ACS) was exposed (Figure 2.16; Ponce et al. 2011). The bulk of this area is in the south (the ACS extends approximately 880 km beyond the current shore at the latitude of the Malvinas/Falkland Island), and its exposure made Patagonia half again as large as it is presently. This not only increased habitable land area, but also affected weather patterns across Patagonia east of the Andes, creating a much more continental climate than today's.

Like the present coastline, the Pleistocene Atlantic coast was heterogenous, characterized by diverse environment types (Ponce et al. 2011). The majority (~65%) of the ACS is sand, and large portions of the LGM coast were extensive sandy beaches. The second most common substrate is gravel (~12%), with large stretches of now-submerged gravel beach between 46° S and 56° S. A small proportion (~2%) of the LGM coastline was characterized by rocky islands, islets, and outcrops that likely hosted sea mammal rookeries and seabird breeding grounds. The silts and clays near estuaries, bays, and gulfs, were prime habitat for shellfish (Ponce et al. 2011).

As temperatures warmed and glaciers retreated at the end of the LGM, sea levels began to rise. By around 15,000 cal BP, just before the earliest widely-accepted occupation at Monte Verde (Dillehay 1997), sea levels had risen roughly 40 m (to −90 m) and the ACS was reduced by 65%. Still, an area of approximately 400,000 km^2 remained exposed and, despite rapid marine transgression pushing coastlines ever farther west, a large and likely resource-rich

coastal plain remained habitable. Between Santa Cruz Province and Tierra del Fuego, the water's edge remained between 40 and 90 km to the east of its current position; to the north, in Río Negro and Chubut, the exposed coastal shelf was still 200 km wide on average (Ponce et al. 2011).

Seas continued to rise rapidly between 15,000 and 11,000 cal BP—at a mean coastline recession rate of 27 m per year—and, by the end of the Late Glacial period (ca. 11,000 cal BP), the exposed ACS was just 105,000 km^2 (17% of its fully exposed extent; Ponce et al. 2011:372). Still, at this time, the coastline at the latitude of Tierra del Fuego was 15 km farther east than it is presently and ~25 km east of the current Santa Cruz coast. Seas continued to rise, forming the Straits of Magellan around 10,200 cal BP. The ACS was fully submerged by ~9000 cal BP (Ponce et al. 2011).

The injection of cold, fresh glacial meltwater cut off Tierra del Fuego from the Patagonian mainland and drowned substantial portions of the Patagonian landscape. It may also have temporarily altered ocean salinity, marine currents, and associated ecosystems (De Pol-Holz et al. 2006). How these complex dynamics affected early inhabitants of Patagonia is not yet clear. For that matter, neither is it clear how—or even whether—the simple, though dramatic, reduction of coastal real estate affected prehistoric people. If people were living on the exposed ACS or in now-submerged portions of the southern or western coasts, evidence of their behaviors, cultures, and affinities may be lost forever. We cannot currently say with any confidence whether the mixed terrestrial-coastal subsistence strategy observed in sites along the present east coast—particularly those inhabited around the time of sea level stabilization (ca. 8000 cal BP)—owes to coastal people having been driven inland, marine encroachment on terrestrial hunter-gatherers' territories, or initial occupation by groups that developed a hybrid strategy in situ. More generally, it seems clear that present-day coastal environments were inhabited during the middle Holocene, but does this simply reflect the timing of sea level stabilization, the expansion of growing interior populations into new ecosystems, or something else? Techniques for underwater exploration have improved dramatically in recent decades (Bailey and Fleming 2008; Benjamin 2010; Josenhans et al. 1997) and will perhaps bring clarity to some of these issues.

River Dynamics

Interior hydrologic systems were likewise affected by glacial activity. Glacial remodeling in the Andes affected rivers' headwaters (Coronato et al. 2008), and exposure of the ACS during the LGM may have altered their channels as well. Ponce and colleagues (Ponce et al. 2011) suggest that, during previous glaciations, the Colorado and Negro rivers may have merged on the exposed continental shelf, while other rivers appear to have been captured by larger drainage basins. Considering there is currently no widely-accepted evidence of a human presence in Patagonia prior to approximately 13,000 cal BP, these particular changes are only relevant to the extent that they highlight both the dynamism and the newness of the Patagonian fluvial system; the major river systems as we know them today developed largely following the Last Glacial Maximum (Coronato et al. 2008).

Major rivers might always have been focal points of human activity in Patagonia, particularly on the arid steppe where water is otherwise relatively scarce. During deglaciation, rivers likely swelled with meltwater, transporting large amounts of sediment downstream. Any archaeological sites that might have been present along their banks could have been washed away by floodwaters or deeply buried beneath overbank deposits. Moreover, any meandering of the rivers' channels would further confound interpretations of prehistoric behaviors, through destruction of sites on the one hand and potential dissociation of sites and relevant landforms on the other (e.g., a site's present location relative to rivers might not accurately reflect its past location relative to rivers).

Lastly, as with Holocene glacial readvances, riverine dynamics since the LGM have affected the landscape and archaeological record in ways similar to those just described (e.g., burial beneath deep overbank deposits). As such, riverine sites of all periods, not just early ones, may have been disproportionately disturbed.

Volcanoes

Beyond glacier-related landscape changes, several modeling agents have shaped, and continue to shape, the Patagonian landscape. Among them, Holocene volcanism is particularly important to our understanding of Patagonia's human past. Two of the four Andean volcanic zones lie within Patagonia: the Southern Volcanic Zone (SVZ) and the Austral Volcanic Zone (AVZ). The SVZ extends from approximately 33° S to 46° S and is the result of subduction of the Nazca Plate under the South American Plate. There is a volcanic dead zone—the Patagonian Volcanic Gap—between 46° S and 49° S, south of which the Antarctic Plate is subducted below the South American Plate, creating the AVZ, which extends to Tierra del Fuego. This zone is generally less active than the SVZ, though volcanoes in this zone periodically produce ash and pyroclastic material (D'Orazio et al. 2000).

The extent and duration of environmental impacts of prehistoric volcanic eruptions are unknown in most cases. We can, however, look to modern events for insights. Effects of the 1991 eruption of Volcán Hudson (~45°54' S) on plant and animal communities in southern Patagonia are well documented, for example (Pearson 1994). Immediately following the major 1991 Hudson eruption, violent winds redistributed the ash, leaving deposits 5 to 15 cm thick across approximately 100,000 km² of Argentina's Santa Cruz Province. Tephra deposition choked streams, causing them to dry up in many places, cutting off important water supplies to the arid region and killing off vegetation vital to commercial livestock grazing (Pearson 1994). Lago Buenos Aires/General Carrera (~46°30' S) was still ash-covered more than a year later.

Pearson (1994) studied the impact of the Hudson eruption on small mammals, reporting that 16 months after the eruption, hare, pichi, and skunk were all thriving, perhaps because predators had not yet recovered or because of reduced food competition from grazers (guanaco and domesticated sheep), whose numbers were reduced by effects of the eruption. From the 1991 Hudson event we might hypothesize that Patagonian volcanoes' effects can be widespread and devastating. Nonetheless, these effects may be spatially restricted and the area(s) affected determined in large part by wind patterns (already a major factor in Patagonian climates). The recent Hudson eruption also suggests that the negative effects of even major eruptions can be relatively brief. Of course, humans' responses to volcanic eruptions may not be solely, or even primarily, governed by practical considerations or physical effects of eruptions; such events may have had longer-lasting psychological and cultural effects than warranted by physical environmental changes.

Indeed, some eruptions appear to have had dramatic effects on prehistoric human populations. Cardich (1985; see also Prieto et al. 2013) hypothesized that a middle Holocene (ca. 7800 cal BP) eruption of Volcán Hudson led to a dramatic decline in human populations in central Patagonia, perhaps on account of the 20 cm thick tephra that blanketed parts of Tierra del Fuego, over 800 km to the south (Stern 2004; Prieto et al. 2013). This Hudson eruption is a particularly dramatic example from what appears to have been a pulse of increased volcanism in the SVZ during the middle Holocene (Coronato et al. 2008). Durán and Mikkan (2009) presented geomorphological and geochronological data indicating a spate of eruptions between 7800 and 5600 cal BP in far northern Patagonia (southern Mendoza Province, Argentina). A subsequent study (Durán et al. 2016) shows that each of these middle Holocene eruptions deposited tens of centimeters of tephra (up to 3 m in one instance) many kilometers from the ejection sites, and Durán and colleagues cite this as a potential cause of the coincident decline in the region's cultural radiocarbon dates.

Earthquakes and Landslides

Most of Andean Patagonia is seismically active, with a zone of relative inactivity between 45° S and northern Tierra del Fuego, corresponding roughly (and not surprisingly) to the Patagonian Volcanic Gap. The historic record indicates more than 400 earthquakes of magnitude M = 4 (where M is Richter magnitude) or higher since 1969. While paleo-seismicity is more difficult to document, appreciable quakes may have been at least as frequent in the past (Perucca and Bastias 2008). Paleo-seismicity is documented through primary evidence at the faults themselves, but also through secondary evidence including landslides, rock falls (from cliff faces and cave roofs), liquification, and the creation of dikes and sills. Beyond damage caused directly by a quake, these secondary effects clearly affect people, too, perhaps even more profoundly.

Perucca and Bastias (2008) report that the minimum quake force necessary to cause landslides is M = 4.5, which, as we just saw, is a very common earthquake occurrence today. González Díaz and colleagues (2005) provide evidence that quakes of at least this magnitude were common in the past as well. They report that northern Andean Patagonia has been prone to landslides since the start of the Holocene. For example, in Neuquén Province, between 36° S and 38° S, they documented nearly 50 rock avalanches since the Pleistocene. These would have been a significant risk to people living in Andean and foothills river valleys, and even if no one was present at the time, the quake may have buried evidence of previous occupations.

In addition, landslides significantly alter landforms through the displacement of large amounts of rock and soil. Because slides often occur in valleys, displaced debris can dam waterways and create lakes where previously none existed. Natural dams often subsequently fail under the force of accumulated water, again potentially affecting hunter-gatherer groups living in the area and/or archaeological sites in the path of these torrential floods. In a dramatic instance of this, a great middle Holocene landslide covered roughly 8 km² between Mendoza and

Neuquén Provinces, blocking the Río Barrancas and creating a large lake. The rock dam failed catastrophically in 1914 CE, flooding the lower Barrancas to the Río Colorado valley and destroying much life and property downstream (González Díaz et al. 2001). As with volcanism, seismicity and landslides may have been particularly frequent during the middle Holocene (Salemme and Miotti 2008).

In far southern Patagonia, quakes and landslides are also significant. Although modern seismicity is relatively low along the Magallanes-Fagnano fault (Lodolo et al. 2003), which runs the length of the Strait of Magellan, earthquakes may have posed periodic threats to the islands' prehistoric inhabitants. The temblors themselves likely caused dangerous landslides and avalanches, but human groups appear to have been small and highly mobile through much of prehistory, potentially diluting the impact of such events. Coastal sediment geomorphology on the east coast of Isla Grande, however, suggests that a subduction zone 2,300 km east of Tierra del Fuego—the Scotia-South Sandwich Island plate boundary—may have produced occasional tsunamis of moderate energy during the last 6,000 years (Bujalesky 2012).

Wind

If glaciers were the primary landscape-modeling agent of the past, Patagonian winds are likely the most important present one, for both their strength and constancy (Coronato et al. 2008). Winds erode and transport loose soils, excavating deflation hollows and accumulating large dunes. On the steppe in particular, high winds inhibit soil formation, leaving nothing but exposed bedrock in places. Winds contribute to evaporation and aridity, which leads to further erosion, and they generate waves at sea and in large lakes, which erodes shorelines and cause cliffs to recede. These effects are cumulative and have significant effects on archaeological records.

All of these forces—wind, seismicity, volcanism, fluvial geomorphology, eustasy (global sea level change), and glaciations—shaped the Patagonian landscapes to which prehistoric people adapted and across which their cultures changed through time. Importantly, while the earliest inhabitants may not have perceived the global-scale significance of the melting ice or the particular middle Holocene frequency of volcanoes and earthquakes, these and other changes occurred on timescales relevant to people. Perhaps northern Patagonians avoided the uplands on account of frequent volcanic eruptions (Durán et al. 2016); perhaps Fuegians avoided camping at the bases of hills to reduce the risk of landslides (cf. McCartney and Veltre 1999). We should be mindful, though, as we try to reconstruct and interpret prehistoric human distributions, that many of the landscape modeling forces described in this section affect site preservation as well: if we find there are no sites at the bases of hills, will it be because people avoided making camp there or because the landslides themselves have created a preservation bias? The final section of this chapter presents radiocarbon trends in Patagonia and provides a baseline understanding of how landscape dynamics and other postdepositional factors might have affected the archaeological record. Knowing this helps us better interpret available evidence in terms of human behavior and cultural change.

Temporal Trends

The radiocarbon database that I refer to throughout this book contains 1,840 dates derived from the published literature. The list is extensive, but almost certainly not exhaustive. Nonetheless, the data make clear that there are significant spatial and temporal gaps in our understanding of Patagonian prehistory.

Figure 2.19 shows the spatial distribution of all the dates in the database. Immediately obvious is the fact that large portions of interior Río Negro and Chubut Provinces, Argentina, and much of Chilean Patagonia remain archaeologically unknown, with the exception of northern Aysén and southern Magallanes administrative regions. Across Patagonia, dated locations likely reflect both site preservation and the historical

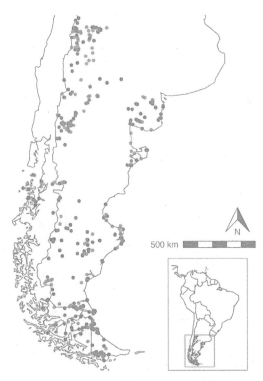

FIGURE 2.19. Geographic distribution of radiocarbon dates in the database compiled for this book (n = 1,840). Each point is semitransparent. Heavier (more saturated) icons indicate multiple dates at a particular location.

regions of particularly intensive dating. Points on the map are semitransparent, so the darker the icon, the more dates available for a particular location. In some cases, this is because there are several sites in close proximity, and in others, because single sites have large numbers of dates (see Chapters 5 and 7). Sites of course differ in the amount of material available for dating, and projects differ in their duration, budgets, and scopes. Certain regions become research attraction basins. This is certainly not unique to Patagonia (Garvey 2019; Haas and Kuhn 2019), but we should bear in mind the effects of attraction basins in our interpretations of Patagonian prehistory.

Figure 2.20 presents the 1,840 radiocarbon dates in 1,000-year intervals between ~15,000 (12,890 ^{14}C BP, Piedra Museo) and 0 cal BP. This set of panels presents a clear pattern of increasing radiocarbon frequency through time. This might owe to growing human populations, to loss of archaeological data through time, or a combination of the two. In the following chapters, I explore each of these possibilities at particular moments in Patagonian prehistory, and discuss them in greater detail in Chapter 7.

Our understanding of the first important "moment" in Patagonian prehistory—initial human colonization—rests heavily and somewhat uncomfortably on an incomplete and likely impoverished radiocarbon record. I attempt to remedy this by incorporating unconventional lines of evidence, as described in Chapter 4, following Chapter 3's discussion of bodies of theory that motivate this book.

distribution of research attention. Patagonia is a vast landscape, parts of which have limited infrastructure. Survey access can be incredibly challenging and some of the gaps in the radiocarbon record are places that simply have not yet been tested. Also evident in Figure 2.19 are

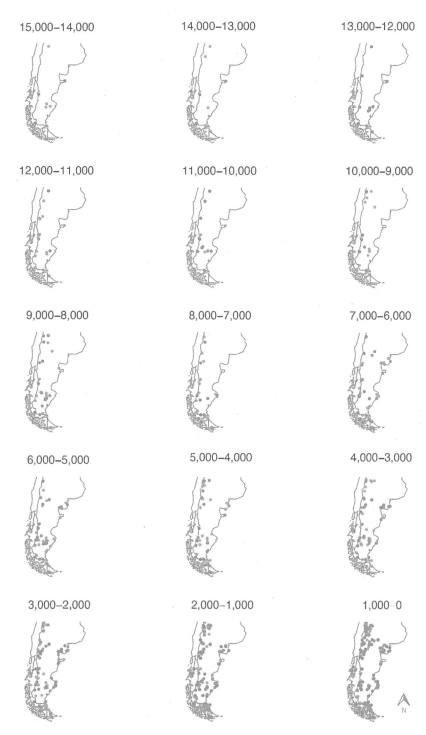

FIGURE 2.20. Geographic distribution of Patagonia's radiocarbon dates presented in 1,000-year increments (e.g., the top left panel depicts all dates between 15,000 and 14,000 cal BP). Heavier (more saturated) icons indicate multiple dates at a particular location.

3

The Evolutionary Perspective

Nothing about culture makes sense except in the light of evolution.
—Peter Richerson and Robert Boyd (2005:252)

This book takes an evolutionary perspective. "Evolution," at its most basic, is simply change through time. To call special attention to this book's evolutionary perspective might seem unnecessary, then, since *most* archaeology deals with change through time on one level or another. There is even a long history in anthropology of drawing parallels between cultural and biological evolution, as this book does: Nineteenth century "progressive social evolutionary theory," for example, was sometimes referred to as "social Darwinism," and proponents believed human groups evolved progressively through stages of savagery, barbarism, and civilization (e.g., Morgan 1877; Powell 1885; Spencer 1864). Functionalists of the early to mid-twentieth century viewed all components of culture, including seemingly maladaptive cultural "oddities," as adaptations to local resources (e.g., Freeman 1971; Piddocke 1965; Rappaport 1968; see also Bettinger et al. 2015; Garvey and Bettinger 2014). While evolutionary views are not new to archaeology, this book's evolutionary perspective differs fundamentally from historical "change-through-time" approaches, and it is worth clearly defining these differences here at the start. To do so, this chapter attends to three basic questions: (1) What is an evolutionary perspective? (2) How can an evolutionary perspective help us understand prehistory? and (3) Which specific models are most useful for addressing the questions about Patagonian prehistory posed in this book?

What Is an "Evolutionary Perspective"?

My approach to Patagonia's archaeological record is rooted in the works of Darwin (1859, 1871), contributors to the modern evolutionary synthesis (e.g., Dobzhansky 1947; Huxley 1942; Simpson 1944; see also Chapter 1), and more recent founders of the multidisciplinary field of cultural evolution (e.g., Boyd and Richerson 1985; Cavalli-Sforza and Feldman 1981). Central to their views of evolution, and to mine, are "population thinking" and explicitly defined evolutionary processes.

Population thinking is the term Ernst Mayr (1959) used to describe a radical cognitive shift attributable to Darwin, away from ideal archetypes (e.g., species, human groups) and toward material variation within "types." According to this view, descriptions of species can be informative, but they are really little more than statistical summaries that do not describe individuals very well. Moreover, Darwin believed that variation within populations—rather than central tendencies and typological ideals—is the real matter of interest, and the raw material on which evolution works (Hey 2011). In anthropology, this view differs fundamentally from traditional approaches to cultural change that treat cultures as homogenous wholes (all members of a group are culturally identical), and change as both monolithic (all group members

50

change in the same ways simultaneously) and progressive (goal oriented; groups ultimately become "civilized" because it is the best thing to be). Population thinkers believe, instead, that human groups are composed of individuals who, jointly, carry a pool of culturally acquired information (Richerson and Boyd 2005:59). Individuals' information differs in part because we learn different things and from different people, and in part because we may each learn differently, relying more heavily on either socially- or independently-acquired information. How information is acquired and from whom, and how it is then adapted and retransmitted, are some of the processes that account for cultural evolution.

Recall from Chapter 1 that scientists associated with the 1930s' modern evolutionary synthesis demonstrated mathematically that evolutionary mechanisms, natural selection in particular, can carry advantageous traits through populations (of individuals) over time. In their application of these principles to cultural evolution, Cavalli-Sforza and Feldman (1981), Boyd and Richerson (1985), and many others since have shown that a variety of mechanisms—including selection, but also forces particular to cultural evolution—carry cultural traits, including nonadaptive or even maladaptive ones, through populations over time. The identification of evolutionary mechanisms and formal assessment of how they might effect cultural change is another way this book's approach differs from historical ones in which change was viewed as inevitable, requiring no special explanations (forces), or else the result of a "prime mover," a singularly important force external to the evolving culture (e.g., climate change). Prime movers, including climate change, are certainly responsible for some of the cultural change we see in the archaeological record. But culture is one of the most complex adaptations on earth and its evolution is a correspondingly complex process, involving not only external forces (e.g., selection via environmental change) but also demographic factors (population size and connectivity) and forces that are purely cultural (e.g., biased transmission of cultural information). I describe some of these evolutionary forces in a later section of this chapter and throughout the book in the specific case of Patagonia. The next section, though, describes some of the distinct benefits of interpreting the Patagonian record—or any record, for that matter—from an evolutionary perspective.

How Can Evolutionary Perspective Help Us Understand Prehistory?

This chapter's epigraph, a quote from two pioneers of dual inheritance theory, is a nod to Theodosius Dobzhansky, a prominent geneticist and evolutionary biologist associated with the modern synthesis who, in 1973, published an article titled "Nothing in biology makes sense except in the light of evolution" (Dobzhansky 1973). Boyd and Richerson's adaptation, "nothing about *culture* makes sense except in the light of evolution," (Boyd and Richerson 2005; my emphasis) is also a fine summary of the power of the evolutionary approach in the study of culture. Evolutionary theory helps us understand not only Culture with a capital "C"—what it is, when and how it evolved, how it benefits humans, and at what cost—but also the details of any given culture (lowercase "c"), both at a particular moment and as it changes through time.

Nonevolutionary approaches certainly afford valuable insights, too. Even if we were to take a completely atheoretical approach, we could describe a culture, c, at time t and, with adequate knowledge of things going on elsewhere in the relevant sphere of influence (e.g., among neighboring groups prehistorically; in the rest of the world during the modern era), we can arrive at logical explanations for elements of c. We could even peer backward, to time t-1, to identify potential causes of the things we identified as causal in our description of c at time t—and so on into a more remote past, t-n, until we have a lengthy string of historical causes and effects leading to c.

There are some problems with this approach, though. First, we are likely at some point to lose the thread. We can only peer backward so far and, probably, the farther back we look, the less reliable our associations between events due to information attrition. Still, even if our information were perfectly reliable, and our associations perfectly accurate, all the way back to the most distant *t-n*, we cannot in this way ever arrive at the *ultimate* explanations of *c*'s elements. Not ones that are meaningful, anyway: "Big Bang leads to pyramids at Giza" is flashy, but vapid.

More problematic, however, is the fact that an atheoretical approach provides no framework for distinguishing important from unimportant information. This is precisely the job of theory, to condense the sea of facts—many of which are irrelevant and, anyway, could never be described in full—to a coherent set of data. Even in the otherwise atheoretical example above, describing *c* at time *t* and in terms of *t* requires that the historian choose a subset of facts on which to focus (e.g., which elements of *c* are important). Still, if we are interested in how *c* and another culture, geographically distant *d*, came to resemble one another, or we want to understand ultimate causes of *c*'s characteristics, we need a tool more powerful than historical description.

Evolutionary theory is one such tool and, as Boyd and Richerson (2005) argue, the most appropriate one for the study of culture because culture does not just change, it *evolves*: a variety of forces act on variation within cultures to change the frequencies of particular variants through time. *Culture* itself can be difficult to define completely and in a way that attends to all of its possible states and uses (cf. Sperber and Claidière 2008), but it certainly includes socially acquired information that is stored in human brains and cultural objects (Richerson and Boyd 2005). "A culture," then, includes the pool of all such information and objects held by a population of varied individuals. So, to explain properties of either Culture or "a culture," we need to understand how day-to-day events in the lives of individuals shape the pool of information and objects (Richerson and Boyd 2005). This requires careful accounting since the population-level consequences of individuals' choices and behaviors day-to-day can be difficult to intuit; "group consequences do not follow in any simple

way from individual intent" (Bettinger and Richerson 1996:226–227). Modeling is one particularly effective way to scale up from individuals to groups while taking advantage of things we already know about humans' biology and psychology, culture, and the mechanics of evolution.

Models

Models are deliberate simplifications that allow us to explore complex causal relationships through the isolation and manipulation of variables. Models can be formal (mathematical) or informal (conceptual), and each kind has a place in the study of prehistory. Formal models rooted in principles and methods derived from evolutionary biology, genetics, and population ecology (e.g., Boyd and Richerson 1985; Cavalli-Sforza and Feldman 1981; Henrich and McElreath 2003; Richerson and Boyd 2005) have fundamentally changed our understanding of the mechanisms of cultural evolution, and these are perhaps the most powerful and versatile tools in the evolutionary scientist's toolkit. They can be used to simulate evolutionary outcomes and to formulate hypotheses whose predictions can then be tested against empirical data. Because formal models require clearly specified parameters, they can provide a level of understanding that is difficult to achieve through observation alone, allowing us to explore how outcomes change as we change parameter values, or the parameters themselves. In modeling cultural phenomena, we distill "the unnumbered complexities of reality to a tractable number of abstractions" in order to make predictions to which we can then compare cultural data (Garvey 2008:11; Friedman 1953). As an exploratory tool, this can be particularly useful in archaeology where our remove from past behaviors is such that we cannot fully appreciate their complexity through observation alone. Importantly, too, modeling can reveal unanticipated—even counterintuitive—causal relationships, leading to novel hypotheses.

It is true, though, that archaeological data are not always perfectly suited to this kind of modeling, whether for specifying parameters or assessing models' predictions. In the case of assessing predictions, the issue is really that many models of cultural evolution imagine person-to-person exchanges of information while archaeological data most often represent aggregations of many such exchanges, accumulated over years, centuries, or even millennia; their respective scales seem mismatched. In recent years, archaeologists have developed evolutionary models specifically tailored to archaeological circumstances (e.g., aggregated and time-averaged records), which has helped to bridge the gap between theory and data and should facilitate formal modeling going forward (Bettinger and Eerkens 1997, 1999; Eerkens and Bettinger 2001, 2008; Eerkens and Lipo 2005; Garvey 2018a).

There are also instances in which conceptual models are better suited to our purposes. Conceptual models, often derived from formal ones, specify more general relationships between variables: "x should have a positive effect on y," or even "a twofold increase in x should result in a similar increase in y," rather than "the effect of x on y is precisely. . . ." That is, conceptual models help us understand the direction and magnitude of the effects of one thing on another. This kind of modeling is also powerful; we formulate hypotheses, make predictions, and evaluate them using archaeological data, just as we would with formal models, and we can do so even lacking very specific information about appropriate starting parameters or values for certain variables. Archaeologists already make good use of this kind of model, and conceptual models will likely have a place in archaeology even as we continue to identify archaeologically relevant units of observation and analysis for use in formal models.

Lastly, while evolutionary models are powerful tools for exploring cultural evolution in archaeological contexts, they are supplements to, not substitutes for, standard archaeological inference and deduction. Good old-fashioned excavation and analysis generate critical information about prehistory, without which evolutionary theory and modeling remain largely hypothetical. However, without theory and models, archaeological data will never truly

make sense and, as Bruce Winterhalder suggests, "we are just beginning to tap the promise of evolutionary social science" (2018).

Evolutionary Principles and Models Applied in This Book

Humans are subject to the same evolutionary forces as other animals. We are, as evolutionary anthropologist Robert Foley (1987) says, just another unique species. Yet, at the same time, our uniqueness seems . . . *extraordinary*: we exhibit unprecedented adaptive and cultural variation, and humans are clear outliers in many domains, even relative to other large-brained and highly social animals. Burnside and colleagues refer to this as our "dual nature" (Burnside et al. 2012). This duality demands application of a variety of models in concert to identify and understand the ways in which human culture shapes our interactions with the natural world. The models used in this book are particularly effective in this regard, and can be classed broadly as macroecological, microeconomic, and co-evolutionary.

Macroecological models identify important ecological relationships at large spatial and temporal scales, defining their effects on species distributions and densities. Conversely, microeconomic models identify individual-level adaptations in more specific ecological context, that is, on a much smaller scale, but with similar underlying assumptions. Both classes of model are predicated on the idea that most features we observe (e.g., species distributions, behaviors) are the result of adaptation, whether unconscious—as when a species' range is restricted by the physical environment—or consciously, as when species make decisions in light of options' relative profitability. The two classes of model are complementary: macroecological models provide a sense of the environmental variables and ecological relationships worth paying attention to at the local scale, and microeconomic models are a source of explanations for macroscale patterns. Likewise, both acknowledge the unevenness of resource distributions—across the Earth and in local environments, respectively—and both assume the effects of resource patchiness will be reflected at the scale of the model (global- and local-scale species distributions and abundances, as well as individuals' foraging and reproductive decisions on the micro scale). There is room in both kinds of model for cultural parameters. Both are quite good, in fact, at identifying the *effects* of culture on species distributions and behaviors, but neither is designed to explicitly address nonadaptive behaviors or "purely" cultural relationships (those not necessarily affected by the physical environment). This requires a third type of model: co-evolutionary.

Co-evolutionary models are not only different in scope, they are also explicitly multiscalar. Firmly rooted in Darwin's population thinking, co-evolutionary models specify individual-level processes and scale them up to multigenerational populations to understand group-level and long-term evolutionary consequences. These models, sometimes referred to as "dual inheritance" models, are designed to explore cultural ecology—adaptations to both physical and cultural elements of the environment—and feedback between our culture and biology, since we do not simply adapt to our environment, we change the very environment to which we physically and culturally adapt (Lewontin 1983; Odling-Smee 1988). Moreover, this body of theory acknowledges that, while much of our behavior is adaptive, some aspects of culture are decidedly nonadaptive—maladaptive, even. Neither of the other two classes of model is equipped to explain such phenomena and, clearly, all three classes are relevant to the study of prehistory.

From this book's approach to Patagonian prehistory, two main themes emerge: the distribution of people across the landscape through time and the evolution of material culture. These themes are closely related because human demographics likely affect rates of cultural evolution and overall cultural complexity, as I describe next and in case studies throughout the book. The following sections describe specific macroecological, microeconomic, and co-evolutionary models that can help us understand cultural evolution and human distributions in prehistoric Patagonia.

Macroecological Models

Biogeographical studies of nonhuman animals indicate that environmental factors account for a substantial portion of the variation observed in species distributions (cf. Hubbell 2001). This is because variables like temperature and precipitation affect the abundance, timing, and dispersion of resources, which, in turn, affects the abundance and distribution of the species that consume those resources. Since, as Burnside and colleagues (2012) note, humans are subject to the same evolutionary forces and natural laws as other animals, it is worth assessing the degree to which these forces affect human distributions and densities in light of our "second nature": culture. Simple macroecological models can quickly indicate general trends in human population distributions relative to environmental variables. They can also reveal outliers, or human groups that deviate substantially from a general trend. Both trends and outliers can be very informative.

Macroecological trends indicate possible limiting factors—conditions that limit species' abundances or distributions, such as available moisture in dry environments and average low temperatures during the coldest part of the year. In both of these examples, dry and cold environments, humans have found ways to overcome the limiting effects (e.g., well-digging, clothing), which is partly why many of the macroecological models that are good at predicting nonhuman animals' distributions find little or no expression among human groups. It is likewise true that a single variable (e.g., aridity) might have little effect on its own, but a significant effect on human densities and dispersions when combined with one or more other variables (e.g., aridity *and* temperature). Simple models are nonetheless informative as first-order approximations of the importance of environment in a given case and as indicators of variables worth incorporating in more precise models.

In the archaeological literature, a handful of variables are frequently fingered as potential limiting factors, including precipitation, effective temperature, and primary biomass.

Probably most of us could readily think of three reasons these would *not* be very good predictors of worldwide distributions and densities of human hunter-gatherers. Still, it is worth assessing this formally in light of these variables' frequent appearance as "prime movers" in the archaeological literature.

Binford (2001) provided a convenient source of both environmental and demographic data related to 339 ethnographic groups from around the world. The selection of environmental variables considered here are mean annual rainfall, mean rainfall during the driest month of the year, primary plant biomass (g/m²/year), and four temperature measures: annual average, averages during the hottest and coldest months of the year, and effective temperature. I have included the driest month's rainfall because population growth among nonhuman animals is often limited by the scarcest resource (or period of least availability in the case of rain), rather than total resource availability. This is Liebig's law of the minimum (Gorban et al. 2010). For similar reasons, we might expect temperature extremes to have a greater effect than annual mean temperatures, so I have included them, too. Effective temperature is a composite variable, calculated as a function of temperature extremes (warmest and coldest month means; Bailey 1960), and is considered a more reliable measure of growing season and environmental productivity than annual average temperature (Binford 2001). These variables' relationships to the ethnographic groups' population densities (individuals per 100 km²) are presented in Figure 3.1, alongside equivalent correlations between environmental variables and primary plant biomass, for comparison.

The upshot of this modeling exercise is that environmental variables are better at predicting primary plant biomass than they are at predicting human biomass. Neither is plant biomass itself a very good predictor of human population densities ($r^2 = 0.27$), despite its use as proxy for food availability (cf. Kelly 1983). This is not especially surprising and probably owes in large part to culture, which can both facilitate unprecedented population growth

in relatively low-quality habitats (i.e., where biomass is naturally low), and stifle growth in high quality habitats (e.g., through rules regarding fertility). Nonetheless, some interesting information emerges from these models. For instance: (1) Most (85%) of the groups in the Binford dataset live(d) at population densities below 0.5/100 km². It is not clear whether this reflects late-prehistoric-through-modern era distortions of previous human densities (e.g., the spread of agriculture and effects of European/Euroamerican disease and aggression on New World populations) or something else. (2) Mean warm month temperature has essentially no effect on population density, but the relationship between density and mean cold month temperature is modestly positive ($r^2 = 0.19$). Approximately 40% of all groups in the Binford sample live in places where the coldest month's average temperature is below 0°C and, among these groups, the cold month average is a reasonable predictor of population density ($r^2 = 0.44$). Lastly, (3) human population densities are most variable where rainfall and primary plant biomass are lowest. That is, where mean annual rainfall is low, humans live at both very low and (relatively) very high densities—in fact, the highest densities in this sample of ethnographic hunter-gatherers. A significant proportion of all groups (43%) live in places that receive no appreciable rain (<5 mm) during the driest month of the year. The same proportion live in places where primary plant biomass is less than 5,000 g/m²/year (the lowest 8% of the biomass scale) and, while nearly all (96%) of these groups live at population densities below 0.5/100 km², some live at densities as high as those of populations living where biomass exceeds 35,000 g/m²/year.

These findings lead us to two important conclusions. Firstly, despite their simplicity, univariate macroecological models can explain a nontrivial amount of variance among ethnographic hunter-gatherer groups' densities. Of course, there is quite a lot of unexplained variance, too. In a few cases, this is simply a matter of model-fitting; nonlinear models better describe some of the relationships in Figure 3.1. However, most "prime-mover" arguments assume a simple,

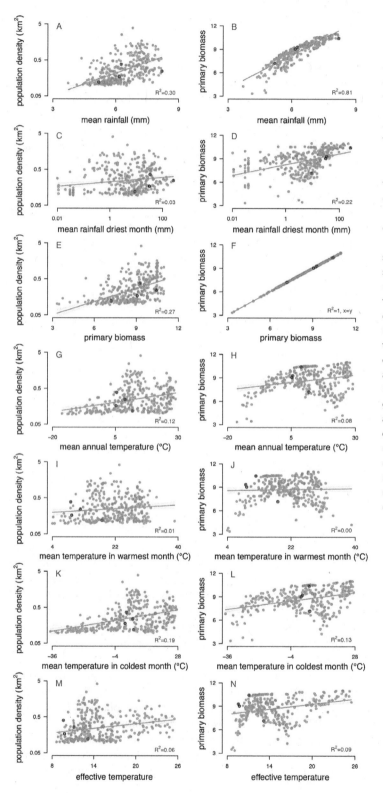

Figure 3.1. Relationships between (left column) population density and (A) mean annual rainfall, (C) mean annual rainfall during the driest month of the year, (E) primary biomass, (G) mean annual temperature, (I) mean warm month temperature, (K) mean cold month temperature, and (M) effective temperature; and (right column) between primary biomass and the same seven environmental variables (biomass is regressed on biomass simply as a placeholder). The significance of each (linear) relationship is indicated in the lower right hand of the corresponding panel (use of linear models is described in the text). Lines and shading depict mean predicted values and 95% confidence intervals. Data points for Patagonian groups listed by Binford (2001) are outlined in black: A = Alacalouf (Káwesqar), O = Ona (Selk'nam), T = Tehuelche (Aónikenk, Gununa'Kena, and Mecharnúekenk), Y = Yaghan (Yámana). Data from Binford (2001).

proportional relationship between human densities and environmental variables, and this exercise highlights potential problems with that approach. Meanwhile, in other cases, the lack of strong correlations (i.e., large amounts of unexplained variance) between major climatic variables and human population densities likely owes to interactions among environmental variables. The second major, and perhaps more important, conclusion we draw from this exercise is that human culture can clearly mitigate (or amplify) environmental effects in ways that make univariate environmental models relatively weak for prediction.

In macroecological studies of nonhuman species' densities and distributions, latitude is frequently used in place of single environmental variables. Latitude is, in a sense, a composite variable because it is correlated (to varying degrees) with multiple environmental variables (e.g., temperature, seasonality) that affect the abundance, timing, and dispersion of resources. In exploratory studies, latitude can be a useful starting point, simplifying the accounting related to, say, annual variations in both temperature and rainfall. Importantly, too, in the study of prehistoric humans' distributions, latitude captures the potential influence of history in a way that environmental variables cannot, since, with important exceptions, environmental data measure present conditions while species distributions are partly a result of past environments and interactions with other species (Blackburn et al. 1999; Harcourt 2012). Compelling patterns that emerge from latitudinal studies form the basis of basic ecological principles that, in turn, motivate hypotheses regarding species density and dispersion. An example relevant to our study of human distributions is the observation that, on average, there is greater species diversity at low latitudes than at high, a phenomenon Harcourt (2012) calls the "Forster effect," crediting Johann Forster's observation of the latitudinal gradient of diversity in 1778. Granting that human groups are all part of the same species and that genes typically flow readily between human groups, cultures can remain surprisingly discrete and are analogous to species in certain

ways. Allowing this analogy, the Forster effect is present among human groups as well. Collard and Foley (2002:375) analyzed a sample of over 3,800 cultures and found a significant relationship between latitude and human cultural density (i.e., diversity; $r = -0.93$, $p < 0.001$); there are many more cultures in the tropics than there are at higher latitudes (Figure 3.2).

Simply noting such relationships can help us make predictions about certain aspects of human culture, as I explore below and in the coming chapters. The underlying causes of these macroecological relationships can, of course, have important implications, too. There are several possible explanations for the Forster effect, and Harcourt (2012) explored their applicability in the case of human cultural diversity. Among humans, the latitudinal diversity gradient might be explained by greater environmental stability at low latitudes (i.e., reduced seasonality), which tends to promote diversification. Alternatively (or additionally), the Forster effect among human groups might owe to the positive correlation between geographic range size and latitude—this is the "Rapoport effect," the tendency for species' range sizes to increase with increased latitude (Rapoport 1982)—coupled with the fact that culturally distinct human groups' ranges tend not to overlap. Large, non-overlapping ranges suppress diversity because space is simply insufficient to host many such wide-ranging groups. The Rapoport effect is not universally accepted as an ecological rule (e.g., Gaston et al. 1998), but seems to have reasonable empirical support among species at latitudes above ~40°, and the effect itself may be explained by a variety of factors including increased seasonality, decreased productivity, and deceased competition at higher latitudes (Grove et al. 2012; Nettle 1999; Pearce 2014). In humans, range size is positively correlated with latitude (Figure 3.3; Binford 2001; Collard and Foley 2002; Harcourt 2012; Mace and Pagel 1995), likely as a result of seasonality and environmental productivity. Where plant resources are relatively scarce, animals must range farther to meet their caloric needs, and humans must range farther in response (Garvey 2018b).

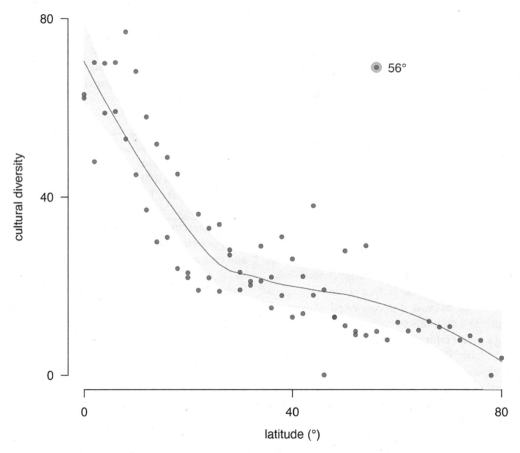

FIGURE 3.2. Relationship between cultural diversity and latitude (degrees north or south of the equator). The shaded area depicts a local polynomial regression line and 95% confidence intervals using α = 0.75 (the default setting of loess in the R {3.5.2} package). The highlighted point is 56° S; there are far more cultural groups in Tierra del Fuego than predicted by the Forster effect (see text). A second order polynomial regression demonstrates that cultural diversity is significantly negatively related to latitude ($\beta_{latitude}$ 3 SE = −1.63 ± 0.22; $\beta_{latitude^2}$ ± SE = 0.012 ± 0.003; n = 70 groups; R^2 = 0.69; $p < 2.2 \times 10^{-16}$). Data derived from Collard and Foley (2002).

Humans at higher latitudes also tend to move farther each time they move within a range (Figure 3.4; Burnside et al. 2012).

Another set of explanations for the diversity gradient highlights the important possibility that underlying causes of macroecological phenomena are not necessarily uniform across space or through time. In 1950, Theodosius Dobzhansky (of modern evolutionary synthesis fame) posited that species diversity is most limited by competitors, predators, and disease at low latitudes where biodiversity is high, and by the physical environment (e.g., temperature, available biomass) at higher latitudes (Dobzhansky 1950). Robert MacArthur (1972) later refined the hypothesis in the specific context of North American species, writing that species' southern boundaries are determined by interactions with other species (i.e., competitors, predators, and diseases), and their northern ones by environmental tolerances. Binford was among the first to suggest that this might also be true of human groups (Binford 2001), a hypothesis only very recently tested formally. Tallavaara and colleagues (Tallavaara et al. 2018) used structural equation modeling to evaluate the relative contributions of environmental productivity, species diversity, and pathogens on patterns of hunter-gatherer densities and dispersions. They found that, indeed, environmental productivity is not the best predictor of human demographics across environment types, disease burden being far more important than productivity in highly productive areas (i.e., low latitudes).

Environmental productivity does appear to be important at Patagonian latitudes and may have affected distributions and abundances of prehistoric hunter-gatherers there. However, for the ethnographic period, at least, southern Patagonia is an outlier on the latitudinal diversity gradient. Recall that Collard and Foley (2002) found a significant relationship between latitude and human cultural diversity ($r = -0.93$). The negative correlation between latitude and cultural diversity (Forster effect) predicts Patagonian cultural diversity should be low, in part because groups' range size requirements tend to increase with latitude to meet resource needs (Rapoport effect). But, according to the Collard and Foley study, cultural diversity (groups per 10^6 km^2) between 52° and 56° southern latitude is surprisingly high (see Figure 3.2). Tierra del Fuego, in particular, is a clear outlier: there are far more cultural groups there than predicted by the Forster effect. With the exception of Antarctica and a handful of small islands (including the Falklands, which appear not to have been inhabited before 1764 CE; Goebel 1971), Tierra del Fuego is the only landmass south of 52° S. This makes high-latitude Southern Hemisphere diversity all the more surprising, since cultural groups are concentrated in a very small geographical area, made smaller still where islands' interiors are uninhabitable (see Chapter 2; Garvey 2018b).

Exaggerated diversity in southern Patagonia might be a product of the considerable environmental heterogeneity there (Chapter 2), coupled with apparent cultural insularity, which may itself have either ecological or historic roots. At contact, there were four named cultural groups in Tierra del Fuego—the Yámana, Selk'nam, Manek'enk, and Kawéskar—who spoke mutually unintelligible languages (Cooper 1946). Each of these was further subdivided into dialect groups and social units that were smaller still. The Yámana alone were divided into five territories where groups spoke mutually intelligible but distinct dialects. Within each territory, Yámana lived in small, independent family groups that were relatively isolated from one another. Social gatherings of any size were rare and occurred primarily to observe initiation rites or to partition a beached whale. Cooper (1946) indicates that the Yámana expressed a deep sense of individual independence. These generalizations are supported by Binford's (2001:246) data on the aggregated and dispersed sizes of the world's hunting and gathering groups. The Yámana average aggregated group size was 24 people, and dispersed groups contained 13 on average, both of which are on the low end of the spectrum represented in the Binford dataset (see also Garvey 2018b). Whatever the origin of this diversity, it likely had significant cultural evolutionary implications, as I describe in the section on co-evolutionary models, below.

The Forster and Rapoport effects and other global-scale patterns can help clarify the relative effects of cultural and environmental factors on human distributions and densities by identifying trends as well as outliers. Analyses based on either latitude or particular environmental variables can be used to formulate hypotheses related to mobility, range size, and relative isolation. These, in turn, have implications for other important aspects of culture and cultural change. It is nonetheless important to keep in mind both that these models are meant only as first approximations of general human-environment relationships, and that these approximations are only as good as the data used to generate them. The Binford (2001) dataset, for instance, may be better suited to making predictions for northern hemisphere groups than for southern, given the underrepresentation of southern groups in that sample (Figure 3.5). Moreover, neither the northern nor the southern hemisphere subsample is a balanced representation of all latitudes; there are peaks at approximately 40° N and 20° S. Whether this is

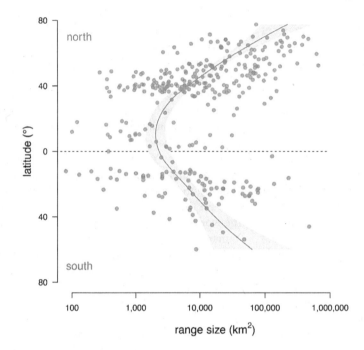

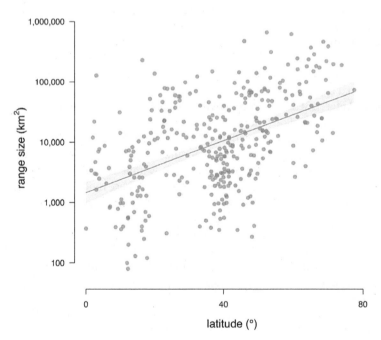

FIGURE 3.3. Relationship between latitude and range size (mean total kilometers of yearly moves). Blue points indicate foraging groups above the equator; orange points indicate those below. The top panel depicts the size of forager group range size (km^2) across the latitudinal range, demonstrating a clear trend towards larger range sizes at high latitudes. The shaded area in the top panel depicts a local polynomial regression line and 95% confidence intervals using $\alpha = 0.75$ (the default setting of loess in the R {3.5.2} package). The bottom panel shows range size is significantly positively correlated with absolute latitude (linear model, $\beta_{latitude} \pm$ SE = 0.05 ± 0.005; n = 339 ethnographic groups; $R^2 = 0.23$; $p < 2.0 \times 10^{-16}$). Line and shading depict mean predicted values and 95% confidence intervals. Data from Binford (2001).

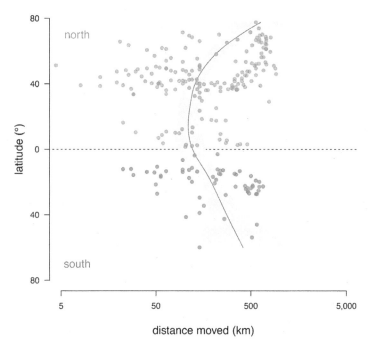

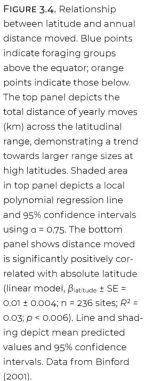

FIGURE 3.4. Relationship between latitude and annual distance moved. Blue points indicate foraging groups above the equator; orange points indicate those below. The top panel depicts the total distance of yearly moves (km) across the latitudinal range, demonstrating a trend towards larger range sizes at high latitudes. Shaded area in top panel depicts a local polynomial regression line and 95% confidence intervals using a = 0.75. The bottom panel shows distance moved is significantly positively correlated with absolute latitude (linear model, $\beta_{latitude} \pm$ SE = 0.01 ± 0.004; n = 236 sites; R^2 = 0.03; p < 0.006). Line and shading depict mean predicted values and 95% confidence intervals. Data from Binford (2001).

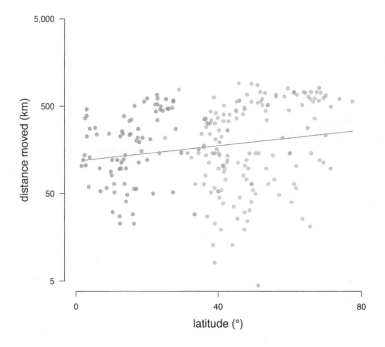

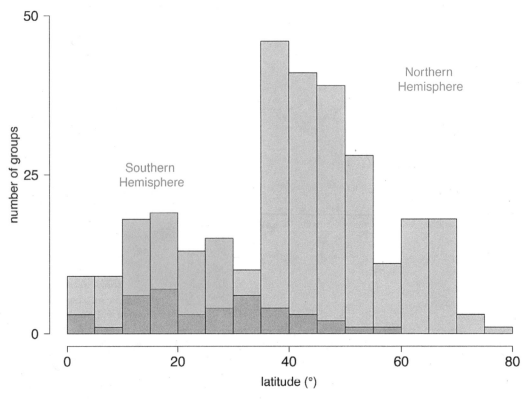

FIGURE 3.5. Histograms depicting the representation of ethnographic groups from the Northern (blue) and Southern (orange) Hemispheres in the Binford (2001) database.

a result of sampling bias or a reflection of actual ethnographic hunter-gatherer densities (which would, incidentally, violate the Dobzhansky-MacArthur principle described above), it is noteworthy that there is more variation in range size and distance moved at latitudes for which there are more observations (Figures 3.3 and 3.4). Perhaps there would be more variation across the board (and, therefore, weaker predictive models) if we had more data at other latitudes. Or perhaps there is really something worth paying attention to at 40° N and 20° S.

A final caveat related to the Binford dataset: Many intergroup comparisons now use the Standard Cross Cultural Sample (SCCS; Murdock and White 1969) rather than large cultural datasets to draw general inferences about cultural evolution. The SCCS is a carefully selected sample of 186 cultural groups from around the world considered relatively independent from

one another. Murdock and White compiled the list in an attempt to avoid "Galton's problem" in cross-cultural analysis—the fact that many groups in larger cultural lists are not independent on account of cultural connections including trade, cultural borrowing, copying, conquest, and homology (inheritance from a common ancestor). This is a problem because, with such autocorrelation, we cannot always tell whether traits shared by neighboring groups owe to similar adaptations to similar environment or to an historical relationship between the groups. Nonetheless, I have chosen to use the larger Binford dataset because my analyses are limited to examinations of basic ecological relationships rather than specific cultural expressions and, in this case, more data are more likely to indicate true patterns than fewer data. It is true that groups' range sizes might not be independent, in the sense that space is finite and groups rarely have overlapping territories. Nonetheless, we would not necessarily expect this to result in a Rapoport-like pattern (large high-latitude/small low-latitude ranges) in the absence of ecological factors.

For all their shortcomings (confirmed and potential), simple macroecological models nonetheless provide some compelling hypotheses regarding human distributions and densities. They are not meant to diagnose causal relationships, but to identify variables worth paying attention to in subsequent modeling exercises. Indeed, most cultural phenomena are likely the result of complex interactions among social, demographic, and environmental variables rather than of simple human-environment relationships. Macroecological models are also useful for identifying outliers: groups that deviate significantly from observed trends (i.e., from modeled predictions) can be sources of novel hypotheses related to both microeconomic behaviors and gene-culture co-evolutionary scenarios. This is certainly true in the case of the unexpected cultural diversity in southern Patagonia, as I describe below.

Microeconomic Models

The previous section alludes to culture's role in human groups' deviations from the predictions of macroecological models. Obvious examples are major cultural developments like agriculture, which increases productivity per unit land and the number of people the land can support, and medicines that improve survivorship in the tropics. These and similar developments can "artificially" increase population densities, diluting macroecological trends and producing outlier groups that deviate substantially from observed patterns. Culture can additionally affect macroecological patterns in subtler ways, as through group-level differences in subsistence technologies, foraging strategies, and other cultural manifestations that change the availability of environmental energy. On an even smaller scale, individuals within groups differ in their tool-making and hunting skills, access to and retention of ecological knowledge, and a wide range

of other factors. So, where macroecological models explain adaptive trends at large spatial scales, microeconomic models predict individuals' responses to local environmental conditions. And while microeconomic decisions underlie many macroecological patterns, the individuals themselves are generally invisible in macroecological models. Conversely, individuals are precisely the unit of analysis in microeconomic models.

In fact, microeconomic models center on a very specific kind of individual: idealized, hyper-rational, optimizing ones faced with decisions related to the allocation of scarce resources. Typically, the resources involved are time and energy, both of which are assumed to be limited relative to the individual's demand for these and other resources (e.g., mating opportunities). Modeled individuals consistently make optimal decisions, ones that maximize benefits relative to costs, and these individuals are endowed with superior reasoning skills, which allow them to eliminate all irrational impulses. Clearly, this idealized actor—*Homo economicus*—is fictional. Humans are not unerringly rational, narrowly self-interested optimizers. Most evolutionary scientists who employ microeconomic models not only acknowledge the fiction of *H. economicus* but embrace it as a key component of a methodology designed to isolate the variables most relevant to a particular problem, and to winnow the predictively irrelevant chaff (Friedman 1953).

The microeconomic focus on an idealized type, *H. economicus*, might at first seem to be at odds with Darwinian "population thinking." Recall that Darwin's preoccupation with variation within "types" was a radical departure from the then-standard descriptions of species in terms of an archetype, and that he believed variation to be the raw material on which evolution works. In fact, one of the goals of microeconomic modeling in archaeology is to identify deviations from modeled optima. Understanding the ways in which real world outcomes differ from idealized ones helps us understand the decision-making process, both in specific circumstances and in general (e.g., do we behave more optimally in, say, subsistence-related contexts than in others?). Ultimately, it is the variation in individuals' behaviors we would most like to understand, to then assess the effects of variation at the population level.

Because individuals vary in their knowledge and abilities, they are important loci of selection and reproduction (genetic and cultural). Individuals learn and pass on distinct cultural variants (behaviors, ideas), some of which are better suited to particular circumstances and so are reproduced at higher rates than other variants, such that their frequency in the population increases over time. The microeconomic models used in this book derive from optimal foraging theory (OFT), which centers on variation among foraging behaviors, specifically. OFT assumes that "foraging behavior [in a general sense] has been 'designed' by natural selection to respond to changing conditions in a way that yields the greatest possible benefit for the individual forager's survival and reproductive success (Darwinian fitness)" (Smith 1983:626). Foraging models, in turn, examine choices among specific foraging behaviors, weighing the costs and potential benefits of each to determine what a forager *should* do under very specific circumstances if (s)he is trying to maximize benefits relative to costs. Importantly, in archaeology, optimal foraging models are not meant to describe actual foraging behaviors, but to generate predictions regarding optimal behaviors under specific conditions. We then compare archaeological data to models' predictions, keeping in mind that departures from modeled optima can be at least as informative as perfect coincidence between predictions and empirical data. That is, behaviors that appear suboptimal (i.e., data that do not match our predictions) are important sources of novel hypotheses regarding things that influence and constrain decision making.

As I have mentioned, individuals' foraging behaviors vary along multiple lines, but many of these are archaeologically invisible, which makes technology a particularly important source of variation in archaeological interpretations. Even so, we do not study prehistoric technology simply because it is often all that is left to study; technology is legitimately central to the calculation of foraging costs and benefits. As Steward (1936, 1955) long ago noted, technology's role in the extraction of environmental energy is so important that, holding environment constant, foragers equipped with different technologies effectively live in different environments. In optimal foraging terms, tools can have profound effects on the cost-benefit ratios of particular decisions and, therefore, our predictions for a particular place and time. For example, bow-and-arrow technology makes small, arboreal species more accessible, but may be ineffectual in the pursuit of whales. Storage technology increases the value of a place, but limits potential encounters with other resources if it requires that the forager stay put to defend the stash. Yet, technology is not always acknowledged or incorporated in foraging models, a point to which I return shortly.

Three foraging models make frequent enough appearances in the coming chapters to warrant introduction here at the start: the diet breadth model, marginal value theorem, and ideal free distribution. My aim in this section is to provide a general overview and reference for the models as they are used in subsequent chapters. Those interested in learning more about the models and their formal application (how to "do the math") should consult the primary references cited below (see also Bettinger 2009a for a primer on the diet breadth [and other] model[s], and Bettinger et al. 2015 for summaries and applications).

The Diet Breadth Model

The diet breadth model (DBM) is perhaps the most widely applied foraging model in archaeology. According to the model, for every time and place there is an optimal set of resources that, when targeted to the exclusion of all others, will maximize energetic gain relative to energy expended in the food quest (MacArthur and Pianka 1966). Food items are ranked according to their profitability; calorie- and/or nutrient-dense foods are higher-ranked than those that provide fewer calories or nutrients per unit of "post-encounter handling time" (time spent in pursuit and processing). Previously ignored, lower-ranked foods become part of the optimal set (are pursued on encounter) as higher-ranked foods grow scarce.

In light of this decision landscape, the DBM predicts the optimal behavior when a forager encounters a potential food item: pursue/collect the item or keep looking for a higher-ranked one. In the moment, the decision should not be difficult since the forager is assumed to have all the relevant information including (1) how much energy the encountered food item offers, (2) how much time or energy it will take to extract the food item's energy, (3) the rates of return for all other food items in the environment (energy per unit extraction effort), and (4) how abundant "better" food items are on the landscape. Or, perhaps more realistically, the forager knows in the moment whether the item encountered is in the optimal set and should be taken, or not in the set and should therefore be ignored. To do otherwise—to pursue resources not in the optimal set or ignore ones that are—results in a smaller energy payoff for the amount of time and energy spent foraging. Over the long run, making such nonoptimal decisions can lead to energy deficit (insufficient energy for future foraging or other life-sustaining activities) and, ultimately, death. We assume, then, that foragers make wise decisions on average.

Archaeological accounting related to these decisions can be a bit tricky. This is partly due to the fact that, like human groups, animal species are composed of individuals that vary in size, body composition, state of health, wariness, and so on. Most often, though, we keep track at the species level, ignoring important interspecies variation, when in fact the DBM assumes a ranking based on post-encounter return rates, which almost certainly overlap among species (e.g., small representatives of large-bodied species may yield no more calories per unit handling time than large representatives of medium-bodied species). It is also true that, depending on the kinds and numbers of resources in an environment (biodiversity and amount of "return rate overlap" as just described), determining the optimal set might

hinge on precise estimates of search times for the highest-ranked items. We rarely have access to this level of detail in modern scenarios, much less archaeological records. Still, the DBM has provided novel insights and formed the basis of compelling hypotheses through both detailed calculations of profitability and simple ratios of large- to small-bodied animals (e.g., Broughton et al. 2010). That is, cautious use of even coarse-grained approaches to dietary breadth can tell us something about prehistoric economics.

A Patagonian example helps to illustrate the point. The steppe, which accounts for 75% of the Patagonian landmass, is home to dozens of species of mammals, reptiles, birds, and plants (Chapter 2). Many of them were likely food items, habitually or situationally, for prehistoric Patagonians. Because a full accounting is impractical, particularly in this brief illustration, I will focus on those routinely encountered in archaeological records, namely, guanaco, rhea, pichi, and small rodents. We have reasonable estimates of guanaco (Borrero 1990; Neme and Gil 2002; see also Chapter 2) and rhea (Giardina 2006, 2010a, 2010b) profitability, but less concrete information related to pichi and "small rodents" (e.g., *Phyllotis* sp., smaller species of *Ctenomys*). Broughton and colleagues (2011) show that body size is a reasonable proxy for post-encounter returns, so, given the limited overlap in these animals' body sizes, we can reasonably rank them according to body size until we have more complete information. The descending rank order of our steppe resources in this simple example is: guanaco, rhea, pichi, small rodents.

Ranking in this way (or with actual post-encounter handling estimates) allows us to predict the addition and subtraction of food items in the face of changed environmental conditions. In a perfect world, where all resources are in unlimited supply, the optimizing forager should only ever pursue the highest ranked resource—we will assume a high tolerance for repetition ("Guanaco *again*?!"). Of course, supply is rarely unlimited, or at least not for long (see Chapters 4 and 7), and as guanaco become scarce, our forager has to deduct time and energy lost to searching from the expected payoff. Eventually the time/energy lost to searching will reduce the overall foraging return rate to a level that makes the inclusion of #2-ranked rhea optimal for maximizing foraging returns. The forager should, of course, continue to pursue guanaco when encountered, but if (s)he comes across rhea, the search for guanaco should be discontinued and rhea pursued. Abundant guanaco in the archaeological record, then, probably indicate a productive environment (abundant resources), while few guanaco and abundant pichi or small rodents may indicate resource stress.

Our lowest-ranked class in this illustration, small rodents, points to important limitations of the DBM, particularly in archaeological applications. Firstly, we generally assume ranking is based on the post-encounter return rate for a single food item, which is partly what makes body size a good proxy for resource ranking much of the time. However, mass capture fundamentally changes the definition of "food item" from an individual to a group (e.g., from a single fish to a shoal). Mass capture makes return rates density-dependent (Madsen and Schmitt 2003). Small rodents are more profitable when congregated (as during a mast event; see Chapter 2) than when solitary. Some species are always aggregated in relatively dense groups (e.g., grass seeds), so large numbers of them in archaeological records almost certainly indicates mass capture. Some species, though, occur in groups of various sizes—even guanaco groups fission and fuse throughout an average year—so interpreting their numbers in archaeological sites can be tricky and likely requires multiple lines of dietary, technological, and environmental evidence.

Small rodents are an interesting case in another regard, too: they are effectively "hunted" using passive technologies. In the United States Great Basin, a region ecologically similar to parts of the Patagonian steppe, micromammals including rodents were an important dietary item (Janetski 1997). Evidence from dry caves, such as bundles of sticks from Lovelock Cave in Nevada (Loud and Harrington 1929; Spier 1955), suggests rodents were at least sometimes caught in traps and snares that could be set and left, rather than actively pursued. Costs and benefits associated with passive technologies are distinct from those associated with active foraging. Trapped and snared resources—even vegetal windfall collected in baskets, skins, or blankets—have much lower handling times than they would otherwise and so are higher ranked under these circumstances.

Clearly, technology is an important, but sometimes overlooked, variable in the foraging calculus: holding environment constant, two otherwise identical foragers might have very different optimal diets when equipped with different technologies (Winterhalder and Bettinger 2010). Similarly underplayed, and just as important, are human energy budgets. Two foragers equipped with identical technologies might have very different caloric needs (energy budgets) which could result in very different foraging strategies. Yet caloric need, when considered at all, is often glossed as static, universal, or inconsequential. Basal metabolic rate (BMR) is the energy required to maintain essential body functions (e.g., brain activity, respiration, circulation, immune function, thermoregulation) of an individual at rest. BMR is a useful metric for assessing and comparing energy budgets, because it typically constitutes a large majority of total caloric expenditure and can be thought of as a threshold, below which health and longevity are increasingly threatened (Garvey 2018b; Leonard et al. 2007). BMR varies by individual according to age, sex, body composition, and reproductive state (e.g., gestation, lactation; Garvey 2018b), and it is sensitive to ambient temperature:

> Controlling for body size and composition, high-latitude populations tend to have elevated BMRs relative to low-latitude populations (Galloway et al. 2000; Leonard et al. 2002; Snodgrass et al. 2008), suggesting an adaptation to chronic cold stress. Moreover, a recent study among the Yakut (Sakha) of northern Siberia suggests that this effect may be amplified seasonally among prime-aged adults, likely as a result of changes

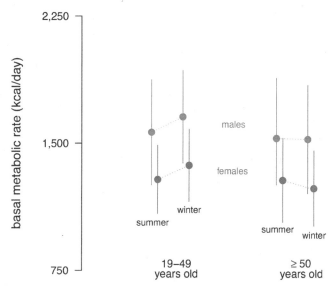

FIGURE 3.6. Variation in basal metabolic rate (kcal per day) as a function of season in the Yakut (Sakha) of Northeast Siberia. Plots shows basal metabolic rate of males (blue) and females (red) in summer and winter months, with individuals aged 19–49 years old plotted on the left and individuals ≥ 50 years old on the right. Data from Leonard and colleagues (2014).

in both thyroid hormone activity (associated with decreased temperature and photoperiod) and physical activity ([Figure 3.6]; Leonard et al. 2014). Ethnographically and very likely prehistorically, food availability also fluctuated seasonally, often even among groups that relied on storage, such that populations living in cold climates may have experienced significant periods of negative energy balance and weight loss. (Garvey 2018b:24)

Like all budgets, energy budgets are characterized by the zero-sum property. Energy allocated to BMR, subsistence activities, and other aspects of somatic maintenance is unavailable for other functions, including reproduction (Ellison 2003). Women in negative energy balance (experiencing frequent episodes of resource shortfall) may have compromised reproductive function (Rosetta 1993:71) for at least two reasons. Human pregnancy is energetically costly and results in an elevated BMR, due in part to

"increased oxygen consumption because of enhanced work with respect to maternal circulation, respiration, and renal function and to the increased tissue mass," as well as to increased cardiac work and serum concentrations of thyroid hormone (Lof et al. 2005). Meeting these higher energy requirements can be difficult, particularly during seasons of restricted resource availability. Moreover, ovarian function is directly affected by energetic state (Ellison 2001; Ellison et al. 2005) and women in negative energy balance may have reduced fertility. Cultural or behavioral apparatuses that mediate the negative effects of cold stress and resource shortfall on health, longevity, and reproduction can lead to archaeologically visible diversity, either directly, as evidence of larger populations and the changed social dynamics they may necessitate, or indirectly, through material cultural outcomes of larger populations (Garvey 2018b). The importance of BMR and instances of feedback between BMR/biology and technology are described in more detail below and in Chapter 4.

The Marginal Value Theorem

Where the DBM makes predictions about what a forager should eat, the marginal value theorem (MVT; Charnov 1976) predicts how long a forager should remain in a given resource patch and how far (s)he should be willing to travel to get to a new one. Foraging in a patch, catching and consuming its resources, decreases the amount of energy remaining there. The forager could catch and consume every last available calorie before leaving a patch but, by virtue of diminishing returns—the fact that each next unit of foraging time yields less energy—it may be smarter to leave in search of a new patch before the first patch is completely depleted. In fact, there is an *optimal departure time*, determined by the amount of energy available in the environment as a whole (i.e., across all possible patches) and its distribution across patches. When the within-patch rate of energy intake (amount of energy acquired per unit time) is equal to that of the environment as a whole (i.e., energy gained relative to the sum of all travel, search, and handling costs), the forager should move to a new (pristine) patch (Figure 3.7).

An important variable in the calculation of total environmental energy is the cost of traveling to a new patch. In fact, travel time between patches (a function of patch density) is a reasonable proxy for environmental quality: rich environments are associated with low travel costs and poor ones, high travel costs. And it is environmental quality that determines what the forager should do when the environment changes. The traditional interpretation of the model is that when environment degrades, the optimizing forager should remain longer in a given patch and extract more of its resources before moving to a new one. If environmental quality improves, the forager should move more frequently between patches and use fewer of the resources in each before moving. This was a compelling and somewhat counterintuitive prediction of the original model's because many informal (nonmathematical) interpretations suggest just the opposite: stay put when "the gettin' is good" and move often when resources are scarce. A recent reevaluation of the model, though (Bettinger and Grote 2016; Bettinger et al. 2015) shows that the solution actually is more complicated than initially thought.

As it turns out, solution of a marginal value problem hinges on two things: the nature of environmental change and the proportion of the forager's time given to handling. When environmental change affects patch quantity (i.e., number of patches on the landscape increases or decreases) the traditional interpretation of the MVT holds: When there are fewer patches (environmental degradation), travel time between remaining patches increases, so the optimizing forager should remain longer in a given patch and exploit it more completely (consume a greater fraction of its resources before moving). Conversely, when patch count increases (environment improves), travel time between patches is decreased and the forager should move more often, exploiting each less fully (Bettinger et al. 2015; Charnov 1976; Garvey 2008, 2012a, 2015a).

In some cases, though, environmental change affects patch quality (within-patch resource abundance) rather than patch quantity. This is where a forager's energy allocation comes in. When foraging entails no handling, environmental degradation that is uniform across patches would not effect a change in forager behavior. This is because, although there are fewer resources available in any given patch, this is true of all patches. So long as patch count remains constant, foragers will remain in patches as long as before, extract the same fraction of available resources before leaving, and travel as far as before. Foragers may be doing worse on the whole, but there is no better solution and no behavior that would increase the rate of energy intake in this situation. If, however, foraging entails at least some handling, within-patch foraging time (but not foraging intensity, the fraction of resources used) should increase as handling time increases. This is because increasing handling time decreases the rate at which total patch energy is depleted (Bettinger and Grote 2016). Of course, most foraging entails at least some handling, and precisely how much can be very difficult to determine archaeologically. As in the case

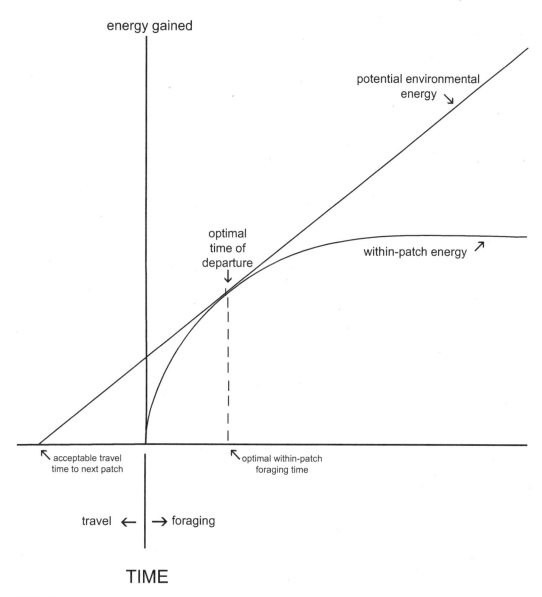

energy gained

potential environmental energy ↘

optimal time of departure ↓

within-patch energy ↗

↖ acceptable travel time to next patch

↖ optimal within-patch foraging time

travel ← | → foraging

TIME

FIGURE 3.7. Graphical representation of the standard marginal value theorem (adapted from Bettinger et al. 2015; Charnov 1976). As patch resources are depleted (time increases to the right of the origin), the rate of energy acquisition decreases (within-patch energy curve). The optimal time of patch departure is reached when the within-patch rate of intake falls to the rate obtainable from the whole environment (potential environmental energy), at which point a forager should leave the patch or face diminshing returns.

of dietary items for which we have incomplete calorie/nutrient information, we can sometimes make reasonable predictions using estimated hunting-to-gathering ratios. If evidence suggests a forager (foraging group) relies heavily on hunted foods, which generally require less handling time, within-patch time should be less than if the forager (group) relies more heavily on gathered foods with lengthier processing times. Calculating (or even estimating) within-patch time for the forager who relies equally heavily on hunting and gathering could be quite complicated.

The Bettinger-Grote reanalysis of a classic model makes clear that the MVT's predictions are not as straightforward as we once thought. It is also true that, when we lack precise information about a region's resources or past environmental changes, the "more completely" and "less long" of foraging effort can be tricky to parse. This aspect of cost-benefit analyses of archaeological cases is, itself, a tradeoff: unless we have solid contextual data (resources, environment), assigning precise values to the costs and returns of foraging decreases model reliability, while imprecise estimates of costs and benefits provide more reliable predictions but ones that are, well, less precise. This is certainly not to downplay the utility of optimality models. Cost-benefit analyses can be very powerful tools and excellent sources of hypotheses regarding behaviors and associated archaeological patterns. Perhaps ironically, they can be most useful for predicting behaviors in areas and circumstances about which we know the least. I demonstrate this in Chapter 5's discussion of a controversial middle Holocene occupational gap in northern Patagonia's record.

The Ideal Free Distribution

The ideal free distribution (IFD) simultaneously predicts when to move and to where, and the model is correspondingly more complex than either the diet breadth model or marginal value theorem. It also explicitly accounts for other actors' behaviors, which neither of the others does, and involves multiple time steps. Perhaps because of this added complexity, it has been slow to gain popularity among archaeologists, though it was introduced to biology many decades ago (Fretwell and Lucas 1970) and has recently been applied to archaeological cases with compelling results (e.g., Codding and Jones 2013; Kennett et al. 2006). It likewise offers some interesting hypotheses regarding Patagonia's initial colonization (Chapter 4), responses to middle Holocene climate changes (Chapter 5), and mobility where hunter-gatherers lived adjacent to farmers (Chapter 6).

The IFD predicts how individuals—birds in the original model and people in our case—should distribute themselves among resource patches that differ in their quality. Patches are ranked much as resources are in the DBM: those that provide the highest returns on foraging effort are highest ranked. However, in the IFD, patch rank is also a function of the number of other foragers already in the patch and how quickly they are consuming its resources. Unsurprisingly, the model predicts that a forager entering the landscape should select from the mosaic of patches the one that offers the highest rate of return at that time (the "ideal"). In a pristine (previously unoccupied) environment, the highest-ranked patch is occupied first and exclusively. Additional foragers should continue to join the highest-ranked patch until resource depletion causes the return rate there to fall to the level of the next highest-ranked patch. At that point, foragers should occupy the second-ranked patch until its profitability falls to the level of the third-ranked, and so on until all available patches are filled (Bettinger et al. 2015:123; Fretwell and Lucas 1970). We assume people are able to move, unimpeded, between patches (i.e., that they are "free") and that, at equilibrium (when people are no longer moving between patches and the population is stable), the distribution of individuals across patches will be proportional to the resources available in each (i.e., more people in rich patches, fewer in poorer patches).

While more complex than the other foraging models presented in this chapter, the IFD is, in a sense, just a formalization of something rather intuitive: when given the choice (and motivated primarily by subsistence needs), foragers should prefer to live where the ratio of food to people is good and to avoid until necessary places where resources are harder to come by. Indeed, this is precisely what O'Connell and colleagues (1982) hypothesized for the initial colonization of the Great Basin even without reference to the IFD: habitats characterized by low-ranked resources should be colonized relatively late. The advantage of the IFD is that it offers explicit and testable predictions rooted in a well-attested body of theory.

Nonetheless, determining which of Patagonia's habitats are highest ranked, now and in the prehistoric past, can be tricky, and it is tempting to use archaeological site densities and colonization sequences as proxies for habitat quality (e.g., the earliest-colonized and most densely occupied places must be highest-ranked; Borrero 2004; Gil et al. 2005; Martin and Borrero 2017). While the IFD does predict early and continuous occupation of high-ranked areas, there are many reasons the archaeological record might not accurately reflect actual colonization history (see Chapters 2, 4, and 7). For example, preservation might simply be better in some places than others, and unless there is a strong, positive correlation between preservation and habitat quality, the archaeological record might present a skewed view of quality. This is another advantage of using the IFD. By making predictions about where we might expect early sites and assessing them in light of archaeological data, rather than the other way around, we avoid potentially misleading tautologies (see Chapters 4 and 7).

Because we suspect Patagonian population densities were low, at least initially and perhaps throughout prehistory, it is worth mentioning a variant of the IFD that includes an "Allee effect." The standard IFD assumes that, from the modeled individual's perspective, each additional forager is a detriment to patch quality because they catch and consume resources that would otherwise have been available to our forager. Though this is always true, the negative effect is sometimes offset by benefits associated with having a few extra foragers around. When populations are relatively small, additional foragers might actually *increase* patch quality if communal hunting improves foraging returns or cooperative groups pool risk and resources (Winterhalder 1986a). More individuals might also provide additional mating opportunities and defense against predators and enemies. When this is true, the addition of more individuals increases patch quality until it reaches "peak suitability," at which point the addition of more foragers begins to decrease patch quality

and foragers should begin to distribute themselves as in the standard IFD, moving to lower and lower ranked patches until equilibrium is reached (Allee and Bowen 1932; Bettinger et al. 2015; Courchamp et al. 2008). So, Allee effects delay movement into new patches. While delays themselves might be invisible at archaeological time scales, density-dependent (Allee) effects were likely relevant to the initial colonization and subsequent settlement of Patagonia, and should be included in our analyses as additional testable hypotheses (Chapters 4 and 7).

Another point related to the initial colonization of Patagonia: the IFD, like many optimization models, makes a number of simplifying assumptions that require careful consideration when applied in archaeological contexts. In this case, I refer to the "ideal" part of the model—the assumption that foragers are aware of the number and respective quality of patches available in the environment. In reality, this may not hold, particularly for foragers entering a landscape for the first time, as during initial colonization. It is reasonable to assume that groups send scouts to reconnoiter unknown parts of a landscape and that, even at low population densities, people can have very detailed information about areas they have never themselves visited. Through information sharing, some Inuit of the North American arctic reportedly have accurate information about upwards of 650,000 km^2, though their first-hand experience is limited to a small fraction of that area (Aporta and Higgs 2005; Meltzer 2009). Until full assessment of a landscape can be made, the scale of IFD decisions (or DBM and MVT decisions for that matter) may be relatively more local than regional. This fractal property of the model's predictions— the fact that they are self-similar at increasingly small scales—means that modeling colonization according to the IFD might require efforts to match time scales to spatial scales. For example, the very earliest arrivals to an area might behave according to predictions of the IFD, but only on a local scale, since the sphere of knowledge does not yet cover the whole of Patagonia. Once sufficient knowledge has been accumulated through landscape exploration, we might expect an IFD at the regional scale. This makes the traditional equation of "early occupation" to "high-quality habitat" all the more problematic, although it is possible that the exploration period is so rapid as to be irrelevant in terms of the model. These are areas for exploration and improvement as we develop archaeologically appropriate versions of optimal foraging models, many of which were developed to study real-time behaviors among relatively short-lived species.

Segue to Co-evolutionary Models

Since its introduction to anthropology via biology in the 1970s, microeconomic modeling has met with some resistance. A recurrent criticism is that the approach, developed for the study of nonhuman animal behavior, downplays or outright ignores the importance of culture and human agency (e.g., Hockett 2016; Ingold 2000). While it is true that culture is not always a salient feature in optimization analysis (we might say rarely, even), culture can have a profound effect on both calorie/nutrient "supply" and "demand." As I described in the section on dietary breadth, technology in particular, but also ecological knowledge, the organization of work, and other cultural elements, have significant effects on foraging efficiency, handling times, and other important variables. In both the MVT and IFD, rates of patch depletion are tied directly to handling times, which, of course, depend heavily on available technologies, just as in the DBM. Likewise, culture affects caloric and nutrient "demand"—basal metabolic rate in particular (e.g., through clothing, shelter), but also caloric expenditure and the efficiency of work (e.g., hauling and transportation technologies). So while the roles of human agency and historical contingency are seldom explicit in microeconomic models, they are nonetheless central to foraging outcomes. Where technologies "come from"—how innovations spread and material culture evolves—and how technology (or any aspect of culture) and biology affect one another are the subjects of the third kind of model introduced here: co-evolutionary.

Co-evolutionary Models

Human culture is one of the most complex traits ever to have evolved. Early notions of cultural evolution grew out of the writings of Herbert Spencer (1864), a prominent Victorian philosopher and political theorist who believed the evolution of human culture could itself be explained very simply: Societies—like elephants, and embryos, and *everything*—inevitably transform from simple, undifferentiated entities into complex, heterogeneous ones when environmental pressures are sufficient to require it. As the discipline matured and as scientific, cross-cultural analyses became common, the inevitability of cultural transformation was shown to be wrong. Still, environmental pressures remain central to our understanding of *why* culture changes, and this is probably as it should be. The physical environment is clearly an important driver of cultural change and a fair bit of culture is probably adaptive. The natural environment likewise has a place in explanations of *how* culture changes, because it is a strong selective force no matter how sophisticated our technologies and social institutions. Nonetheless, the macroecological models I described earlier show, and even Spencer would agree, that culture affects how we experience the environment. Adjusting variables in our microeconomic models to reflect culturally mediated handling times or caloric needs, we get a better sense of just how significant culture's effects can be. We find that culture not only allows us to meet in novel ways the needs we share with other animals (eating well, surviving, and producing offspring), and even to regulate the needs themselves (e.g., by changing basal metabolism), it also creates needs not present among asocial animals (e.g., the need for judicial systems). Following this logic out farther still, we come to the realization that culture, in fact, shapes the very environment to which our biological selves adapt (Lewontin 1983; Odling-Smee 1988). Culture modifies selection pressures and adaptive landscapes, and this is precisely the co-evolutionary dynamic this final set of evolutionary models is designed to explore. Co-evolutionary models are also more explicit in their assessment of *how* culture changes, acknowledging the importance of the physical environment but centering on person-to-person exchanges of information and how these influence the suite of traits a group possesses at any given time.

The Evolution of Cultural Complexity

Spencer and the others cannot really be faulted for thinking that cultural evolution is an inevitable, progressive march towards "complex" civilization. It is in fact true that cultural complexity—measured approximately by the number of interconnected cultural constituents—has increased through time in most places across the globe, and there are real benefits to increased complexity. Complex tools and toolkits, concepts explored in detail below, are generally more efficient than their simpler counterparts. Complex social systems organize work in ways that makes it more efficient, too, and elaborate social institutions provide services essential for the long-term survival of large groups of mostly unrelated individuals. The historical distribution of relatively simple societies even suggests that environment might have something to do with the rate at which groups "progress" (cf. Porter and Marlow 2007), although this may have as much or more to do with conquest, the spread of disease and farming, and other relatively recent historical interactions than with ecology. So, assuming that all groups are capable of becoming more complex, how do we explain the worldwide variation in levels of complexity, if not in terms of environment and inevitability?

The spread of ideas, practices, and technologies offers partial explanation of worldwide patterns of complexity, as I mentioned, but it obviously does not explain everything. Even if most complexity were a result of conquest or diffusion—and this certainly seems not to be the case—"original" complexity would require some alternative explanation. The co-evolutionary approach treats complexity like any other cultural trait and models its evolution as a process whereby forces acting on diversity at the individual level lead to trait distributions at the group level. The basic equation is one borrowed directly from evolutionary biology and designed to track the effects of evolutionary forces on trait distributions through time:

$$P_{t+1} = P_t + \sum_{i}^{n} forces$$

where P_t is the frequency of a trait at time t (the proportion of individuals possessing the trait), and $\sum_{i}^{n} forces$ is the force or forces that increase or decrease the frequency of trait P between time t and time $t + 1$, when its frequency is measured again (Eerkens et al. 2014:1129). "Forces" can be anything from aesthetic preferences to functional requirements to unconscious learning biases (how and from whom we acquire cultural information). Learning biases have been studied extensively (e.g., Boyd and Richerson 1985; Cavalli-Sforza and Feldman 1981; Henrich and McElreath 2003, 2007) and include what may be an adaptive propensity to preferentially copy successful individuals. In an elaboration of the basic model above, Henrich (2004) provides a framework for exploring how this particular learning bias (preferential copying) can lead to increased cultural complexity.

Henrich's model centers on selective choice of cultural models—the fact that people tend to model their behaviors on those of particularly skilled or successful individuals (Henrich and Gil-White 2001)—and on imperfect imitation. Though we may emulate the skilled and successful, we vary in our own perceptions and skill and so, also, in our ability to faithfully reproduce cultural models' behaviors. Because of imperfect imitation, novice individuals (those attempting to learn a behavior) will, on average, be unable to match the behavioral model's skill level, and this constrains the rate of technological evolution in a population. The more complex the behavior (e.g., the more steps or parts it has), the more pronounced this evolution-dampening effect. Through occasional "lucky guesses or errors," however, a novice's behaviors (or tools) might be *superior* to the behavioral model's, at which point the novice becomes the preferentially copied model and the superior behavior (tool) becomes the emulated version (Henrich 2004:201). Over time, consecutive lucky leaps lead to the cumulative evolution of culture.

Henrich's model also demonstrates the importance of group size in the evolution of culture (cf. Andersson and Törnberg 2016; Collard et al. 2014). Because highly skilled individuals are, ostensibly, relatively rare in most populations, the larger the population, the more common such individuals are likely to be. As groups of social learners grow, the number of skilled individuals increases, leading to increased rates of cumulative cultural evolution. Conversely, the effects of losing skilled individuals by chance are greater in small populations. The fewer such individuals there are, the more likely their loss would result in a group-level decrease in average skill and, perhaps, in outright losses of cultural components (Henrich 2004).

A key factor in the evolution of cultural complexity, specifically, is the cumulative nature of human social learning. That is, we not only learn from our conspecifics, we improve upon the things we learn and pass on these modified versions, ratcheting-up complexity each time. The novice's "lucky guesses" retain the best elements of the previous model's version and improve upon them to produce a new version that is then copied, and eventually further improved by others. Complexity can manifest in most any domain of culture. Many of these are archaeologically invisible, though. In Patagonia, stone artifacts dominate most records, making technological complexity the most readily accessible domain.

Wendell Oswalt (1973, 1976) introduced the concept of "technounits," which are individual parts of a complete artifact. He then defined technological complexity in terms of technounits per tool type: more complex technologies have more units per tool. Others have since expanded the study of technological complexity to include toolkit "diversity" or the number of tools per kit (Shott 1986; Torrence 1989); more complex technologies, of course, have more tools per kit.

To assess drivers of technological complexity, Oswalt (1976) himself made a cross-cultural comparison and observed a positive correlation between the number of technounits in a toolkit and the mobility of targeted prey. Torrence (1983, 1989), Bleed (1986), and others (e.g., Eerkens 1998) later built on the idea that prey species' characteristics affect toolkit complexity, adding the timing of resource availability and risk associated with resource shortfall as key variables. These studies suggest that tools are often made to be "reliable" when foraging failure would be costly. Tools are designed to minimize the likelihood of failure in high-risk situations through redundancies and "over-designing" (e.g., making tools stronger than necessary). Risk of resource failure is tied to seasonality (and therefore latitude), and the prediction that technological sophistication (high reliability, technological complexity, and toolkit diversity) should track with seasonality is empirically supported. For example, using the same dataset Oswalt (1976) studied, Torrence (1983) found a significant positive correlation between toolkit complexity and latitude, and concluded that it was a result of increased reliance on animal resources at higher latitudes, itself a result of decreasing plant biomass with distance from the equator. Collard and colleagues (2005) compared four competing hypotheses for toolkit complexity (characteristics of food resources, risk of shortfall, human mobility, and population size) and likewise demonstrated a strong positive correlation between tool complexity and latitude, which they cautiously attributed to risk of resource failure, as Torrence had.

Following publication of the Henrich model (Henrich 2004), demographics (population size, density, and connectivity) became central to the debate regarding the evolution of technological complexity. Indeed, a subsequent study by Collard and colleagues (2013) found a strong positive correlation between toolkit complexity and group size among a sample of 40 small-scale food-producing groups from around the world. Likewise, Kline and Boyd (2010) conclude that population size is the best predictor of technological complexity, having demonstrated that larger populations' toolkits typically have a much higher mean number of technounits than smaller populations' kits. This follows from the logic that, because cultural evolution is largely a product of the gradual accumulation of socially transmitted information, rates of cultural change should covary with population size. As groups of interacting social learners grow, rates of change should increase as a function of both information accumulation and the increased probability of innovations in larger groups (Henrich 2004). Population density and cultural connectivity (network size) are also important variables, since innovations can travel more quickly through denser populations, and between-group connectivity ensures access to innovators even when group size is relatively small (Baldini 2015; Henrich 2004; Powell et al. 2009; Shennan 2015). Conversely, small, scattered, and loosely connected groups' cultures should change more slowly, because innovations are statistically less frequent, the diffusion of innovations can be slower in dispersed groups, and random losses of innovators or preferentially copied cultural models can have a greater effect on smaller populations (Richerson et al. 2009). Larger and better-networked groups should have larger and richer toolkits and their cultures should be more robust in the face of demographic fluctuations (cf. Collard et al. 2014; Read 2008, 2012).

Cultural Complexity in Patagonia

According to the relationship between cultural complexity and latitude reported by Oswalt (1976), Torrence (1983), Henrich (2004), and Collard and colleagues (2005), Patagonian material culture should be relatively complex, particularly in the far south. More precisely, the linear model derived from the Oswalt dataset predicts an increase in the number of technounits per group from the equator (~5 units) to the high arctic (~250 units), and approximately 150 technounits at 55° S, the approximate center of the Yámana's distribution. In fact, though, the Yámana toolkit only consisted of 69 technounits at European contact (Oswalt 1976), which is strikingly low for that latitude. A comparison of the contact-period Yámana with a contemporaneous, same-latitude group of maritime foragers at the opposite end of the globe illustrates the relative simplicity of the Yámana toolkit.

The Yámana occupied the southern coast of Isla Grande de Tierra del Fuego and numerous adjacent islands, comprising a land area of roughly 11,000 km² between 54° and 56° S. The Aleutian Islands are located between 51° and 55° N, and comprise a total land area of approximately 17,700 km². The regions' climates are similar: both are relatively cold, though temperature seasonality is moderated by the marine environment. Both archipelagos are subject to frequent high winds, dense cloud cover, intense winter storms, and regular summer snows. Resource availability is likewise comparable (cf. McCartney 1975) and includes a wide range of sea mammals, fish, sea birds, marine invertebrates, seaweeds, and limited terrestrial plants and animals.

Despite very similar climates and resource regimes, the Yámana and Unangan toolkits could scarcely have been more different. The Yámana subsistence toolkit was relatively small and simple, consisting of spears and clubs for seals; wooden gorge hooks, pole snares, and clubs for birds; and pronged forks for urchin. Mussels were gathered by hand, as were fish, often, though women sometimes baited kelp stems or sinew lines to draw fish to the surface and scooped them up in baskets. Unmodified sticks were used for extracting clams and limpets; unmodified stones were used opportunistically in place of clubs or manufactured projectiles when necessary; unmodified mussel shells were frequently used as expedient tools (Oswalt 1973). The Yámana lacked fishhooks; rarely worked stone, with the exception of crudely made projectile points and scrapers; and did not rely on storage except for small amounts of dried fungi and oil (Cooper 1946; Garvey 2018b). They traveled almost exclusively by boat, but their sewn bark canoes "leaked much" (Cooper 1946:88) and were generally used for moving from camp to camp and in near-shore subsistence activities rather than open water navigation or hunting.

Conversely, the Unangans' hunting toolkit was extensive and specialized, with technologies well designed for efficient procurement of a wide variety of marine and littoral resources (e.g., toggling harpoons, atlatls, fishhooks, basketry). They made lightweight, seaworthy kayaks of skins over wooden frames that facilitated hunting of both fish and sea mammals on the open ocean, as well as sea lions and other animals on offshore rocky outcrops. Storage was an important component of the subsistence routine (Binford 2001; McCartney and Veltre 1999).

It is possible that the linear model derived from the Oswalt (1976) dataset—the one that predicts more than twice the number of technounits than were actually observed among the Yámana—is flawed. Recall that the Oswalt dataset is the common denominator among studies showing a relationship between complexity and latitude (Oswalt 1976; Torrence 1983; Collard et al. 2005). Indeed, Collard and colleagues (2005) were cautious in their support of the relationship precisely because the Oswalt data are biased towards the northern part of the western hemisphere; only a handful of southern hemisphere groups are included. So our expectation for greater technological complexity in southern South America might be unrealistic. Still, so striking a contrast between groups living in such similar environments (the Yámana and Unangan) is intriguing. I hypothesize that it owes to ecological constraints on and/or cultural beliefs about group size and connectivity, culturally mediated differences in fertility, and feedback between demographic variables and technological innovation, which led to less and more favorable conditions for cumulative cultural evolution among the Yámana and Unangan, respectively (Garvey 2018b).

Group Size and Connectivity

It is reasonable to think that both the Yámana and Unangan were foraging efficiently according to the technologies each possessed. However, the Unangans' large and specialized toolkit allowed them to access a greater portion of available energy than the Yámana, and their (the Unangans') reliance on storage likely alleviated

seasonal or periodic resource shortfall. The fact that the Yámana either never developed or else lost the capability for offshore hunting and fishing kept carrying capacity much lower in Tierra del Fuego than in the Aleutians (Steager 1963; Yesner et al. 2003).

Indeed, population size and density in the two areas differed dramatically. The Yámana numbered approximately 3,000 when the first estimates were made in the 1830s (Europeans initially encountered the Yámana in the early sixteenth century but no census was taken until the nineteenth century). In contrast, the Unangan population was five times larger, numbering roughly 15,000 at contact with Russian fur traders in the mid-eighteenth century (Lantis 1984). The disparity between their respective population densities—28.4 per 100 km^2 among the Yámana and 54.7 people per 100 km^2 among the Unangan (Binford 2001)—is not quite so pronounced, but still significant.

In the section on macroecological models, I described the Yámana as an internally differentiated and linguistically diverse group, the members of which lived in small, independent family units that remained isolated most of the time (Binford 2001; Cooper 1946). Conversely, the contact period Unangan lived in longhouses that accommodated multiple family groups within large, permanent villages. Technological similarities suggest cultural continuity and contact both among the islands of the chain and between the chain and Alaskan mainland (Turner 2008) despite there having been a number of different dialects and tribes across the islands. In contrast to the Yámana's small average group sizes, Unangan aggregated groups were relatively large (average = 55 people).

Differences in the groups' respective sizes, densities, and levels of intergroup connectivity probably owe to both (culturally mediated) ecological differences and social factors that may be impossible to know at this point. Whatever their cause, these population variables may have led to greater cultural complexity among the Unangan because "cultures that better facilitate sociality, information sharing, and effective teaching [are] better able to maintain complex technologies and skills" (Baldini 2015:330; Henrich 2010; Pearce 2014).

Fertility and Feedback

Difference in the groups' respective abilities to mitigate negative effects of chronic cold (e.g., elevated BMR, compromised fertility) might also have contributed to the observed differences in their respective cultural complexity. Clothing may have been particularly important. Gilligan (2007) has suggested that small differences in ambient temperature inside fitted clothing make a significant difference in basal metabolic rates and overall energy budgets. At contact, the Yámana wore only seal, sea otter, or fox pelts draped over the shoulders, pubic coverings, and occasionally leggings. They smeared their bodies with fat to further protect against snow, rain, and temperatures that were routinely below freezing. Conversely, the Unangan made and wore expertly tailored bird- and sea mammal-skin clothing and watertight outerwear. Gilligan (2007:501) indicates that clothing fitted to the limbs is two to five times more thermally resistant than simple, draped clothing, so the Unangan's wardrobe may have afforded them a considerable advantage in the cold climate. Fitted clothing would have reduced adult and infant mortality due to direct cold stress and decreased metabolic upregulation (i.e., it held BMR more or less constant), thereby limiting episodes of negative energy balance and compromised female fertility. Additionally, warm and watertight clothing might have facilitated Unangan mobility, particularly offshore hunting, while the lack of such garments might have further limited the Yámana's ability to navigate and hunt on the open water. Clothing's effects on temperature regulation (and possibly hunting ability) likely promoted greater health and fertility, and therefore larger populations, among the Unangan relative to the Yámana. As described above, larger and more connected populations are better able to preserve existing technological complexity and more likely to produce innovations, which in turn raise local carrying capacities and improve survivorship and fertility, thereby further increasing innovation rates. This feedback between culture and biology

may have fostered greater cumulative cultural evolution among the Unangan. (For an extended discussion, see Garvey 2018b.)

Implications

It is possible that prehistoric Fuegians at one time had but subsequently lost the knowledge and tools necessary to produce fitted clothing. Archaeological evidence indicates initial occupation of Tierra del Fuego around 12,500 cal BP (northern Isla Grande; Massone et al. 1999), and for roughly 2,500 years Fuegian groups could have maintained contact with larger populations to the north. By 10,000 BP, postglacial sea levels had risen sufficiently to cut Tierra del Fuego off from mainland Patagonia (Ponce et al. 2011), after which time contact may have been limited, while Fuegian populations themselves began to diversify (Charlin et al. 2013). It is relevant that Tierra del Fuego is isolated in a more general sense, too. That is, the total land area between 50° and 55° southern latitude is vanishingly small relative to that of the same latitudinal range north of the equator (Chapter 2; Figure 2.3). The northern hemisphere's subarctic, for example, is vast, and developments in one part of the region could easily have spread to others, even if groups had little direct contact with one another. It was simply a larger effective population of people experiencing similar environmental conditions—a larger "idea pool" where the potential for beneficial innovations was greater.

Social and geographical isolation in southern Patagonia likely restricted the flow of people and ideas between groups, holding innovation rates low, as described in Henrich's (2004) model. This effect would have been exacerbated by chance events such as natural disasters, which can remove cultural models from populations. Recall from Chapter 2 that southern Patagonia is seismically and volcanically active. Earthquakes caused periodic landslides and avalanches, and sediment geomorphology on the east coast of Isla Grande suggests that a subduction zone east of Tierra del Fuego may have produced occasional tsunamis (Bujalesky 2012). Volcanic eruptions are associated with apparent population decline in central and southern Patagonia (Cardich 1985; Prieto et al. 2013). If Fuegian populations were small, as they appear to have been through much of prehistory, such natural disasters would have had a disproportionately large effect on cultural evolution there, perhaps leading to the loss of fitted clothing and other technologies.

Alternatively, clothing might never have been present in prehistoric Tierra del Fuego. There is currently no archaeological evidence to suggest tailored clothing was ever produced by the ancestral Yámana, as would be indicated by needles, awls, and blades. Conversely, the earliest sites on the Aleutians are microblade sites—microblades having recently been linked to clothing production (Yi et al. 2013)—and it is likely that the islands were first colonized by people who already had fitted cold-weather clothing. Genetic evidence suggests that all Native Americans descended from Siberian populations (Goebel et al. 2008) who almost certainly had tailored clothing (Hoffecker 2005). It is possible, then, that the tropics, and perhaps the lower midlatitudes, were an ecological barrier to the production of fitted clothing. I explore this and related topics in Chapter 4.

Patagonian Cultural Complexity in Deeper Time

Whether ancestral Fuegians (and other Patagonian groups) had fitted clothing or not, the fact remains that cultural complexity among the contact-period Yámana could have been dampened by negative feedback between cultural and biological spheres, which limited population growth and, therefore, cultural evolution and vice versa. As archaeologists, we are also interested in knowing whether similar coevolutionary forces affected populations farther back in time and, assuming they did, how this might have influenced human ecology and longer trajectories of technological evolution.

Many direct records of prehistoric Patagonian technology are limited to the stone component and the odd bone tool, all other technologies having succumbed to destructive agents. This makes it difficult to accurately assess

prehistoric technological complexity. We know, for example, that site type, occupation duration, and stone conservation behaviors can affect the numbers of kinds of tools found in archaeological sites (e.g., Andrefsky 1994, 1998) and that tool counts might therefore be inaccurate measures of toolkit diversity (complexity). Numbers of technounits may be even more problematic, since stone tools themselves typically represent a single technounit, whether as stand-alone tools (e.g., handheld scrapers) or parts of composite tools (e.g., arrows). Alternatively, we could create a stone-tool-specific complexity typology to include, say, a ranking of flaking patterns (e.g., random vs. parallel oblique), blade treatments (e.g., straight vs. serrated), or haft elements (e.g., triangular vs. corner notched) but, for most times and places, there are likely a lot of "intermediate" attributes whose ranking would be hard to resolve. Moreover, while the production of more elaborate bifaces (for example) is likely a more complex *process* than the production of simpler ones, it is not clear whether the elaborations themselves represent differences in *complexity* per se.

Still, it is a worthwhile exercise to think, at a general level, about how complexity might be reflected in a stone-dominated record. It probably matters, for example, whether the environment is stone-rich or stone-poor, and whether materials for organic tools or tool components are easy or hard to come by. In a forest where local stone is sparse and of low quality, stone tools might be infrequent to begin with and less likely to be elaborated through time, while wood and fiber technologies might see substantial investment and development. On the Patagonian steppe, conversely, which constitutes about 3/4 of the Patagonian landscape, stone is abundant, organic materials are relatively sparse, and important prey species are effectively hunted with projectile technologies. In this context, we might expect greater investment in the stone component of the toolkit. These assumptions are rooted in the logic of optimization and can be formalized using microeconomic models, such as the model of technological investment, which predicts increased investment with increased tool use (Bettinger et al. 2006; Garvey 2015a; Ugan al. 2003; see also Chapter 2). Deviations from modeled expectations are fertile source of hypotheses.

I have wondered, for instance, whether bifacial projectiles might have been subsidiary to bolas in Patagonia. Bola stones were sometimes pecked and abraded in ways that make them recognizable not only in stratified sites but also in surface contexts. We certainly have record of their prehistoric use, including bolas in early deposits at Cueva Fell (Bird 1988) and depictions of their use at Cueva de las Manos (UNESCO 2019). During the contact era, though, some bolas were simply unmodified, naturally rounded cobbles placed in a leather pouch that was then drawn shut and attached to the cords. These cobbles might go largely unrecognized, particularly in surface contexts where they would be little different from the background distribution of stones. The contact-era stone-in-bag construction, which consists of more technounits than the pecked-and-lashed type, may represent evolution towards greater technological complexity despite a *decrease* in elaboration of the stone component itself. Archaeological interpretations of the evolution of projectile technology in Patagonia might be doubly confounded, then, if bolas were the more important technology. Bifacial technology changed little and slowly, while bolas changed substantially but in ways that are archaeologically invisible.

Yet another hypothesis regarding the relative lack of change in projectile typology in Patagonia is directly linked to the co-evolutionary principles described above. Stone tool attributes, including levels of investment and elaboration, evolve via the same processes as things more obviously related to complexity (e.g., increased number of technounits per tool). If Patagonian populations were relatively small and poorly connected, we would expect relatively low rates of cultural change because innovations are statistically less common, diffusions of innovations are slower in dispersed groups, and random losses of innovators or preferentially copied cultural models may have been paralyzing. Because subsistence technologies are so tightly linked to foraging returns and therefore to carrying capacity and group size, low rates of technological evolution in prehistoric Patagonia could have checked population growth, leading to the same kind of negative feedback cycle described in the clothing example above.

In the following chapters, we will explore a variety of Patagonian puzzles, from initial colonization to apparent gaps in middle Holocene records and reasons Patagonians might have remained foragers despite having lived side by side with farmers for at least 2,000 years. The macroecological, microeconomic, and co-evolutionary models described here will help us understand why people settled where they did initially, how they spread from there, and how their technology and other aspects of culture evolved in subsequent millennia.

4

Initial Colonization:
Explorers of an Empty Landscape

Patagonia is the farthest place to which man walked from his place
of origins. It is therefore a symbol of his restlessness.

—Bruce Chatwin (1977)

The New World is the last of Earth's major land-masses to have been colonized and, in light of modern humans' migration out of Africa as early as 200,000 years ago (Herskovitz et al. 2018), the peopling of the Americas is surprisingly recent. Just *how* recent, though, is highly controversial. Some archaeologists say initial colonization happened little more than 13,000 years ago (Fiedel 2017), while others claim that an unidentified species of *Homo* might have been here on the order of 130,000 years ago (Holen et al. 2017). Professional stakes are high and the evidence, equivocal.

To be sure, this is more than just professional wrangling; the details of New World colonization are important. Knowing when people first arrived, under what climatic conditions, by which route(s), in what numbers, and how quickly they spread across two continents, we stand to learn a lot about human adaptive capacity. The colonists experienced a tremendous range of environments and climates, most of them very different from the late-glacial homeland; depending on how quickly people moved through the Americas, they may have been essentially flying blind through this new world. By some estimates, colonization was so fast that people would have been forced to adapt largely without the benefit of knowledge accumulated by generations of social learners—a pool of information that far exceeds what any individual could acquire independently in his or her own lifetime.

In fact, some of the most compelling colonization questions hinge on dispersal speed, which makes Patagonia a pivotal waypoint. Genetic evidence indicates that a small founding population diverged from eastern Siberian stock during the Last Glacial Maximum and remained isolated in eastern Beringia for a few thousand years before moving into the Americas (Eshleman et al. 2003; Llamas et al. 2016; Moreno-Mayar et al. 2018; Schroeder et al. 2009). Because Patagonia is, indeed, the farthest place to which the colonizers traveled from their place of origin, one obvious way to estimate colonization speed is to subtract the earliest known Patagonian dates from our best approximation of when people started south from eastern Beringia. However, as is obvious to anyone with even a passing familiarity with New World peopling issues, this equation's solution simply does not jibe with all of the available evidence. This is part of the reason the subject is so captivating—and controversial—and also what makes Patagonia's earliest record so important to our understanding of the colonization process.

Nonetheless, Patagonia's role in mainstream peopling debates has been sharply bipolar: appropriately central on the one hand, unfortunately marginal on the other. Patagonia has been central in the sense that, since the mid-1990s, any attempt to explain New World colonization must account for evidence from Monte Verde, the earliest widely accepted archaeological site

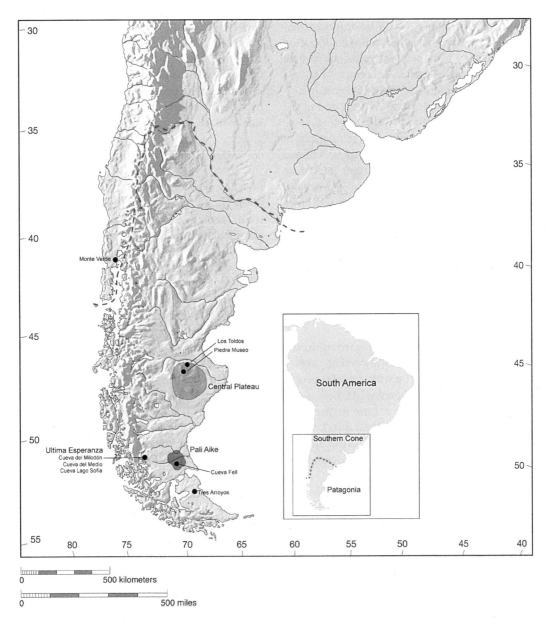

FIGURE 4.1. Map of early sites and archaeological regions mentioned in the text.

in the Americas, located on the northern border of Chilean Patagonia (Figure 4.1). Yet, it has been marginal in that Patagonia's early record does not otherwise feature prominently in the peopling literature. This is unfortunate because Patagonia's earliest colonization has much to contribute to traditional peopling debates, from the timing of first entry to the route(s) of colonization. As I describe in the next section, these debates are long-running and often acrimonious. It is unclear whether simply generating more of the same kinds of data will be sufficient to resolve standing disputes. At times like these, bringing other, less conventional, lines of evidence and argumentation to bear on an issue can provide some clarity, or at least new directions to explore. Likewise, an unconventional approach to Patagonia's own colonization can provide a fresh perspective on subsequent cultural developments in the region.

In this chapter, I analyze Patagonian colonization both at the regional level and in the broader context of New World peopling, comparing the Patagonian record to predictions of the ideal free distribution. I also pick up a thread from the previous chapter—whether Patagonia's first arrivals wore fitted clothing—to explore New World colonization speed and technologies' niche-constructive properties, considering how our culture can change the adaptive environment and lead to powerful feedback loops between culture, biology, and environment.

Peopling Debates and the Invisibility of the Patagonian Record

In broadest strokes, debates regarding initial colonization of the New World currently center on precisely when and by what route(s) people first arrived. Most archaeologists now agree that evidence supports a human presence roughly 14,500 years ago (Wheat 2012), which is about a thousand years before the appearance of Clovis, the earliest well-documented human occupation in North America (O'Brien et al. 2014). There are some, though, who feel the available evidence is inadequate to describe this 14,500-year-old occupation at Monte Verde as anything more than a one-off—a failed colonization attempt (e.g., Fiedel 2017). Still others believe that, to account for the earliest known site(s)—which are almost certainly not the earliest occupations (see below)—the first people must have arrived much earlier, perhaps on the order of 16,000 years ago or more (Dillehay 2012). Part of the problem is that both potential routes of first entry, land and sea, were periodically complicated by environmental conditions and it is currently hard to reconcile archaeological evidence with the timing of the routes' respective availability. The details are all misaligned but the topic is so divisive that efforts are not always directed at their alignment. It is also true that the long-dominant paradigm, which

sees Clovis as the earliest undisputed cultural manifestation in the New World (Potter et al. 2017), has so profoundly influenced our expectations for early sites that we may be overlooking important evidence. Indeed, these expectations may be the reason Patagonia has largely been sidelined.

Rise of the Clovis-first Paradigm

Peopling debates can be traced all the way back to the initial collision of cultures in the late fifteenth century, when Europeans began to explore and colonize what was, to them, a "New World." From the first, Europeans pondered the identities and origins of the peoples they encountered—and probably vice versa, though much less has been written on that side of the story. Until the mid-1800s, the endeavor was largely idle and speculative, though debates were sometimes heated, as between three prominent Dutchmen who, in the 1640s, argued bitterly about whether Natives originally hailed from Scandinavia, Spain, or Polynesia (Wilmsen 1965). Others fancied them descendants of the Lost Tribes of Israel (Adair 1775; Huddleston 1967; Willey and Sabloff 1993), and, of course, there were supernatural explanations, too, as were favored for Patagonian groups (Pigafetta 1524). Most people believed, though, that the Earth was a very young place, and colonization of the New World a relatively recent phenomenon. Migration at some point in the past was implicit, but the goal of this speculative period was to establish their place of origin, not how, when, or under what circumstances people migrated.

This all began to change in the mid-1800s with the publication of Lyell's (1833) *Principles of Geology*, which radically altered our understanding of the Earth's age, and Darwin's *On the Origin of Species* (1859) and *The Descent of Man* (1871), which made a strong case for the antiquity and malleability of humankind. Lyell's and Darwin's concepts paved the way for a more scientific study of the human past, which, in Europe, led to convincing demonstrations of humans' coexistence with extinct fauna (e.g., at Brixam Cave, England; Meltzer 1993). As a direct result of

these Old World discoveries, New World scholars seem to develop a touch of "antiquity envy"
and a desire to prove that New World sites were
every bit as old and important as European ones.
Celebrated Argentine naturalist and paleontolo-
gist Florentino Ameghino went so far as to argue
that humans not only have a long history in the
New World but *evolved* here. Ameghino's "au-
tochthonous theory" was roundly criticized by
Aleš Hrdlička, influential physical anthropologist, curator at what would become the Smithsonian National Museum of Natural History, and
vocal watchdog with a penchant for pointedly
discrediting claims of great antiquity in the New
World. Nonetheless, for the moment, American
archaeologists were riding an especially buoyant
wave, exploring deep time in the New World,
and seeing evidence of an "American Paleolithic"
in every overturned stone.

The surge of unbridled optimism crashed in
1890 when William Henry Holmes, respected
scientist with the United States National Museum and Bureau of American Ethnology, published a trenchant criticism of one such claim
for great New World antiquity. Archaeologist
and naturalist Charles Abbott believed he had
discovered a 20,000- to 30,000-year-old human
occupation near Trenton, New Jersey, based on
the crudeness of tools discovered in what Abbott
described as glacial till (Abbott 1889; Wilmsen
1965). Holmes had been trained in both geology
and archaeology, and his own work at quarry
sites in the eastern U.S. led him to reject Ab-
bot's claim. Holmes argued that the crude implements at Trenton were quarry rejects left by fully
Archaic (or later) people, if they were even tools
at all (Holmes 1892; Willey and Sabloff 1993).
Holmes, like Hrdlička, became an "American
Paleolithic" watchdog and was especially critical
of claims of great antiquity based solely on the
crude appearance of the chipped stone tools. The
two men were contemporaries, in fact, and their
prominence in their respective fields as well as
the force of their criticisms—which, especially
in Hrdlička's case, could be witheringly scorn-
ful—created an atmosphere of apprehension in
the archaeological community. Quite justifiably,
Holmes and Hrdlička had high standards of

scientific rigor, demanding that claims for great
antiquity be backed by unimpeachable evidence
(Willey and Sabloff 1993). The result, however,
was a growing reluctance among archaeologists
to pursue the topic.

Nonetheless, in the early 1920s, artifacts
were found in association with the bones of
extinct fauna at Lone Wolf Creek in Texas. Excavations at this site convinced archaeologist
Jesse Figgins of a human presence in the New
World contemporaneous with Pleistocene animals. Yet, the Lone Wolf Creek excavations were
not performed by trained archaeologists and the
contemporaneity of the artifacts and bones was
largely discounted (Dixon 1999). Very shortly
thereafter, a find in Wild Horse Arroyo near
Folsom, New Mexico, was brought to Figgins's
attention. Several years earlier, rancher George
McJunken had discovered artifacts in association with the bones of a very large bison. When
Figgins learned of the site in the 1920s, he immediately made a connection between the Wild
Horse materials and those of Lone Wolf Creek.
So as not to let a second opportunity fall to
the same criticisms, Figgins left some of Wild
Horse materials in situ and invited Hrdlička to
observe the association himself. This, the first
"site visit"—now an important rite of passage for
sites thought to be very old—marks the turning
point in peopling studies: having witnessed a
projectile point in direct contextual association
with the remains of *Bison antiquus*, Hrdlička
was convinced of the antiquity of humans in
the New World (Dixon 1999). Soon thereafter, at Blackwater Draw (New Mexico), Clovis
points were found clearly associated with mammoth remains in a stratum directly below one
containing Folsom points in association with
(extinct) *Bison antiquus* remains (Cotter 1937,
1938; Dixon 1999).

Blackwater Draw firmly established the
Pleistocene antiquity of humans in the New
World (Boldurian 2008). It also contributed
to the burgeoning view of first-Americans-as-
super-hunters, for which the distinctive Clovis
point became emblem. Indeed, as more Clovis
sites were discovered and their distributions
mapped, a robust peopling narrative emerged,

bolstered by a growing body of paleoenvironmental information: At the end of the last ice
age, small bands of Clovis big-game hunters
walked across the Bering Land Bridge before it
was swallowed up by seas rapidly swelling with
glacial meltwater. As the massive Cordilleran
and Laurentide ice masses subsided, a passage
opened between them, funneling Clovis hunters directly from eastern Beringia (in the vicinity of the Mackenzie Mountains, northwestern
Canada) onto the North American Great Plains,
from which region they rapidly spread in pursuit of megafauna. This hypothesis, now known
as "Clovis first" in opposition to claims of still
greater New World antiquity, quickly gathered
mass because it seemed to account neatly for all
available evidence. When radiocarbon dating
became available in 1950, and as paleoenvironmental techniques continued to develop through
the 1960s and 1970s, the primary research ob-
jectives were to date Clovis more securely and
to better characterize late glacial environments
(e.g., Beringia, the ice-free corridor). Each new
datum in favor of Clovis first—including finds in
far southern South America—edged alternative
models farther and farther out of contention.

In 1936, just a few years after Blackwater
Draw was discovered, Junius Bird began his excavations at Cueva Fell near the Strait of Magellan. In the lowest stratum, which has since been
dated to between approximately 12,900 and
12,400 cal BP (Bird 1988), Bird found distinctive,
fluted "fishtail" projectile points (Figure 4.2)
in association with extinct horse and ground
sloth. Similar Patagonian finds in the following
decades, including at Los Toldos (Cardich et al.
1973; cf. Borrero 2008; Menghin 1952), seemed
perfectly aligned with the hypothesis that the
first colonists were fluted-point wielding super-
hunters. The South American sites presented a
slightly different cast of characters, in terms of
both the megafaunal species and the people who
hunted them, but the story was Clovis-like in all
the important ways.

Beyond fueling the Clovis-first hypothesis, fishtail points in southern South America
may have had the ironic effect of sidelining
Patagonian peopling research. Initially, before

FIGURE 4.2. Stylized versions of (left) a fluted fishtail
point, relatively common in early South American
sites, and (right) a Clovis point. Illustrations by Emily
Wolfe.

sites with fishtail points could be dated absolutely, the assumption was that, given their geographic position relative to the ice-free corridor,
they must postdate Clovis and must, therefore,
be derivative; studying them would tell us little
about initial colonization. When eventually
these sites were dated and found to be largely
coeval with Clovis (Waters and Stafford 2007),
the most logical explanation was that colonization was incredibly rapid as a result of people's
having "mapped on" to Pleistocene megafauna
(sensu Binford 1980), making local adaptations
largely irrelevant. This did little to improve
negative perceptions of Patagonia's potential to
yield revelatory information related to initial
colonization. And so, while fishtail points were
often mentioned in support of the Clovis-first
hypothesis, mainstream discussions centered on
refining the Clovis chronology in North America, searching for a Clovis progenitor in Siberia,
and characterizing the Beringian and subglacial
landscapes.

Decline of the Clovis-first Paradigm

Even as the Clovis-first hypothesis was gathering steam, evidence started coming to light
that cast doubt on aspects of the model, leading

some archaeologists to question whether alternative peopling scenarios might be feasible. In the 1960s and 1970s, a few paleoenvironmental reconstructions indicated that both the Bering Land Bridge and the ice-free corridor may have lacked sufficient vegetation to support large herbivores or, therefore, humans (Colinvaux 1996). Data now suggest Beringia was a shrub tundra suitable for human habitation (Elias and Crocker 2008), but opinions remain divided regarding the viability of the ice-free corridor. A recent analysis of DNA from lake sediment cores within the corridor shows that steppe vegetation, mammoth, and bison were absent before approximately 12,500 cal BP (Pedersen et al. 2016; cf. Heintzman et al. 2016), which means that, even if the corridor had been open before then, it was almost certainly not the route taken by the group that inhabited Monte Verde roughly 14,500 cal BP, and not likely how Clovis people arrived, either, since the earliest Clovis sites predate a viable corridor by a thousand years (Buchanan et al. 2014). Moreover, we simply do not see the progression of dates from north to south that we would expect if people migrated from Alaska through the corridor into subglacial North America (Beaudoin et al. 1996).

The 1970s also saw the introduction of an alternative route of initial entry: the Pacific Coast. Knut Fladmark (1979) hypothesized that the coast would have been largely ice-free, and subsistence resources would have been available much earlier on the coast than on the mainland (Ames and Maschner 1999; Dixon 1993; Fladmark 1978; Josenhans et al. 1997). The updated perspective, sometimes referred to as the Pacific Coast model or "kelp highway" hypothesis, is informed by a more nuanced understanding of modern and ancient coastal conditions, as well as mounting archaeological evidence. Erlandson and colleagues (2007), for example, describe a highly productive corridor of kelp and mangrove forests from Beringia to Tierra del Fuego, which they believe could have supported groups of late Pleistocene colonists traveling south along the coast (see also Braje et al. 2017). A recent study of lake core data from Sanak Island in the western Gulf of Alaska, which would have been a high point on the Beringian coast, indicates that the coast was ice-free and resource-rich by 17,000 years ago (Misarti et al. 2012).

Based solely on their respective dates of availability, then, the Pacific Coast hypothesis would seem to have the upper hand as the only one currently able to account for Monte Verde's 14,500-year-old occupation. Still, until recently, there was little archaeological evidence to support it. Of course, this is not really surprising, given how dramatically sea levels have changed since the Last Glacial Maximum. As Fladmark himself explained when he first proposed a Pacific coastal route, most coastal sites predating roughly 9,000 years ago (when seas reached postglacial high stands) are now likely submerged beneath more than 100 m of sea water or else were washed away by rising postglacial tides (Fladmark 1979:62).

Nonetheless, a handful of early coastal sites have been found that provide clear evidence of a coastal or maritime adaptation during the late Pleistocene, including very early coastal villages on Triquet Island (British Columbia; 14,000 cal BP; Katz 2017) and at Quebrada Jaguay (Peru; ca. 13,000 cal BP; Sandweiss et al. 1998). And, while direct evidence of boat technology (e.g., boat parts or tools unequivocally related to boat manufacture) remains elusive, there is circumstantial evidence of boat use. It is clear that *Homo sapiens* had boat technology and sophisticated navigational abilities by at least 50,000 years ago (Bird et al. 2018) and potentially as early as 65,000 years ago (Clarkson et al. 2017), when Australia was colonized via open ocean voyage. Of course, this does not mean that everyone everywhere had boats by this time, but compelling New World evidence of boat use comes from several relatively early sites on islands not connected to the mainland, even at the height of glaciation. Examples include the Anangula Blade site (Ananiuliak Island, Alaska; Gómez Coutouly 2015), Kilgii Gwaay (Cohen 2014), and sites on California's Channel Islands (Erlandson et al. 2011). Moreover, Braje and colleagues (2017) cite commonalities among stemmed and tanged points around the Pacific Rim, which they believe further support a coastal migration.

Debate regarding initial routes of entry is clearly tied to the timing of particular deglaciation events, and the archaeological data remain somewhat equivocal on this point. For this reason, many have turned to other lines of evidence for clues regarding the timing of initial entry. Genetic data in particular have provided estimates to which archaeologists can compare existing data. Raghavan and colleagues (Llamas et al. 2016; Raghavan et al. 2014) suggest divergence of Native American stock from Siberian between roughly 23,000 and 18,500 years ago, a "standstill" in eastern Beringia—a period of isolation and genetic differentiation beginning no earlier than 23,000 years ago and lasting no longer than 8,000 years—and ultimate expansion into the New World between 16,000 and 13,500 years ago. Coastal route proponents note that the earlier side of this window—but not the later—provides ample time for people to reach Monte Verde (Braje et al. 2018) since the coast was ice-free by 17,000 years ago and the corridor may not have been viable until 12,500 years ago. Clovis-first proponents note, however, that genetic evidence also indicates two lineages—one northern, corresponding to Arctic and Subarctic groups, and one southern, to which Clovis people are related—neither of which supports an older-than-Clovis migration (Potter et al. 2018). Braje and colleagues (2018) contend, though, that genetic data are estimates based on unpredictable variation in mutation rates; divergence dates provide general guidelines but, ultimately, the route(s) and precise timing of initial colonization can only be determined archaeologically.

Archaeological support for an older-than-Clovis occupation is growing now, too, if somewhat haltingly. In the late 1990s, Monte Verde was formally accepted by the archaeological community as legitimately older than Clovis (Meltzer et al. 1997). The site's acceptance was hard-won through an exhaustive and meticulous 20-year research effort, culminating in a site visit in the spirit of Figgins and Hrdlička at Wild Horse Arroyo (Dillehay 1989, 1997; Meltzer et al. 1997). Since then, other sites—for example, Bluefish Caves (Bourgeon et al. 2017), Debra L. Friedkin (Waters et al. 2011), Gault (Collins and Bradley 2008; Collins et al. 2013), Manis (Waters et al. 2011), Meadowcroft Rockshelter (Adovasio and Page 2002), Page-Ladson (Halligan et al. 2016), and Paisley Caves (Jenkins et al. 2012)—have weathered the intense criticisms of Clovis-first proponents, and the older-than-Clovis hypothesis has gained traction since the turn of the twenty-first century. Nonetheless, the date of initial entry remains controversial, even among those who accept an older-than-Clovis migration (Wheat 2012).

So it is that a clear understanding of the peopling process eludes us despite decades of dedicated, high-budget research and reams of reports. At times, opposing camps interpret the same data differently, and at times each simply dismisses the evidence another puts forward. Professional consensus sometimes seems utterly unattainable and, while one camp occasionally pronounces another dead (Braje et al. 2017), several recent publications, including a high-profile exchange in *Science*, suggest we may be as far from consensus as ever (Braje et al. 2017, Braje et al. 2018; Dawe and Kornfeld 2017; Fiedel 2017; Morrow 2017; Potter et al. 2018; Potter et al. 2017; Reid 2017).

The Clovis-first Legacy

Clovis remains the "earliest unequivocal widespread cultural manifestation south of the ice sheets" (Potter et al. 2017:1224), and the burden of proof lies with older-than-Clovis proponents. In the decades following the introduction of radiocarbon dating, and in the spirit of Holmes and Hrdlička, a new cohort of watchdogs has emerged whose criticisms of older-than-Clovis claims (and claimants) can likewise be scathing. They have assembled a list of criteria for evaluating purportedly early sites: (1) radiocarbon measures that are reliable and consistent; (2) concurrence between these radiocarbon measures and the site's stratigraphy; (3) incontrovertible human artifacts and/or features; (4) "direct and unimpeachable contextual association of the artifacts, features, and radiocarbon dates and the sediments associated with them" (Dillehay 1997:767); and (5) a living/use surface that is contextually sound within its geological stratum, showing little or no postdepositional disturbance (Dillehay 1997; also Adovasio and Pedler 1997:574; Haynes 1969:714; Lynch 1990; Meltzer 1995a:32; Stanford 1983:65). Some of the cited authors note that it would be best, of course, if there were also dateable human remains. Granting that directly dated human remains should be harder to dismiss, so far the only evidence of the kind is human coprolites from the Paisley Five Mile Point Caves in Oregon, which date to between 12,750 and 14,300 cal BP (Gilbert et al. 2008; Jenkins et al. 2012), and there have certainly been attempts to discredit this find, too (Goldberg et al. 2009; Poinar et al. 2009).

It is telling that "of the 50 sites identified in 1964 as older than Clovis, only 4 made a 1976 version of that list, and none made a 1988 list" (Krieger 1964; MacNeish 1976; Meltzer 1995a:22; Morlan 1988). Dozens more purportedly pre-Clovis sites have since been dismissed for failing to meet the criteria listed in the previous paragraph. The criteria are stringent, to be sure, but this is as it should be. Still, there may be a sixth criterion, seldom articulated but understood, that may be unduly hampering our study of New World colonization.

This "sixth criterion" centers on *visibility* (Adovasio and Pedler 1997; Lynch 1990; West 1996), or widespread evidence of a recognizable lithic technology or other material cultural trait. There are obvious problems with requiring visibility of sites of great antiquity. Preservation, for one, makes it unlikely we will find basketry, footwear, clothing, and the like—things potentially identifiable as particular to a culture, which is to say "visible"—at even a single site, let alone several that could then be compared. What we are really talking about, then, is a visible lithic technology and, to date, "the small sample of pre-Clovis sites has yet to produce a coherent technological signature with the broad geographic patterning that characterizes Clovis" (Braje et al. 2017:593). It is on these grounds that some Clovis-first proponents reject claims of an older-than-Clovis occupation.

Basing acceptance of older-than-Clovis claims on whether they show evidence of a recognizable lithic (or other) technology is a legacy of the long reign of Clovis-first. Like the Clovis-first model itself, the "sixth criterion" presupposes cultural homogeneity among the first people to reach the Americas and, by extension, either a very rapid migration or strong selection pressure on tool form (e.g., success in hunting megafauna; cf. Kelly 1988; Kelly and Todd 1988). Indeed, given the extensive literature on potential Clovis-progenitor technologies (e.g., Bradley and Stanford 2004), the expectation seems to be that the visible technology will be related to projectile weaponry, which assumes a subsistence focus on game hunted with spears or darts. Less charitably, we might say the criterion actually stipulates that any older-than-Clovis migration ought to look, in broad strokes, just like Clovis-first.

In fact, there are good reasons to think that an older-than-Clovis migration *should* resemble the Clovis-first model. Genetic evidence suggests a small founding population ($\approx$1,000–5,000 people, effective size; Kitchen et al. 2008) that was isolated in a relatively small area in eastern Beringia for several millennia before moving into the Americas (Llamas et al. 2016; Moreno-Mayar et al. 2018; Schroeder et al. 2009). A visible technology could easily emerge (or be preserved) under the circumstances. "Mapping on" (*sensu* Binford 1980) to large-bodied, wide-ranging fauna, including Pleistocene megafauna would solve the problems of (1) landscape unfamiliarity (Kelly and Todd 1988) and (2) a lack of experienced neighbors one might otherwise ask for advice and help (Meltzer 2009). It is not hard to imagine how, jointly, these conditions and strategies might lead to the rapid dispersal of a relatively culturally homogenous population with a visible technology. Indeed, it would be puzzling if older-than-Clovis colonists fit this description yet remained cryptic for several millennia, which is precisely the Clovis-first proponents' point. However, emerging evidence suggests that older-than-Clovis occupations represent a rather more generalist adaptation and that this, combined with the visibility criterion, might be hiding them in plain sight.

Monte Verde is now widely accepted as the earliest known occupation in the New World

(Wheat 2012). It is older than Clovis by at least a thousand years (see also Dillehay et al. [2015] for a description of a possible occupation ca. 18,000 BP). Three things are noteworthy in light of the current discussion. First, the lithic toolkit would not likely meet the visibility criterion, even if identical tools of similar age were found in other places. The assemblage is largely composed of naturally broken or minimally modified cobbles that were taken directly from nearby Chinchihuapi Creek, used expediently to perform some task, then discarded (Collins 1997; Dillehay 1997). Additionally, there are bola stones, which are grooved in this case but, in other times and places across southern South America—potentially including sites contemporaneous with Monte Verde—bolas were simply rounded stones placed in skin bags. When the bolas are indistinct from local stones, there is a high probability of this technology going unrecognized.

The second noteworthy point related to the visibility criterion is that a large proportion of the Monte Verde assemblage is perishable. Plant parts, cordage, hide, and wood would not have been preserved were it not for the rapid but low-energy covering of the site in a slurry that inhibited the breakdown of organic remains. With only slight changes to the depositional environment (or project budget, or any number of other factors) Monte Verde would not likely have been accepted as older-than-Clovis and may well have been nearly invisible—perhaps missed altogether. Other such early sites could easily be overlooked or, at least, not studied at the same level of detail as Monte Verde.

Thirdly, the Monte Verde faunal assemblage suggests a much broader diet than is consistent with the big-game specialist scenario associated with a Clovis-first-like colonization. While gomphothere (*Cuvieronicus*) and paleo-camelid (*Paleolama* sp.) are present in the bone assemblage, they are outnumbered by seeds, fruits, seaweeds, and terrestrial plants representing tens of different species (Dillehay et al. 2008). Other early sites' assemblages (e.g., Broken Mammoth, Tanana River Valley, Alaska) reflect similarly broad diets (Holmes 2001). Exacerbating the relatively low visibility of small game compared to megafauna—and coming back around to the first point regarding technological visibility—if colonizing groups relied on foraging, scavenging, fishing, and/or hunting small game with snares, slings, nets, or bare hands, then the production of projectile points or other specialized, nonperishable tools may have been unnecessary.

Acknowledging that early sites might be difficult to see and might, when we find them, look very different from expectations derived from any Clovis-first-like colonization model, we can recalibrate our expectations and tailor future research designs to maximize the likelihood we will recognize such occupations. Optimality models can also be effective antidotes to expectation biases. If the visibility criterion steers us toward environments known to have been suitable for large- and medium-bodied animals during the late Pleistocene, or makes us less likely to question apparently late dates of initial occupation in other habitat types, we may be inadvertently limiting our own ability to understand New World colonization. Because optimality models can be specified in ways that neutralize expectation biases, they can counteract our preconceptions and generate novel hypotheses regarding the timing, nature, and details of colonization at local and regional levels. The ideal free distribution model, for example, provides fresh insights into the process (sequence) of New World colonization and, therefore, dispersal speed, at the same time highlighting particular benefits and challenges of the Patagonian landscape.

The Ideal Free Distribution

The Patagonian landscape is highly diverse (Chapter 2), and its ecoregions can be ranked according to various criteria (e.g., food availability) for use in particular behavioral models. Habitat ranking is central to the ideal free distribution (IFD) model, and here I specify and compare two IFD models of colonization, first assuming prehistoric people's preference for calorie maximization, then assuming the alternative of risk minimization. Existing archaeological data are better aligned with predictions of the calorie-maximization IFD model of Patagonian colonization than those of either the risk-minimization version or a neutral model that assumes a more or less random colonization process. Here, I describe rankings of Patagonia's ecoregions, the three models' respective predictions, and available archaeological data in light of these rankings and predictions.

As I outlined in Chapter 3, the IFD predicts that in a pristine (previously unoccupied) environment, the highest-ranked patches will be occupied first and exclusively. Other patches should be occupied in rank order, the second-ranked occupied only once overcrowding and resource depletion reduce the suitability of the first-ranked to the initial suitability of the second-ranked. The process continues, with people occupying lower and lower ranked habitats, for as long as new foragers continue to join, through both migration and population growth (Fretwell and Lucas 1970).

Recall, too, that suitability is measured in terms of individual fitness (survival and reproduction), which is a function of both the presence of positive attributes (e.g., availability of food, water, shelter, mates, and helpers) and absence of negative ones (e.g., parasites, predators, competitors; Winterhalder et al. 2010). Because habitats are ranked according to their suitability as experienced by the first inhabitant (i.e., the first inhabitant's fitness; Fretwell 1972), archaeologists must use proxies for habitat suitability—we do not have access to detailed information related to most of the factors affecting the first occupant's fitness, much less to the actual fitness of the first occupant themself.

Precisely calculating the prehistoric suitability of each of Patagonia's ecoregions is complicated. Even leaving aside the truly thorny ingredients like mate and hunting-partner availability, we lack detailed information on the prehistoric abundance and distribution of subsistence resources in each ecoregion (e.g., total available calories and nutrients, reliable fresh water, construction materials). Assessment at a much more general level and a bit of back-of-the-envelope accounting are nonetheless informative, as I explore below, but estimating

habitat suitability is also complicated in this case by our skewed understanding of prehistoric resource use in Patagonia. We feel more confident in our interpretations of what people on the steppe were eating, for example, than we do our interpretations of forest diets because more sites have been located and excavated on the steppe (i.e., statistically, the steppe sample is more reliable), and because preservation is generally worse in forests. So, even if we had perfect information regarding prehistoric resource availability in all environments, unless we know which of those resources were, in fact, targeted, our estimates of habitat suitability might be artificially inflated. For example, all potential west coast resources might sum to an incredibly rich and virtually inexhaustible food supply, but unless prehistoric groups had efficient boats that could navigate open stretches of difficult water, the effective food supply is substantially smaller and the habitat's rank substantially lower.

Lastly, it is worth repeating a sentiment first explored in Chapter 2: Within each of Patagonia's several ecoregions, a host of variables (e.g., site aspect, wind exposure) contribute to the development of microenvironments that may not reflect average conditions. Average conditions also fluctuate through time, both seasonally and on longer timescales. So, while precise accounting and formal modeling are preferred in many instances and often tractable at a local level, they are largely inaccessible for this regional-level analysis of late Pleistocene Patagonia. Nonetheless, well-justified estimates and general assessments provide relative habitat rankings useful for distinguishing two alternative colonization hypotheses centered on the IFD, one where habitats are ranked according to calorie maximization, and another that ranks them according to risk minimization.

Patagonian Habitat Ranking

Under the hypothesis that Patagonian colonists' settlement decisions were primarily motivated by maximization of foraging returns, habitats are ranked according to biomass availability. Biomass is the total mass of living matter in a given unit of space. Primary productivity is the rate at which biomass is produced, a proxy for food availability, and a more commonly used variable than biomass in ecological studies. As we saw in Chapter 3's discussion of macroecological models, primary productivity is also a fair predictor of human population density. Population densities tend to be higher in habitats where primary productivity is higher, which supports the IFD model's prediction that, at equilibrium, the number of people in a habitat should reflect the abundance of resources available there. Because the IFD also predicts that the highest-ranked habitat (the one with the highest primary productivity, in this case) should be occupied first, we can assess initial colonization in light of the model even though, by definition, colonizing populations are not at equilibrium.

The majority of Patagonia's terrestrial ecosystems are characterized by relatively low primary productivity. The steppe comprises roughly 75% of the Patagonian landmass, and annual average precipitation there is very low (100–200 mm/year), winds are high and constant (exacerbating evaporation), and, in places, there is substantial cloud cover much of the year (Chapter 2). All of these factors restrict primary productivity. Primary productivity in Aónikenk territory on the Argentine steppe (ca. 46° S) ranks 285th (16th percentile) among the 339 locations in Binford's (2001) ethnographic sample—just above the territories of the Alaskan Inuit, Siberian Eskimo, and Karadjera of western Australia. Nonetheless, the steppe does host large herds of guanaco, flocks of ratites (*Rhea* spp.), and, prehistorically, large-bodied megamammals (e.g., ground sloth, paleolama, extinct horse). Indeed, though their numbers are presently much smaller, there were an estimated 30 to 50 million head of guanaco in Patagonia at initial contact with Europeans (ca. 1500 CE; Sarno et al. 2015). Riparian, lacustrine, and other wetland zones (e.g., seasonal marshes) also offer a range of plants, small animals, and birds that may have been attractive to humans. Moreover, the steppe offers patchy but reliable water despite the arid climate (e.g., rivers with Andean headwaters; see Chapters 2 and 5), as well as lithic resources, rock shelters, and relatively easy travel and way-finding.

Like the steppe, the unforested Andes are sparsely vegetated. This is particularly true in the north and above the tree line. The mountains host fewer and generally smaller-bodied animals than the steppe, although guanaco do move into the Andes seasonally. Because of their lower biomass, seasonally restricted habitability, and the negative effects of steep, uneven terrain and hypoxic conditions above ~2,500 masl, mountains are generally considered undesirable for human habitation (cf. Chala-Aldana et al. 2018).

Patagonian forests are characterized by relatively high primary productivity and higher biodiversity than other terrestrial habitats. Nonetheless, several Patagonian archaeologists argue that the resource structure in Patagonian forests was not conducive to long-term human habitation (Borrero 2004; Mena 1995; Méndez, Reyes, Nuevo Delauney et al. 2016). In particular, they note that forest game species are smaller and more solitary than their steppe counterparts, making hunting in forests less profitable. Conversely, the forest-steppe transition might have been highly desirable since, as with all ecotones, positioning oneself in a boundary zone provides access to resources from both adjoining environment types. Yet the location of the forest-steppe boundary is highly sensitive to environmental change and anthropic disturbances (e.g., burning; Iglesias et al. 2014), so attempting to stake a claim in the prehistoric boundary zone would have been difficult, particularly as populations grew. Archaeological identification of explicit boundary zone use is also difficult, and requires detailed paleoenvironmental reconstructions at all sites in both the westernmost steppe and easternmost forest.

Patagonia's marine ecosystems, and the west coast in particular, are more productive than its terrestrial ones. In fact, the Humboldt Current is one of the most biologically productive ocean currents in the world (Chavez et al. 2008) and, considering modern levels of commercial fishing associated with the Humboldt Current, west coast resources likely were virtually inexhaustible at prehistoric levels of fishing, hunting, and gathering. The west coast is also forested, and so provides both coastal and forest resources. Conversely, Patagonia's east coast is generally more accessible than the steep and forested west, though the marine bounty is not quite as rich as that supported by the Humboldt Current. On both coasts, fresh water is naturally available at river mouths and these may have been preferred settlement locations. Rainwater could have been managed to ensure fresh water access elsewhere, particularly in the west where precipitation is higher and more reliable. To take full advantage of either coast, however, prehistoric people would have needed efficient boats, although littoral resources are accessible without much specialized technology.

Model Predictions: Calorie-maximization IFD

Given this broad-strokes, subsistence-focused assessment of Patagonian habitats, and assuming the initial colonists were primarily interested in maximizing foraging returns, colonists *with boats* should have settled in marine habitats first and exclusively until growing populations reduced their suitability to that of the second-ranked habitat. More specifically, freshwater outlets likely were particularly high-ranked, as were embayments suitable for canoe haul-outs and flat ground for camping, that latter of which is relatively rare on the west coast (Winterhalder et al. 2010). However, the Pacific Coast appears to have been overrun by mountain glaciers until well after other parts of Patagonia had been colonized (Borrero 2008). This would, of course, render the west coast completely unsuitable for initial colonization regardless of available technologies. The east coast was not directly affected by glaciers and would have been highly ranked in terms of productivity, but the late Pleistocene east coast is not accessible by traditional archaeological methods since it is now located as much as 880 km offshore and up to ~250 m below the modern sea surface (Ponce et al. 2011). Indeed, even if future paleoenvironmental reconstructions were to show that part of the Pacific Coast was ice-free earlier than is currently understood, both coasts were affected by rising postglacial

tides and significant landscape erosion (Chapter 2). Our ability to assess early prehistoric use of these habitats is presently quite limited.

The coasts' inaccessibility—the west coast's unavailability to initial colonists and the Pleistocene east coast's unavailability to modern archaeologists—effectively makes the second-ranked Patagonian habitat the first-ranked. This is because, according to the IFD, people should continue to join a region's first-ranked habitat exclusively until its suitability is reduced to that of the second-ranked habitat, which should then be colonized. Based on projected prehistoric densities of guanaco and Pleistocene megafauna, plus the availability of stone for hunting implements and of caves for shelter from the westerlies (Martin and Borrero 2017), the steppe is the most likely second-ranked habitat despite its relatively low primary productivity. If people did in fact colonize the coast first, calorie-maximizing colonists should have spread next to the steppe.

When available paleoenvironmental and archaeological data limit us to a fairly coarse habitat ranking, as is the case for late Pleistocene Patagonia, it can be helpful to combine predictions of the IFD with those of other models to triangulate on a most likely colonization scenario. Original colonists prioritizing foraging returns should also have relatively narrow diets centered on a habitat's highest-ranked resources. Following initial colonization, and as a habitat fills with people competing for the same high-ranked resources, diets will broaden, but the earliest record, at least, should indicate selectivity (narrow dietary breadth).

Model Predictions: Risk-minimization IFD

If Patagonia's initial colonists' settlement choices were based on risk minimization, the early record should look very different from what is predicted if we assume calorie maximization was the goal. Entering a landscape about which one has little information can trigger risk aversion, resulting in decision making that favors known but lower foraging returns over unknown but potentially higher ones. In late Pleistocene (terrestrial) Patagonia, this would equate to a diet centered on low-ranking but easily accessible resources (e.g., small mammals and plants) rather than high-ranked but potentially elusive ones (e.g., guanaco). The behaviors of large-bodied, wide-ranging herbivores are different enough in different environments to require a fair bit of learning before one is a proficient hunter in a new setting (Meltzer 2009). Even "mapping on" to members of this guild initially entails some uncertainty as one moves between environments. Rather than specializing in such resources and targeting the habitats in which they are dominant—the strategy for maximizing foraging returns—a risk-averse forager should diversify the diet, to spread foraging risk across multiple species and increase the likelihood of bagging *something* on any given foraging bout.

By the same logic, a risk-averse forager should rank habitats according to their biodiversity rather than their productivity. Biodiversity is correlated with ecosystem stability in the sense that productivity is less variable through time the more diverse the ecosystem, which decreases subsistence-related risk (Tallavaara et al. 2018). Productivity and biodiversity are correlated to some degree, but not perfectly, and, more importantly, Patagonia's (effective) first-ranked habitat for the diversity-loving forager is distinct from that of the calorie-loving forager. I say *effective* first-ranked habitat because the actual first-ranked habitat in terms of biodiversity is, again, the coast but, for all of the reasons explored in the previous section, the coasts' inaccessibility (prehistoric and modern) exclude them from this analysis. So, for reasons also explored in the previous section, we can in good conscience focus on what is likely the second-ranked habitat: in this case, the forest.

Patagonian forests are surprisingly biodiverse (Villagrán and Hinojosa 1997), offering a wide range of plant and animal species, including nut- and fruit-bearing trees and bushes, small mammals, birds, frogs and lizards, fish, and medium-bodied ungulates (huemul deer and guanaco). While most forest species are relatively small and many of them solitary (e.g., huemul), making each potentially less profitable than larger and more gregarious steppe species (Borrero

2004; Mena 1995; Méndez, Reyes, Nuevo De-launey et al. 2016), the habitat's unusual biodiversity would have made it highly attractive to risk-averse initial colonists. Incidentally, in their study of worldwide hunter-gatherer carrying capacities, Tallavaara and colleagues (2018) predict high forager densities in temperate forests.

In acknowledging some amount of foraging uncertainty, the risk-averse version of the IFD model relaxes the assumption of perfect knowledge that guides calorie-maximizing foragers to the most productive habitats. Nonetheless, the risk-averse IFD still assumes colonizers know the difference between, and where to find, highly productive versus highly diverse environments (when the two do not overlap perfectly). It is possible that, through scouts and reconnaissance missions—perhaps leaving so ephemeral a record as to be invisible themselves—colonists did essentially have perfect, or at least perfectly sufficient, information. If so, they could have moved swiftly to the most suitable habitat, potentially without making an archaeologically confusing mess along the way.

Plausibly, though, initial colonists had no information about the landscape beyond what they had already experienced and could presently see. This is essentially a random walk, in which there is an equal probability that the next "step" will be in any one of a set number of directions. This neutral model is consistent with the "wave of advance" hypothesis for initial colonization, which sees movement as a product of building population pressure behind the wave front such that even a random walk moves the wave, on balance, forward (Young and Bettinger 1992). This alternative is explored in more detail in the *Squaring IFD predictions with observed dietary breadth* section, below.

The Archaeological Record of Patagonian Colonization

Archaeological data from Patagonia currently support the calorie-maximization IFD. The region's record reportedly begins roughly 15,000 cal BP (12,890 ^{14}C BP) on the steppe—specifically, the Central Plateau (Deseado Massif) of Santa

Cruz Province, Argentina (Miotti 1996; Miotti et al. 2003). Throughout much of the late Pleistocene, Patagonian sites appear to have been restricted to three regions: the steppe's Central Plateau and Pali Aike volcanic field (Argentine-Chilean border north of the Strait of Magellan), and the Última Esperanza region (Magallanes, Chile), situated in the Andean foothills and forest-steppe ecotone (Figure 4.1).

The Piedra Museo site (Central Plateau) is currently the earliest accepted occupation in Patagonia, dating to approximately 15,000 cal BP (12,890 ^{14}C BP; Miotti 1996; Miotti et al. 2003). The associated assemblage includes two biface fragments, large end- and side-scrapers, and bones of guanaco, extinct horse, ground sloth, and rhea (both American and Darwin's, the latter no longer present in southern Patagonia; Borrero 2008). The Los Toldos site, also on the Central Plateau, is reportedly as early (ca. 14,900 cal BP) and contains similar materials, including side-scrapers and bones of extinct fauna (Cardich and Miotti 1983). However, some are skeptical of the association between the cultural materials and the early date (Borrero 1999). Just south of Los Toldos, the Cerro Tres Tetas site dates to about 13,300 cal BP and contains primarily unifacial tools in association with guanaco. Projectile points and now-extinct animals are absent (Borrero 2008).

The Pali Aike region's record begins coincident with the Cerro Tres Tetas occupation, approximately 13,300 cal BP. Though not colonized quite as early as the Central Plateau, once the record begins, occupation of Pali Aike appears to have been continuous and intense (Martin and Borrero 2017). Our understanding of this region's early occupation is based in part on the record at Cueva Fell, excavated by Junius Bird in the early 1930s (Bird 1938). At Cueva Fell, there is a clear association between artifacts, including fishtail points and a host of other tools, and the bones of extinct horse and ground sloth (Bird 1988), all dating to about 12,800 cal BP (Borrero 1999, 2008).

Martin and Borrero (2017) hypothesize that these two regions—the Central Plateau and Pali Aike (but particularly the former)—were highly ranked locations on account of abundant high quality lithic raw materials and rock shelters, and "adequate biotic resources" (Borrero 2012; Martin and Borrero 2017:90). They argue that as initially small colonizing populations grew in these regions, they required larger and larger foraging ranges, which ultimately led to population expansion into other Patagonian regions, including Última Esperanza and Tierra del Fuego. Unlike the Central Plateau and Pali Aike, Última Esperanza and Tierra del Fuego have only ephemeral late Pleistocene records followed by apparent multimillennial abandonments (Martin and Borrero 2017).

The early occupation of Última Esperanza is recorded at two sites in close geographic proximity: Cueva Lago Sofía, which may have been in the forest-steppe ecotone, and Cueva del Medio. The early occupation at the Cueva Lago Sofía rock shelter dates to between roughly 13,300 and 11,500 cal BP and consists of hearths, lithics, and bones of guanaco, extinct horse, and ground sloth (Massone and Prieto 2004; Prieto 1991). The assemblage at Cueva del Medio (ca. 12,800 to 10,900 cal BP), just a few kilometers to the south, is very similar and consists of hearths and lithics in association with animal bone, primarily guanaco but also extinct species of horse, ground sloth, and camelid (Nami 1987; Nami and Nakamura 1995).

The Tierra del Fuego record is intriguing. A very early occupation, circa 15,500 cal BP, has been suggested but remains unsubstantiated (Coronato et al. 1999). There is a well-accepted occupation dating to approximately 12,500 cal BP and then an apparent hiatus until the late middle Holocene. An early cultural level at the Tres Arroyos site near the Strait of Magellan dates to circa 13,600 cal BP, but the site is more consistently dated to about 12,500 cal BP (Borrero 1999; Massone 2004). The later dates are associated with what may be a fragment of fluted fishtail point, as well as several hearths and bones of guanaco, horse, sloth, and extinct fox. Following the early Holocene occupation, evidence of people on Tierra del Fuego is scant until 6800 cal BP on the coast and 2000 cal BP inland (Borrero and Barberena 2004). Borrero

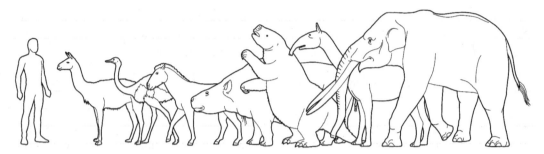

FIGURE 4.3. A selection of extant (living; L) and now-extinct (E) animals from southern South America (from left to right): *Lama guanicoe* (L), *Rhea* sp. (L), *Hippidion* (E), *Toxodon platensis* (E), *Mylodon* (E), *Macrauchenia* (E), gomphothere (E). Illustration by John Klausmeyer.

(2012; Salemme and Miotti 2008) believes this pattern may represent a failed colonization attempt by a small, founding population unable to adapt to climate change in an already harsh environment. Failure is attributed in part to Tierra del Fuego's having been cut off from mainland Patagonia around 10,000 cal BP (Ponce et al. 2011) as sea levels rose during the late Pleistocene and early Holocene, ultimately forming the Strait of Magellan.

Synthesizing the above, Patagonia's colonization sequence begins in the late Pleistocene, when small groups of mobile hunter-gatherers arrived on the steppe (Borrero 1999, 2008; Salemme and Miotti 2008). These groups appear to have been drawn to guanaco, ignoring large-bodied, now-extinct animals. The sites they left are characterized by low artifact densities—assemblages composed primarily of debitage, cores, informal tools, and rough bifaces. There are no well-defined projectile point styles securely dated to this period (Prates et al. 2013), and high quality nonlocal lithic materials occur at low frequencies. Sites are few on the landscape, suggesting a small founding population (Borrero 1999, 2008).

By about 12,500 years ago, there was a well-established human presence in Patagonia, as interpreted from the increased number of occupations as well as sites' broader distribution across Patagonia, including the Andean foothills and forest-steppe transition (Prates et al. 2013). Between 12,800 and 11,500 cal BP, people appear to have spread to far southern Patagonia (Tierra del Fuego; Borrero 2003) and far northern Patagonia (Neuquén Province; Barberena, Borrazzo, Rughini et al. 2015), though the record remains sparse between roughly 40° S and 48° S (Borrero 1999). It is during this millennium that the distinctive fluted "fishtail" points first appear, often in association with extinct animal species, though megafauna still do not constitute a significant portion of the bone record (Prates et al. 2013). The east coast record does not begin until approximately 8200 cal BP, and sites in the mountains and on the west coast are rare before 2000 cal BP.

Squaring IFD Predictions with Observed Dietary Breadth

Patagonia's archaeological record indicates that the game-rich steppe was the first habitat colonized, while the most biodiverse terrestrial habitat, forests, may not have been colonized before about 10,500 cal BP and, even then, the record remains sparse through the Holocene. The risk-averse IFD—where colonizers prefer biodiversity to caloric profitability—does not find much support here. Instead, early colonization of the steppe appears to reflect an ideal free distribution motivated by foraging returns. However, as I suggested earlier, we would expect foraging returns-driven colonizers to target not only the highest-ranked resource patches, but also the highest-ranked resources according to the diet breadth model. Early sites' occupants' preference for guanaco appears to violate this expectation.

On a virgin landscape, and assuming the colonizing population was fairly small, initial hunting pressure was likely insufficient to trigger a broadening of the diet immediately upon arrival. So, on the late Pleistocene steppe, the largest-bodied animals should dominate early faunal assemblages (see Chapter 3 and Broughton et al. 2011). In fact, though, a comparatively small animal (guanaco) dominates many early records despite the availability of several megafaunal species (Figure 4.3). Bones of megafauna are present in some sites, but their associations with humans are often questionable (Borrero 2009). Even when associations are clear, remains are few, and it is possible these animals were taken only opportunistically (e.g., when found injured or trapped) or scavenged.

The first Patagonians' diets were suboptimal relative to predictions of the diet breadth model, raising the possibility that colonization decisions were *not* centered on foraging returns. Accordingly, we need to test the alternative that the colonization process was neutral with respect to environment type, rather than driven by calorie maximization to the most profitable habitat. With available data, the best test of this neutral model is a comparison of known sites' locations and dates of earliest occupation. If the colonization process was neutral—essentially a random walk—sites' proximity should be a good predictor of how similar they are in age: sites of similar age should be nearer to one another than to sites of less similar age across Patagonia, reflecting an advancing wave-front indifferent to environment types. To perform this test, I calculated pairwise differences in both site age (calibrated radiocarbon date) and location (UTM coordinates) between each site in the Patagonia radiocarbon database (Chapter 2) between 15,000 and 11,500 cal BP (12,000 and 10,000 ^{14}C BP). The resulting regression of difference-in-distance on difference-in-age is presented in Figure 4.4. There is no relationship between the two variables ($R^2 = 0.01$); site proximity tells us nothing about site age during the terminal Pleistocene-early Holocene, as it would under a strategy-neutral wave of advance.

Granting the unlikelihood of a neat, perfectly coordinated forward march, a more nuanced version of the wave-of-advance—reflecting a complex process of advances, back-migrations, frog-leaps, and subsequent in-fillings—should actually produce a *stronger* correlation between site age and proximity than a wave of advance. This is because, along a wave front, contemporaneous sites can be quite distant from one another, particularly in northern Patagonia where the landmass is up to 750 km wide. It is more likely, therefore, that the lack of a relationship between site age and proximity at the regional level (i.e., across all habitat types) supports calorie-maximizing IFD hypothesis for colonization. Indeed, there is evidence that, even within the first-ranked terrestrial habitat, people were seeking the best patches. A pairwise comparison including only sites on the steppe (i.e., excluding all other ecoregions), slightly decreases the strength of an already very weak correlation (Figure 4.5; $R^2 = 0.01$). Again, there is virtually no statistical relationship between site age and proximity, suggesting targeted patch use *within* the steppe and further supporting the hypothesis that the initial colonists were motivated by a desire to maximize foraging returns, despite what seems like only casual use of the highest-ranked resources.

In fact, a bit of further reflection shows that ignoring megafauna could well have been the optimal decision. As Bird and O'Connell describe (2006), risks and costs associated with hunting the very largest animals can be high and may simply have been unjustifiable on the late Pleistocene steppe, perhaps because human groups were too small to hunt megafauna safely, to defend kills against scavengers, or to efficiently process and consume such large meat packages before they spoiled.

Alternatively, the return rate for hunting megafauna may have been higher but only over unacceptable time frames. If one could expect larger game to return, say, 25,000 kcals every five days, and guanaco 9,000 kcals every two days, larger game would have a higher return provided one could wait five days between kills. If food was required every two days, guanaco

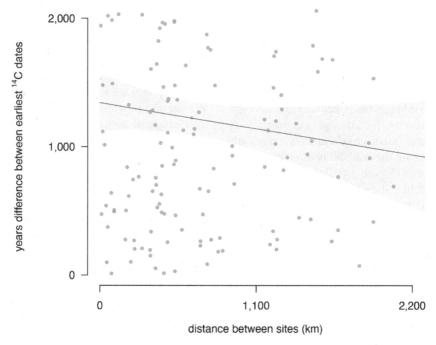

FIGURE 4.4. Pairwise comparisons of the distance between sites and the difference in their earliest radiocarbon dates for all sites with dates between 15,000 and
12,000 BP. Sites in closer proximity have larger differences in their earliest radiocarbon
dates, but the effect is very small (β_{DIST} ± SE = –0.18 ± 0.13; n = 18 sites; p = 0.16) and distance explains very little of the variance in difference in earliest radiocarbon date (R^2 =
0.01).

would be superior. When these costs and considerations are part of the foraging calculus,
it is possible that, on average, guanaco were the
highest-ranked resource on the steppe despite
their smaller size.

Finally, it is possible that megafauna *were*
an important resource among the colonists, but
that big animals were killed and processed elsewhere, their bones left at the kill site and only
(or mostly) soft tissues transported to the caves
where most early sites have been found (see also
Chapter 5 for a discussion of cave sites' repre-
sentativeness). Such "invisible" behaviors are a
perennial complication and faunal analysts have
a long history of working through and around
related issues (e.g., Lyman 1994). Historically,
though, we archaeologists have been relatively
slow to incorporate routine study of prehistoric
plant use (via macrofossils, pollen/phytoliths,
residues), artificially rendering invisible a whole

category of prehistoric subsistence—one that
was likely central to settlement (colonization)
decisions, and to the very survival of our species,
besides.

Theoretically and empirically, men's and
women's optimal foraging strategies differ because their mating strategies do: men's reproductive success depends on access to mates
while women's depends on successful rearing
of offspring (for an archaeological discussion
of first-principles, see Zeanah 2004). Generally, this equates to women's focus on reliable,
if lower-ranked, resources including small
game and plants, plus littoral/near-shore resources in coastal environments. Because
women's provisioning of offspring is vital for
group survival, it is likely that the availability
of these resources drove settlement decisions
during (and well beyond) Patagonia's colonization, as O'Connell and Allen (2012) argue was

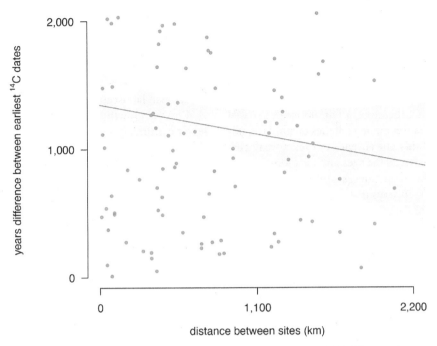

FIGURE 4.5. Pairwise comparisons of the distance between sites and the difference in their earliest radiocarbon dates for all sites with dates between 15,000 and 12,000 BP located south of 34° S and east of 72° W (the approximate boundaries of the Patagonian steppe). Sites in closer proximity have larger differences in their earliest radiocarbon dates, but the effect is very small ($\beta_{DIST} \pm SE = -0.21 \pm 0.15$; n = 15 sites; $p = 0.16$) and distance explains very little of the variance in difference in earliest radiocarbon date ($R^2 = 0.01$).

the case during the Pleistocene colonization of Sahul, for example.

As in so many other world regions, the historical focus in Patagonia on archaeological datasets associated with "traditionally male" activities (e.g., larger game and projectile weaponry) has limited our understanding of prehistoric subsistence and all associated behaviors (e.g., mobility). In recent years, we have begun to incorporate field and laboratory methods designed to recover and identify small-bodied prey and plant remains/residues (e.g., Belmar 2019; Lema et al. 2012; Llano 2011, 2014; Llano and Barberena 2013; Llano et al. 2019) and, with this increased attention to "traditionally female" resources, our understanding of Patagonian prehistory will surely improve. Indeed, increased attention to plant and small animal records could fundamentally change our understanding of the region's colonization.

Effects of Research Effort and Taphonomy

In addition to complications associated with the "invisible" foraging behaviors discussed above, other factors have influenced the archaeological patterns that underlie our interpretations of colonization. As every archaeologist knows, our data rarely sum to a straightforward account of past human activity because they also reflect research effort and taphonomy—where we look and what is there to be seen. This is evident in the pairwise comparison of site age and proximity on the steppe (Figure 4.5). As I have described, we would expect a strong correlation between sites' ages and locations if Patagonian colonization was a strategy-neutral wave of advance, and a weaker correlation if returns-maximizing colonists were targeting especially rich patches within the steppe. On reflection, however, even targeted patch use within the steppe should produce at least a weak correlation, the strength of which should be proportional to the degree of spatial autocorrelation among rich patches. The orientation of the Andes relative to dominant weather patterns (Chapter 2) produces fairly linear bands of productivity—west-east clines—and, therefore, a fair amount of spatial autocorrelation among patches of similar quality. Given this, the absence of even a weak correlation between the ages and locations of early sites on the steppe suggests the record might be incomplete in ways that complicate our understanding of Patagonia's initial colonization.

Patagonia is a big place with limited infrastructure; large portions of the region remain untested. We do not yet know the extent to which the clustered distribution of early sites (see Figure 2.19) owes to prehistoric settlement decisions versus modern research foci and site preservation. So, for example, while Patagonian colonists may well have targeted the Central Plateau for the food, stone, and natural shelters available there (Martin and Borrero 2017; Salemme and Miotti 2008), it is unclear whether other places also attracted early colonists and how the occupation of such places might relate to the occupation of known sites. Complicating things further is the fact that regional-level data related to negative findings—places that have been surveyed or tested but that did not produce dates and cultural materials—are often unavailable. Some of the voids between site clusters evident in Figure 2.19 might reflect places that were in fact avoided prehistorically, while others are simply testing gaps.

The patchy distribution of early sites in Patagonia likely also owes, in part, to poor preservation. Describing the North American landscape, Whitley and Dorn (1993) note that, at the Pleistocene-Holocene transition, normal erosion was intensified by glacial meltwater, which resulted in rapid down-cutting and changed patterns of sediment deposition. "The result is that there would have been few places at the close of the Pleistocene in North America where nondestructive sedimentary processes, conducive to the preservation of archaeological deposits, could have operated" (Whitley and

Dorn 1993:634). The same is true of Patagonia, and perhaps to an even greater degree given how relatively narrow (W-E) the landform is, and the ladder of major rivers that run from the Andes to the coasts. As I described in Chapter 2, the Patagonian landscape was dramatically remodeled by the growth and retreat of glaciers. Sea levels continued to rise and rivers to overrun their banks, meander, and erode landforms well into the early Holocene. The middle Holocene may have been a time of increased volcanism, seismicity, and landslides (see Chapters 2 and 5). These and any number of more recent factors— including modern human alterations of landscapes—may have profoundly affected the record of colonization.

Granting that the colonization record is incomplete, and that this may complicate our understanding of the process within Patagonia, the timing of colonization is compelling in light of the ideal free distribution. Patagonia appears to have been colonized at least as early as neighboring regions and possibly earlier (ca. 15,000 cal BP, at Piedra Museo; Miotti 1996; Miotti et al. 2003). The region's early colonization is incongruous with its reputation as one marginal for human habitation. Patagonia is demonstrably less productive and less biodiverse than other parts of South America, and if late Pleistocene Patagonia was as desolate and difficult as has been described (e.g., Salemme and Miotti 2008; Saxon 1976), why would people move into Patagonia before absolutely necessary? Both the IFD and conceptual models (e.g., Borrero 1999) predict movement into marginal habitats only after more favorable ones have become uncomfortably full. By this logic, Patagonia should not have been occupied until relatively late in the sequence of New World colonization. Patagonia's early sites would imply, then, either incredibly rapid population growth and the swift filling of preferred habitats, or a significant older-than-Clovis presence in the New World.

Like many interesting questions surrounding the peopling of the New World, our interpretation of movement into apparently marginal habitats hinges on colonization speed. The Clovis-first model assumes an incredibly fast migration, on the order of hundreds of years, which would suggest that Patagonia was colonized early either because it was not, in fact, marginal, or because more profitable habitats filled up quickly. Conversely, interpretations based on the geographic, technological, and subsistence diversity of older-than-Clovis sites suggest a much slower dispersal, on the order of thousands of years (e.g., Borrero 1989; Dillehay 2000), which may mean Patagonia *is* relatively marginal and, therefore, colonized fairly late in the sequence. As described above, decades of dedicated research have yet to resolve issues of timing, and it now seems reasonable to pursue unconventional lines of evidence, as I do in the next section.

Colonization Speed and Inferences from an Unlikely Source: Clothing

Knowing, even in a general sense, whether the colonization process was rapid, protracted, or varied in speed across space and through time can help us understand adaptive capacities and humans' use of marginal habitats. Importantly, too, a better handle on colonization speed would help us manage expectations regarding early sites' visibility—in the "sixth criterion" sense of a "coherent technological signature with ... broad geographic patterning" (Braje et al. 2017:593)—because visibility should reflect colonization speed. The faster people dispersed, the more likely there will be a clear and widely dispersed technological signature. Many colonization rates have been proposed (Bettinger and Young 2004; Hassan 1981; Haynes 1966; Martin 1973; Whitley and Dorn 1993) and, while a comprehensive review is not one of my goals here, it is helpful to briefly summarize the extremes.

The straight-line distance from the Bering Strait to Tierra del Fuego is roughly 16,000 km (~10,000 miles). Harcourt (2012:44) estimates the trip could have been made in under 200 years, based on Binford's (2001) sample of the world's foragers, who average(d) eight moves per year at a mean distance of 13 km per move. The overland distance between Beringia and southernmost South America is, of course, greater than the straight-line distance, and colonizing groups were not moving within territories about which they had extensive information, as groups in Binford's sample were. Nonetheless, it is within the realm of possibility that, through a combination of rapid migration and population growth, people spread across the Americas in a few hundred years.

Conversely, the diversity reflected in older-than-Clovis sites, as well as the level of landscape familiarity evident at several (e.g., Monte Verde), suggests that New World peopling was a protracted process of exploration and colonization that took several thousand years (Borrero 1989; Dillehay 2000). For example, Dillehay (2000) believed a New World entry on the order of 16,000 years ago was necessary to achieve the level of landscape and resource familiarity evident at Monte Verde 14,500 years ago, and his more recent report of the site's occupation roughly 18,000 years ago (Dillehay et al. 2015) aligns well with this sentiment. This earlier date is, however, hard to reconcile with current best estimates of coastal deglaciation (ca. 17,000 years ago; Misarti et al. 2012).

Variable colonization speed across space and through time is both more realistic and a more complex model than either of the ones just described. Bettinger and Young (2004; Young and Bettinger 1995) used computer simulation to produce a predictive model of population expansion based on a variable migration rate. Their model assumes rapid diffusion—largely via rapid population growth—at lower latitudes and slower diffusion (population growth) at higher latitudes. Using the timing of important deglaciations (as understood at the time of their writing) to determine an appropriate "launch" date, their variable rate accurately predicted the accepted date of initial occupation at Monte Verde (ca. 14,500 years ago).

Quite logically, most colonization rates are anchored by key events (e.g., deglaciations). Rates are refined as our understanding of the late glacial period improves, and reconstructions of deglaciation and postglacial conditions become more reliable with each new analysis. However, while paleoclimatic reconstructions are invaluable to peopling studies, many of them are based on relatively small sampling locations within a truly vast expanse, across which local conditions can be highly variable. Other sources of auxiliary data, including linguistics (Greenburg et al. 1986; Gruhn 1988; Nichols 1990) and genetics (Eshleman et al. 2003; Llamas et al. 2016; Moreno-Mayar et al. 2018; Schroeder et al. 2009), also provide helpful guidelines for studies of colonization speed, but the mutation rates on which they are based are unpredictably variable. In the end, archaeological data are the only true means of resolving the timing of New World colonization but, as I described in the previous section, our data are not simply a record of past human behaviors, but also reflect postdepositional processes and archaeological research effort.

The effects of taphonomy and research effort on our understanding of a region's colonization history both scale with time: the longer ago a site was occupied, the greater the likelihood it has since been affected by postdepositional processes, and the longer a region has been the subject of active research, the more likely it is that this time-ravaged early record will have been located and tested. There are important exceptions to both trends, and we have learned a fair bit about Late Pleistocene-Early Holocene life in the New World through some of these "happy accidents" (e.g., Dillehay 1997) although, ironically, these exceptions make it harder to estimate and manage the potentially offsetting effects of taphonomy and research effort (Martin 1993; Maxwell et al. 2018). We can, however, make some useful generalizations (Table 4.1).

Firstly, the potential archaeological record—the total number of sites that could be found assuming no postdepositional losses and perfect archaeological coverage—is a function of the colonizing population's size and dispersal rate: a small, fast-moving population will create fewer sites than a larger, slower one. Dispersal rate also affects site composition, further biasing against fast-moving groups' sites since they tend to be more ephemeral, decreasing the likelihood they will be preserved and discovered. Secondly, the larger the potential record, the less

detrimental the effects of research effort and taphonomy on our understanding of colonization. Say we can reasonably expect to find 10% of the potential record (cf. Martin 1993). It is likely that 10% of a large number of sites would give us a better sense of early life in the New World than 10% of a small number, simply because the total number of sites found is larger. However, and thirdly, the effects of taphonomy and research effort on our understanding of a region's colonization history also scale with colonization speed.

If colonization was very rapid, finding only 10% of a small potential record might actually be less problematic than finding 10% of a bigger record left by a slower-colonizing group. There are two reasons for this. First, because the faster group's sites are more tightly clustered in time, it does not matter much that we are highly unlikely to ever record earliest New World occupation (Meltzer 2009); the earliest sites we find should fairly accurately represent the date of initial colonization. Yet, if colonization was much slower, the difference between the dates of the actual earliest and the earliest-known sites could be significant. This would, of course, mean that our estimates of initial colonization are wildly inaccurate, and that our interpretations of adaptive pressures are flawed as well.

The second reason decimation of a faster group's smaller record might not matter much is that rapid colonization is more likely to result in a "visible" record in the sense described in the earlier discussion of the Clovis-first legacy—a widespread, recognizable lithic technology or other material cultural trait. A slower group's potential record is more likely to be diverse; the sites would reflect a much wider range of adaptations and material variants, so the weight of each lost or unfound site is greater. Ultimately, then, the faster colonization was, the less it matters that research effort and taphonomy have decimated the potential record.

Estimating relative colonization speed is clearly important. Considering the obstacles to finding early sites—and the fact that we do not currently agree on what constitutes valid evidence, even—it makes sense to use multiple lines

TABLE 4.1. Generalized effects of relative colonization speed on our ability to find and interpret the archaeological record of colonization. "Potential record" is the total number of sites that could be found assuming no post-depositional losses and perfect archaeological coverage. "Prop. decim. effect" is the proportional decimation effect, or the effect of decimation by taphonomy and research effort on our ability to find and interpret the colonization record; the effect is greater on small potential records than on large ones. "Temp. cluster" is temporal clustering, the overall spread of colonization sites in time; "high" indicates a higher degree of site contemporaneity across the New World. "Visibility" is meant in the "sixth criterion" sense of a widespread, recognizable lithic technology or other material cultural trait. "Decim. import" is decimation import; the relative degree to which decimation of the record ultimately affects our ability to correctly interpret the colonization record.

	potential record	prop. decim. effect	temp. cluster	"visibility"	decim. import
fast	small	high	high	high	low
slow	large	low	low	low	high

of reasoning, including some unconventional ones, in order to get at least a general sense of whether the process more likely resembles Harcourt's estimate or Dillehay's. Using data related to prehistoric and traditional clothing—specifically, the spatial and temporal distribution of *fitted* clothing—is one such unorthodox approach to estimating colonization speed.

Benefits and Costs of Tailoring

Clothing that was fitted to the limbs and layerable was indispensable in late glacial eastern Siberia (Hoffecker 2005a, 2005b). Its value may have decreased as people approached the tropics, only to increase again with increasing (southern) latitude, through the temperate zone and into Patagonia. Because fitted garments are costly to produce, the distribution of tailoring may reflect colonization speed: rapid dispersal across both continents could have preserved the technology even in places where it is not necessary for survival, while slower dispersal might have resulted in loss of the technology where tailoring was less beneficial. Whether colonizing Patagonians had but later lost fitted clothing, or arrived without it, also has important implications for subsequent population growth and technological evolution in the region.

In the daily lives of some prehistoric foragers, clothing technology was arguably as important to survival as hunting accoutrements. Indeed, clothing technology can influence when and how people hunt (see Chapter 3 and, e.g., Yi et al. 2013); so it is, in a sense, part of the subsistence toolkit. Clothing may be especially important at latitudes above 40° because it can positively affect human basal metabolism (BMR), or the energy required to maintain essential body functions (Chapter 3). In cold climates, clothes reduce cold stress, thereby also reducing metabolic upregulation (i.e., holding BMR more or less constant) so that the body does not have to work as hard to maintain core temperature. Because it is fitted to the limbs, tailored clothing (e.g., coats, pants) provides two to five times the thermal resistance of simple, draped clothing (e.g., cloaks, loincloths; Gilligan 2007:501). Fitted clothing also allows greater freedom of movement, both in the sense of maintaining body coverage (warmth) while preserving range of limb motion and by allowing people to stray farther and longer from shelters and fires (Garvey 2018b; Yi et al. 2013). The improved mobility—particularly winter mobility—afforded by tailored clothing provides access to resources in places and at times they would otherwise be inaccessible.

Tailored clothing is expensive, though. Wilder (1976) describes traditional Inuit methods of garment production, which include time- and labor-intensive, multistep processes to remove odors from, soften, and tan hides; amass and assemble pieces to fit a pattern; and sew and maintain the finished garments. Many of these steps require tools that themselves must

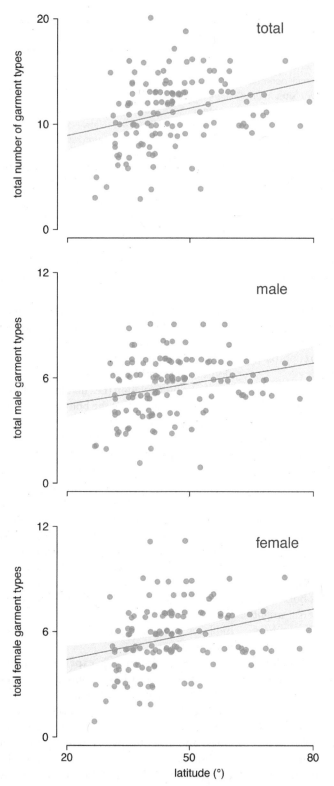

FIGURE 4.6. Relationship between total number of garment types and latitude. Top panel: total number of garment types is significantly positively correlated with latitude (linear model, $\beta_{LAT} \pm SE = 0.09 \pm 0.03$; n = 139 groups; $R^2 = 0.09$; $p = 0.0007$). Middle panel: total number of male garment types is significantly positively correlated with latitude (linear model, $\beta_{LAT} \pm SE = 0.04 \pm 0.01$; n = 139 groups; $R^2 = 0.06$; $p = 0.004$). Bottom panel: total number of female garment types is significantly positively correlated with latitude (linear model, $\beta_{LAT} \pm SE = 0.05 \pm 0.01$; n = 139 groups; $R^2 = 0.08$; $p = 0.0009$). All data from Paterek (1994).

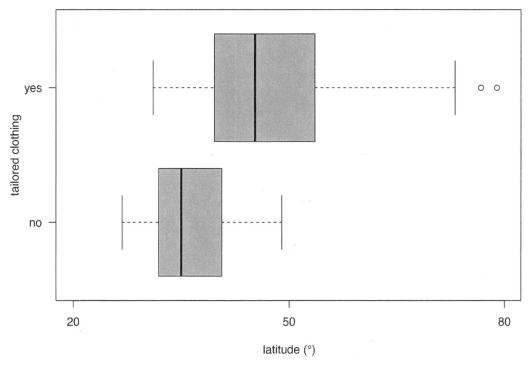

FIGURE 4.7. Presence of tailored clothing as a function of latitude. Sites further from the equator are significantly more likely to have tailored clothing (logistic regression: $\beta_{LAT} \pm SE = 0.19 \pm 0.06$; n = 139 sites; Nagelkerke's $R^2 = 0.29$; $p = 0.005$). All data from Paterek (1994).

be produced and maintained. In cold climates, survival would not likely be possible without fitted clothing. Elsewhere, clothing can be beneficial but unless there are significant stretches of "down time," as during an Arctic winter, clothing entails significant opportunity costs that might not be justifiable in warmer zones. That is, investment in clothing technology should decline with clothing's declining importance for survival: where need is relaxed, tailoring should be less common. This certainly appears to be true of clothing produced in the northern hemisphere during the late prehistoric and early historic periods. Between southern Florida (25° N) and eastern Siberia, the total number of garment types per group increases significantly at higher latitudes (Figure 4.6). The presence of tailored clothing also shows a significant positive relationship with latitude; groups farther from the equator are significantly more likely to have tailored clothing (Figure 4.7; $R^2 = 0.29$).

Latitude is also a good predictor of whether a group produces watertight clothing (Figure 4.8; $R^2 = 0.52$), which is a particularly involved process (Wilder 1976), but an indispensable technology where getting wet could be fatal.

Tailored Clothing and New World Colonization

Many of the benefits and costs of tailored clothing production scale with latitude. At the end of the last glacial age, when the New World was colonized, the benefits associated with fitted and layerable clothing would have warranted the costs associated with its production in both the eastern Siberian homeland and in Patagonia. This may not have been the case at intervening latitudes however, and this section presents archaeological and ethnographic evidence to infer colonization speed from spatial and temporal distributions of tailoring.

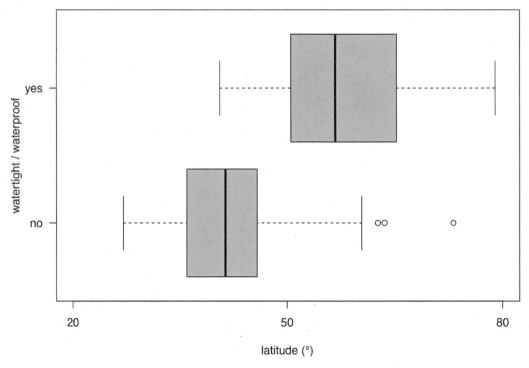

FIGURE 4.8. Presence of water-resistant clothing as a function of latitude. Sites further from the equator are significantly more likely to have watertight/waterproof clothing (logistic regression: $\beta_{LAT} \pm SE = 0.18 \pm 0.03$; n = 139 sites; Nagelkerke's $R^2 = 0.52$; $p < 0.0001$). All data from Paterek (1994).

Eastern Siberians had Tailored Clothing

Colonization of eastern Siberia would not have been possible without clothing technology. Today, even as global temperatures reach record breaking highs with increasing frequency, the average cold-month daily minimum temperature in Tiksi, Russia is −36.1°C (−32.8°F); the average mid-summer night's low is just above freezing (2.9°C; 37.2°F). Tiksi is in the vicinity of several early archaeological sites in eastern Siberia near 70° N, including Yana RHS (ca. 31,700 cal BP, or 28,000 ^{14}C BP; Pitulko and Pavlova 2010) and Bunge-Toll (ca. 48,400 cal BP, or 45,000 ^{14}C BP; Pitulko et al. 2016), both occupied during the last glacial age. Conditions that were already much colder than today's continued to get colder in Siberia as the glacial period reached a crescendo between roughly 31,000 and 23,000 cal BP (Clark et al. 2009). Goebel (2002) argues that Siberia was simply too cold,

dry, and resource-poor for humans during this time, and that the region was largely abandoned, to be recolonized approximately 21,800 cal BP by groups with a distinctive technology: microblades.

Goebel (2002) suggests that microblades were instrumental in the recolonization of Siberia because they facilitated a highly mobile lifestyle, which was necessary to pursue relatively scarce postglacial game. Indeed, microblades are frequently linked to high mobility in harsh environments because they provide many times more cutting edge per unit weight than other stone technologies (Elston and Brantingham 2002) and because they are typically used in composite tools, which can more easily be repaired on the fly. Yi and colleagues (2013) add that, in north-central China, the occurrence of microblades increases dramatically during the Younger Dryas glacial readvance (12,900–11,600 BP). Given that there is no corresponding increase in hunting evident at these sites, and that all of the known microblade-edged tools are knives rather than projectile weapons, the authors conclude that microblade technology was indeed linked to mobility, but in this case through the production of tailored clothing. Yi and colleagues (2013) argue that, due to effects of the changed climate on key resources, Younger Dryas foragers in north-central China became "serial specialists" (*sensu* Binford 1980) who needed to remain winter-mobile in pursuit of game, a strategy greatly facilitated by tailored clothing. Tailored clothing, as I mentioned, allows people to stray from fires and shelters, and to forego overwintering in a place where they might otherwise have "geared up." Microblades are superior for fine craftwork like tailoring, and they may have been a key technology among serial specialists who needed to turn garments out relatively quickly (Yi et al. 2013).

The origins of microblade technology are disputed. Kuzmin and colleagues (2007) argue for a Siberian origin around 40,000 cal BP. Tailored clothing would certainly have been beneficial in Siberia at that time. However, Goebel (2002) questions the contexts of these early dates and maintains that the earliest securely dated microblade industries date to 21,000 cal BP (17,500 ^{14}C BP) in the southern Baikal region. Moreover, post-LGM microblades in Siberia are associated with dispersed groups of highly mobile hunters but, contrary to sites in north-central China, there is clear evidence of their having been used in projectile weaponry. Nonetheless, many northeastern Eurasian microblade assemblages also contain bifacial points, and this apparent technological redundancy might indicate that, in fact, microblades were used in sewing instead of—or at least in addition to—hunting (Yi et al. 2013).

Like fitted clothing, microblade technology is itself costlier than other kinds of stone tool technologies. Firstly, it requires very high-quality raw materials that can entail high procurement costs. Moreover, core preparation is extensive, and blade removal requires both finesse and, often, indirect percussion techniques. On account of these costs, microblades may have been dropped from the toolkit when their use time (in, say, the production of clothing) dropped below a certain level (Bettinger et al. 2006; Garvey 2015a). Many of the earliest sites in the North American Arctic and Subarctic contain microblades, often in addition to bifaces. Magne and Fedje (2007) argue that the technology spread in the early Holocene from eastern Siberia into central Alaska, the Northwest Coast, western Canadian Plateau, and coastal western United States (Washington and Oregon). Microblade sites are relatively common in these areas until the middle Holocene (ca. 5500 cal BP on the Northwest Coast and ca. 3000 cal BP farther south)—a period characterized by increased global temperatures. In some places, though, microblades persisted into the historic period. Interestingly, their distribution overlaps most significantly with a cold-month (January) low isotherm of −15 to −10°C (5 to 15°F). Microblades are not generally associated with Clovis points, although large blade technology is.

Contact-Period Patagonians Did Not Have Tailored Clothing

Many historical accounts of Patagonian groups at contact (or during the Mission period) describe Patagonians' use of clothing as sparing, typically consisting of only capes, loincloths, and footwear. Perhaps most famously, the Yámana of southernmost Tierra del Fuego wore only seal, sea otter, or fox pelts draped over the shoulders plus pubic coverings, and, occasionally, leggings. They smeared their bodies with fat to further protect against snow, rain, and temperatures that were routinely below freezing. There is no evidence of needles, awls, or microblades in the earliest Patagonian occupations. Awls are occasionally found in later deposits, but needles and microblades are completely absent from the Patagonian record.

There is also limited evidence to suggest that some Patagonians—Fuegian groups including the Yámana and Kawéskar—may have had physiological adjustments to cold, suggesting biological adaptations to habitual exposure. Hernández and colleagues (1997) analyzed craniofacial morphological traits among 32 human groups from around the world. They report that the Yámana and neighboring Kawéskar exhibit relatively high, narrow nasal passages, morphologically similar to those of the Greenlandic Inuit ("Eskimo" in Hernández et al. 1997), and the two (Fuegians and Inuit) differ significantly from other groups in this dimension. The authors interpret this as a cold adaptation, an association that has since been corroborated by Noback and colleagues (2011), who show a correlation between bony nasal cavity morphology and temperature. Additionally, Hernández and colleagues (1997:114) note that members of Fuegian groups exhibit "thick, subcutaneous deposit[s] of fat, high basal metabolic rates, and high body temperature" (see also Hammel 1964; Hammel et al. 1960), which may also reflect adaptations to cold exposure.

Tailoring Was Potentially "Lost" in the Tropics

Because average January lows do not fall below freezing at latitudes below roughly 40° N, the thermal properties of clothing may have been less important in the subtropics and tropics than in temperate, sub-Antarctic/Subarctic, and Arctic climates. To be sure, clothing has benefits beyond insulation: it minimizes sun exposure in open areas and, in forested environments, it affords some protection against biting insects, snakes, and plant residues that cause allergic reaction on exposed skin (e.g., urushiol). It may be, though, that the costs of wearing animal-skin clothing in hot environments—less effective heat dissipation, increased skin irritation, and harboring of parasites, for example—outweigh any potential benefits. Conceivably, plant products could have been substituted for animal skins as early colonists moved from their Arctic homeland—where they probably wore primarily skin clothing (Wilder 1976)—into warmer environments. So long as available fibers could be manipulated in ways similar to skins, it is possible that tailoring persisted despite a hypothesized switch from hide to textiles. However, there are arguments against this technological development.

Processing and manipulating plant fibers to produce textiles may not have been part of the cultural repertoire in late glacial eastern Siberia. In that case, colonists would have had to invent the technology, learn which plants to use, and how to process them in ways that made them simultaneously pliable and hard-wearing. The information, techniques, and skills required to produce effective, durable garments from plant fibers would have taken generations to accrue. Moreover, some plants offered alternatives to clothing at far lower production costs. Plants such as mugwort (*Artemesia vulgaris*) and sweetgrass (*Hierochloe odorata*) are effective against biting insects (American Chemical Society 2015; Mardones 2007), and plant-based topical solutions can prevent and treat plant-residue rashes (e.g., yarrow [*Achillea millefolium*] and jewelweed [*Impatiens capensis*]; Smith 1933). Where available, these may have been preferred to clothing, since they offer similar (or better) protection without impeding heat dissipation. So, costs associated with both skin and textile clothing and benefits afforded by clothing alternatives may have acted against the preservation of tailoring at lower latitudes.

The opportunity costs of clothing production also reduce the likelihood of tailoring in warm climates. In places where tailored clothing is not essential to survival, it may have been abandoned when its production conflicted with activities related to the food quest. As seasonality decreases in the tropics, groups tend to invest less in storage and more in year-round foraging, and gathering increases significantly (Figure 4.9). In many ethnographic cultures, gathering is primarily done by women (cf. Bliege Bird and Codding 2015), as is the production and maintenance of tailored clothing, in the Arctic (Fair 2006) and historically among the Tehuelche (the Gununa'Kena, Mecharnúekenk, and Aónikenk; Prieto 1997). Certainly other cooperative divisions of labor—gender-based or otherwise—could have developed in response to particular circumstances (Bliege Bird and Codding 2015), but the net benefits of tailored clothing may not have warranted the costs, regardless of who performed which tasks.

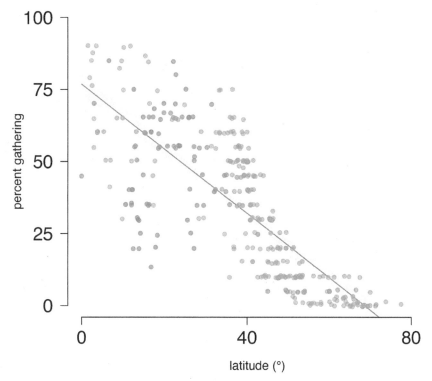

FIGURE 4.9. Importance of gathering (percent of diet comprising gathered foods) as a function of latitude. Blue points indicate foraging groups above the equator; orange points indicate those below. Importance of gathering is significantly negatively correlated with latitude (linear model, $\beta_{LAT} \pm SE = -1.11 \pm 0.05$; n = 339 sites; $R^2 = 0.62$; $p < 2.2 \times 10^{-16}$). All data from Binford (2001).

If knowledge and tools associated with the production of tailored clothing were indeed lost as people moved into and through lower latitudes, these would not be the only things to have gotten caught in the tropical filter. A recent study of domesticated dogs (Mitchell 2017) indicates that colonizing humans lost them, too, as they moved through the Neotropics, where the canine versions of distemper, trypanosomiasis, rangeliosis, and visceral leishmaniasis are prevalent. Despite a well-documented presence in parts of North America by at least the early Holocene, there is no evidence of domesticated dogs anywhere in South America before about 5000 cal BP, and they appear to have been completely absent from Patagonia prior to European contact (Mitchell 2017).

Inferring Colonization Speed from Evidence for Tailoring

If Patagonia was colonized as part of a rapid late glacial migration out of eastern Siberia, the retention of knowledge related to the production of tailored clothing and associated technologies (e.g., needles, awls, microblades)—even through low latitudes, where these might have been both less beneficial and more costly—would have been more likely than if colonization were slow. Fitted clothing would certainly have been advantageous at the end of the Pleistocene, particularly in southern Patagonia, yet Borrero notes (2012:66) there is "no evidence of clothing for that early period, and it is notable that there is a lack of bone technology—for instance,

needles—usually associated with clothing production." This, as well as evidence of physiological adaptations to cold among some Fuegian
groups, suggests colonization was slow enough
for the technology and knowledge to be lost.
Precisely *how* slow will likely remain a matter
of debate for the foreseeable future, but even
a relative sense of speed helps us think about
colonists' adaptive strategies and calibrate our
interpretations of the Patagonian record.

For example, under a fast migration model,
general-level knowledge of animals and plants
would have had much broader geographic
relevance than the very specific knowledge of
Beringian resources the first migrants undoubtedly also had. However, it is unlikely that even
the colonizing Beringians' most general ecological knowledge would have been sufficient to
facilitate a two-century surge (Harcourt 2012)
through environments as diverse—and distinct
from late glacial Arctic environments—as the
Sonoran Desert and Amazon rainforest. Assuming a very rapid migration, an effective
adaptation (perhaps the *only* viable adaptation) would have been to map on to relatively
large-bodied animals, including megafauna and
ungulates (e.g., horse, bison, deer, and camelids; Kelly and Todd 1988). With such an adaptation, the New World environment would,
in important respects, be largely invariant from
eastern Siberia to Tierra del Fuego. Granting
that the behaviors of large-bodied prey can differ between environments, the basics of tracking, hunting, weapons production and the like
would still apply. Social learning (acquiring
cultural information from group-mates) would
have been highly effective and efficient, elimi-
nating the need for much individual trial-and-
error learning.

Conversely, under a slow migration model,
environmental differences between eastern Siberia and Tierra del Fuego likely mattered much
more. Rather than being "technology oriented"
and tuned to generalized knowledge of animal
behavior, as Kelly and Todd (1988) argued for
the Paleoindian period in North America, slower dispersal would have permitted a broader diet
and may have favored trial-and-error learning,

resulting in far more material cultural diversity
than under the fast-migration scenario.

Clothing and Cultural Succession

This unconventional line of inquiry—whether
colonizing Patagonians had tailored clothing—
also has implications for subsequent population
growth and technological evolution in the region. This is because, in a sense, founding populations' technologies are like seeds in ecological succession. *Ecological succession* is gradual
change in plant (and animal) communities that
results from species' modifications of their own
environments and often trends in the direction
of increasing community complexity. Rates and
trajectories of successional change are influenced
by many factors, some of which are fairly predictable while others are stochastic. For example,
following a forest fire, colonizing species tend to
be fast-growing ones with ample dispersal ranges,
and postfire communities typically lack diversity.
As the colonizers alter soil chemistry and create
microenvironments, species diversity increases
and forests change predictably from herb fields or
grasslands to shrubland to mature forests (Bazzaz
1996). However, *which* species colonize might owe
largely to chance (e.g., a particular storm track
or where seed-dispersing animals happened to
be feeding the day before); which of the colonists
then thrive might depend on the weather in the
subsequent days and weeks, and whether a mature
forest ever develops is likewise contingent on past
developments and present conditions. Similar
logic applies in the case of human colonization of
previously unoccupied spaces, making succession
a useful metaphor for cultural evolution because
it is also a product of both historical/random
factors and more or less predictable forces, often
tending towards increasing complexity through
time (Richerson and Boyd 2005). A broad characterization of Patagonia's colonizing population,
then, can help us generalize about rates and trajectories of subsequent cultural change.

As inferred from the region's early record
and genetic evidence, Patagonia's founding population was small (Borrero 1999; de la Fuente
et al. 2018; Salemme and Miotti 2008), regional

differentiation (population isolation) occurred in some places shortly after initial occupation (de la Fuente et al. 2018), and tailored clothing was not part of the colonizers' toolkit (Borrero 2012; Garvey 2018b). Each of these characteristics is linked to ecology and, therefore, predictable to a degree: population size is related to carrying capacity (cf. Chapter 7), weak intergroup connectivity is related to limited information relevance across environment types (Chapter 2), and tailoring may have been lost in the tropics due to scheduling conflicts with other subsistence pursuits. Importantly, though, these characteristics of Patagonia's colonizing population also reflect the size of the group(s) that originally left eastern Beringia, colonization speed, and stochastic fluctuations in subsequent population growth and dispersal across the New World, each of which is random with respect to Patagonia per se, much as storm tracks and seed-disperser behaviors are random with respect to our hypothetical patch of burned forest. Nevertheless, effects of the colonizing group's initial characteristics on subsequent population growth and technological development in Patagonia are amenable to modeling.

Recall from Chapter 3 that evolutionary models predict positive relationships between technological complexity and both group size and intergroup connectivity. Specifically, while innovators and highly skilled cultural models are rare in most populations, their numbers will be greater in larger groups simply as a function of population size. Moreover, connections between groups effectively increase each group's size and provide broader access to innovators and skilled cultural models. Several empirical studies demonstrate these relationships (Collard et al. 2013; Kline and Boyd 2010; Powell et al. 2009; Shennan 2015); ethnographic groups that are large and/or well-networked have more complex behavioral repertoires and tool kits, and are less susceptible to cultural losses, than small and poorly connected groups (Henrich 2004).

Human populations have the capacity for exponential growth and, when resources are ample relative to people, populations can grow very quickly. Resources' ampleness is determined, in part, by existing adaptations (technologies, knowledge, behaviors, etc.), so culture has a direct effect on population size, as anthropologists have always known. As we have seen, clothing—fitted clothing in particular—can improve survivorship in cold environments and contribute to population growth in a variety of ways: by improving access to food resources through freedom of movement (both bodily and of foragers to food); by increasing food resources' utility through reduced metabolic upregulation (i.e., each unit of resource goes farther because well-clothed people require fewer calories than poorly-clothed people). Recall, too, that even among Arctic groups with sophisticated clothing (e.g., the Yakut of northern Siberia; Leonard et al. 2014), basal metabolism increases seasonally due to hormone fluctuations (Figure 3.6). Prehistorically, the seasonal increase in BMR would have overlapped seasonal lows in resource availability, and prehistoric groups living in cold environments likely experienced significant periods in negative energy balance, during which the body must draw on stored fat to maintain basic functions and fuel work (Garvey 2018b). These effects would have been acute among groups that lacked tailored clothing and did not store foods for consumption in the lean season, as was the case in prehistoric Patagonia.

Seasonal energy deficit affects not only survivorship but fertility (Chapter 3), and the thermal advantage of tailored clothing in cold environments may be particularly important among reproductive females. Energetic state can affect ovarian function, and women in negative energy balance may have reduced fertility (Ellison 2001; Ellison et al. 2005). Moreover, human pregnancy and lactation elevate a woman's BMR, and meeting these increased energy requirements can be difficult, particularly during a lean season. A lack of tailored clothing in cold environments could reduce lean-season fertility, resulting in higher incidence of conception when resources rebounded in spring. This would, in turn, result in more winter births and, because this is precisely when resources tend to be scarcest, a potential increase in infant mortality. Children born to mothers experiencing frequent episodes of negative energy balance may be underweight, weaned sooner, and generally more susceptible to environmental stressors.

Had colonizing Patagonians been equipped with tailored clothing, they would have experienced higher fertility and survivorship. Well-dressed colonizers would also have had greater access to winter resources. As it happened, though, colonizing Patagonians' lack of tailored clothing probably limited when and where people could forage during the coldest months of the year, thereby limiting carrying capacity, and a small colonizing population may have been held relatively small by both this foraging limitation and compromised fertility during each cold season. Given the relationship between population size and rates of cultural evolution—exacerbated in the Patagonian case by apparent early isolation, both within Patagonia and, potentially, between Patagonia and neighboring regions—relatively low innovation rates/technological complexity might further have limited carrying capacity, and so on in a negative feedback cycle. The colonizing "seed" in our ecological succession metaphor, combined with subsequent environmental factors (including, potentially, the Younger Dryas [Heusser 2003] and/or Antarctic Cold Reversal stadial [Pedro et al. 2015]) and stochastic events (e.g., volcanic eruptions, landslides), profoundly affected rates and trajectories of subsequent cultural change in prehistoric Patagonia.

Conclusions

It is well worth noting that, while tailoring appears never to have been a part of the Patagonian cultural repertoire, sewing certainly was—at least by the Contact era and perhaps throughout prehistory. The ethnographic Aónikenk (southern Tehuelche) for example, were renowned for their finely made guanaco skin cloaks (*quillangos*). Each quillango was produced with the hides of up to thirteen newborn guanaco calves (or near-term fetuses) that had been skinned from head to hoofs and expertly dovetailed to minimize both imperfections in the cloak and wastage of guanaco hide (Prieto 1997). In a report from the early twentieth century, Hatcher (1903:268–269) describes the process in detail:

> When a sufficient number of skins, usually eleven or thirteen, have been … dressed and painted, they are trimmed so that the neck of one fits nicely between the hind legs of the one in front, and the skins of the fore and hind legs between the legs on either side of adjoining skins. These skins are fitted and sewed with such skill that, when completed, there is not the slightest wrinkle anywhere in the entire mantle.

It is not clear when quillangos were first produced in this way, but archaeological evidence (motifs in rock art and on pottery) suggests that this may date to at least 500 cal BP (Prieto 1997).

Beyond cloaks, prehistoric Patagonians may well have sewn other equipment including bags, quivers, hides for use in the construction of shelters (e.g., "tent covers"), and any number of other accoutrements. Some hide equipment requires trimming, fitting, and stitching skills well beyond those necessary to make a simple tunic, for example, as is clearly true of the Aónikenk quillangos. This makes it all the more curious that Patagonians did not wear tailored clothing prior to Contact, when they acquired it from Europeans. It has been suggested that, in the far south where precipitation is significant and sea spray is unavoidable, the adoption of European wool clothing in fact hastened the decline of groups like the Yámana (Cooper 1946); fitted clothing of any kind, hide or textile, *when wet* may be worse than no clothing at all, despite temperatures that are routinely below freezing. And, while reinvention of tailored clothing at high latitudes following initial colonization might not have been beyond the capabilities of even small, poorly connected groups, the invention of *watertight* clothing—imperative for survival in coastal northern latitudes but the product of tremendously involved processes—may well have been hindered by population size and connectivity.

5

The Mysterious Middle Holocene

Adaptation seems to be, to a substantial extent, a process of reallocating your attention.

—Daniel Kahneman (2005)

Challenging as Patagonia's late glacial environment was for the initial colonists, the middle Holocene may have been even more arduous. Between roughly 9000 and 4500 cal BP (8000–4000 ^{14}C BP; Anderson et al. 2007; Méndez, de Porras, Maldonado, Reyes, Delaunay, García 2016; Zárate et al. 2005), many world regions, including large swaths of Patagonia, saw marked increases in temperature and aridity (e.g., Albanese and Frison 1995; Anderson et al. 2007; Antevs 1948; Butzer 1957; Sandweiss et al. 1999). People living in areas affected by this climatic optimum surely experienced changes in the distribution and abundance of resources and, in some places, the result appears to have been a decline in human populations.

Reports of middle Holocene population decline, through abandonment or increased mortality (e.g., Salemme and Miotti 2008; Zárate et al. 2005), are intriguing in part because they are in stark contrast to images of New World colonization. Where the initial colonists are often portrayed as industrious and intrepid, hardy trailblazers determined to expand across a challenging and unfamiliar landscape, gaps in middle Holocene archaeological records suggest that foragers of the time were unable or unwilling to adapt to changed conditions, despite greater landscape familiarity and more robust social networks on which to rely when the going got tough (Miotti and Salemme 2004). Gaps in archaeological records

demand our careful attention because instances of population decline can help us identify the limits of human adaptive flexibility, understand culture's role in determining carrying capacity, and address related, fundamental anthropological questions. However, misattributing gaps to demographic change when, in fact, they owe to archaeological sampling or poor preservation can instead lead to detrimental misunderstandings of human adaptive capacity. So, while it is certainly possible that, in some places, resources were so severely affected by increased temperature and aridity that populations declined, recent studies of climate change/archaeological gap co-occurrences suggest reassessment of the "demographic hypothesis" is warranted in some regions (Garvey 2012a, 2020; Garvey and Bettinger 2018; Kintigh and Ingram 2018).

In this chapter, I survey a range of responses to middle Holocene climate changes from across Patagonia before taking a deep dive into archaeological data from the region's northwest, where the middle Holocene was characterized by pronounced heat and aridity and scholars report a protracted archaeological hiatus.

The Environmental Context

The Holocene Climatic Optimum was a multimillennial, global-scale climate event characterized by elevated temperatures, particularly at higher latitudes, and variable precipitation, with some regions experiencing severe droughts. Increased aridity was due in part to changed weather patterns near the equator, in turn caused by changed insolation (solar radiation) associated with normal Milankovitch cycles (Silva Dias et al. 2009). Precipitation across the middle latitudes (between roughly 23° and 66°) in both the Northern and Southern Hemispheres is affected by the Intertropical Convergence Zone (ITCZ), the equatorial convection front where the hemispheres' respective weather patterns meet. During the middle Holocene, the ordinary north-south migration of the ITCZ was reduced, exacerbating aridity in already-dry midlatitude regions (Grimm et al. 2001) including Patagonia.

Data from across Antarctica indicate a primary warming event between 11,500 and 9000 cal BP (the end of the last glacial period), with secondary optima between 7,000 and 3,000 years ago (Masson et al. 2000). To understand how these warming events—registered in polar ice caps—played out in Patagonia, Waldmann and colleagues (2010) analyzed lake core sediments from Lago Kami (Lago Fagnano, 54° S) on Tierra del Fuego's Isla Grande. Their petrophysical, sedimentological, and geochemical reconstructions of middle Holocene climates are consistent with results of previous palynological studies (Unkel et al. 2008) and glacial reconstructions (Heusser 1989), all of which indicate significant increases in temperature and aridity in Patagonia between 9000 and 6000 cal BP.

Local records, however, indicate that, while average middle Holocene conditions across Patagonia may have been warmer and drier, the period is best characterized as one of increased variability, particularly as regards precipitation (Mancini et al 2005; Tonni et al. 1999). Considering Patagonia's environmental diversity (Chapter 2), with six major ecoregions and unnumbered microclimates, it is not surprising that effects of the Holocene Climatic Optimum differed in kind and degree across the region. For example, both far northern and far southern Patagonia (Mendoza / Neuquén and Tierra del Fuego, respectively) saw a pronounced increase in temperature and aridity (Zárate et al. 2005).

On the Central Plateau of Santa Cruz Province (Argentina), temperatures may have increased while precipitation remained largely unchanged through the first part of the middle Holocene, decreasing only after circa 7500 cal BP (Mancini et al. 2005). Intermediate latitudes (e.g., Lago Cardiel, 49° S; coastal Chile near 41° S) also saw higher temperatures during the middle Holocene, but some regions were actually wetter, probably as a result of increased westerly winds drawing more moisture in from the Pacific (Waldmann et al. 2010). The westerlies themselves intensified around 7000 cal BP (Bertrand et al. 2008), and this has been linked to a period of glacial readvance in parts of the southern Andes (Waldmann et al. 2010). Clearly, rather than a uniform increase in temperature and decrease in humidity as is sometimes assumed, the middle Holocene is better described as a time of widespread, but spatially and temporally varied, change (Sandweiss et al. 1999).

Postglacial climate change had equally important secondary effects as glaciers and polar ice melted. One effect was a dramatic rise in sea levels through the first half of the middle Holocene, some levels stabilizing only around 6500 cal BP. Accordingly, coastlines continued to recede towards the Andes and upslope where the mountains run into the sea. The greatest loss of real estate was along the east coast, where the continental shelf is vast and gently inclined (Chapters 2 and 4).

Other middle Holocene landscape remodeling was largely unrelated to global climate change. Lake core and sediment records indicate that the period was characterized by frequent volcanic and seismic events. Among the most extensively studied is a major eruption of Volcán Hudson (45°54'; Aysén, Chile) approximately 7600 cal BP (Waldmann et al. 2010). With a volcanic explosivity index of 6, similar in magnitude to the 1883 eruption of Krakatoa and the 1991 eruption of Pinatubo, the so-called H1 event was so violent it deposited a thick ash layer as far south as Tierra del Fuego, roughly 1,000 kilometers away. In fact, Cardich (1985) hypothesized that the H1 ash is the primary cause of a sparse middle Holocene archaeological record across affected parts of Patagonia. Similar but smaller-scale eruption-induced population decline is reported elsewhere, too. In northern Patagonia, for example, evidence suggests increased volcanism between 7800 and 5700 cal BP, which appears to have had long-term effects on vegetation and, as a result, human populations (Duran et al. 2016). Durán and Mikkan (2009) demonstrate that a major eruption around 7800 cal BP choked the region's *vegas* (upland marshes/meadows) with ash and negatively affected the availability of wild ungulate browse. They argue that the region did not recover before the onset of the 6500 cal BP neoglaciation, and hypothesize that this sequence of events discouraged would-be colonizers until after glacial retreat at the start of the late Holocene.

Seismic events were also more common during the middle Holocene (Coronato et al. 2008; see also Chapter 2). Salemme and Miotti (2008) report extensive evidence of cave and rockshelter roof collapse in southern Patagonia during this time, and Waldmann and colleagues (2010) show that landslides and mass wasting events were common. González Díaz and colleagues (2005) report similar phenomena in northern Patagonia. As discussed in more detail in the case study below, slide and wasting deposits occasionally dammed rivers, creating temporary lakes that may have been draws for human activity … until the dams forming them ruptured. Catastrophic dam failure releases large volumes of water, sediment, and stone, which further changes the landscape and potentially causes significant losses of life, habitat, and archaeological sites.

Middle Holocene Cultural Changes

The complexity of Patagonia's middle Holocene climate and environment is reflected in the diversity of human responses. Across Patagonia, responses varied in proportion to the severity of climate change (i.e., resource depression relative to population size), as a function of groups' existing adaptations. Where the middle Holocene was broadly characterized by increased aridity (e.g., Tierra del Fuego, northern Argentine

Patagonia), peoples' reactions were shaped in part by the effectiveness of existing water-use strategies under the new (middle Holocene) precipitation regime. Groups previously dependent on water supplies tightly linked to local precipitation (e.g., rain-fed basins, anthropic rainwater capture) would have been affected to a greater degree than those dependent on allochthonous water, which may have been immune to local drought because it originates elsewhere (e.g., rivers with Andean headwaters). Nonetheless, even groups with plenty of drinking water could have been affected by droughts if the plants and animals on which they depended became locally scarce, or if neighboring human groups moved in, searching for reliable water or food. It is not surprising, then, that some areas appear to have been abandoned during the middle Holocene (Zárate et al. 2005), while others saw the advent of "new technologies, artistic innovation … and perhaps population growth" (Mena 1997:49).

Coastal Environments

The earliest evidence of a truly coastal adaptation (as opposed to mere coastal occupation) in Patagonia dates to the middle Holocene: circa 5700 cal BP on the west coast (Reyes et al. 2015), circa 8000 cal BP in the east (Gómez-Otero 2006), and circa 8200 cal BP in Tierra del Fuego (Bjerck et al. 2016; Piana et al. 2012). In most places, these adaptations were coastal from the start, although, in Tierra del Fuego, evidence from at least two sites (Imiwaia I and Binushmucka I) suggests that maritime/littoral-adapted foragers were preceded by foragers with a terrestrial adaptation (Bjerck et al. 2016). Still, even in Tierra del Fuego, a specialized maritime/littoral adaptation seems to have appeared quite suddenly during the middle Holocene, and to have developed quickly in places like Estrecho de Magallanes, Seno Otway, and Isla Navarino (Figure 5.1) where, by that time, people were regularly exploiting marine invertebrates, sea birds (cormorants and penguins), and marine mammals (*Otaria* and *Arctocephalus*) using a toolkit that included multi-barbed harpoons with

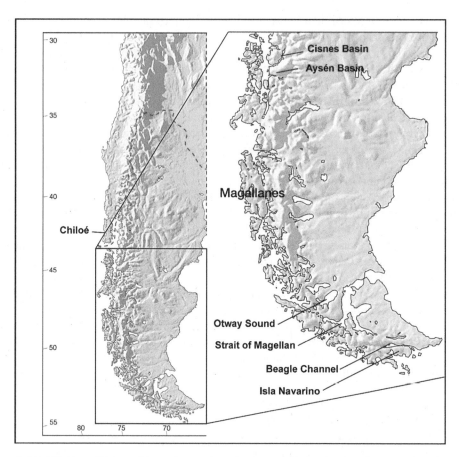

FIGURE 5.1. Map of Patagonia's western and southern coasts, indicating locations mentioned in the text.

detachable heads, chisels, wedges, and (likely) bark watercraft (Mena 1997).

Relatively late use of Patagonia's coastal resources can be interpreted in a number of ways. First, it is possible that the coastal lifeway developed rapidly during the middle Holocene in response to resource stress in the interior (i.e., a tension-triggered "push"). Researchers in several interior regions report diminished archaeological evidence during the middle Holocene (Gil et al. 2005; Salemme and Miotti 2008; Zárate et al. 2005), and this has in some cases been interpreted as a response to drought-induced declines in prey abundance.

Conversely, the timing of Patagonia's coastal occupation could reflect an abundance-triggered "pull." In central Chile, the middle

Holocene is characterized by a one-to-four-degree decrease in average sea surface temperatures, which would, in principle, have been a draw for certain large fish species. It is unclear what the effect would have been across southern Patagonia given that the southern westerlies complicate teleconnections (long-distance climate linkages) between the eastern tropical Pacific and southern South American Pacific Coast (Carré et al. 2012). One possibility is that marine resource availability increased on average during the middle Holocene, resulting in rapid development of the observed coastal lifeway.

Yet another alternative is that the marine/littoral lifeway developed for reasons wholly unrelated to resource abundance, although the near-simultaneous appearance along Patagonia's extensive coastline suggests that the explanation lies at least partly in climatic or environmental change.

The circumstances that precipitated coastal adaptation are much debated (Orquera and Piana 2006), partly because the adaptation's precise timing (see above) and geographic origin remain unclear. Whether it developed in and spread from the south (Beagle Chanel area and/or the western third of Magellan Strait and associated inland seas; Orquera and Piana 2005), the Chiloé archipelago (Legoupil and Fontugne 1997), both places quasi-simultaneously (Ocampo and Rivas 2004), or another area altogether (Figure 5.1) has real implications for the conditions under which coastal and littoral resources became centrally important. Even while research teams work to clarify where the adaptation first appeared, there seems to be a general sense that it developed among formerly inland-dwelling Patagonian groups, as opposed to an in-migration of coastal peoples from outside Patagonia.

Decades of excellent archaeological research notwithstanding, disuse of the coast prior to the middle Holocene is itself difficult to test directly. This is because (1) large sections of Patagonia's vast coastline have yet to be surveyed, (2) previously occupied landscapes may now be underwater, because sea levels continued to rise into the latter half of the middle Holocene, or (3) those landscapes may have been otherwise disturbed by middle Holocene and subsequent landscape remodeling (e.g., landslides). These factors complicate detection of potentially earlier marine/littoral adaptation in coastal habitats, and indicate a need for alternative hypotheses. For convenience, I treat the following alternative hypotheses separately, though it should be kept in mind they are not mutually exclusive.

Sections of Patagonia's east and south coasts have been extensively surveyed (e.g., Arrigoni et al. 2006; Favier Dubois et al. 2006; Gómez-Otero 2006; Piana and Orquera 2006), but much of Patagonia's coastline remains understudied, particularly in the west where high winds, rough seas, and dense forests make survey particularly challenging (Reyes et al. 2015). As we continue to expand the survey effort and more coastal sites are discovered, our understanding of the coasts' initial colonization and the origins of the coastal adaptation will surely improve.

Holocene sea level rise poses a more serious challenge (Voorhies and Metcalfe 2007). In some places, postglacial sea levels did not stabilize until roughly 6000 BP, and Holocene high stands were several meters above modern sea level, so many middle Holocene (and earlier) sites may be submerged or located on raised beaches that are difficult to identify and access (Mena 1997). Here, again, the west coast presents particular challenges because reconstructing former coastlines—a method that can guide predictive modeling and subsequent research design in this incredibly difficult environment—depends not only on estimates of eustatic (global) sea level rise as on the east coast, but also on local, glacier-driven isostasy (depression/uplift of Earth's crust) and Holocene seismic events. These forces may have dramatically altered the positions of former beaches and terraces (Rabassa et al. 2003), but necessary local-level reconstructions remain few.

Marine transgression has certainly affected our modern ability to identify archaeological sites. It likely also affected the prehistoric distribution of habitable terrain. Sea level rise was, at times, quite rapid: 15 m per 1000 years on average until circa 8000 cal BP, at which point the rate of rise generally decreased (Lambeck et al. 2014). Where terrain is steep, the rate of marine terrace formation probably limited coastal population growth until sea levels stabilized. Estuaries were likely favored for their often-gentler slopes, access to fresh water, and unique suite of food resources. However, river and stream mouths are limited in their distribution, highly dynamic, and especially affected by high sedimentation rates, most notably during glacial retreat at the end of the middle Holocene (see Environmental Context, above). Finding sites in these areas is complicated by these processes and by the regular tectonic activity that characterizes the region.

In sum, while it is clear that coastal resources were routinely targeted by at least 6000 cal BP along much of Patagonia's coastline, it is difficult to determine whether the apparent middle Holocene colonization of the coast is real and not due to the invisibility of older occupations (Salemme and Miotti 2008; see also Chapter 4). Recent advances in underwater archaeology (Bailey and Fleming 2008; Benjamin 2010; Josenhans et al. 1997) might help us better understand human use of this landscape, both during the middle Holocene and at other times.

Andes Cordillera

As local climates became warmer and drier across Patagonia, the Southern Andes (Chapter 2) may have provided middle Holocene refugia. Plant communities often migrate upslope in response to increased temperatures (Parmesan and Yohe 2003), and people could have repositioned their settlements in response. Water would have been more reliable in the mountains, too, since significant evaporation east of the foothills would have been exacerbated by decreased local precipitation (see below). At the same time, the middle Holocene saw several episodes of glacial readvance in the Southern Andes—including a substantial one between 6500 and 4900 cal BP, and a lesser one between 2600 and 2200 cal BP (Espizúa 2005). Glaciers are barriers to transmontane movement and restricted mobility on smaller scales, as well: glaciers limit options for future moves, precluding moves toward the glacier itself (Borrero 2004; Salemme and Miotti 2008; cf. Dawe and Kornfeld 2017).

Even where glaciers are absent, movement in the Southern Andes can be strenuous, with high energetic costs owing to steep, uneven terrain, and, above roughly 2,500 m, to hypoxia (see Chapter 2). Mountains, particularly glaciated mountains, present real challenges for human habitation, and some scholars have argued that Patagonia's montane environments were used infrequently and only opportunistically until the late Holocene, when regional populations outgrew their preferred habitats and were forced into less desirable ones (Neme and Gil 2008a). However, in some parts of Patagonia this interpretation rests on incomplete information (Garvey and Bettinger 2018), partly because of mountain environments' dynamism.

As glaciers grow, they accumulate large amounts of earth and stone, which are left as lateral and terminal moraines with glacial recession. These processes bury and destroy evidence of previous human activity. Valley glacier moraines can dam river channels, creating proglacial lakes. During the arid middle Holocene, these new water sources probably attracted large numbers of birds and other fauna (including people), but eventual failure of the dams that formed them would have destroyed archaeological records, both locally and potentially far downstream. During glacial retreat, melting ice creates stream channels where before there were none, existing channels are downcut, and over-bank deposits accumulate where meltwater exceeds existing channels' capacities. As when earthen dams fail, meltwater discharge following middle Holocene glacier growth may have washed away or deeply buried any previously deposited archaeological evidence along waterways. So, while glacial meltwater may have improved resource availability in areas hard hit by middle Holocene droughts, preferentially locating settlements along river channels would have exposed middle Holocene sites to the meltwater's destructive effects. Ultimately, while the Andes could have been a refugium for middle Holocene foragers, data are currently too few to test this hypothesis adequately.

Forests

As described in Chapter 2, Patagonian forests remain understudied relative to other ecoregions (Méndez, Reyes, Delaunay, Velásquez, Trejo, Harmazábal, Solari, and Stern 2016). Relatively few stratified sites have been excavated, but what information is available suggests Patagonian forests were primarily used during the late Holocene (after roughly 3000 cal BP). Méndez, Reyes, Delaunay, Velásquez, Trejo, Harmazábal, Solari, and Stern suggest the late Holocene move into forests may have been prompted by climate change on the neighboring steppe, though lack of preservation of earlier sites cannot be ruled out (2016; Barberena, Prates, and de Porras).

Chile's Aysén Region encompasses roughly a third of all Patagonian forests. Research there indicates earliest forest use during the middle Holocene. In the Río Ibáñez basin, for example, La Fontana rock shelter (Mena 2000), Las Guanacas cave (Mena 1983), and Alero Largo (Río Ibáñez-6W; Garvey 2016) were all initially occupied between roughly 7400 and 6800 cal years ago, and Las Quemas rock shelter in the Cisnes basin shortly thereafter, around 6000 cal BP (Méndez, Reyes, Delaunay, Velásquez, Trejo, Harmazábal, Solari, and Stern 2016; see Figure 5.1). Interestingly, each of these sites displays a protracted occupational hiatus following initial occupation (~5,600-year gap at Las Guanacas, ~3,400 at La Fontana, ~4,500 at Alero Largo [but work here is ongoing], and ~3,200 at Las Quemas), their use apparently resuming only in the late Holocene. Changed conditions on the steppe may have provoked initial use of adjacent forests, but these early colonization attempts failed, perhaps because forests were growing during the middle Holocene and reached their maximum extent and density at about this time (de Porras et al. 2014). Patagonian forests are generally seen as marginal for human habitation (Borrero 2004; Scheinsohn et al. 2009). During the middle Holocene, when they were even larger and denser, already-elusive and solitary prey (e.g., huemul) may have been even harder to find, and human movement within forests prohibitively difficult.

Incidentally, the expansion of Patagonian forests is coincident with the circa 6500 cal BP pulse of glacier growth cited in the previous section, both attributed to the increased effective moisture that resulted from intensification of the westerlies. The apparent abandonment of Aysén's forests following the 7400–6800 cal BP "colonization event" could simply be related to decreased sedimentation rates in caves as a result of increased precipitation, and the apparent increase in site frequencies around 3000 cal BP related to the onset of drier local conditions. As with Patagonia's montane environments, we currently lack sufficient information

to determine whether the forest pattern reflects actual histories of occupation, incomplete survey, and/or postdepositional processes.

Steppe/Plateau

The Deseado Massif (Central Plateau, Santa Cruz Province, Argentina; Figure 5.2) has been the focus of extensive archaeological research, and patterns observed in the Deseado record inform hypotheses regarding prehistoric use of the steppe. Three middle Holocene trends are compelling. Firstly, during the middle Holocene, people appear to have moved from the steppe into adjacent regions and social networks apparently broadened. Secondly, the middle Holocene is characterized by a major change in material culture, including a dramatic reduction in bifacial technology. Thirdly, as in other parts of Patagonia (e.g., forests, the far north), protracted middle Holocene occupational gaps are reported in some of the steppe's archaeological records. I describe each in more detail below.

First, though, a sense of middle Holocene climatic and environmental characteristics across the subregion provides context for these trends. The steppe—arid even under non-drought conditions (~200 mm of rain annually)—was even drier during the middle Holocene. Changes in precipitation were spatially and temporally variable: aridity intensified across the region, but the drying trend started around 9,000 years ago in some places and not until approximately 7400 cal BP in others (Mancini et al. 2005). The north-south temperature gradient was sizable, as it is today (Soto and Vázquez 2000), but an increase in shrub vegetation across the steppe indicates widespread elevated temperatures between 9000 and 6800 cal BP (Mancini et al. 2005). Lastly, the middle Holocene uptick in volcanic and seismic activity evident in the Andes also affected the steppe. For example, ash from the H1 eruption of Volcán Hudson (ca. 7500 cal BP) appears in cave deposits on the Deseado Massif (e.g., Los Toldos Cave 3; Naranjo and Stern 1998), and numerous instances of cave and rock shelter roof collapse date to this period (Salemme and Miotti 2008). In sum, while the

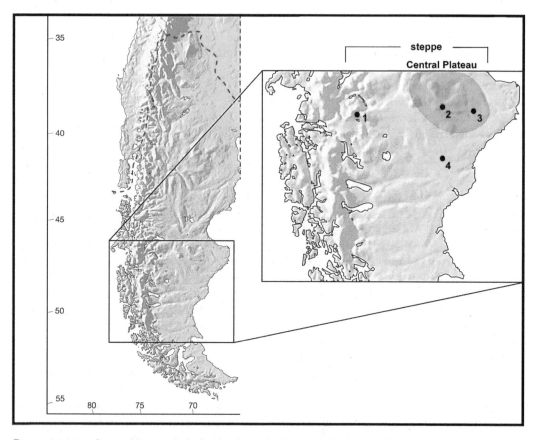

FIGURE 5.2. Map of central Patagonia, indicating Argentina's Central Plateau and important middle Holocene sites in the region: (1) Cerro Casa de Piedra 7, (2) Cueva Maripe, (3) Piedra Museo, (4) La Martita.

timing and magnitude of climate change was not uniform, the middle Holocene steppe environment seems clearly to have been distinct from that of other periods.

The early-to-middle Holocene transition on the steppe is characterized by an increase in sites across northern and central Patagonia (e.g., El Verano cave, Cerro Casa de Piedra 7, and La Martita, all occupied toward the beginning of the middle Holocene, ca. 8900–8000 BP). Salemme and Miotti (2008:463) state that "for the first time the most noticeable, intense and long-lasting human adaptive exploration ... became visible." This is evidence, they argue, of populations expanding into new areas. Importantly, during the middle Holocene, some of the movement is into areas generally considered marginal for human habitation such as the

lacustrine basins in the Andean foothills (~46° S and 48° S). Meanwhile, materials from the coast and nonlocal obsidians appear in sites on the steppe, leading Miotti and Salemme (2004) to argue that the period between 9500 and 3700 cal BP was an important time of range expansion and/or network development.

Steppic material culture also changed during the middle Holocene, most notably from a toolkit that contained projectile points to one that lacked them. The Casapedrense material cultural complex, dated to between circa 8000 and 5500 cal BP (Cardich 1985; Cardich et al. 1973), is characterized by unifacial tools with abrupt dorsal retouch, often on distal margins of flakes and large blades (typically listed as "endscrapers" in functional typologies; Menghin 1952). And, while the primary stone weapon associated with the earlier Toldense toolkit was a subtriangular projectile point, the subsequent Casapedrense lacks points but includes abundant bolas. Hermo and Mangin (2012) note, however, that among the unretouched blades, scrapers, and pecked and polished bola stones from Cueva Maripe, a middle Holocene site on the Deseado Massif, are a few flakes indicative of bifacial retouch (see also Hermo 2008). Regardless, bifacial technology is certainly sparse in middle Holocene toolkits on the Central Plateau.

High frequencies of both scrapers and blades in the Casapedrense toolkit are also intriguing. Scrapers are generally associated with the preparation of animal skins for use in clothing, carrying technologies (e.g., bags, baby slings), and weaponry, including slings and bolas. Ethnographically, Patagonian bolas were made by attaching stones to long, plaited strips of leather. The stones themselves were either unmodified and placed in leather pouches drawn together and affixed to the plaited cords, or pecked around the middle to allow for secure tying directly to the cords. Scrapers would have been an essential part of this technology, for rendering hides hairless and pliable. Likewise, blades, with their long straight sides, may have been ideal for cutting the long strips of hide necessary to make bola cords. Granting that microwear studies can be problematic (e.g., Van Gijn 2014) and that few such studies have been performed on Patagonian blades, small blade-like knives from Cueva 13 in the Los Toldos Locality (ca. 6300 cal BP; Central Plateau) have wear patterns consistent with cutting hides (Cueto et al. 2017). It is possible that both scrapers and blades were auxiliary technologies during the middle Holocene/Casapedrense and that their increased frequency is directly related to the redoubling of bolas production.

Why, then, the increase in bolas technology (and decrease in projectile points) during the middle Holocene? Mena hypothesized that the switch is indicative of guanaco specialization and possibly communal hunting, which, he argues, would have "conferred a distinct competitive advantage wherever it was adopted" (Mena 1997:49). Communal hunting, meanwhile, could

have arisen consequent to middle Holocene temperature and precipitation variability, which caused resource stress and heightened intergroup competition. Alternatively, or additionally, the middle Holocene rise in bolas use might have been in response to intensification of the southern westerlies during this period, bolas being more effective in windy conditions since they do not require the accuracy of darts (see Mayr et al. [2007] and Moreno et al. [2010] regarding intensification of the westerlies).

The third salient feature of middle Holocene records on the Patagonian steppe is gaps in archaeological records. For example, Salemme and Miotti (2008) report an occupational hiatus between 7800 and 6300 cal BP in the Deseado Massif area, which they interpret as population movement to previously unoccupied regions (e.g., the Andean foothills and Atlantic coast), perhaps due to heightened aridity on the steppe or as a result of increased volcanism and seismicity. The archaeological records are sparse and/or spotty elsewhere, too (e.g., Gil et al. 2005; Neme and Gil 2008a; Zárate et al. 2005), which has historically been interpreted in terms of abandonment due to droughts.

In summary, the middle Holocene on the steppe is characterized by settlement reorganization (colonization of previously unoccupied areas, possibly from the steppe, and reduced residential mobility; Cueto et al. 2017), consolidation of social networks, and changed hunting patterns, including a distinct stone toolkit. The sum of these changes makes the middle Holocene on the steppe difficult to interpret. Some changes suggest resource stress (expansion into lower ranked habitats, augmentation of social networks, archaeological gaps, reduced residential mobility), while others might indicate a relatively productive habitat (guanaco specialization). The record of middle Holocene steppe use currently comes primarily from caves, and additional research might clarify these apparent discrepancies. Presently, I take up the idea of occupational gaps in another part of Patagonia; some of the lines of evidence used there might prove relevant for future studies on the Deseado Massif/Central Plateau and elsewhere.

A Case Study: The Middle Holocene in Northern Patagonia

Occupational gaps at scales detectable in archaeological records have profound implications for our understanding of human adaptive capacities. Identifying local climate conditions and their potential effects on water and game can help us model human responses and, ultimately, to better understand how mobility, dietary adjustments, and other behaviors trade off against each other under changed conditions. However, as the following case study illustrates, unless we can confidently distinguish the archaeological effects of demographic decline (death or abandonment) from those caused by taphonomic or other biases, we risk misinterpreting humans' adaptive strategies and capabilities.

In arid northern Patagonia, archaeological gaps are reported between circa 9000 and 4500 cal BP, during the Holocene Climatic Optimum (Gil et al. 2005). This finding is consistent with (and, in fact, contributes to) patterns reported in two recent meta-analyses of radiocarbon trends in the Andes and adjacent environments between 16° and 44° S. In the first of these, Méndez and colleagues (2015) compiled radiocarbon data from sites located between 29° S and 35° S. They note significant radiocarbon troughs between 7850 and 6300 cal BP on the Chilean coast and in the valleys west of the Andes, and between 7700 and 6000 cal BP in the foothills and plains east of the Andes. Both troughs occur during a prolonged period of above-average aridity evident in regional pollen profiles, which lasted from approximately 9000 to 5500 cal BP (Heusser 1990; Jenny et al. 2002; Kim et al. 2002; Lamy et al. 1999; Maldonado and Villagrán 2006; Valero-Garces et al. 2005; Veit 1996; Villa-Martínez and Villagrán 1997). A subsequent study by Barberena and colleagues (2017) expanded the analysis to include sites between the latitudes of 16° S and 44° S. At this larger scale, they likewise identified troughs between 7600 and 7200 cal BP, after which point occupations (dates) increased dramatically before decreasing to another low between 6800 and 6400 cal BP. Barberena and colleagues found, too, that

the pattern holds when the data are analyzed in three smaller latitudinal bands. Patterns as widespread and pervasive as these affirm there is something different about the middle Holocene across western South America.

Radiocarbon gaps at sites located between roughly 32° S and 37° S—a region that includes northern Argentine Patagonia—have historically been interpreted in terms of regional abandonment or population decline triggered by drought-induced habitat deterioration (Gil et al. 2005; Neme and Gil 2008a). However, as is true of similar gaps in other world regions, causality was not initially tested because the decrease in radiocarbon dates coincides with an episode of major climate change (Kintigh and Ingram 2018). In fact, aspects of the region's archaeological and geomorphological records suggest that a confluence of factors might have created a radiocarbon gap despite the continued presence of people through the middle Holocene. I describe these factors in detail following a description of southern Mendoza's environment and climate.

Regional Overview

Mendoza Province is ecologically diverse, due in part to abrupt changes in elevation, temperature, and precipitation from west to east, as the rugged and sparsely vegetated Andes descend to a relatively cool, moist piedmont, which itself gives way to a low, arid plain.

The Río Atuel Valley is the focal landscape in this case study (Figure 5.3). The Atuel is one of several major rivers originating in the Andes and flowing east across the piedmont and plains. The Andes are rugged at this latitude, averaging between 2,000 and 4,000 m (~6,500 ft to 13,000 ft) and reaching a maximum of 5,189 m (17,024 ft; Cerro el Sosneado). The highest elevations are perennially glaciated, and much of the landscape above ~2,500 m is characterized by glacial topography (e.g., cirques, trunk valleys, moraines, narrow river valleys). Most everywhere, slopes are steep, soils are thin and unstable, and the terrain is generally rocky and uneven. Rapid, near-complete runoff holds

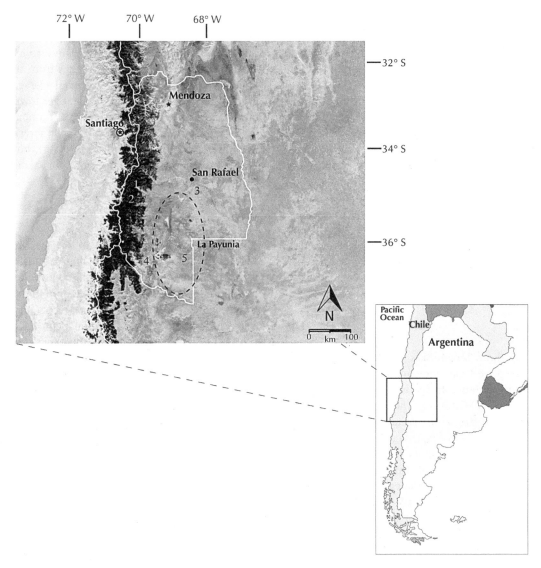

FIGURE 5.3. Map of Mendoza Province, Argentina, indicating the five previously-known sites with middle Holocene deposits: (1) Arroyo Malo-3, (2) Arroyo el Desecho-4, (3) Gruta del Indio, (4) Gruta de El Manzano, (5) Cueva Delerma. La Payunia volcanic field is indicated by the dashed oval.

primary biomass low, except around extant glacial lakes and *vegas* that form when glacial and seasonal melt pools in poorly drained soils.

Other major landforms in the Atuel Valley include the foothills (2,000–1,400 m; Volkheimer 1978), a piedmont fringe (1,400–1,200 m), and the Depresión de los Huarpes ("Huarpes Basin," hereafter "Depresión"). In the

foothills, winds and solar radiation are less intense, slopes are gentler, and soils are better developed relative to the higher Andes, and they support a higher biomass as a result. Numerous arroyos and springs provide water year-round. The piedmont comprises a series of broad alluvial fans, sand dunes, and an open, grassy plain (Gil et al. 2005). The adjacent Depresión is a closed basin with irregularly distributed lakes (permanent and seasonal), dry lake beds, and salt flats, transected by a number of major rivers, including the Atuel. Both the piedmont and Depresión are arid and, today, sparsely populated.

To the southeast of the Atuel Valley is an extensive volcanic field, La Payunia, characterized by volcanic cones, sprawling basalt fields, and a handful of known obsidian sources. Intriguingly, these sources appear to have been ignored until the late prehistoric (after 4400 cal BP) despite having been accessible year-round, in contrast to Andean sources, which are available only seasonally but were used extensively throughout prehistory (Giesso et al. 2011; cf. Garvey and Bettinger 2018). Of the habitats described here, La Payunia receives the least precipitation and produces correspondingly little vegetation.

Climate

Southern Mendoza is arid to semiarid, with a steep west-east moisture gradient, decreasing with distance from the Andes (Neme 2007; Neme and Gil 2009). The mountains receive up to 1,000 mm of precipitation annually, chiefly as winter snow (Espizúa and Pitte 2009; Wäger 2009). The piedmont averages ~350 mm annually, falling uniformly throughout the year, primarily as rain. On the eastern plain, summer storms bring nearly all of that environment's ~250 mm of annual precipitation. The precipitation gradient is partly due to the fact that weather in the Andes is governed by the Southeast Pacific Subtropical Anticyclone (Chapter 2), while the lowlands are under the influence of the Atlantic Anticyclone, which circulates around a high-pressure core in the southern Atlantic Ocean and brings moisture to eastern South America. The boundary between these two weather systems delimits a band of maximum aridity because each has lost most of its moisture by the time it reaches the boundary. This so-called Arid Diagonal currently parallels the eastern flank of the Andes from approximately 27° S to 40° S and then extends southeastward, reaching the Atlantic Coast at 44° S (Bruniard and Osuna 1982; Mancini et al. 2005).

Temperatures in the region also decline across a steep gradient, but in the opposite direction, from east to west. On the plain (750 m; city of San Rafael), temperatures range from an annual average low of 8°C to an annual average high of 23°C. In the piedmont (1,425 m; town of Malargüe), the annual mean is 12°C (annual average low of 5°C, high of 20°C; Wäger 2009). Data are fewer for the Andes (2,250 m), but Wäger (2009) estimates a mean annual temperature of 8°C.

Hydrology

The Río Atuel has its headwaters near the Argentine-Chilean border (4,041 m; Capitanelli 1972), and it drains an area of roughly 13,000 km². Its discharge is governed by precipitation in the Andes, which it collects at its headwaters, and also from a number of perennial tributaries (Volkheimer 1978). Accordingly, the river's discharge is highly variable by season (highest from October to March; Neme 2007). Between 1941 and 1998, the Atuel's mean annual discharge at El Sosneado Dam was 35.8 m³/s (maximum observed = 67.9 m³/s; minimum = 17.1 m³/s (Vich et al. 2007; for reference, the Amazon's mean discharge is 209,000 m³/s, and that of North America's Mississippi River is ~17,000 m³/s). Below 2,000 m, no snow- or glacier-fed tributaries reach the Atuel, and the river's volume downstream is determined largely by evaporation, with little contribution from local precipitation.

In the Andes, snows begin in February and persist until December; the winter snow line is at 2,000 m and, even during the brief summer, storms can be unpredictable and severe. Seasonal melting of the snowpack and alpine glaciers feeds the major rivers and glacial lakes that are perennial freshwater oases, attracting large numbers of migratory water birds. The *vegas* (upland meadows / marshes) that dot the upper Atuel Valley and its tributary valleys have historically attracted local pastoralists, but modern human use of the area is generally limited to the summer months and elevations below 3,000 m.

A handful of shallow lakes currently occupy natural depressions on the plains. These tend towards saline and alkaline on account of high evaporation and dissolution of minerals accumulated during the dry season, and lake depths vary year to year according to local precipitation. Numerous *salares* (salt pans) on the plains also collect water in exceptionally wet years. Like lakes in the uplands, plains lakes draw large numbers of water birds each year.

Far less is known about subsurface water in Mendoza, but it appears to be a crucial part of the region's hydrology (e.g., Allekote et al. 2002; Violante et al. 2010). Relevant to our understanding of human responses to middle Holocene droughts, much of the Río Atuel's discharge percolates through its sand and gravel alluvial fan as it exits the foothills, recharging an aquifer beneath the piedmont and plain. Fluvial waters from the Andes reappear close to plains lakes' margins as springs and "wells" or natural upwellings in depressions typically tens of meters in diameter and one or two meters deep (Violante et al. 2010:653).

Flora and Fauna

Biotic zones show two basic arrangements in Mendoza: vertical in the Andes and horizontal on the plains. In the Andes and, to a lesser degree, the adjacent foothills, resource zones change abruptly with elevation. At the highest elevations, terrain is steep. Runoff, poor soil development, high winds, and solar radiation produce a flora consisting primarily of low, slow-growing plants adapted to withstand extreme conditions. Birds (large raptors, migratory waterfowl), guanaco (*Lama guanicoe*), and puma (*Puma concolor*) are among the few animals found at these elevations. For all but a few months of the year, the entire ground surface is snow-covered, which deters herbivores and their predators. Temperatures, length of growing season, and primary productivity are low, contributing to a low, patchy, and highly seasonal edible biomass at high altitudes. This, combined with a winter snow line at 2,000 m, restricts human use of the Mendozan Andes to a small portion of the year. Between 2,300 and 1,500 m, the Andean foothills are characterized by more diverse flora and fauna, despite lower annual precipitation, because conditions are generally milder (Neme 2007). Fauna include guanaco, ñandú and choique (*Rhea americana* and *R. pennata*, respectively), *culpeo* (Andean fox; *Lycalopex culpaeus*), and puma. There are numerous small mammals in the region, but the extent of their prehistoric use is uncertain.

In contrast to the vertically stratified Andes, piedmont and plains resources are arranged horizontally. Both piedmont and plains receive little rainfall, but the numerous scattered water features described above break up the dry expanse. Seed-bearing grasses and waterfowl (both resident and migratory) are common in these areas. Edible plant resources decrease with increased distance from riparian and lacustrine zones but guanaco, rhea, pichi (*Zaedyus pichiy*), and *algarrobo* (*Prosopis* sp.) are available both within and outside water-based biomes. Most of the vegetation around lowland lakes is xerophytic/halophytic, including *Atriplex* spp. and *Prosopis* spp., which may have been important foods prehistorically, and the largest lakes have been registered as "wetlands of international importance" to protect the tremendous abundance of water birds they support each summer (RAMSAR 2002). These aquatic birds, as well as resident passerines, terrestrial fauna, and fish, form a rich lacustrine ecosystem within the arid plain (Garvey 2012a).

Middle Holocene Climate

For much of the middle Holocene, the Atlantic Anticyclone was disrupted, reducing summer rains across the region (Grosjean and Núñez 1994; Grosjean et al. 1997; Mancini et al. 2005; Thompson et al. 1998). The Southeast Pacific Subtropical Anticyclone, on the other hand, was periodically dominant (Villagrán 1993) and, during those pulses, winter precipitation increased in the Andes, leading to glacier growth. Conditions east of the Andes were particularly arid during readvances, when much winter precipitation—which would otherwise have flowed east each summer—was locked up in glaciers and summer precipitation was reduced. Glacial records suggest that the driest interval was between 6800 and 4400 cal BP, when glaciers were actively advancing (Gil et al. 2005). Smaller-scale fluctuations at the intersection of the Atlantic and South Pacific subtropical anticyclones—that is, fluctuations in the position of the Arid Diagonal—likely caused annual or decadal climate variability as well. For example, while conditions were generally hotter and drier, there is evidence for "low-frequency, heavy storms" throughout the middle Holocene (Messerli et al. 1997:232; Núñez et al. 2001).

While paleoclimatic studies in the Atuel Valley remain few, available data likewise indicate a hot, dry middle Holocene. A proliferation of desert taxa evident in regional pollen records suggest increased temperatures and decreased summer rains through the middle Holocene. In southern Mendoza, both mountain (Markgraf 1983) and piedmont (Gruta del Indio; D'Antoni 1983) pollen sequences indicate that middle Holocene conditions were generally arid, and that shrubs (Schinus, Verbena, Ephedra, Larrea) and halophytes (Chenopodiaceae, Poaceae; Mancini et al. 2005; Zárate and Paez 2002) were dominant. On the eastern plains, middle Holocene pollen records show an increase in Asteraceae and Larrea, with some Prosopis and Cercidium, all of which flourish in dry climates (Mancini et al. 2005).

The middle Holocene increase in volcanism and seismicity described previously is clearly evident in northern Patagonia. Durán and Mikkan (2009) and Durán and colleagues (2016) present geomorphological and geochronological data that indicate numerous volcanic eruptions between 7800 and 5700 cal BP, each of which deposited a thick blanket of tephra (20–300 cm thick) over many kilometers. This surely affected human populations, and some regions may not have recovered for centuries (Durán et al. 2016).

Middle Holocene seismic events were also significant, causing landslides and the collapse of numerous cave and rock shelter roofs, as in southern Patagonia. Interestingly, while landslides surely had negative short-term effects, some appear to have had beneficial side effects. For example, Gosse and Evenson (1994) interpret two geomorphological features in the upper Atuel Valley to be debris slides that dammed the Río Atuel during the middle Holocene, creating a lake that spanned the 1.5 km wide river valley. Such a lake would have attracted significant waterfowl and terrestrial fauna. Humans would have been among the species attracted to the lake, both for the concentration of food resources and because the dam itself limited the flow of vital Andean water across the drought-stricken plain.

An alternative interpretation, offered by Volkheimer (1978) and Stingl and Garleff (1978, 1985), is that the features are glacial moraines, rather than slide deposits. This would indicate a major but geographically isolated readvance on par with that of the last glacial maximum, resulting in the opposite ecological effect to a lake and making middle Holocene occupation of an icy middle Atuel Valley highly unlikely. Either phenomenon, slide-dam or major glacial readvance, would negatively affect the middle Holocene archaeological record. The ultimate failure of an earthen dam would have swept away or deeply buried any evidence of people living locally and downstream. Likewise, major glacial retreat would have raised river levels to flood volumes, with the same effect. More generally, when glaciers retreated and summer rains resumed at the end of the middle Holocene, sites along river and arroyo channels would have been both flooded and eroded, deleting a major portion of the region's archaeological record.

Southern Mendoza's Middle Holocene Record

Gil and colleagues (2005; Neme and Gil 2009; Neme et al. 2011) report 91 radiocarbon dates associated with human activity in southern Mendoza. These span the period between roughly 13,000 and 280 cal BP, but the middle Holocene is underrepresented: the period 9000 to 4500 cal BP accounts for more than 36% of the time since initial occupation, but only 17% (n = 16) of reported dates fall within the middle Holocene (Garvey 2008, 2020; Garvey and Bettinger 2018). Gil and colleagues (2005; Lagiglia 2001;

Neme and Gil 2009) have described this pattern in terms of demographic decline or major population reorganization.

Southern Mendoza's 16 middle Holocene dates derive from five sites: Gruta del Indio, Cueva Delerma, Arroyo Malo-3, Arroyo el Desecho-4, and Gruta de El Manzano. The first two sites provide limited information regarding human behavior during the middle Holocene, and I include only a very brief description of each, followed by more detailed summaries of the other three.

Gruta del Indio is a cave site in a steep-sided canyon of the Río Atuel Valley (660 m), south of the city of San Rafael. Occupation of the cave spans the Holocene, and the region's cultural chronology is based in large part on its occupational sequence (Gil 2000; Lagiglia 1977; Neme 2007; Semper and Lagiglia 1962–1968). The site has been the subject of intensive study, yielding nearly a third of the region's radiocarbon dates (n = 29); only two of them fall within the middle Holocene (ca. 8400 and ca. 8200 cal BP). These dates derive from noncultural specimens and are associated with few cultural remains. Geomorphological evidence suggests a stratigraphic unconformity between the early and late Holocene deposits (Gil et al. 2005; Neme and Gil 2009).

Cueva Delerma is a small cave ($\sim$8 m^2) in the Payunia volcanic field. Gil (2000) excavated a 2 × 1 m unit inside the cave, from which he obtained a single radiocarbon date (ca. 8400 cal BP) from a hearth. No artifacts were found in association with the dated material.

Arroyo Malo-3 is a rock shelter (approximately 13 m wide by 7.5 m deep) located in the Andes ($\sim$2,000 m) adjacent to Arroyo Malo, a tributary of the Río Atuel. This elevation marks the approximate boundary between distinct phytogeographic and biogeographic communities. The site's prehistoric inhabitants were likely drawn to the resulting range of available resources, including fresh water, guanaco, chinchilla (*Lagidium* sp.), possibly rhea and armadillo, edible plants (e.g., Chenopodiaceae, *Oxalis*), and firewood (e.g., *leña amarilla, Adesmia pinifolia*).

Twelve dates are reported, including five that correspond to the middle Holocene (Gil et al. 2005). Within the site's middle Holocene date range—approximately 8400 to 5200 cal BP—there are a series of gaps of various lengths, the longest lasting roughly 2,300 years.

The faunal assemblage at Arroyo Malo-3 (n = 1,660) displays heavy processing, perhaps for marrow extraction (Neme 2007). In fact, the assemblage is so fragmented, less than 10% of the bones could be identified to any taxonomic level. The genus *Lama* (including guanaco) is the most abundant. Granting that the number of identified specimens (NISP) of most species is small (Neme 2007), if the proportion of each species reflects its relative contribution to the diet, guanaco constitute over 60% of the total meat portion of the diet during the middle Holocene. This figure falls to 50% in the late Holocene, and to 30% during the most recent occupation (Neme 2007). Taxonomic diversity falls at the start of the late Holocene, rising again in the most recent occupations.

Lithic data shed further light on middle Holocene behavior, indicating a shift from a largely expedient middle Holocene technology produced on local basalt to one characterized by formal tools and finer-grained, nonlocal materials later in time (Garvey 2012a).

Gruta de El Manzano (hereafter El Manzano) is a rock shelter located on the northwestern edge of the Payunia volcanic field (ca. 1,500 m; Figure 5.3). It is situated south of Arroyo del Manzano and just west of the arroyo's confluence with the Río Grande, one of the major west-east trending rivers in the Province (Gambier 1985). Flora in the area includes species of *Adesmia, Larrea,* and *Prosopis* (Böcher et al. 1972; Roig 1972), as well as *Ephedra ochreata* (*solupe*), and *Berberis gravilleana* (*peje,* barberry; Gambier 1985:120). The local fauna is diverse, including guanaco, rhea, pichi, and *mara* (*Dolichotis patagnum*; Gambier 1985; Roig 1972).

Ten dates are reported for the site. These indicate frequent or persistent use of the cave during the early middle Holocene (ca. 9000 to ca. 7800 cal BP) and a protracted occupational gap between approximately 7800 BP and

TABLE 5.1. Radiocarbon dates from Gruta de El Manzano.

cal BP	14C	σ	material	sample	references
1181	1300	50	charcoal	LP-1662	Gil et al. 2008; Gil et al. 2011
1477	1629	33	wood	AA-73204	Gil et al. 2008; Gil et al. 2011
2035	2100	70	charcoal	LP-1663	Gil et al. 2008; Gil et al. 2011
7857	7070	170	charcoal	Gak-7532	Gambier 1985; Gil et al. 2011
7894	7110	180	charcoal	Gak-7530	Gambier 1985; Gil et al. 2011
7972	7190	130	charcoal	Gak-7531	Gambier 1985; Gil et al. 2011
8112	7330	150	charcoal	Gak-7529	Gambier 1985; Gil et al. 2011
8568	7835	44	charcoal	AA-73202	Gil et al. 2008; Gil et al. 2011
8722	7940	45	charcoal	AA-73203	Gil et al. 2008; Gil et al. 2011
9036	8141	44	charcoal	AA-73201	Gil et al. 2008; Gil et al. 2011

2000 cal BP (Gambier 1985; Neme et al. 2011; Table 5.1).

Neme and colleagues (2011) report unusually high taxonomic diversity at El Manzano, particularly in the earliest occupations. Fifteen taxa are represented across all levels. Among the zooarchaeological remains, Rhea eggshell, Dasipodidae (armadillo) scutes, catfish vertebrae, and Camelidae (likely guanaco) bones are most common. Both taxonomic diversity and the artiodactyl index (ratio of Camelidae to Camelidae plus all other taxa) decreases from the earliest to the most recent occupations. Plant diversity is also high, and peaks in the most recent occupations, perhaps due to preservation.

A comprehensive analysis of El Manzano lithics shows that—like the Arroyo Malo-3 assemblage—there is a shift in the relative proportions of basalt and obsidian through time (Garvey 2012a). The earliest occupations are characterized by roughly equal proportions of basalt, obsidian, and cryptocrystalline silicates (CCS), followed by a clear shift to obsidian in more recent levels, in which basalt is conspicuously rare. Informal tools outnumber formal ones during the initial occupation(s) of the cave, which, coupled with the proportions of local (basalt) and nonlocal (obsidian) materials, might indicate longer stays at El Manzano during the early middle Holocene. Interestingly, projectile points are relatively rare at the start of the middle Holocene (~25% of formal tools compared to ~40% in later components) but camelid remains are more frequent, suggesting that perhaps another hunting technology was preferred during the middle Holocene, as bolas seem to have been in southern Patagonia (see above).

Arroyo el Desecho-4 is the only known open air site in southern Mendoza with a middle Holocene component. It is located at the confluence of arroyos El Desecho and Las Leñas (~2,100 m), which form the Río Salado beyond this point. Given their similar elevations, resource availability would have resembled that described for Arroyo Malo-3. However, the river and arroyo valleys surrounding Arroyo el Desecho-4 are broader than others in southern Mendoza and the area may have provided different opportunities. The distinct landform might also have contributed to its protection from late Holocene erosion. The reported date range is narrow, solidly in the middle of the middle Holocene (ca. 7100–5900 cal BP; Garvey 2012a; Méndez et al. 2015).

Trends and Caveats

Trends evident in southern Mendoza's archaeological record are partly the result of human responses to middle Holocene climate changes. However, they suggest that research and taphonomic biases contribute to the radiocarbon gap as well. On the one hand, the five stratified sites with middle Holocene deposits share features that suggest settlement and subsistence changes in response to increased heat and aridity during this period: With the exception of Cueva Delerma—the ephemeral site in La Payunia volcanic field—all of the stratified middle Holocene sites are located near water. Moreover, all are located in the foothills and lower elevations of the Andes (between ~1,500 and 2,200 m)—again with the exception of Cueva Delerma and, also, Gruta del Indio, whose middle Holocene component is similarly sparse. The foothills provide access to a wide range of upland and lowland food resources, reliable water, and firewood, which may explain why these sites have middle Holocene occupations where others apparently do not. Lastly, both the Arroyo Malo-3 and El Manzano lithic assemblages show high proportions of locally available, lower-quality stone during the middle Holocene and a shift to nonlocal, high-quality material later in time. These features contribute to a picture of reduced mobility and persistent use of well-watered upland sites during the middle Holocene, a pattern elaborated more fully in the section below titled *An Alternative Hypothesis.*

Another commonality among the stratified sites—that all but one is in a natural shelter—suggests that sampling biases may be contributing to the appearance of an occupational hiatus. In fact, 71% of *all* sites in Gil and colleagues' (2005; Neme and Gil 2009; Neme et al. 2011) database of radiocarbon dates from the Atuel Valley are from natural shelters. Natural shelters, especially ones with well-stratified deposits, are invaluable sources of information, but they are also relatively rare on most landscapes including Mendoza's, and are therefore unlikely to reflect the full suite of prehistoric behaviors in any region. That is, while southern Mendoza's *caves* might have been used less frequently during the middle Holocene it would not necessarily follow that the region as a whole experienced population decline.

Furthermore, there is reason to believe that intrasite sampling may have biased against middle Holocene radiocarbon dates across the region. Note, for example, the considerable variation in the number of radiocarbon dates per site in southern Mendoza. In the database published by Gil and colleagues (2005; Neme and Gil 2009;

Neme et al. 2011), 55% of all radiocarbon dates derive from three sites—Gruta del Indio (n = 29), Arroyo Malo-3 (n = 12), and Gruta de El Manzano (n = 10)—and the mean number of dates per site is 3.8 (SD = 6; range = 28). When the three outliers are removed, the mean falls to 2 dates per site (SD = 1.1; range = 4). In many places around the world, an economical and quite logical means of assessing the range of a site's occupation is to date the uppermost and lowermost strata, a practice that biases against middle Holocene dates for any site occupied from the start to the finish of the Holocene. In the Atuel watershed, most site chronologies are anchored by two or fewer dates and, as shown in Figure 5.4, the number of radiocarbon dates reported for a particular site is a strong predictor of whether at least one of those dates falls within the middle Holocene (negative binomial GLM, $\beta_{n.dates} \pm$ SE = 0.33 ± 0.07; n = 24 sites; $p < 0.0004$).

The prevalence of "bracket sampling" is probably also a function of greater research attention on the earliest and latest occupations in southern Mendoza, greater time and resources being devoted to initial colonization and human association with megafauna on the early end, and the introduction of plant domesticates on the latter end. Keen interest in these periods also explains why the traditional regional chronology lumps the 6,000-year stretch between initial colonization and the rise of agricultural "proto-producers" (Atuel IV) into a single cultural phase, imprecisely subdivided into Early, Middle, and Late Preceramic (Gil et al. 2005; Lagiglia 2002; Neme 2007).

New Lines of Evidence

The potential biases described in the previous section invited a closer look at the middle Holocene record, as well as new research designed specifically to address the reported occupational gap.

Regional Surface Survey

The overrepresentation of caves and shelters in southern Mendoza's archaeological record

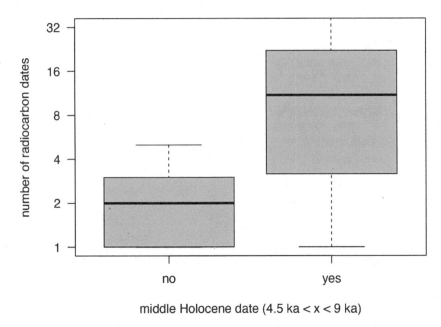

FIGURE 5.4. Boxplot of the number of radiocarbon dates for Mendozan sites that do (right box) and do not (left box) contain a middle Holocene radiocarbon date (i.e., a date between 9,000 and 4,500 cal BP). Sites lacking middle Holocene dates have fewer radiocarbon dates than sites containing at least one middle Holocene date (median$_{no}$ = 2, median$_{yes}$ = 11; n_{no} = 20, n_{yes} = 4; Mann-Whitney U = 16; p = 0.059). Note: the Mann-Whitney is a conservative, non-parametric test. With the small sample size, this does not quite reach standard value for statistical significance but the result is nonetheless clear. Further, analysis of the total number of radiocarbon dates and the number of middle Holocene dates is significantly positive (negative binomial GLM, $\beta_{n.dates}$ ± SE = 0.33 ± 0.07; n = 24 sites; p < 0.0004).

makes it difficult to determine whether the observed radiocarbon gap reflects changed regional demography, a change in the use of caves and shelters, or something else. Elsewhere in southern South America, where mid-Holocene archaeological gaps are also reported, shifting the scale of analysis from individual sites to broader regions suggests that, while some kinds of sites were abandoned during the middle Holocene, occupation persisted at others. For example, Grosjean and colleagues (2005) report that caves in both the Puna de Atacama and adjacent Atacama Desert—among the driest places on Earth—were abandoned at the onset of middle Holocene droughts, but that better-watered valleys remained occupied, suggesting intraregional population reshuffling rather regional-level population decline.

Until relatively recently, southern Mendoza had not been sampled sufficiently to determine whether intraregional population reshuffling might be a potential explanation for gaps in the region's cave record. To generate the sample necessary to assess this and other middle Holocene hypotheses, and to tap the previously unrealized potential of northern Patagonia's extensive surface record, I designed a regional survey that covered the full range of environments below 2,500 m in the Río Atuel Valley. Survey targeted a large number of randomly selected 1 × 1 km units from within a 140 × 20 km corridor centered on the Río Atuel (n = 33). The river was centrally important to the research design because it probably always served as a focal point of human activity in arid southern Mendoza, especially during middle Holocene droughts.

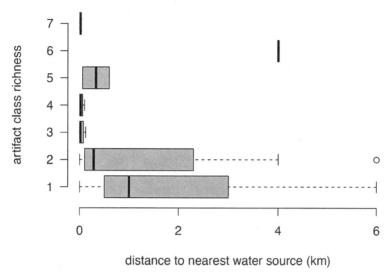

FIGURE 5.5. Boxplot illustrating the relationship between distance from the nearest water source and artifact class richness (number of artifact types) for sites located during survey in southern Mendoza, Argentina. Sites with only one or two artifact classes are located at a much wider range of distances from water than richer sites, which are typically located within 1 km of water.

Survey located 67 previously undocumented archaeological sites, all of them open-air sites in parts of the Atuel drainage not typically sampled by the conventional survey methodology. Survey also revealed six distinct environment types: riverine, alluvial fans, lacustrine, plains, foothills, and montane. The distribution and characteristics of sites found across these environment types is revealing. Most significantly, (1) riverine sites are much rarer than anticipated (n = 1, 1.5% of all sites), suggesting a taphonomic bias and, (2) in contrast to the southern Mendoza radiocarbon record, the middle Holocene is overrepresented in the survey sample, particularly in the foothills and lower elevations of the Andes.

The single riverine site encountered is large (~5,000 m²; the range of site sizes located during survey is < 1 m² to ~315,000 m²), and site size generally decreases as distance from water increases. Archaeological locations within 1 km of water are of a wide range of sizes, from isolated artifacts to sites with surface areas up to 315,000 m². Conversely, all sites located farther than 1 km from water are 100 m or less in maximum dimension, with only two exceptions.

Artifact class richness is also highest within 1 km of water—richness defined here as a simple count of artifact categories meant to distinguish limited use sites from ones where more diverse activities were performed. With one exception, sites located farther than 1 km from water contain just one or two artifact classes (mode of 1; Figure 5.5), whereas sites within 1 km of water commonly have four or more. As expected (Jones et al. 1983), artifact class richness is positively correlated with site size (richness ~maximum dimension; R^2 = 0.52; Figure 5.6). However, when isolates and lithic scatters smaller than 5 m in diameter are removed from the sample, there is a nearly bimodal distribution: richness across sites less than 2,000 m in maximum dimension is between 1 and 4 (mode = 1), while richness in larger sites (maximum dimension >2,000 m), is between 4 and 7 (mode = 4). These modes may represent distinct site types, smaller logistical camps and larger base camps, the relative distributions of which are linked to water availability.

Given the relationship between water availability (site proximity to water) and both site

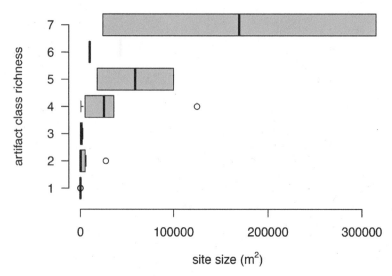

FIGURE 5.6. Boxplot illustrating the relationship between site size (m²) and artifact class richness (number of artifact types). Granting small sample sizes in some cases, larger sites are much richer than smaller ones.

size and richness, it is surprising that we located only a single riverine site despite having surveyed many 1 × 1 km units along the river. Opportunistic survey of river cut-banks both within riverine units and traveling between them likewise failed to reveal cultural evidence, suggesting that the pattern is real and the result of taphonomic biases. The Río Atuel floodplain is several kilometers wide and the river channel has meandered across it for millennia (Stingl and Garleff 1985), eroding and burying sites, reducing the sample of middle Holocene archaeological deposits that once existed. This is particularly problematic given the tendency for human activity to concentrate along watercourses (in greatest proximity to the destructive forces of water), particularly during droughts (e.g., the middle Holocene).

Temporal Trends

Because radiocarbon is not effective in dating surface sites, and well-defined projectile typologies are lacking in southern Mendoza, the best prospect for a preceramic chronology for the extensive surface record is obsidian hydration (Garvey 2012b; Garvey et al. 2016). Granting

the hydration process is more complicated than suggested by early models (Friedman and Long 1976; Friedman and Smith 1960), recent research presents ways to control for confounding factors including ambient temperature and intrinsic water (for recently developed controls see Liritzis 2014; Rogers 2007; Stevenson et al. 2013; Stevenson and Novak 2011). My colleagues and I, therefore, developed preliminary hydration rates for two sources (Garvey 2012b; Garvey et al. 2016), which I used to estimate the ages of survey finds. In measuring the hydration rim widths of artifacts found during survey, we took particular care to target surfaces unaffected by weathering, including small internal cracks in flake platforms, which hydrate at the same rate as external flake surfaces but are protected from subsequent weathering.

Fourteen archaeological locations (sites, small scatters, isolates) located during survey contained obsidian artifacts whose ages could be estimated using our preliminary hydration equations. Of the 45 age estimates, 67% fall within the middle Holocene (71% when dates are calculated at two standard deviations), and nearly 80% of all dateable locations have middle Holocene-aged obsidian artifacts (93% at two standard deviations; Table 5.2; Garvey and Bettinger 2018). In short, the middle Holocene is overrepresented in the obsidian hydration dated survey sample, whereas it is underrepresented in the radiocarbon record from stratified sites.

Noteworthy, too, is that younger sites are richer (have more kinds of artifacts) on average than older ones. While this might reflect a greater human presence in later prehistory, preservation is also a likely factor: older sites have been exposed longer increasing the likelihood that older artifacts have been displaced, scavenged, or buried (see also Chapter 7). One implication of preservation bias is the high probability that small middle Holocene (and earlier) sites will be particularly elusive, further complicating our understanding of prehistoric foragers' use of the region during this period.

A final trend worth mentioning is that sites dated to the middle Holocene are located primarily in the foothills and mountains, and range in size from approximately 20 m^2 to 25,000 m^2. Their lithic assemblages are dominated by local materials, particularly basalt, and artifact densities per square meter are relatively high (variable but generally >10 artifacts per m^2). This pattern suggests low residential mobility during the middle Holocene. Small sites with low artifact class richness are likely logistical camps, located in the foothills and on the plains. These supported larger base camps, located primarily in the foothills and mountains (above 2,000 m), perhaps reflecting less severe winters during the middle Holocene. This is taken up again in the following section.

Because radiocarbon data from southern Mendoza suggest that intrasite sampling (especially "bracket dating") may be contributing to the appearance of a middle Holocene gap, I was interested in developing an approach to offset this. Most of the >400 obsidian samples used in the development of our hydration rates derive from radiocarbon-dated levels in southern Mendoza's stratified sites (see Garvey [2012a, 2012b] and Garvey et al. [2016] for details). If local radiocarbon gaps represent occupational hiatuses, similar gaps should be evident in the obsidian record: leaving more precise age estimates aside,

there should be specimens with thick hydration rims (early Holocene) and ones with thin rims (late Holocene), but none of intermediate thickness (middle Holocene). However, this is not the pattern that emerges.

Gruta de El Manzano is exemplary in this regard. Recall that the site's ten radiocarbon dates indicate a protracted occupational hiatus between circa 7800 and 2000 cal BP (Neme et al. 2011). The original excavation removed essentially all of the cultural fill from the cave's interior (Gambier 1985), making it very difficult to redate the site using radiocarbon. There are, however, numerous obsidian artifacts throughout the sequence. If the site was abandoned for over 5,000 years as the radiocarbon record suggests, El Manzano obsidian hydration rims should also show significant discontinuity.

Granting the effects of intrinsic water on hydration rates and the potential for native water to vary within sources (Stevenson et al. 2019), there is an historical precedent for controlling for obsidian source as a means of constraining hydration rate variability. So, as part of this project, I used X-ray fluorescence to assign obsidian artifacts—from El Manzano and many other sites across the region—to their most likely sources. Of the El Manzano artifacts, 90% are from a single source location (Laguna del Maule), which provided a reasonable sample (n = 57) for this assessment of the middle Holocene gap. Simply arranging the hydration rim values from smallest to largest reveals a nearly continuous sequence of rim thicknesses between 1.5 μm and 10 μm (Figure 5.7; Garvey and Bettinger 2018:852). According to the preliminary hydration rate for Laguna del Maule obsidian, this suggests use of the cave throughout the Holocene, between roughly 12,600 and 400 cal BP.

When the same form of analysis is applied to a larger sample of obsidian (n = 219), the result similarly contradicts the regional-level radiocarbon pattern. As with the El Manzano sample, the regional sample shows a nearly unbroken sequence of obsidian hydration rim values (Figure 5.8). All of the artifacts in this larger sample have been assigned by XRF to one of two sources, Laguna del Maule and

TABLE 5.2. Obsidian hydration age estimates and environment types of sites found during surface survey.

	site	environment	date
early Holocene	A7	plains	10,452
	F2	foothills	9436
	F2	foothills	9381
	F7	foothills	9307
middle Holocene	M3	mountains	8398
	ALM5	mountains	8330
	M6	mountains	8098
	M6	mountains	8087
	P14	plains	7691
	F4	foothills	7450
	F7	foothills	7214
	F2	foothills	7189
	F2	foothills	7174
	F2	foothills	7169
	F2	foothills	7166
	F2	foothills	7166
	F2	foothills	7148
	F2	foothills	7135
	F7	foothills	7119
	ALM3	mountains	7116
	F2	foothills	7110
	F2	foothills	7101
	F2	foothills	7100
	F7	foothills	7088
	F2	foothills	7077
	F2	foothills	7060
	F2	foothills	7045
	T7D1	plains	7004
	F2	foothills	6998
	F2	foothills	6954
	ALM3	mountains	5444
	M3	mountains	5293
	ALM1	mountains	5007
	ALM4	mountains	4750
	ALM1	mountains	4725
	T7D2	plains	14,357[a]
	ALM2	mountains	4356[a]
late Holocene	ALM3	mountains	4012
	ALM4	mountains	4012
	ALM2	mountains	3385
	ALM3	mountains	2929
	ALM2	mountains	2571
	ALM1	mountains	2566
	ALM1	mountains	2562
	M3	mountains	2432

Hydration ages are calculated using rates in Garvey et al. 2016.

[a] Date falls between 9000 and 4500 cal BP (middle Holocene) when calculated at two standard deviations.

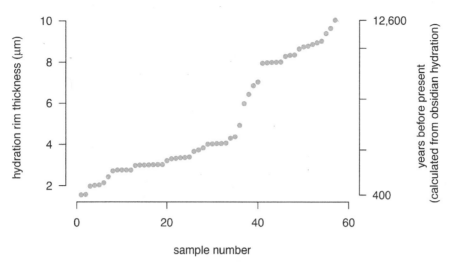

FIGURE 5.7. Hydration rim measurements from El Maule obsidians at El Manzano, dissociated from their spatial and temporal contexts. According to preliminary hydration equations, the site appears to have been occupied throughout the period from ca. 12,600 to 400 BP.

Las Cargas. According to these sources' respective preliminary hydration rates, the regional obsidian sample suggests that southern Mendoza was occupied throughout the Holocene, from approximately 13,000 cal BP to European contact. In fact, fully *half* of this larger sample falls between 9000 and 4500 cal BP (the middle Holocene) when ages are calculated at two standard deviations (45% at one SD), and nearly 60% of all sites from which samples were drawn contain obsidian artifacts dated to the middle Holocene (Garvey and Bettinger 2018:852), a figure that far exceeds that of the radiocarbon sample (16%).

Finally, it is worth highlighting the fact that, when compared side by side as in Figure 5.8, the radiocarbon record shows more and longer gaps than the hydration record. The two small middle Holocene gaps in the hydration record are more likely due to sampling or stone procurement behaviors than to demographic decline or abandonment during these times (Garvey and Bettinger 2018), given that there are hydration gaps of similar duration during the last 2,000 years when people were certainly present and, in fact, their populations may have been growing rapidly (Neme and Gil 2008b; see also Chapter 6). Changed stone procurement behaviors are an important component of an alternative hypothesis for southern Mendoza's sparse middle Holocene record, as I describe next (see also Garvey 2015a).

An Alternative Hypothesis

The traditional interpretation of Mendoza's radiocarbon record centers on population decline (rising death rates, falling birth rates, regional abandonment; Gil et al. 2005), as is true of similar archaeological phenomena elsewhere (Barrientos 2001; Guráieb 2004; Núñez and Grosjean 1994; Núñez et al. 1996; Yacobaccio 1998). Here, I offer an alternative hypothesis: the middle Holocene in southern Mendoza was, in fact, well attended, the appearance of a gap having been created by various biasing factors on the one hand and prehistoric human behaviors on the other. This hypothesis is supported by three primary conclusions drawn from the above analyses, and by predictions of optimal foraging models. In summary, these conclusions are:

(1) Bracket sampling reduces the likelihood of middle Holocene dates, both as a function of the law of large numbers and because "brackets"

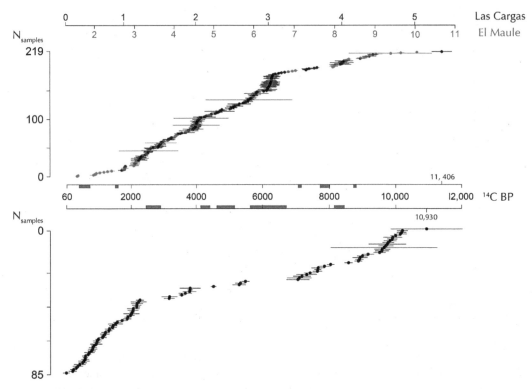

FIGURE 5.8. Hydration rim measurements and associated hydration age estimates of 219 obsidian artifacts sourced to Las Cargas and El Maule compared to 85 radiocarbon dates (plus and minus two standard deviations) from 35 stratified sites in southern Mendoza. Gaps in the respective records are highlighted in gray on the shared x-axes (from Garvey and Bettinger 2018, reprinted with permission).

over-sample early and late deposits; sites with two or fewer radiocarbon dates tend not to have middle Holocene dates, whereas sites with several radiocarbon dates do. Moreover, obsidian hydration age estimates fill radiocarbon gaps, both within and across sites in southern Mendoza.

(2) Even if an amplified program of radiocarbon dating / obsidian hydration age estimation failed to identify more middle Holocene components in the region's cave record, results of the probabilistic survey described above show that the historical over-sampling of caves is itself contributing to the appearance of a gap. Of all sites in Gil and colleagues' dates database, 71% are caves/shelters, only five of which produced middle Holocene radiocarbon dates. If real, a relative disuse of caves during the middle Holocene would be intriguing, but it still would not necessarily support population decline. This

is made clear by the fact that, of the dateable sites found during survey—100% of which are open-air sites—80% have middle Holocene-aged artifacts.

(3) Both the survey data and data from the few stratified sites with known middle Holocene deposits indicate a preference for locating longer-term occupations (e.g., residential base camps) near reliable water. This is unsurprising given southern Mendoza's arid climate. The survey data also suggest that many such sites located along rivers could have been lost to the rivers themselves. If middle Holocene droughts drew people to rivers' margins, as I describe below, loss of these sites would contribute to the appearance of a sparse middle Holocene record.

Our understanding of southern Mendoza's middle Holocene will improve as ongoing research generates more dates and results of systematic surveys. Still, knowing that human behavior can serve as a powerful counter to drought-induced resource scarcity, we can use behavioral models to generate predictions that can be tested against current datasets—and retested as more data become available. Rather than simply adjusting their populations, humans can adjust aspects of their settlement, subsistence, and technology when local conditions change, and two microeconomic models provide principled expectations for southern Mendoza's middle Holocene.

The Marginal Value Theorem Predicts Reduced Middle Holocene Mobility

Recall from Chapter 3 that the marginal value theorem (MVT; Charnov 1976) can be used to predict optimal patch residence time—how long a forager should remain in a patch, catching and consuming its resources, before incurring the cost of moving to a fresh patch. Depending on the structure of the local resource base and the nature of environmental change, at least two outcomes are possible: (1) If environmental change reduces the number of available patches, optimizing foragers should remain in a given resource patch longer and be willing to travel farther to get to a new patch; and (2) if, instead, environmental change reduces within-patch resource abundance equally across all patches, optimizing foragers' behaviors should track with handling time, patch residence time increasing with increased resource handling (Bettinger and Grote 2016).

Southern Mendoza's paleoenvironmental data are currently insufficient to provide a detailed picture of specific middle Holocene changes in resource abundance and distribution. Projections based on the current resource structure, estimates of middle Holocene drought severity, and information from the few known archaeological sites with deposits dating to between 9000 and 4500 cal BP suggest the first scenario (patch reduction) might be the more accurate description of environmental change during this time. Most of Mendoza's local plants and animals are drought-adapted, so food resources may not

have been significantly affected by decreased precipitation during the middle Holocene and, in fact, the highest-ranked resource (guanaco) appears to have remained a subsistence focus (Neme and Gil 2009), suggesting consistently high prey densities. Water, however, has probably always been a limiting resource in southern Mendoza, particularly during the hot, dry middle Holocene. Water also has high transport costs, so longer-term residential sites should be located near water sources in times of water scarcity. Accordingly, resource patches likely centered on reliable water sources—margins of rivers, large arroyos, and lakes, for example—the number/size of which decreased during the middle Holocene as a result of drought.

Perhaps counterintuitively, water-based patches, while fewer, might have become more productive during the middle Holocene. Decreased precipitation and increased evaporation reduce stream and river discharge, which can promote marsh formation (Grosjean et al. 2001; cf. Betancourt et al. 2000) and increase the salinity of the region's shallow lakes, making them more attractive to waterfowl (Kingsford and Porter 1994). Lowered water levels also expose nutrient-rich and permanently saturated soils along the margins of waterways and in backwaters, and these may have supported wetland vegetation and wildlife that was richer, more diverse, and more localized—which is to say easier to procure—during the middle Holocene than before or after (Bettinger et al. 2015; Bettinger et al. 1997; Brown 1985; Brown and Vierra 1983; Grosjean et al. 2005; Jefferies 2008; Orians and Pearson 1979). Modern marshes in southern Mendoza's lowlands host seed bearing grasses (e.g., saltbush, bulrush, dropseed), as well as cattails and tubers, small rodents, mara (*Dolichotis* sp.), pichi, ducks, geese, swans, and millions of migrant waterfowl each breeding season. These might have been very attractive places prehistorically.

Whether or not extensive marshes formed, local ecology predicts a middle Holocene preference for living near reliable water, a hypothesis archaeologically supported in ecologically analogous regions that were also affected by middle

Holocene droughts (e.g., the U.S. Great Basin; Jones et al. 2003). Under the circumstances, foragers should have responded by moving less often, exploiting local resources until within-patch foraging returns were low enough to warrant the travel costs necessary to get to the next patch. So, a reduced radiocarbon signal during the middle Holocene—if real—might simply reflect a reduction in the overall number of sites, each occupied longer. That is, evidence presented in this chapter shows there was a greater middle Holocene presence than is indicated by the traditional cave site/radiocarbon record, but even if future research confirms a relatively weak middle Holocene signal, it would not, a priori, confirm low middle Holocene population densities.

A Model of Lithic Raw Material Procurement Supports the Marginal Value Theorem's Predictions

Dovetailing with predictions of the MVT, a microeconomic model of lithic raw material procurement predicts decreased use of high-quality, nonlocal stone during the middle Holocene, either because reduced mobility effectively increased the cost of procuring it or because the food resources in broadened middle Holocene diets did not require fine lithic materials (Garvey 2012a, 2015a; cf. Bettinger et al. 2006).

In brief, this model of stone procurement predicts the amount of tool use necessary to warrant trips to distant sources when serviceable, but lower-quality, stone is locally available. Incorporating high-quality, nonlocal materials before this "critical use time" is reached results in a lower rate of return (i.e., is inefficient) because the time and energy required to procure it offsets benefits afforded by its use. As use time increases, though, it pays to invest in the costlier resource. Use of high-quality, nonlocal stone might also increase if costs associated with its procurement are reduced (e.g., through mobility or trade).

Obsidian and basalt are the two most common materials in many of southern Mendoza's archaeological deposits. Across the region, obsidian occurs in both the Andes and La Payunia volcanic field, south of the Atuel Valley. Nonetheless, and despite their inaccessibility during winter, Andean sources are far better represented in archaeological deposits than plains ones, which are available year-round (Barberena et al. 2019; Giesso et al. 2011). Basalt, on the other hand, is ubiquitous (Rodríguez and Ragairaz 1972) and easily obtainable from many archaeological sites; its procurement costs are far lower than those of the region's Andean obsidians. Relative to obsidian, though, local basalt tends to be grainy, which reduces the control one has when knapping tools, potential sharpness of cutting edges, and the efficacy of resharpening/reworking tools. That is, basalt return rates (i.e., use efficiency) are low compared to those of obsidian. According to the stone procurement model, these materials' respective return rates relative to the time it takes to procure and craft tools from them define a critical use time that must be exceeded for obsidian procurement to be worth the effort. Obsidian should be preferred when groups live close enough to sources for procurement costs to be relatively low or when fine, sharp tools are important enough (or the social value of obsidian high enough) to warrant the trip to a far-away source. Conversely, basalt should dominate lithic assemblages when mobility is limited or use of fine, sharp tools (or the social value of fine materials) is below the critical threshold (see Garvey 2015a for an extended discussion).

The restricted middle Holocene mobility predicted by the MVT would have increased obsidian procurement costs. Given the west-east flow of the Atuel River and arrangement of resources across the region (see above), middle Holocene foragers tethered to water features, might simply have tracked seasonally available resources along the river, from upland valleys (summer) to the plains (winter). Such a pattern would have reduced the frequency of foraging near Andean obsidian sources, none of which are in the Atuel Valley. With restricted movement, costs associated with resource excursions beyond the Atuel Valley may have been too high to justify trips to distant obsidian sources.

Moreover, restricted middle Holocene movement likely required a broadening of the diet to include not only guanaco but also smaller game, fish, and more plant foods (Jones et al. 2003), and this more generalized diet might have obviated the need to procure obsidian for specialized hunting tools. Marsh resources, for example, could be procured using nets or snares or simply gathered by hand. For middle Holocene assemblages, then, the model predicts relatively small amounts of obsidian and higher proportions of local stone like basalt.

Archaeological Data from Southern Mendoza Align with the Models' Predictions

Several lines of archaeological evidence related to southern Mendoza's middle Holocene support both the MVT prediction of longer stays at sites, preferentially located near water, and the procurement model prediction that, accordingly, use of local stone should be common.

With few exceptions, middle Holocene sites are located between 1,500 and 2,500 m above sea level (the foothills and lower elevations of the Andes), in the valleys of major water courses. Water sources here tend to be more reliable (i.e., less likely to have dried up during the middle Holocene) than streams and playa lakes in the lowlands. Arroyo Malo-3, Gruta de El Manzano, Arroyo el Desecho-4, and 80% of the middle Holocene sites located during survey all fit this profile. The foothills provide easy access to both upland and lowland resources and, although current climate restricts year-round habitation to elevations below 2,000 m, the middle Holocene climatic optimum may have permitted winter occupation at higher elevations. During summer, the foothills would have been cooler than the plains and permitted relatively easy logistical access to marsh resources, including grass seeds, cattails, and an abundance of terrestrial and water birds that breed and molt on shallow plains lakes/marshes each year. From the foothills, the upland meadows (*vegas*) where herds of guanaco likely grazed would also have been easily accessible. In winter, the foothills would have provided shelter from

the high winds on the plains and heavy snows in the mountains. Guanaco winter in the foothills for these same reasons, and would not have required lengthy logistical forays for people with foothills base camps.

One of the middle Holocene-aged sites found during survey is a relatively small lithic scatter on the plains, hydration-dated to circa 5900 cal BP. Cueva Delerma and Cueva del Indio (previously identified cave sites with middle Holocene radiocarbon dates but few associated cultural materials; see above), are located on the plains and, like the lithic scatter found during survey, may have been associated with logistical foraging during the middle Holocene to support base camps at higher elevations.

None of previously identified middle Holocene cave sites is especially large, but their artifact assemblages suggest either prolonged stays or frequent serial reuse during the 9000 to 4500 cal BP window. Of the middle Holocene-aged sites located during survey, two in the foothills are fairly large (~25,000 m²). All of the middle Holocene survey sites have dense and rich assemblages (i.e., many artifacts per unit area and many distinct artifact types), reflecting a range of subsistence behaviors consistent with ethnographic base camps. This pattern suggests low residential mobility and, given the abundance of local raw materials, a correspondingly high cost of obtaining nonlocal stone during the middle Holocene.

Consistent with the procurement model predictions, the lithic assemblages at middle Holocene sites, such as Arroyo Malo-3, El Manzano, and the survey sites in the foothills, are dominated by high proportions of basalt, likely procured locally. At El Manzano, informal tools also outnumber formal ones, the tool:debitage ratio is high, and the faunal record indicates a broad diet (high-ranked guanaco plus lower-ranked armadillo, rhea eggs, fish, and plants), all of which supports the hypothesis that mobility was reduced during the middle Holocene (Andrefsky 1998; Kuhn 1991).

Lastly, it is worth noting that at both El Manzano and Arroyo Malo-3, raw material use changed significantly after the middle Holocene,

with a substantial increase in the presence of obsidian. This implies either increased mobility,
as the MVT predicts for climate amelioration,
or more specialized tool use corresponding to
a narrower subsistence focus, or both. That is,
increased mobility would have brought people
into more frequent contact with both obsidian
and larger-bodied, wide-ranging prey (e.g., guanaco), both of which would have increased use
of obsidian during the late Holocene relative to
the middle Holocene.

Summary and Conclusions

Prehistoric foragers were likely affected by
middle Holocene climate changes in southern
Mendoza. However, the multiple lines of evidence presented here suggest that the effect of
these changes was not population decline, as has
been argued (e.g., Diéguez and Neme 2003; Gil
et al. 2005; Neme and Gil 2001). Instead, southern Mendoza's middle Holocene foragers appear to have deliberately positioned themselves
relative to a key resource—water—which had
cascading effects on other aspects of prehistoric
behavior and on the archaeological record. This
perspective allows us to reinterpret not only
southern Mendoza's middle Holocene record,
but also potentially those of ecologically similar regions where middle Holocene gaps have
been observed.

Analogous gaps have been reported for parts
of Chile's coast (20–27° S; Grosjean et al. 2007),
the Puna de Atacama (Grosjean et al. 2005;
Grosjean et al. 2007; Yacobaccio and Morales
2005), southern Africa (Deacon 1974; Humphreys and Thackeray 1983; Wadley 1986, 2000)
and, in the United States, the High Plains (Kelly
2013), southern High Plains (eastern New Mexico and northwest Texas; Bender and Wright
1988; Frison 1975; Meltzer 1995b, 1999), and
Great Basin (Aikens and Madsen 1986; Antevs
1948; Baumhoff and Heizer 1965; Benson et al.
2002; Grayson 1993; Grayson and Louderback
2008; Louderback et al. 2010). Increased heat
and aridity during the middle Holocene are
likewise reported for each of these regions.
Because these radiocarbon gaps occur in areas

that are presently arid, many interpretations
rest on the assumption that dry places, inhos-
pitable to begin with, were virtually uninhabitable during the middle Holocene, and that
people were unable or unwilling to adapt to
changed conditions. Certainly, restricted access
to water poses problems. Humans need water.
In arid climates, the average adult loses 7–12 L
of water per day; bouts of exercise can cause
additional losses of 1–3 L per hour, which can
lead quickly to dehydration and associated life-
threatening complications (Sowell 2001). Water
is also difficult to transport in large quantities,
so drought can pose real challenges to mobile
foragers, particularly those who have to cross
water-poor expanses (Larson 1977; Meltzer
1999; Schmidt-Neilsen 1964). What is less clear,
as the southern Mendoza case study illustrates,
is whether reduced precipitation in such areas
would necessarily trigger population decline or
abandonment, as is often assumed.

Firstly, macroecological models of human
distribution across the globe suggest that
hunter-gatherer populations are not limited by
the abundance or timing of rainfall. Recall from
Chapter 2 that foragers live at both very low and
relatively high densities where mean annual
rainfall is low, and that nearly half of all groups
in the Binford (2001) dataset live in places that
receive no appreciable rain (<5 mm) during the
driest month of the year. Certainly, the distribution of foragers included in the Binford dataset is
influenced by a variety of factors (e.g., the spread
farming at the expense of foraging), but the
point remains that hunter-gatherers can live at
reasonably high densities in water-poor places.

Secondly, reduced middle Holocene precipitation in already arid areas may not have provoked abandonment because arid-land species
and ecosystems are equipped to survive even
prolonged droughts. While it is true that deserts
are characterized by low species diversity and
primary productivity, desert plants and animals
are adapted to environmental extremes, including large thermal amplitudes (daily and annual)
and low water availability (seasonal and inter-
annual). Desert animals tend to be generalists,
ranging widely and foraging opportunistically;

desert plants have an array of drought- and mineral-tolerant adaptations and seed-banking capabilities (Sowell 2001). Plants and animals—including people—with long histories in arid climates tend to be well-adapted to relative resource scarcity, and many of their physical and behavioral traits are conditioned not by average conditions, but by below average ones (Bettinger 1980; Odum 1959; Sowell 2001).

Thirdly, it is worth noting that drought is typically defined in terms of rainfall but decreased precipitation does not always result in water deficit. Across much of eastern Patagonia, for example, river discharge is regulated by precipitation in the Andes, which is determined by weather patterns distinct from those responsible for precipitation on the eastern plains. During the middle Holocene, rivers may have continued to flow normally across the lowlands (e.g., Mendoza's eastern plain and the Patagonian steppe) despite below-average rainfall, and aquifers, which are resistant to evaporation and typically recharged by mountain runoff, may have ensured reliable surface water even at the height of middle Holocene droughts (Meltzer 1995b).

None of this is to say that Patagonia's middle Holocene droughts were inconsequential—only that the assumption that arid lands are marginal to begin with and simply get worse with decreased rainfall may be unfounded. Kintigh and Ingram (2018) have shown that, while causal links between climatic downturns and major cultural changes are commonly suggested in the literature, statistical analysis fails to support the relationship in even a single instance in their analysis. Notably, the cases in their study all involve claims of drought-induced change, most of them not scrutinized because of the obvious coincidence between cultural and climatic change. "Indeed, the logic of these arguments sometimes seems so compelling that a critical examination of the question appears unnecessary" (Kintigh and Ingram 2018:29). As Kintigh and Ingram are careful to note, though, their results do not necessarily mean that there is no relationship between drought and cultural change, only that temporal coincidence is insufficient to demonstrate causation. And, as the southern

Mendoza case study shows, links between climate and cultural or behavioral change can be subtle, secondary, and easily misinterpreted if not thoroughly examined.

In southern Mendoza, a relatively minor behavioral adjustment may have had disproportionately large effects on archaeological visibility. If human responses were similar elsewhere in Patagonia, the effect would have been the same: decreased mobility would have resulted in an overall reduction in the number of sites produced during the middle Holocene, correspondingly reducing the statistical likelihood of finding sites dating to that period. The three things that compound this problem in southern Mendoza likely have the same effect in other parts of Patagonia. These are (1) trends in sampling and research foci, (2) an historical emphasis on cave sites, when local ecology predicts that middle Holocene sites are more likely to be found near reliable water, and (3) the very fact that middle Holocene sites were preferentially located near water predisposed them to erosion and deep burial, particularly as middle Holocene glaciers melted and proglacial lakes' dams failed.

It is infeasible to exhaustively date every site we excavate but, as I demonstrated above, we must be aware of the potential effects of bracket dating as we interpret regional records. Indeed, among radiocarbon dates in the Patagonian database introduced in Chapter 2 (n = 1,982), whether a site has at least one date within the middle Holocene range is well predicted by the total number of dates reported for that site; sites with two or fewer radiocarbon dates tend not to have middle Holocene dates, whereas sites with several radiocarbon dates do (Figure 5.9; $p < 2.2 \times 10^{-16}$). Moreover, the model best fit to these data predicts that, above 15 radiocarbon dates, the likelihood that a site will have a middle Holocene date is about 95% (Figure 5.10, $p < 2.0 \times 10^{-16}$).

As in southern Mendoza, what we know about the broader-Patagonian middle Holocene is based largely on data from natural shelters. Radiocarbon gaps in these sites' records might owe to sampling, as just described, or to true disuse of shelters that were simply too far from

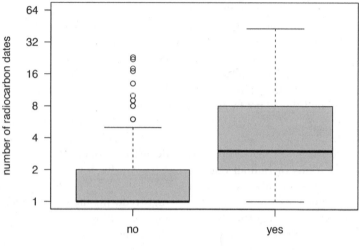

FIGURE 5.9. Boxplot of the number of radiocarbon dates for sites that do (right box) and do not (left box) contain a middle Holocene radiocarbon date (i.e., a date between 9,000 and 4,500 cal BP). Sites lacking middle Holocene dates have significantly fewer radiocarbon dates than sites containing at least one middle Holocene date (median$_{no}$ = 1, median$_{yes}$ = 3; n_{no} = 522, n_{yes} = 120; Mann-Whitney U = 16,812; p < 2.2 x 10^{-16}).

reliable water to have been used at archaeologically visible intensities during the arid middle Holocene. Additionally, increased seismicity (Salemme and Miotti 2008:447) made some caves unlivable due to roof fall—or the threat of it, anyway. Even one instance of catastrophic roof collapse might have been sufficient to discourage the use of caves, perhaps even well after the period of frequent, perceptible tremors. In sum, to the extent that they cannot be explained by sampling bias, middle Holocene gaps in cave records are an intriguing problem, but they are not in themselves sufficient evidence that gaps in regional archaeological records reflect population decline.

Strategic encampment near reliable water is likely also biasing against middle Holocene sites across the region. If wetlands formed in river valleys as rivers slowed due to droughts (Grosjean et al. 2005), when precipitation rebounded during the late Holocene, sites in the vicinity would have been negatively affected. This is especially problematic in areas that experienced late middle Holocene or early late Holocene

glacier readvance since subsequent glacial retreat damages archaeological records through both scouring and overbank deposition.

There is more at stake here than correcting potential misinterpretations of regional prehistories. Real gaps in archaeological records can help us define human adaptive capacities, and isolating the effects of taphonomic and other biases is correspondingly critical. So, while this chapter's epigraph—"adaptation seems to be, to a substantial extent, a process of reallocating your attention" (Kahneman 2005)—captures the essence of north-Patagonians' response to middle Holocene environmental change, it is also a constructive reminder to all of us that we must sometimes reallocate our attention—and recalibrate our expectations (Garvey 2020)—in light of new information.

Final Thoughts

Whether gaps in Patagonian records are real or illusory, the region's middle Holocene record stands in stark contrast to those of many other

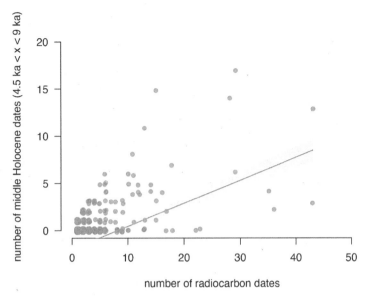

FIGURE 5.10. Scatterplot of the number of middle Holocene dates (i.e., dates between 9,000 and 4,500 cal BP) versus the total number of radiocarbon dates. There is a significant positive relationship between the total number of radiocarbon dates and the number of middle Holocene dates (negative binomial GLM, $\beta_{n.dates} \pm SE = 0.24 \pm 0.02$; $p < 2.0 \times 10^{-16}$). Line and shading depict GLM mean predicted values and 95% confidence intervals.

world regions. During the same 4,000-year period, many places saw dramatic increases in technological and social complexity. Extractive metallurgy began approximately 8,000 years ago, developed rapidly, and spread widely. Agriculture reached Europe's Atlantic Coast and the Nile Valley where ensuing demographic and social changes were profound. Even just to the north and east of Patagonia, populations appear to have grown and cultures to have changed dramatically during this time. In Brazil's Río de la Plata Basin and adjacent littoral zones, social complexity first emerged with the Sambaquis and Cerritos moundbuilding cultures circa 6800 cal BP. These are contemporaneous with early urban societies and monumental architecture on Peru's coast (Iriarte et al. 2017:294; Moseley 2001; Sandweiss and Quilter 2012). The trend of increasing complexity continued in Peru, of course, leading ultimately to the formation of the largest New World empire, that of the Inca. The Inca empire cast a long shadow and, while it is not clear the extent to which the Inca influenced Patagonian cultures during the late Holocene, the juxtaposition of expansionist agrarian state in the north and relatively small groups of hunter-gatherers in the south is intriguing. Could it be that the Patagonian environment simply would not permit farming, the economic change that seems to have underwritten much of the social complexity seen in other regions? The transition from foraging to farming is one of the most enduring and hotly debated topics in archaeology and, I would argue, studying cultural change in places where agriculture *did not* take root may be as informative as studying cultural change in places where it did. The next chapter is motivated by precisely this, and explores reasons Patagonians might have remained hunter-gatherers.

6

Foragers in a World of Farmers

[Species] evolve exactly as if they were adapting as best they could to a changing world, and not at all as if they were moving toward a set goal.

—George Gaylord Simpson (1964:23)

Patagonians lived as committed hunter-gatherers for millennia, from initial peopling to European contact (ca. 1550 CE). This makes Patagonia one of relatively few world regions beyond the Arctic/Subarctic where farming never took root. This observation is all the more intriguing because, at least in the north, Patagonian foragers lived alongside and interacted with agriculturalists for at least 2,000 years. Nonetheless, we seldom ask *why* Patagonians did not farm. Perhaps it is because of the region's reputation as a windswept wasteland; environmental severity seems explanation enough, harsh conditions having made traditional farming (i.e., without draft animals, mechanized plows, or extensive irrigation) superlatively unprofitable. That is, agriculture would have been advantageous if only it had been possible. Alternatively, noting the relative sparsity of Patagonian's archaeological record, we might reason that, possible or not, agriculture was simply unnecessary because populations remained small throughout the Holocene, never reaching a point at which agriculture would have been worth the effort. Either way, Patagonian foraging owes to straightforward economics: farming was either so costly, or foraging so beneficial, that it was a foregone conclusion.

As you might imagine, considering there is a whole chapter devoted to the persistence of foraging in Patagonia, the reality is far more complex—and curious—than that. To be sure,

certain places, seasons, and prehistoric periods are (or were) truly hostile to farming, but the same can be said of equivalent North American latitudes, from the Four Corners region to the Dakotas, where we know people lived as farmers in late prehistory. In fact, Patagonia's environmental and archaeological records indicate that parts of the region are amenable to farming and that foraging efficiency was declining in some places; neither too-costly farming nor too-beneficial foraging is sufficient to explain the pan-Patagonian commitment to hunting and gathering. Nor is ignorance of farming, since, as I mentioned, some Patagonian foragers lived next door to farmers for at least two millennia. As we will see, domesticated plants were part of some foragers' diets, however small. Significantly, too, wild varieties of key Andean domesticates grow readily across much of Patagonia. These were all important ingredients in the development or adoption of farming elsewhere in the world, and this constellation of evidence—that, in some places, physical and economic conditions were right for farming, and both suitable plants (including cultigens) and farming know-how were available—makes space for more nuanced hypotheses. In this chapter, I explore the possibility that social and cultural challenges associated with such a radical reorganization—something I will refer to as "adaptive-peak jumping"—were primarily responsible.

Foraging and farming require very different technologies, schedules, and risk-management strategies, among other major adjustments, particularly where key wild resources are highly mobile, unpredictable, and/or unevenly distributed in space or time. Since Sewall Wright (1931) first introduced the concept, many evolutionary scientists have found a useful metaphor in the "adaptive landscape," a fitness topography on which macroevolutionary change plays out (cf. Gavrilets 2010; Laue and Wright 2019). *Macroevolution* refers to evolutionary change above the level of the individual (i.e., above the microevolutionary level), as when groups transition from foraging to farming. On macroevolutionary landscapes, adaptive peaks are constellations of traits such as the number of residential moves per year, reliance on storage, and calories derived from plant foods, the specific combination and values of which result in high fitness (Chapter 3) relative to adaptive valleys, where trait combinations are deleterious (e.g., extreme residential mobility plus total reliance on storage).

Whether foraging or farming was the higher peak on Patagonia's late prehistoric fitness landscape is precisely the root of the debate. Traditional arguments see foraging as either the higher peak (foraging sufficient to meet all needs) or the *only* peak (farming impossible). But, as I have mentioned and will show presently, neither is entirely true. If both peaks were present on the adaptive landscape and evidence indicates some groups' fitness would have been improved by farming, we need to consider things that might have made it difficult for prehistoric Patagonians to move off the foraging peak and on to the farming one, while avoiding the low-fitness valley between them (e.g., exploring truly unprofitable combinations of traits; Winterhalder and Kennett 2020). In particular, I am interested in social and cultural traits, including resource ownership, risk management, and social coordination, which may contribute more to the peaks' respective fitness values, and account for a greater portion of the valley's depth between them, than previously realized.

The transition from foraging to farming is one of the most enduringly contentious issues

in archaeology, and for good reason. Wherever it happened, the transition was revolutionary, changing not only subsistence and settlement regimes but many aspects of social organization as well, perhaps as a result of increased sedentism and accumulation of stored surplus, both of which have been linked to socioeconomic differentiation and political centralization (Angourakis et al. 2014; Diamond and Bellwood 2003; Winterhalder et al. 2015). It is telling that such an important milestone in the human career—a development likened by some to bipedalism, encephalization, and the evolution of tool use (Winterhalder and Kennett 2006)—remains incompletely understood despite decades of dedicated, innovative, and well-funded research. In some cases, available data are equivocal, and commonalities across cases are few and basic, precluding all but the most simplistic general explanations. Satisfying answers are elusive.

For reasons easily appreciated, most studies of the transition from foraging to farming examine details of incipient food production in a particular region or compare disparate regions as a means of triangulating on precipitating events in each case. I argue that we can also learn a lot about the process through counterfactuals, or prehistoric groups that did *not* transition to farming. Data and theory related to the relatively few world regions where this is true, particularly California (Bettinger 2015) and Australia (Bowles 2015), have been instructive, as I believe the Patagonian case to be as well.

The South American Agricultural Limit

At European contact (ca. 1550 CE), Patagonia's northern boundary (Figure 1.1 and Chapter 2) marked the southern limit of agriculture in South America. North of the Ríos Atuel and Diamante in Argentina and of Chonos Archipelago (coast) / Puerto Montt (mainland) in Chile, native populations' economies centered on farming, while all groups south of these points—that is, all Patagonians—were hunter-gatherers. Traditionally, the contact-period distribution of foragers and farmers has been assumed to reflect the prehistoric one: farming was never practiced south of the Atuel - Diamante/Chiloé/ Puerto Montt (e.g., Lagiglia 1978, 1999; see also Gil, Neme, Ugan, and Tykot 2014). In recent decades, though, new data and approaches have prompted reassessment of the traditional interpretation and sparked debate regarding the true South American agricultural limit, particularly on the Argentine side of the Andes.

The earliest evidence of domesticates at the hypothesized frontier in Argentina is roughly 2,000 years old. In the 1960s, macroremains of four cultigens—maize (*Zea mays*), beans (*Phaseolus* sp.), squash (*Cucurbita* sp.), and quinoa (*Chenopodium quinoa*)—were found in a burial context dated to between 2160 and 1960 cal BP at the Gruta del Indio site in central Mendoza Province (Gil et al. 2018; Lagiglia 1968). Other similarly aged examples have since been found in domestic contexts across the region (Gil et al. 2006; Llano 2011). Contemporaneous archaeological sites north of the Atuel - Diamante (i.e., in northern Mendoza) and into neighboring San Juan Province are associated with semisedentary farmers, as inferred from the widespread archaeological distribution of domesticated plant macroremains (particularly *Zea mays*). These sites also have more substantial residential features (pithouses) and a more elaborated ceramic technology than occurs farther south (Cortegoso 2006; Gambier 2000). For Humberto Lagiglia, an archaeological pioneer in Mendoza, these data summed to a clear picture of the South American agricultural limit: farmers from the north (via San Juan) moved into the Atuel Valley (and no farther; Figure 6.1) approximately 2,000 years ago, cultigens became increasingly important in subsequent centuries as small farming enclaves became corn-fed farming villages, and the pattern culminated in the agricultural Huarpe culture known ethnographically (see below; Lagiglia 1968, 1978, 1999; see also Bárcena 2001; Chiavazza and Cortegoso 2004). Perhaps not surprisingly, what is clear today is that the agricultural frontier is far more complex than Lagiglia's conception.

Firstly, since the initial discovery of agricultural products at Gruta del Indio, the prehistoric distribution of domesticated plant macroremains has been shown to extend not only south of the Atuel - Diamante into southern Mendoza but also into central Neuquén Province in Argentina (ca. 39° S) (Figure 6.1). Llano (2011) reports the regular, if sparse, occurrence of maize macroremains in late Holocene deposits along the flanks of Cerro Nevado in southern Mendoza (Llano and Ugan 2014). In central Neuquén, Lema and colleagues (2012) discovered maize microremains adhering to the surfaces of milling stones from the Michaheo site, which dates to circa 1750 cal BP.

These data confirm prehistoric familiarity with domesticates in at least some parts of Patagonia. Other lines of evidence, though, suggest these agricultural products were more likely acquired by hunter-gatherers through trade or raiding than grown locally. In southern Mendoza, for instance, the late Holocene archaeological record lacks evidence of storage and there are very few domestic structures of any kind, suggesting relatively high mobility, an interpretation largely supported by isotopic studies. One such study compared oxygen isotope values from the bone apatite of 71 human individuals recovered from archaeological contexts spanning the hypothesized agricultural limit (southern San Juan to southern Mendoza) and the last 6,000 years of prehistory (Gil, Neme, Ugan, and Tykot 2014). Oxygen isotope values preserved in human bone—particularly values of $\delta^{18}O$—reflect the values of this isotope present in drinking water consumed by an individual in life. Accordingly, the authors hypothesize that $\delta^{18}O$ values among individuals in their sample should reflect greater sedentism (increased interindividual variation in $\delta^{18}O$) at times and in places where farming was the predominant subsistence activity, namely the northern part of the study area in the last 2,000 years. According to their results, mobility remained high in the southern part of the study area even after maize and other domesticates appear in southern Mendozan archaeological records.

While the presence of domesticated plant macroremains is a clear indication of northern

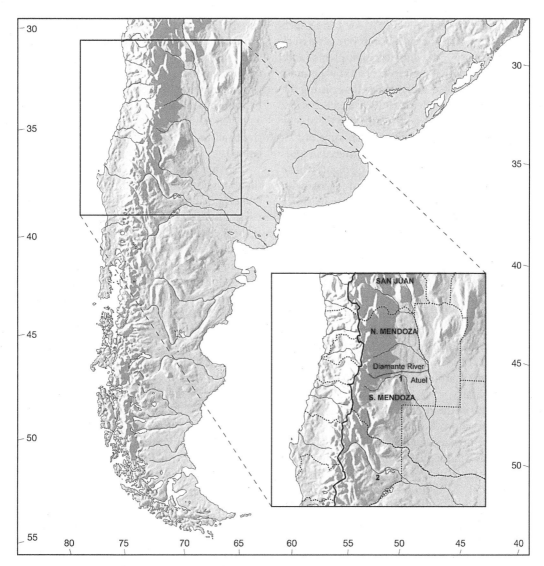

FIGURE 6.1. The hypothesized South American agricultural limit. At European contact, groups north of the Atuel and Diamante Rivers (inset) were farmers, while groups south of the river—including all of Patagonia—were foragers. This is the northern boundary of Patagonia as defined in this book (see Chapter 2). Sites mentioned in the text (inset): (1) Gruta del Indio, (2) Michacheo.

Patagonians' familiarity with these plants, it does not, in itself, provide a sense of their dietary importance in southern Mendoza. Estimating the relative contributions of domesticated versus wild plants to local diets could potentially clarify the southern agricultural limit. However, a series of isotopic studies with precisely this

goal has produced results that are equivocal and, at times, contradictory, owing to their respective skeletal samples and analytical techniques.

Plants have different photosynthetic pathways—3-phosphoglyceric acid (C3), Hatch-Slack (C4), and crassulacean acid metabolism (CAM)—and these discriminate against atmospheric ^{13}C to greater or lesser degree, such that values of δ^{13}C registered in human tissues can give a sense of which types of plants (and/ or herbivores that ate those plants) were most prevalent in tested individuals' diets during the final years of their lives (Hobson and Schwarcz 1986). Most (~85%) wild plants use C_3 photosynthesis, the pathway least permissive of ^{13}C, which means that δ^{13}C values registered in individuals who habitually eat wild C_3 plants will be low relative to those who consume plants with other photosynthetic pathways, particularly C_4 plants. C_4 plants are more permissive of ^{13}C and individuals who consume these will have enriched δ^{13}C values. Maize is one of very few economically important C_4 plants in southern South America, so relatively high δ^{13}C values in human samples are frequently interpreted in terms of maize consumption (Llano and Ugan 2014; Schwarcz 2006). CAM plants' ^{13}C values are intermediate between C_3 and C_4 which, as we shall see in a moment, has led to some confusion regarding the South American agricultural limit.

In one of the region's first isotopic studies, Novellino and colleagues (2004) assessed carbon signatures and dental health among approximately 200 individuals from burial contexts located across Mendoza and Neuquén Provinces (~32° to 40° S) dating to the last 3,000 years. Their broad sampling strategy was designed to capture any changes in carbon enrichment (i.e., consumption of corn) and frequencies of dental caries at the presumed agricultural transition (ca. 2,000 years ago) in the northern part of the study area, while simultaneously providing a foraging-only baseline population from the south, beyond the hypothesized agricultural limit. As predicted, they found a north-south clinal decrease in both the contribution of C_4 plants (corn or animals that ate wild C_4 plants) and frequency of carious lesions. Interestingly, though, they also report a minimal C_4 contribution even among the most northerly populations, who were presumably maize farmers by circa 2000 cal BP (Lagiglia 1968, 1978, 1999). In fact, the oxygen isotope study described

above (Gil, Neme, Ugan, and Tykot 2014) also indicates high mobility in northern Mendoza and southern San Juan throughout the late Holocene. Together, these lines of evidence suggest that farming might not have been as widespread or routine a subsistence strategy in that region as is generally assumed, or that some alternative to all-or-nothing farming was practiced (see below).

Further complicating our understanding of the southern agricultural limit, a different study by Gil and colleagues (2011) found considerable variability in the δ^{13}C values of more than 100 skeletal samples from across Mendoza. Most had relatively low values (consistent with wild plant consumption), but a small number of individuals, notably people buried in northern Mendoza within the last 1,000 years, had elevated values. Additionally, the authors reported discrepancies in the δ^{13}C values recorded in different constituents of bone and in tooth enamel within most tested individuals, which suggests high dietary variability over people's lifespans. From these results, they concluded that maize was unlikely ever to have been a staple in the region, but that some people consumed large amounts of it during some periods of their lives, perhaps reflecting the social or symbolic significance of maize, rather than its role in subsistence.

In response, Llano and Ugan (2014) made the astute observation that consumption of CAM plants, whose ^{13}C values are intermediate between those of C_3 and C_4 plants, can produce isotopic signatures in human tissues that mimic those of mixed C_3 (wild plant) / C_4 (maize) diets. Llano and Ugan show that several varieties of cactus (*Cereus aethiops, Opuntia sulphurea, Maihueniopsis darwinii* var. *hickenii*, and *Pterocactus tuberosus*) have ^{13}C values that overlap those of C_4 plants. These species grow readily in Mendoza and have high energetic returns, and there is evidence of their ethnographic and prehistoric consumption. This raises the possibility that the carbon isotopic signatures of people whose diets were rich in CAM plants such as these cacti would resemble those of people who ate mixed C_3/C_4 diets. Therefore, rather than a primarily wild-food diet supplemented to greater or lesser degree with maize, people across Mendoza—including those northern Mendozans and southern Sanjuanense previously believed to be eating significant amounts of maize—might, in fact, have been eating an almost-exclusively wild diet rich in CAM plants.

Still more recently, Bernal and colleagues (2016) identified a potential weakness common to all of the isotopic studies cited to this point: their reliance on univariate analyses of individuals' signatures relative to a single fractionation value (e.g., δ^{13}C enrichment) for each potential food resource. The authors note that this approach "cannot accurately identify dietary contributions when more than one potential resource is available and ... does not take into account uncertainty and variation in trophic fractionation and isotopic values" (Bernal et al. 2016:230; Layman et al. 2012). As an alternative, they offer a multivariate, Bayesian mixing model that allows the simultaneous estimation of multiple potential food resources in individuals' diets and provides probability distributions for each resource, indicating the most likely proportional contribution of each. By this method, Bernal and colleagues show that the diets of 97 individuals from across Mendoza had isotopic signatures most consistent with a diet centered on animals and C₃ plants, with these two resources in roughly equal proportions south of (approximately) the Diamante River. To the north, animals are the primary resource represented, followed by C₃ plants. Between 1300 and 200 cal BP, maize may have constituted approximately 25% of some individuals' diets. This is at variance with previous studies that suggest maize constituted up to 50% of some northern Mendozans' diets (Gil et al. 2011). Lastly, while they acknowledge the importance of Llano and Ugan's discussion of CAM plants, Bernal and colleagues find that cacti were not a significant component of tested Mendozans' diets.

The picture of the South American agricultural limit that emerges from the evidence described above can be summarized in this way: (1) Archaeological and isotopic data consistently support the hypothesis that people south of Ríos Atuel and Diamante in Mendoza—that is, Patagonians—were mobile hunter-gatherers throughout prehistory. (2) However, recent archaeological finds push the distribution of agricultural products (domesticated plant macroremains) south from the previously understood limit in central Mendoza to at least central Neuquén (ca. 39° S). Importantly, too, I add that much of Río Negro Province, with the exception of the extensively studied coast, is virtually unknown archaeologically (Figure 2.19). In light of the recent finds in Neuquén, it is conceivable that people were familiar with agricultural products across more of Patagonia than we currently appreciate. (3) Archaeological and isotopic evidence appear to be at odds in northern Mendoza/southern San Juan, the area previously believed to have been inhabited by farmers since roughly 2000 cal BP. Pithouses and elaborate ceramic industries typically interpreted as evidence of increased sedentism (cf. Eerkens 2003, 2008 and Morgan et al. 2018) consistent with "place-based" farming (family plots owned and intensively farmed) are reported, while oxygen and carbon isotopes from the region suggest both high mobility and predominant reliance on wild plants and animals. It is possible that northern Mendozans / southern Sanjuanense *were* farmers as early as 2,000 years ago, but rather than place-based, maize-dominated farming, they practiced shifting cultivation, whereby plots are cultivated only temporarily, for two or a few years, and then left fallow while the soil recuperates. There would be sufficient impetus to invest in more permanent house structures (and ceramics) under this system, but lifetime mobility would remain high as farmers moved from plot to plot. In many such precolumbian systems of shifting agriculture, maize was only one of many species planted together in a plot, a strategy that might have been particularly beneficial to *farmers nouveau*, buffering against loss of any particular crop as people learned and manipulated each crop's tolerances. Individuals with particularly enriched δ^{13}C signatures, then, might just be those farmers (among farmers) living in places where maize grew well, rather than being *the* farmers amid foragers. This, of course, is a matter for future study.

What also emerges from available data is an appreciation of the difference between the southern limit of agriculture and the southern limit of agricultural influence. Farming for oneself and acquiring, by one means or another, relatively small amounts of farm products are clearly very different enterprises. It is easy to dismiss farm product acquisition as a relatively low-cost, low-risk pursuit, particularly compared to farming itself; the small number of macroremains and infrequency of maize consumption evident in isotope signatures rule out reliance on maize for survival south of the Atuel - Diamante. However, if the Atuel - Diamante truly was the southern limit of agricultural production, the maize kernels found in Neuquén, for example, traveled at least 400 km; if southern San Juan was the limit, they traveled over 700 km. The long-distance transport of maize implies its great value, if not for subsistence perhaps for reasons better described as social or ritual. Generating trade goods of equivalent value and/or traveling great distances to acquire maize almost certainly required adjustments to existing foraging strategies that, while not likely on par with the adjustments required by the transition from foraging to farming, might nonetheless have been substantial. For example, animals hunted for trade hold different value than those hunted for consumption, at least in the sense that returns are converted to another currency (e.g., kcals protein native to the meat converted to kcals carbohydrates in the plants traded for). Utility of particular animal parts may also change, and trade can incentivize pursuit of resources previously ignored, whether as the trade goods themselves or to replace resources previously consumed but now traded away. Meat transported long distances must be processed to deter rot, further changing the foraging calculus. Nearer the actual agricultural limit, if maize was acquired through raiding rather than trade, this would have involved a host of other costs that might have affected foraging indirectly (e.g., risk of retaliation and

loss of prime-aged hunters, who generally contribute more to group provisioning than they consume; Kaplan et al. 2000).

Assuming that farm product acquisition was always a low-cost, low-risk pursuit, we run the risk of misinterpreting archaeological records, mistaking behavioral changes associated with trade for ones associated with in situ changes in resource availability or need. While farm products may not have contributed significantly to Patagonian diets, our understanding of Patagonian records will be improved by a better understanding of both the geographical extent of agricultural production *and* that of agricultural influence. And the question remains: If maize retained its value 700 km (or more) from where it was grown, why would Patagonian groups not have produced it locally?

Why Didn't Patagonians Farm?: Ecological Explanations

As described in this chapter's introduction, the presumed answer distills to simple economics: either (1) farming was impossible across most of Patagonia and hugely unprofitable anywhere it could be done, due to low temperatures, insufficient rain, thin or rocky soils, steep slopes, or scheduling conflicts with preferred wild foods; or (2) wild foods were sufficient to feed Patagonia's small population, so the higher average caloric yields per unit land associated with farming simply were not worth the extra investment. Although the previous section alludes to a more complicated reality, it is worth probing these historical assumptions first.

Patagonians Didn't Farm Because the Environment Wouldn't Permit It

For nearly every world region where people "failed" to develop or adopt the practice, it is commonly assumed that traditional farming was simply impossible. Glancing at a map of the premodern distribution of farming (e.g., Figure 1 and discussion in Diamond and Bellwood 2003) could certainly leave one with that impression; by about 2,000 years ago, people were farming most everywhere except Alaska, northern Canada, Mongolia, Russia, Patagonia, southern Africa, and Australia, all places characterized by deserts and/or short growing seasons. When we approach the issue scientifically, however, we immediately recognize the danger in concluding that, because *x* did not happen, *x* was not possible. Moreover, when we approach the issue historically, we see that this perspective—well summarized by its converse, "show me arable land and I will show you a farmer"— is rooted in age-old assumptions of agriculture's inherent superiority.

Progressive social evolutionists (e.g., Morgan 1877) saw farming as one of humanity's crowning achievements. The catalyst to "civilization," agriculture freed people from the toils and tedium of gathering food, allowing them to produce it on their own terms, thereby making room for the pursuit of art, literature, science, and industry. Traces of this sentiment can still be seen in discussions of the transition from foraging to food production. Diamond and Bellwood argue, for example, that "food production conferred enormous advantages to farmers compared with hunter-gatherers," citing (1) agriculture's higher yields per unit land and the higher population densities this supports; (2) sedentism, which permits the accumulation of surplus, itself "a prerequisite for the development of complex technology, social stratification, centralized states, and professional armies"; and (3) as a byproduct of living in large, permanent settlements, the development of resistance to epidemic infectious diseases, the lack of such immunity having led to the downfall of many hunter-gatherer groups (Diamond and Bellwood 2003:597). All three facilitate the spread of farming at the expense of foraging (the authors' main point) but otherwise, only the third "advantage" is self-evident: from the group's perspective, fewer people lost to epidemics is generally a good thing. Certainly we can identify benefits of the other two. In addition to its role in improved disease immunity, high population densities have been linked to increased technological complexity (Chapter 3; contra Diamond and Bellwood's assertion that

such complexity follows only from food surplus), and professional armies offer greater protection against outside aggression. But the inherent goodness of social stratification, centralized states, and dense populations has long been a subject of debate (e.g., Marx 1967, 1977; Marx and Engels 1967).

Diamond and Bellwood's thesis, namely that farming readily outcompetes foraging, fuels the sister notion that anywhere foragers were found in the "ethnographic present" must surely be land marginal for agriculture. Or, put another way, the distribution of farmers relative to hunter-gatherers circa 1500 CE is a fairly accurate representation of the distribution of productive versus marginal habitats, respectively (e.g., Lee and DeVore 1968; Porter and Marlowe 2007). It is telling that, nearly a decade into the twenty-first century—and a full century after Boas and his students vehemently rejected progressive, unilineal social evolution, ushering in a new era of anthropological research (e.g., Boas 1896)—Porter and Marlowe (2007) felt compelled to question the presumed marginality of hunter-gatherer habitats. They argue that, if Earth's most productive habitats were acquired by agriculturalists, the average productivity of habitats occupied by foragers and farmers should differ significantly, in favor of farmers. Using the Standard Cross Cultural Sample (Murdock and White 1969) and algorithmically adjusted satellite spectral imaging data to estimate net primary productivity (a measure of habitat quality), the authors found that not only are the habitats of foragers across the globe roughly equivalent to those of farmers, but that, in warmer climates (effective temperature ≥ 13), foragers' habitats are actually slightly *more* productive than those of farmers. Granting the limitations of primary productivity as a measure of habitat quality (Chapters 3 and 7), and that some foraging groups indeed live in resource poor environments, Porter and Marlowe's study makes the important point that, in any given case, we would do well to demonstrate habitat quality empirically rather than arguing, often in circular fashion, that "no farming equals marginal habitat."

If some ethnographic foragers lived in habitats that are as productive or more so than some farmers', it follows that foraging sometimes persisted under farming-favorable environmental conditions. Bowles (2015) shows, for example, that large areas along Australia's northern and eastern coasts were suitable for rain-fed cultivation of millet, sorghum, wheat, and sweet potato, yet Australia remained a "continent of hunter-gatherers" until farming was introduced in the late eighteenth century (Lourandos 1997). Importantly, too, some places occupied by hunter-gatherers during the ethnographic period had in fact been farmed in the preceding centuries. This was true across much of the western United States, where the "reversion" to hunting and gathering was not a failure of farming per se but due to the competitive superiority of intensive foraging (Bettinger 2015). Assuming the marginality of foragers' habitats a priori, we risk gross misunderstandings of both these regions' cultural histories, and humans' adaptive capacities more generally.

Parts of the Patagonian steppe are characterized by low annual precipitation (200 mm or less) and apparently small human populations throughout prehistory (Chapter 2). Assuming this region was marginal for agriculture might seem more reasonable than assuming the same of coastal Australia or California, where hunting and gathering also persisted prehistorically but where, today, farming is economically important. However, large areas of Patagonia were in fact suitable for growing modern varieties of staple crops that were central to the precolumbian farming system in the Andes, including maize, common beans (*Phaseolus vulgaris*), and white potatoes (*Solanum tuberosum*; IIASA/FAO 2010), as I describe in the following section. As in Australia and the western U.S., then, foraging probably persisted in Patagonia for reasons other than environmental marginality.

Farming Was Possible in Patagonia

To this point, our discussion of southern South American agriculture has centered on maize, and for good reason. Maize was domesticated in central Mexico at least 9,000 years ago (Piperno et al. 2009) and spread across much of North and South America in subsequent millennia, becoming the backbone of precolumbian agricultural systems and feeding major New World civilizations (e.g., Inca, Maya, Aztec, Mississippian). It has high food value and, in many instances, high social value as well (D'Altroy 2003; McEwan 2006). For both reasons, maize cultivation profoundly influenced New World prehistory (Bettinger 2015). Maize's influence extended into Patagonia, as I have argued, and although it appears not to have been grown there, it could have been.

Suitability of Maize

According to the Food and Agriculture Organization's (United Nations) Global Agro-Ecological Zones (GAEZ) database (IIASA/FAO 2010), Patagonia's maize-suitable areas extend to approximately 48° S, primarily along Argentina's major rivers (Figure 6.2). Specifically, the middle courses of the Atuel, Grande, Colorado, and Negro rivers (Mendoza and Neuquén Provinces), and a small section of the middle Chubut are characterized by moderate to marginal suitability for maize agriculture. Lower stretches of river valleys as far south as southern Santa Cruz Province, including Río Chico (Chubut) and a portion of the lower Río Deseado, are considered marginal to very marginal (see Table 6.1 for definitions). Granting the relatively low suitability of many of these places, maize farming is nonetheless possible at subsistence levels (i.e., with minimal surplus) even when input is "low" (e.g., rain-only irrigation, traditional land and crop management using labor intensive techniques, no application of fertilizers or pesticides).

Importantly, the GAEZ models probably under-identify lands suitable for maize farming for a number of reasons. Firstly, five arc-minute resolution, while an impressively fine grain for a global-scale evaluation of cropland suitability, necessarily averages key variables (e.g., temperature, rainfall, slope) across units of land much larger than would have been relevant to individual subsistence farmers during prehistory.

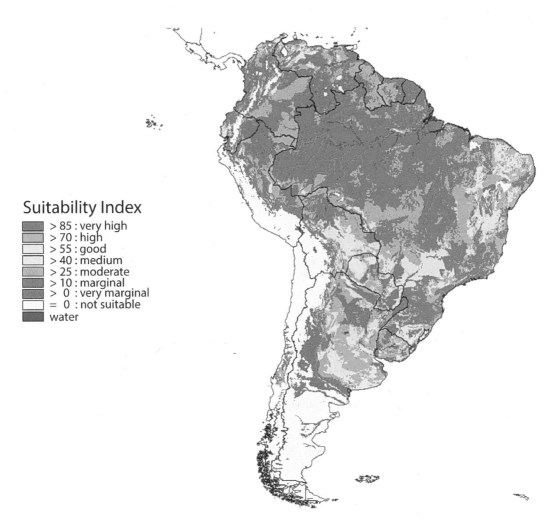

FIGURE 6.2. Suitability of maize (*Zea mays*) farming at five arc-minute resolution. Results of a model that includes local temperature, precipitation, soil type and quality, terrain (rockiness and slope), pests and crop diseases, and assumes rain-fed irrigation and "low" input (traditional land and crop management using labor-intensive techniques, no application of fertilizers or pesticides). Input data on which the model is based is for average climatic conditions for the period 1961–1990. Data and output from GAEZ (IIASA/FAO 2010).

As we saw in Chapter 2, Patagonia is characterized by tremendous variability at multiple scales; small differences in elevation, exposure, and aspect can have significant effects on temperature and water availability, so the grain of the GAEZ analysis is likely masking important within-grid-cell variability. Local suitability may have far exceeded "averaged" suitability within any particular grid-cell, and would-be farmers in prehistoric Patagonia might well have found places suitable for maize farming beyond those indicated in the GAEZ database.

We know, too, that prehistoric Andean farmers were incredibly enterprising: They engineered landscapes to increase productivity and to make naturally unsuitable lands arable. Inca terrace systems are a prime example of water management (Guillet 1987). Many groups, including the ethnographic Huarpe of northern Mendoza and southern San Juan (Canals Frau

TABLE 6.1. Crop suitability index.

suitability index[a]	% of maximum attainable yield[b]
very high	85.1–100
high	70.1–85
good	55.1–70
medium	40.1–55
moderate	25.1–40
marginal	10.1–25
very marginal	0.1–10

Data in Figures 6.2–6.4 are presented in 5 arc-minute resolution and the suitability of a given grid cell is determined by the range within which it falls.

[a]LUT-specific suitability is calculated according to local precipitation and temperature trends, soil type and quality, terrain (rockiness and slope), known pests, and crop diseases.

[b]Maximum attainable yield is the expected yield for a particular crop under best practices for the specified land utilization type (LUT; i.e., crop, water supply, input level, and time period).

1963; Damiani and García 2011; Ponte 2006), offset low rainfall by diverting rivers through extensive canal systems. Raised beds simultaneously managed water and surface temperatures; Erickson (1988; Erickson and Candler 1989) explains that constructing raised beds on the shores of Lake Titicaca, for example, takes advantage of heat stored by the lake during the day, which reduces overnight losses to frost. So, again, the GAEZ projections are conservative, since they do not account for this type of traditional water and temperature augmentation (or the conversion of steep slopes to arable land, etc.), which likely explains why places we know to have been under maize cultivation around the time of European contact are listed as unsuitable in the database (e.g., southern San Juan Province).

Lastly, the GAEZ projections are based on modern commercial strains of maize that may not be good proxies for prehistoric varieties. Across the Western Hemisphere, maize farmers developed landraces particularly suited to local conditions (e.g., Merrill et al. 2009). Some were tolerant of heat and restricted moisture, others well-adapted to cool climates and short growing seasons. The particular strains of maize

cultivated just north and west of Patagonia were likely better suited to growing conditions in Patagonia than are modern commercial varieties, which themselves have been tailored to conditions in the world's key production areas.

By this combination of maize's high adaptability and native groups' ingenious farming methods, maize farming spread north and south from central Mexico across much of the Americas, and new evidence continues to expand its known distribution. Boyd and Surette (2010) recently published evidence of maize as far north as the Subarctic boreal forests of Manitoba and Ontario, Canada (ca. 50° N) by 500 CE, and the authors tentatively acknowledge the possibility of its having been grown locally (Boyd et al. 2008). This latitude is equivalent to Río Santa Cruz, Santa Cruz Province, Argentina and Isla Tarlton, northern Magallanes, Chile and, while the spread of maize across the Northern Hemisphere may have no bearing whatsoever on its spread through the Southern Hemisphere, the North American distribution is nonetheless instructive. It is also fascinating to think how different North American prehistory might have been had maize spread no farther north than it did south (roughly 35° S). In that case, maize agriculture would have been held south of a line between roughly Phoenix, Arizona, and Atlanta, Georgia. All but the southernmost parts of North America would have been without it, including the Four Corners region (37° N) where we know maize to have been the lifeblood of the ancestral Puebloans, and central Illinois, where corn fed the major Mississippian urban center at Cahokia (~38.5° N).

Maize was indeed a game-changer. However, it is worth noting that it was not only the most economically and socially important New World domesticate, it is the most archaeologically visible as well, owing in part to the durability and identifiability of cobs relative to fleshier and less familiar plants, and perhaps also to the long history of its study (i.e., potential research bias). Maize is also one of very few economically important C_4 plants in southern South America, which makes it "visible" in human bone even when plant macroremains are not present in archaeological records. It is possible that other Andean staples spread independently of maize and perhaps beyond maize's known distribution, so it is worth exploring Patagonia's suitability for these crops as well.

Patagonia's Suitability for Other Key Domesticates

Among the domesticated plant macroremains found at the Gruta del Indio site on the hypothesized agricultural frontier (ca. 2000 cal BP) is *Phaseolus* sp. The species is most likely common bean (*P. vulgaris*), which has an independent center of domestication in northern Argentina / southern Bolivia (Bitocchi et al. 2013) and which was another staple of Andean agriculture. In fact, beans often traveled as part of the "milpa" or "three sisters" cropping system, which was centered on maize, beans, and squash (Mann 2005). Like corn, *Phaseolus* sp. has undergone significant regional diversification (Brücher 1988), and varieties have been developed to suit growing conditions on every continent except Antarctica (FAO 2018).

Patagonia's suitability for rain-fed, low-input *Phaseolus vulgaris* is wider-spread than that for maize. Large areas south to approximately 37° S (Río Deseado area) are at least marginal, and beans could be grown at subsistence levels as far south as southern Santa Cruz Province, Argentina (Figure 6.3). More specifically, with the exception of the Andes, much of the land between central Mendoza to the Río Negro-Chubut boundary in Argentina is characterized by marginal to moderate suitability, with pockets of medium and even good suitability in the more northern Andean foothills. Between the Río Chubut and Río Chico (Chubut) is another patch of marginally to moderately suitable land, again punctuated with medium and good parcels. Similar latitudes in Chile are dotted with land marginally good for beans, and the lower stretches of Argentina's major rivers as far south as Río Chico (Santa Cruz), ca. 50° S, are considered very marginal.

For reasons similar to those cited for maize (i.e., grid-cell averaging, farmers' ingenuity, local landraces), it is likely that more places

than are indicated by the GAEZ models would have been suitable for bean cultivation in Patagonia. As we will see in a later section (*The private property problem*), some Patagonian groups were clearly familiar with wild members of the Fabaceae family—of which *Phaseolus* is a member genus—and some genera (e.g., *Prosopis*; common name *algarrobo*, a legume similar to mesquite) may even have been dietary staples in northern Patagonia. Hypothetically, given the greater suitability of Patagonian lands for beans relative to maize and foragers' familiarity with parallel species to *Phaseolus*, bean-centered farming could have been more adoptable in Patagonia than maize farming, unless of course the two travelled as a package, as they seem to have in other times and places. We will return to this point in this chapter's conclusion.

Like beans, tubers were part of the prehistoric Patagonian diet, in at least some subregions (Llano and Ugan 2014), and may well have been in others, though poor preservation limits our understanding of their use (Rumold and Aldenderfer 2016). Potatoes (*Solanaceae* sect. *Petota*) were domesticated in the Andean highlands, though it is not entirely clear when, again on account of poor preservation. Rumold and Aldenderfer (2016) present some of the earliest evidence of potato remains in archaeological context, dating to approximately 5500 cal BP, yet whether the remains derive from domesticated or wild potatoes is unknown. Wild varieties were likely in use long before domesticates emerged. The modern distribution of wild *Solanaceae* extends to roughly 41° S in Argentina, including relatively rare low-elevation species found across the plains and foothills (Hijmans and Spooner 2001; over 90% of all wild potato species grow at elevations above 1,750 m).

The GAEZ database indicates that the distribution of potato suitability is similar to that of the common bean, extending across much of Patagonia south to Río Deseado, primarily at marginal levels (Figure 6.4). The potato suitability distribution is broader and more continuous, though, extending into the Andes, where suitability is medium to good, and out onto the Guaitecas and Chonos Archipelagos. Potato

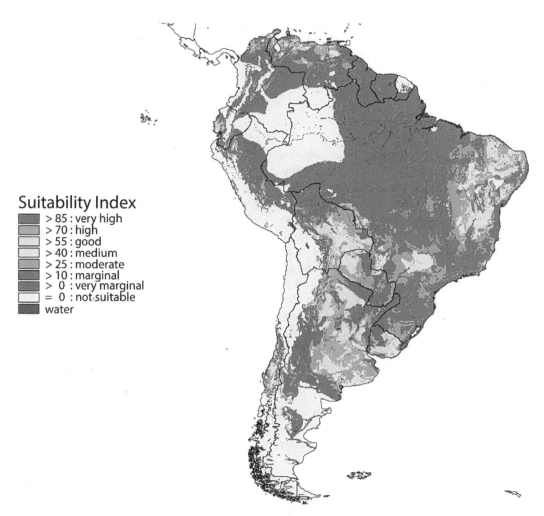

FIGURE 6.3. Suitability of common bean (*Phaseolus vulgaris*) farming at five arc-minute resolution. Results of a model that includes local temperature, precipitation, soil type and quality, terrain (rockiness and slope), pests and crop diseases, and assumes rain-fed irrigation and "low" input (traditional land and crop management using labor-intensive techniques, no application of fertilizers or pesticides). Input data on which the model is based is for average climatic conditions for the period 1961–1990. Data and output from GAEZ (IIASA/FAO 2010).

suitability is generally better across the steppe than bean suitability (it is high even in Andean southern Chubut) though river valleys do not extend potato suitability into southern Santa Cruz as they do for beans.

There are a whole host of other plants domesticated in the Andean highlands that have wild counterparts in Patagonia. None of these is included in the GAEZ database, so I cannot provide detailed accounts of places where their cultivation might have been profitable prehistorically. The three domesticates we have covered, though, make clear that, in Patagonia, (1) foraging persisted even under farming-favorable conditions, and (2) parallel species to staples cultivated in the central and northern Andes grew wild in Patagonia. In the next section, we will consider whether it was the abundance of these and other wild foods, then, that deterred the spread of farming in this region.

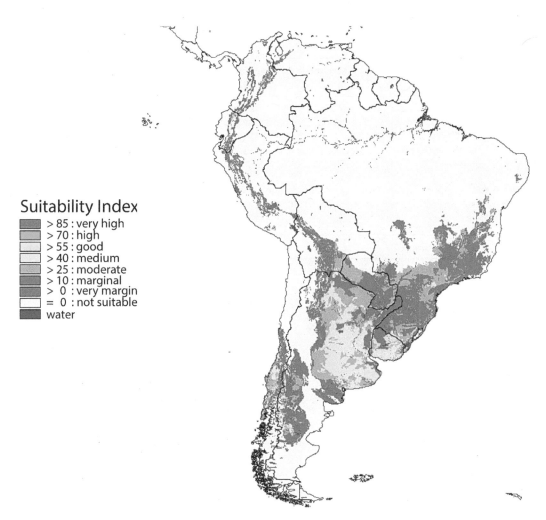

FIGURE 6.4. Suitability of potato (*Solanum tuberosum*) farming at five arc-minute resolution. Results of a model that includes local temperature, precipitation, soil type and quality, terrain (rockiness and slope), pests and crop diseases, and assumes rain-fed irrigation and "low" input (traditional land and crop management using labor-intensive techniques, no application of fertilizers or pesticides). Input data on which the model is based is for aver-age climatic conditions for the period 1961–1990. Data and output from GAEZ (IIASA/FAO 2010).

Patagonians Didn't Farm Because They Didn't Need To

In a sense, the farming impossible/farming unnecessary dichotomy hinges on carrying capacity. If foragers did not farm simply because the environment would not permit it, the implication is that farming would otherwise have been beneficial, which is to say Patagonian populations were hovering around carrying capacity, sometimes exceeding it. In these instances, groups would have experienced resource shortfalls, and the ability to increase the land's productivity through farming would have provided an adaptive advantage. If, instead, foragers did not farm because they did not need to, the implication is that Patagonian populations remained at or even below carrying capacity (see Chapter 7), their needs readily met by available wild resources. Under this scenario,

TABLE 6.2. Comparison of the Patagonian and Wyoming-Colorado (Zahid et al. 2016) databases. Both include data from the last 15,000 years.

	total dates in database	land area km²	dates per km²	dates per year[a]
Wyoming-Colorado	7,900	524,000	0.02	0.53
Patagonia	1,840	1,000,000	0.002	0.12

[a]Total number of dates in the database divided by the number of years represented by the respective databases.

TABLE 6.3. Ethnographic groups falling within the territory considered in the Wyoming-Colorado and Patagonian databases, respectively; two other groups (Noatak Inuit and Karadjeri of Western Australia) included for comparison.

State	Group	C/I[a]	Lat[b]	Long[b]	PP[c]	Pop[d]	Density[e]
Colorado	Antarianunt Southern Paiute	I	38	−111	1434	234	0.03
Colorado	Cheyenne	I	39	−102	6532	2,750	0.05
Colorado	Arapahoe	I	40	−103	7278	3,000	0.08
Wyoming	Crow	I	46	−108	4537	4,650	0.06
Wyoming	Wind River Shoshoni	I	43	−109	4815	1,500	0.02
Argentina	Tehuelche	I	−46	−69	1323	9,000	0.02
Argentina	Selk'nam (Ona)	I/C	−54	−69	8600	3,497	0.07
Argentina	Yámana (Yaghan)	C	−60	−69	10604	2,500	0.28
Chile	Káwesqar (Alacaluf)	C	−50	−75	33546	3,400	0.15
Chile	Chono	C	−45	−74	34098	2,100	0.14
Western Australia	Karadjeri	I	−19	121	1302	536	0.04

All data are from Binford (2001).

[a]Coastal (C) or inland (I).

[b]Lat = latitude; Long = longitude.

[c]Primary productivity (g/m²/yr).

[d]Total population or "ethnic unit size" (Binford 2001)

[e]Population density (number of people/100 km²).

human populations were small, or wild resources were abundant. Of course, both could be true but, as it turns out, it is not clear that *either* is a fair characterization of prehistoric Patagonia.

Evidence of Small Populations and Abundant Wild Resources

The notable scarcity of dated archaeological contexts in Patagonia relative to the region's size and length of occupation suggests it was sparsely populated throughout the Holocene, a point best illustrated through comparison. The radiocarbon database I refer to throughout

this book includes 1,840 dates from across Patagonia's one million square kilometers and the period between ~15,000 cal BP and European contact. In their recent exploration of human population growth in the western United States, Zahid and colleagues (2016) describe a database nearly four times larger for a land area half the size (Table 6.2). Zahid and colleagues' database of 7,900 dates from the last 15,000 years in Wyoming and Colorado (~524,000 km²) equates to approximately 0.02 dates-per-km², and an average of approximately 0.53 dates-per-year since colonization. In contrast, Patagonian dates-per-km² and dates-per-year are vanishingly small

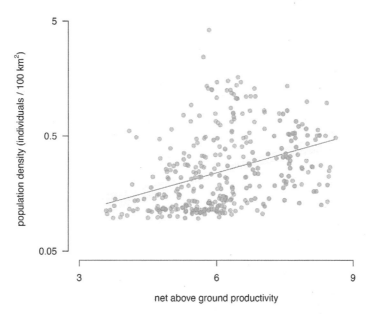

FIGURE 6.5. Relationship between population density (individuals/100 km²) and net primary productivity. Blue points indicate foraging groups above the equator; orange points indicate those below. Population density is significantly positively correlated with the log of net primary productivity (linear model, $\beta_{NPP} \pm SE = 0.26 \pm 0.04$; n = 339 sites; $R^2 = 0.14$; $p < 1.7 \times 10^{-12}$). Line and shading depict mean predicted values and 95% confidence intervals. Data from Binford (2001).

(0.002 and 0.12, respectively). Granting the simplicity of this comparison, the implication is that the prehistoric Patagonian population was quite small (but see below and Chapter 7).

The ethnographic homelands of native groups in Wyoming and Colorado are, on average, three times more productive than those of terrestrial Patagonians (Table 6.3). We might infer, then, that the higher population densities indicated in this analysis of the Wyoming Colorado database are related to greater food availability. In fact, primary productivity on the Patagonian steppe, which constitutes approximately two-thirds of the subcontinent's area, more closely resembles that of the ethnographic homelands of Alaska's Noatak Inuit and the Karadjeri of western Australia (Binford 2001), whose population densities are similar to that of the steppe-dwelling Tehuelche.

Among ecologists, primary productivity is a key indicator of ecosystem function, or "the

capacity for natural processes . . . to provide goods and services, which ultimately meet human needs, either directly or indirectly" (de Groot et al. 2002; Zhang and Wang 2012:230). So, all else equal, places with higher primary productivity should be able to support more people than places where primary productivity is low. However, the macroecological analyses presented in Chapter 3 show that, in a global-level sample of ethnographic groups, the relationship between primary productivity and population density is actually quite low ($R^2 = 0.27$; Figure 6.5; Binford 2001). Probing more deeply, we see that the steppe-dwelling Tehuelche not only lived at a population density nearly identical to those of two Wyoming-Colorado groups whose lands were more productive, but the Tehuelche also lived at densities higher than predicted by the relationship documented in Figure 6.5.

This may be due in part to the Patagonia's ability to support very large herds of herbivores.

Historically, there were over 20 million head of sheep in Patagonia (ca. 1950 CE) and, today, large commercial sheep farming operations on the steppe keep individual flocks larger than 6,000 head on continuously grazed paddocks (Cibilis and Borrelli 2019). Not surprisingly, these and the interspersed smaller farms (between 6,000 and 1,000 head)—as well as generally smaller herds of goats and cattle—have displaced Patagonia's native fauna, particularly guanaco.

Bonavia and Monge (2008) estimate that, before the introduction of domesticated livestock, overhunting, and habitat destruction that began with the nineteenth-century arrival of European settlers, guanaco may have numbered in the tens of millions. Projecting back farther than this is difficult but, given guanacos' drought tolerance, generalist feeding habits, water- and energy-efficient metabolisms, and overall behavioral flexibility (Bonavia and Monge 2008; Raedeke and Simonetti 1988), it is likely their numbers were high prehistorically as well. This bears out in many of Patagonia's archaeological records, which indicate sustained hunting of guanaco throughout the Holocene, at times to the apparent exclusion of all other taxa (Chapters 4 and 5).

Chapter 2 describes the wide variety of animals and plants available across Patagonia, from a range of other drought-tolerant animals and plants on the steppe, to seasonal and pulsed resources in the forests, to the maritime and littoral bounty available on the coasts. If these resources were sometimes foregone, as the record suggests, the implication would be that guanaco were so abundant relative to human populations, there was no need to supplement the diet with species that might have required different technologies (e.g., nets, bows and arrows) that were either unavailable or not worth the production costs (Bettinger et al. 2006). This would suggest, further, that prehistoric Patagonians never turned to food production because foraging returns remained high throughout prehistory, making unnecessary the increased Kcal per unit land generally associated with farming. However, the archaeological record does not align perfectly with this hypothesis either.

At Least Some Patagonian Groups Would Have Benefited from Farming

The Patagonian resource base, if variable across the region, was abundant and reliable in many places. So abundant and reliable, in fact, that wild resources were sufficient to sustain healthy, *growing* human populations.

Evidence that Patagonian Populations Were Not Small

Patagonian populations were likely larger than indicated by the radiocarbon database described above. As many archaeologists have explained, the relationship between radiocarbon date frequencies and human population size/density is not straightforward in most cases (Contreras and Meadows 2014; Crombé and Robinson 2014; Freeman et al. 2018; Hiscock and Attenbrow 2016; Rhode et al. 2014; Steele 2010; Timpson et al. 2014). Taphonomy and research biases are common causes for concern and both have affected the Patagonian archaeological record (Chapters 4 and 5).

Figures 2.19 and 2.20 show large geographic gaps in the distribution of Patagonia's radiocarbon dates. Prehistoric human activity probably accounts for some amount of this patchiness; people do not generally distribute themselves uniformly across a landscape, and some parts of Patagonia were likely used more extensively than others. However, it is also true that the distribution of dates reflects differences in research intensity (see also Chapters 2, 4, and 5). Patagonia is a big place, much of it difficult to access, which limits opportunities for systematic survey. Where possible, though, systematic survey has dramatically increased the number of known archaeological sites (see Chapter 5 and Garvey 2012a, 2015b, 2020; Garvey and Bettinger 2018), and is very likely that the Patagonian dates database will grow to fill these gaps.

The Patagonian database also reflects taphonomic biases, described in detail in previous chapters (especially 2 and 5). While systematic survey might fill in some data gaps, we may never know the full extent to which landscape dynamics have shaped Patagonia's archaeological record. Nonetheless, calibrating our expectations in light of potential losses to natural processes and continuing to incorporate systematic survey and alternative dating techniques, we are likely to find archaeological representation in Patagonia comparable to that of ecologically similar regions, such as Wyoming-Colorado (see above, and Zahid et al. 2016). So, while the Patagonian record, expressed in terms of dates-per-km² or dates-per-year-since-colonization, gives the impression of a vanishingly small population, it is more likely that, in fact, the population was not only larger than we think but, in some parts of the region, people were also experiencing related resource stress (declining returns on foraging effort).

Evidence of Declining Foraging Efficiency

Optimal foraging theory, and diet breadth models in particular, have improved our understanding of foraging efficiency, resource intensification, and transitions from foraging to farming. The process of resource intensification generates increasing caloric yields per unit of space (land area) at decreasing levels of foraging efficiency, since each unit of energy extracted requires increasingly more intensive labor. Often, though not always, the intensification process leads to increased sedentism, reliance on storage, and, ultimately, a shift from foraging to farming as the primary source of food. According to optimal foraging theory, foragers should invest in such activities when doing so improves overall rates of return on subsistence.

In Patagonia, declining foraging efficiency would be signaled by a decrease in the highest ranked foods—guanaco in open areas and huemul in forested ones—relative to lower ranked foods, including (in the interior) small mammals, birds, fish, and plants, and (on the coasts) marine invertebrates. There is mounting evidence to suggest that foraging return rates were, in fact, declining in some parts of Patagonia, suggesting that these groups were at or near carrying capacity and might have benefited from a transition to farming.

Researchers in northern Argentine Patagonia report widespread evidence of declining foraging efficiency in late prehistory (e.g., Giardina 2010a; Gil et al. 2018; Neme 2007; Neme and Gil 2008a, 2008b). Neme (2007) reports that, circa 2000 cal BP, local populations grew substantially (as indicated by radiocarbon date frequencies), concomitant with decreased residential mobility and increased territoriality (more redundant use of particular sites), and that resultant resource imbalances triggered dietary expansion and intensification of plant use (see also Gil, Neme, Ugan, and Tykot 2014; Johnson et al. 2015). Specifically, Giardina and colleagues (2015) report a decrease in guanaco and rhea (the region's highest-ranking prey species) during this time, and greater taxonomic diversity in faunal assemblages, with increased representation of armadillo (*Dasypus* sp.), rhea eggs, fish, and rodents. Plant macrofossil analyses indicate an increase in plant use beginning around 4500 cal BP, as climates ameliorated following middle Holocene droughts, with a notable increase in taxonomic diversity in the last 2,000 years (Llano 2014). Indeed, Bernal and colleagues' (2016) isotopic analyses indicate that, in the last two millennia, most individuals' diets were largely plant-based, consisting of >65% C_3 (wild) plants during the late prehistoric period. Significantly, too, Llano (2014) documents an archaeological transition from assemblages dominated by the region's highest-ranking plant resources (*Prosopis* sp., *Geoffroea* sp.), to assemblages characterized by both greater variety and dominance of lower-ranking taxa such as *Condalia microphylla*, *Ephedra chilensis*, *Opuntia sulphurea*, *Pterocactus tuberosus*, and *Maihueniopsis darwinii*.

In the southern part of the region, too, there is evidence of growing populations and increased incorporation of previously ignored resources. In Santa Cruz Province, Argentina, for example, substantial environmental and climatic changes during the late Holocene appear to have preceded settlement and subsistence changes, including increased population size, sedentism, and dietary breadth. Approximately 2500–2200 cal BP, paleolakes that joined modern lakes Belgrano, Burmeister, and Azara (Aschero et al. 2005), and lakes Salitroso,

Posadas, and Pueyrredón (Horta and Aschero 2010) contracted, coincident with the onset of increasing aridity (Stine and Stine 1990). Cassiodoro and colleagues (2013) report evidence of population growth after 1900 cal BP, as well as reduced mobility (occupational redundancy) and concentration near modern lakes, especially during a period of intense aridity circa 750 cal BP. They also report increased frequencies of both milling equipment and ceramics, and increased species diversity in archaeofaunal records after around 850 cal BP (cf. Otaola et al. 2019).

Meanwhile, on the north coast of Santa Cruz, mollusk shell size decreases in the late Holocene, suggesting intensification of their use. Hammond and Zilio (2016) report that average shell size decreased between approximately 3100 and 300 cal BP in each of three species commonly encountered in the region's prehistoric shell middens (*Nacella magellanica*, *Aulacomya atra*, and *Mytilus edulis*). Ruling out possible environmental causes, the authors interpret their results as evidence of more intensive use of these species, including more frequent and/or less selective collection. Similarly, and farther south still, marine invertebrate use increased in the Beagle Channel region of Argentine Tierra del Fuego, while the importance of guanaco decreased from 4500 cal BP onward (Yesner 2004). This might signal declining foraging efficiency, as marine invertebrates are often considered a low-ranking, "starvation" resource (e.g., Broughton and O'Connell 1999; Erlandson 2001). So, in some parts of Patagonia, it appears that foraging efficiency was declining by the late Holocene.

An Alternative Explanation: Critical Social Infrastructure

The picture that emerges from these examples and from the environmental, radiocarbon, and archaeological evidence presented to this point is that by circa 2000 cal BP, many Patagonian populations had grown substantially, and their settlement and subsistence patterns had changed or were changing, likely in response. In regions ecologically analogous to Patagonia (e.g., California and the U.S. Great Basin; Basgall 1987; Broughton 1994; Janetski 1997; Wohlgemuth 1996), incorporation of small prey, marine invertebrates, and plants, into the inhabitants' diets, and their potential intensification, has been interpreted in terms of resource stress resulting from population pressure. Patagonian groups experiencing wild resource shortfalls would have benefitted from the increased per-unit-land caloric yields afforded by farming, and large areas across Patagonia (north of ~50° S, with the possible exception of the Andes) could have supported subsistence-level farming of modern varieties of key crops in the Andean agricultural system. Still more land could have supported farming of local landraces, particularly using traditional landscape engineering to improve arability. Lastly, we know that northern Patagonians, at least, were familiar with agricultural products and probably with farmers. The fact that foraging persisted under farming-favorable conditions suggests endogenous factors—social structures, values, and beliefs—tipped the scales in prehistoric Patagonia. Here I will describe the effects of risk management, sharing norms, property rights, and social coordination on people's decisions whether to forage or farm, and the population-level consequences of these decisions through time.

At the start of this chapter, I introduced "adaptive-peak jumping" as a framework for exploring alternatives to environment-as-prime-mover explanations for the spread (or not) of farming in far southern South America. Recall that Wright (1931; see also Simpson 1944) imagined the adaptive landscape as a fitness topography where peaks—defined by constellations of continuously varying traits (e.g., degree of reliance on storage, percent meat in the diet)—confer higher fitness than other points on the surrounding landscape. Individuals on peaks are better able to survive and reproduce than those at lower elevations. Both foraging and farming can be, and often are, better characterized as multipeaked mountains; there are multiple ways to be a successful forager in a given time and place. Still, on a fundamental level, the two strategies typically require such different technologies, schedules, and settlement patterns, for instance, that imagining them as discrete peaks is instructive, particularly when exploring a population-level move from one strategy to another.

Challenges associated with moving from the foraging fitness peak to the farming one might explain the persistence of foraging in prehistoric Patagonia. In the standard metaphor, evolutionary "mountain climbers" are blind; they know only whether their last move was up or down—whether a new behavior or technology increased or decreased fitness—and so would have to descend into a valley before reaching the base of one fitness peak and then climbing up to a higher one (Bettinger 2009b). This is a useful way to think about independent inventions of farming, where trial and error can lead foragers into low-fitness valleys before they start to ascend the farming peak. This may be why farming offers no economic advantage initially, and many early farmers' health declined before rebounding (Bowles 2011; Larsen 2006; Larsen et al. 2019; Milner 2019). In instances of agricultural adoption, though, would-be farmers can *see* the adjacent peak, directly observing both the fitness benefits to practicing farmers and many of the traits that form the peak. When farming is adopted rather than invented de novo, foragers can, effectively, jump from peak to peak, avoiding costly exploration of the intervening valley.

In the northern part of the region, Patagonian foragers could see their farming neighbors' growing numbers and link swelling populations to farming's higher yields. They could at least observe farmers, and perhaps even talk to them about tangible components of the lifestyle, including associated technologies and scheduling. On the face of it, all of the necessary information was available for Patagonians to jump quickly from the foraging peak to the farming. There is good reason to believe, though, that even following these things to the letter, Patagonian foragers might not have been able to jump if key farming-favorable social infrastructure was lacking. That is, even to the sighted mountain climber, some critical components of adaptive peaks may be invisible.

Foragers and Farmers Have Incompatible Risk-Management Strategies

People of the prehistoric past were profoundly affected by risk and uncertainty, which stem from unpredictable variation in resource availability and limited information about this variation, respectively (Cashdan 1990). Foragers and farmers typically mitigate risk in very different ways, in part because of farming's extended "production interval" relative to that of many foraging societies (Winterhalder 1990). That is, most foragers generate food on timescales commensurate to the amount of time one could go without food, which is to say that the production interval is roughly equivalent to a baseline human "starvation interval." Farmers, on the other hand, have very long production intervals—considerable time elapses between initial investment and ultimate yield—relative to the starvation interval (amount of time one could go without food), and so must tailor their risk management strategies to this vastly different scale of variability in returns (Winterhalder 1990). In Patagonia, foragers' and farmers' approaches to unpredictable variation may have been an impediment to the adoption of farming for reasons detailed here.

Foragers Share

In most ethnographically known foraging societies, meat is shared widely (Hawkes et al. 2001:113). This has been viewed in terms of "risk-reduction reciprocity," or the sharing out of one's kill with the expectation that the recipient(s) will do the same in future, improving all participants' average foraging returns (Cashdan 1985; Kaplan and Hill 1985a, 1985b; Smith 1988; Winterhalder 1986a, 1986b, 1997). In a now classic paper, Winterhalder (1986a) showed that this strategy of pooling resources among a small group of foragers is much more efficient than managing risk individually.

The diet breadth model (Chapter 3) is widely used among archaeologists to identify, often by comparison, moments of greater dietary specialization or generality, which can in turn indicate the relative quality of the environment. Some observations conform well to the model's predictions (e.g., O'Connell and Hawkes 1984 O'Connell et al. 1982; Winterhalder 1977, 1981), and deviations from modeled optima have led to important epistemological discussions of hunter-gatherer behavior. Nonetheless, the standard diet breadth model assumes that rates of return are fixed when in fact they may be highly variable (Bettinger et al. 2015). When resources are unpredictable in both their timing and their distribution across a landscape, it may be more instructive to model human behavior in a way that reflects risk sensitivity.

Winterhalder (1986a) compares two such models, the Z-score model of optimal foraging and a model of resource pooling among a small group of foragers as a means of risk reduction. The Z-score model incorporates variable rates of return and potential resource shortfall. Variable rates of return are expressed in terms of a mean return rate, u, and its standard deviation, s, rather than fixed values. The amount that a given return rate, n, deviates from the mean, relative to the standard deviation, is that return rate's Z-score:

$$Z = (n - u) / s$$

When modeling human responses to variable returns, n is defined as a minimum rate of return, a "threshold below which survival is increasingly threatened" (Bettinger et al. 2015:148). According to the relationship identified in the equation, then, when mean returns are above the threshold (i.e., when foraging is relatively good), the way to minimize Z (decrease the likelihood of falling below the threshold) is to decrease return rate variability, represented by the standard deviation, s. An effective way to decrease return rate variability in such circumstances is to broaden the diet because a broad diet effectively averages risk among a number of prey types, thereby reducing overall variability.

When an individual has no choice but to forage alone, minimizing risk by expanding

the diet is the optimal approach. Most foragers live in groups, though, and, as it turns out, averaging risk among foragers reduces the effects of stochastic variability in returns without the simultaneous decrease in foraging efficiency that results when risk is averaged among prey types (when the diet is broadened). Winterhalder (1986a, 1986b) demonstrated, through simulation, that when foragers' returns vary independently—that is, when resource distributions make it unlikely all foragers will succeed or fail simultaneously—cooperative alliances with a relatively small number of individuals can reduce the standard deviation of the pooled rate of return to zero; each forager's return rate is constant without having had to incorporate low-ranked food items.

Meat sharing may have been common in Patagonia. Guanaco dominate archaeofaunal records across the region through much of prehistory; their economic importance is clear (Bourlot 2010; De Nigris 2004; Gómez-Otero et al. 2002; L'Heureux and Borrero 2002; Mengoni Goñalons 1999; Santiago and Salemme 2016; Stoessel 2012). Ethnographic accounts indicate that guanaco were sometimes hunted communally (Gallardo 1910; Gusinde 1990 [1937]), as they may also have been prehistorically (Santiago and Salemme 2016). When game is hunted communally, foragers' returns are synchronous rather than independent, and sharing is not an effective strategy against variable returns. Other ethnographic accounts, though, identify solitary hunting as the most frequent strategy during the historic period (Gallardo 1910), and, in these instances, pooling could have been highly beneficial. Guanacos' aggregation patterns and territorial ranges (Raedecke 1978, 1982; Rey et al. 2009; Young and Franklin 2004) make them more predictable than similarly sized game in other places (e.g., Bird et al. 2009). Nonetheless, ethnographic description of solitary guanaco hunting as a near-daily practice (Gusinde 1990 [1937]:252) suggests only intermittent success. Moreover, available hunting technologies might have increased the need to share. Blitz (1988) has argued that bow and arrow technology, which dramatically improved hunting accuracy, spread relatively slowly across North America from northeast Asia, arriving in the southwestern U.S. around 600 CE. If it spread south from there by land, it likely took at least another few hundred years to reach far southern South America. Available projectile technologies, then, would have included atlatls and bolas, and, while we know less about bolas, Bettinger and Eerkens (1999) argue that the atlatl was relatively inaccurate, making meat sharing necessary to offset variability in hunting success.

In becoming farmers, individuals remove themselves from the sharing network, which may be a double-edged sword. Firstly, there is the danger of falling below the starvation threshold that, previously, resource pooling helped the forager-turned-farmer to avoid. Farming is also a risky venture—particularly for those just starting out, as I describe in more detail below—and without a foraging network on which to rely in hard times, the farmer-nouveau may be at a mortal deficit. Secondly, the new farmer's former sharing group is now a forager short, their collective foraging returns reduced, which could easily breed ill will and hostility towards farmers.

Compounding the problem, farmers do not typically pool and divide as foragers often do, which leaves individuals to manage risk alone. One impediment to sharing among farmers is the production interval. Because so much time elapses between initial investment and harvesting, averaging yields across farmers (i.e., pooling resources) is attractive to freeloaders who know both that they will receive a share regardless of the effort they put in and that the production interval makes it difficult to distinguish shirking from bad luck (Winterhalder 1990). This, of course, is strongly discouraging to honest farmers, quickly eroding any system of sharing that might have developed.

Farmers Store

Instead, farmers reduce risk of resource shortfall through overproduction and storage, which smooths intra-annual food availability. To do so successfully, each farmer has to produce enough during each growing season to account for household subsistence between harvests plus seed set-asides for the next year's planting. Yield from year to year is variable, and largely unknowable until harvest time, many months after planting, so the farmer has to make an initial investment large enough to compensate for possible losses to weather, pests, thieves, etc. (Allan 1965; Winterhalder et al. 2015). Overcompensating, though, is costly in terms of labor, resources, and opportunities foregone, making for a delicate balance that likely took time to perfect. In addition, this sort of "variance compensation" is most critical where agricultural production is highly seasonal and crops are largely rain fed (Charles et al. 2010; McCorriston and Hole 1991; Winterhalder et al. 2015), both of which would have been true in prehistoric Patagonia.

Regardless of whether the farmer has correctly predicted the year's needs-plus-variance-compensation, most years' yields will exceed what the farmer can eat immediately, creating a surplus that must be stored. This introduces yet another level of risk for the farmer—the farmer who lives among immediate-return, meat-sharing foragers in particular. Stored resources are susceptible to loss, spoilage, pests, and catastrophes. The level of storage required to see a farmer through from harvest to harvest would also likely be clearly visible to others; it would be hard to squirrel away that much surplus in a way that one can simultaneously monitor and protect. Where foragers' risk aversion strategies include resource pooling, a strong sharing ethos develops (Sherratt 1997; Wiessner 1982). Absent a system of private property rights, this could jeopardize the stores on which farmers depend.

The Private Property Problem

Bowles and Choi (2013) argue that private property rights were impracticable among late Pleistocene foragers but requisite among Holocene farmers, creating a tension that could only be broken by the co-evolution of farming technology and a secure system of individual private ownership. Their argument and co-evolutionary model are compelling. However, the circumstances of agricultural adoption can be quite different from those of de novo invention (the focal circumstance of the Bowles-Choi model), particularly with regards to the critical mass necessary for such co-evolution to occur. Our current understanding of independent developments of farming worldwide is that they were typically gradual processes (Barker 2006). Environmental factors are often cited as catalysts for "origins of agriculture" (e.g., Binford 1968; Richerson et al. 2001). Where major environmental change was an important variable, we might assume relative uniformity in people's receptiveness to farming because everyone would have been experiencing similar environmental stress. This could have, in turn, led to "sufficiently many individuals adopting both the novel property rights and the new [farming] technology so as to overcome the critical mass problem" that occurs when too few people subscribe to a new institution (Bowles and Choi 2013:5). In instances of potential farming adoption, conversely, the possibility exists for both much more rapid uptake of the new technology and greater variation in people's receptiveness to it. Moreover, unless a system of individual property rights is already in place, adoption of the technology, for all of its potential benefits, might be impeded by the critical mass problem: if a majority continue to expect a share of everyone's haul, whether foraged or farmed, would-be farmers have no reasonable guarantee they will retain access to the products of their own labor, making the investment simply too risky (Bowles and Choi 2013).

It is certainly true that some of the world's foragers relied on storage, as both ethnographic and archaeological evidence attests. Binford (2001) reports that 89% of all groups in his global ethnographic sample living above 35° (North and South; n = 214) invest(ed) in storage at "moderate" to "major" levels. This statistic predicts a high likelihood of storage reliance throughout Patagonia, though this is not currently supported by archaeological evidence. The apparent lack of Patagonian storage might simply reflect a prehistoric preference for aboveground storage facilities, storage in perishable

containers (baskets), or stockpiling surplus in caves, all of which are less likely to leave recognizable archaeological traces than belowground storage pits. However, recall that Patagonian groups are outliers in other macroecological comparisons (e.g., number of cultural groups predicted for latitude; Chapter 3), so it is possible that, instead, Patagonians more closely resemble the 11% of Binford's (2001) ethnographic groups that invest(ed) only moderately or not at all in storage. The documented lack of storage among Contact-period coastal Patagonians is consistent with this interpretation; the Yámana, Káwesqar, and Chono, for example, reportedly invested less in storage than groups in ecologically analogous regions elsewhere in the world (Binford 2001). Still, the extent of Patagonian storage around the time of potential agricultural adoption remains to be determined, to say nothing of whether any such storage was *private*, as would be signaled by the movement of storage features from communal spaces into family-level domestic spaces (Bogaard et al. 2009; Earle 2000; Garfinkel et al. 2009; Kuijt 2008; Kuijt and Finlayson 2009).

It is also true that private resource ownership is not strictly a farmers' institution and could have been established in parts of Patagonia prior to the arrival of farmers to the north. In the North American Great Basin, for example, pinyon (*Pinus edulis* and *P. monophylla*) yields were sufficiently predictable (and defensible) that some groves were owned by ethnographic Shoshone (Steward 1933). Likewise, *Prosopis* spp. (mesquite) stands and even individual trees were owned by Cahuilla families in the mountainous region between the Mojave and Colorado deserts of southern California (Bean and Saubel 1972; Strong 1929). Ethnographic and archaeological evidence indicates that araucaria (similar to pinyon pine) and *Prosopis* spp. (especially *P. flexuosa* and *P. algarrobo*) were economically important in northern Patagonia. There is currently no evidence of wild plant management or ownership in the region, but we do know that (1) late prehistoric diets at the agricultural limit (defined above) were comprised of 65% or more of C_3 plants (Bernal et al. 2016), (2) *Prosopis* spp. macroremains are common in northern

Patagonian archaeological records (Llano 2014; Llano and Barberena 2013), and (3) a rise in dental caries in late prehistoric skeletal populations has been attributed to algarrobo intensification (Lema et al. 2012; Novelino et al. 2004). As with storage, this is a fascinating topic for future research. For the moment, though, we have to proceed as though private ownership was not an established institution in Patagonia when corn agriculture arrived in neighboring regions.

Information Exchange and Density Dependence

If foragers' approach to risk is socialist—in the sense that some goods are socially owned or regulated—and farmers' approach is individualist, it is nonetheless true that individual farmers' payoffs are socially dependent. This is obvious in the case of honoring (or not) the institution of individual private ownership, but it may also extend to other aspects of farming.

Like colonizers of a new landscape (Chapter 4), early adopters of farming elect an initially unfamiliar enterprise whose learning curve might have made failure likely in early trials. Even when learned directly from experienced neighbors, local environmental particulars and their interactions with available seed stock, which may be adapted to different conditions, present the novice farmer with challenges (s)he is unprepared to meet. In addition to differences in temperature (means and extremes), moisture (abundance and timing, drought frequency), and available sunlight (day length, cloudiness, aspect, and obstructions), different regions have different climatological challenges (drying winds, frequent hail), blights, and pests. These things require trial and error on multi-season (or longer) timescales in order to develop reasonably reliable strategies for preventing crop loss to these causes—or at least to learn appropriate variance compensation. Even absent droughts and blights and other external challenges, simply perfecting the delicate balance of production to simultaneously minimize costly overproduction and risk of shortfall is no doubt challenging for the uninitiated.

This learning curve could be made steeper (progress accelerated) if novice farmers pooled information related to their experiments, successes, and failures; social learning is often far more efficient than individual trial-and-error learning (Boyd and Richerson 1985; Richerson and Boyd 2005). The larger the pool of farmers sharing information, the better prepared each will be to weather a region's potential hazards. More productive farming enabled by information sharing could also create a system of positive feedback: better information makes better farmers and, as curious foragers witness ever-increasing farming yields, some will decide to become farmers themselves, potentially improving the information pool and average yields, attracting still more farmers, and on and on.

However, while benefits might increase exponentially once a critical number of farmers is achieved, this selfsame density dependence can also make it hard for farming to get started in the first place. Initially, early adopters' inexperience makes it likely that the information exchanged is of relatively low quality. Farmers nouveau might be prone to errant attributions of success and failure, for example. The "burn in" period before information exchange reliably improves average yields might also be prolonged by the fact that some variability in farmers' success will be independent of the amount of information each has (i.e., stochastic variation); some will do poorly even when their information is good, injecting misinformation and, potentially, false doubt into the fledgling system, discouraging would-be joiners/information-sharers. Moreover, stochastic variation is likely to have the strongest negative effect when farming populations are smallest, again making it hard for farming to take root (see Chapter 7, including Figure 7.4).

Stochasticity—and Perhaps the Empire—Strikes Back

Would-be farmers everywhere faced the challenge of achieving critical mass in order to make farming profitable and individual private property a respected institution (Bowles and Choi

2013). Clearly, many were ultimately successful. The new system of risk reduction (storage
and the generation of variance-compensating
surplus) effectively kept many farmers on the
right side of unpredictable variation in resource
availability and allowed farming populations to
grow, often at the expense of foraging ones. So,
if farming was possible and potentially beneficial in parts of prehistoric Patagonia as appears
to have been true, what kept would-be Patagonian farmers below this critical threshold?

Data suggest that, in fact, farmers *were* gathering mass in far northern prehistoric Patagonia, but that they were repeatedly discouraged
by stochasticity, both at the individual level described above and at a larger scale. As we saw in
an earlier section (*The South American Agricultural Limit*), domesticated plants first reached
northern Argentine Patagonia circa 2000 cal
BP. Archaeological and isotopic records show
that, for the next 1,400 years, use of domesticates was highly variable across the region.
Plant macroremains, particularly of maize, are
few and geographically dispersed (Llano 2011,
2014). Isotopic signatures in human bone show
increasing consumption of maize (Gil, Villalba,
Ugan, Cortegoso, Neme, Michieli, Novellino,
and Durán 2014) but also, importantly, significant variation within and between skeletal
populations (Gil et al. 2018). These and other
isotopic analyses from the region (Novellino
et al. 2004; Gil et al. 2011) indicate that some
tested individuals' isotopic values are more consistent with those of mobile foragers, while others individuals show elevated consumption of
maize, and the distribution of "maize-eaters" is
not strongly patterned in space or time. If these
isotopic signatures can in fact be interpreted
in terms of foragers versus farmers (cf. Bernal
et al. 2016), this sort of interdigitation is exactly
what we might expect if some individuals were
experimenting with farming—early adopters intrigued by the fitness benefits observed
among their northern farming neighbors—but,
rather than spreading, farming was repeatedly
thwarted by some combination of bad luck, low-
quality information, and foragers' sharing ethic
interfering with storage. Given the production

interval relative to the starvation threshold discussed above, a single bad season might have
been sufficient to remove a farmer from the
pool, either through discouragement or quite
literally, due to starvation, keeping farmers'
numbers low relative to foragers'. As described
previously, early-adopting farmers' failures
might have discouraged otherwise inclined foragers from attempting farming themselves. It is
also possible that the otherwise-inclined might
have postponed their farming attempts if foraging returns were improved by early adopters'
new pursuit, which relaxes the burden on wild
resources and reduces foraging costs.

Using ethnographic data and a model of
group selection, Soltis and colleagues (1995) estimate that it takes at least 500–1,000 years for a
rare group-beneficial trait to replace a common
one. Roughly 1,000 years after the first appearance of domesticates at the South American
agricultural limit, $\delta^{13}C$ values in the region's
skeletal populations were at their highest, indicating a peak in maize consumption (Gil, Villalba, Ugan, Cortegoso, Neme, Michieli, Novellino,
and Durán 2014). Granting all of the challenges
faced by early adopters of farming (e.g., foragers' sharing ethic, low-quality information)
and the resulting variability in early farmers'
success, the general trend of rising isotope values is precisely what we would expect if the frequency of farming-friendly social institutions
and attitudes were increasing in the region.
It might also reflect the development of locally-
adapted varieties of maize, perhaps as a result
of increasingly-reliable information exchange.
However, roughly 1,500 years into the experi-
ment (ca. 530 cal BP), evidence of maize consumption suddenly and dramatically declined,
coincident with the onset of the Little Ice Age
(ca. 540–200 cal BP or 1370–1750 CE; Gil, Villalba, Ugan, Cortegoso, Neme, Michieli, Novellino, and Durán 2014; for climate data see Espizúa
and Pitte 2009; Fletcher and Moreno 2012). It is
possible that the 1°C decrease in average summer temperatures during this time reduced
productivity enough to make maize farming
unsustainable, as Gil, Villalba, Ugan, Cortegoso, Neme, Michieli, Novellino, and Durán (2014)

argue. Alternatively, it could be that decreased temperatures per se were not the issue—maize was certainly cultivated in places with summer temperatures colder than experienced in west-central Argentina during the Little Ice Age—but that the change in average conditions disrupted the still-fragile system. That is, farmers, of whom there were still few, would have had to revert to trial and error and to tinker with production in order to adjust to the cooler, moister climate because social information was out of sync with changed local conditions.

Notably, the apparent reduction in maize consumption at the agricultural limit is also roughly coincident with southern expansion of the Inca Empire. Between 1471 and 1493 CE, the Empire claimed parts of Bolivia, Chile, and Argentina. On the Chilean side of the Andes, the Inca overtook agricultural groups like the Diaguitas by force until their southward progression was eventually stopped by the agrarian Mapuche in the Battle of the Maule (de la Vega 1609). But, while groups in what is now Chile resisted the Inca by force, the strategy east of the Andes, as the Inca reached Mendoza's Diamante River, may have been one of evasion: mobile foragers are simply harder to dominate and assimilate. So, whatever the reason(s) may have been to that point, in the final decades before European contact, living at the edge of an expansionist state might well have been sufficient impetus for Patagonians to deliberately resist farming.

Conclusions

In light of the preceding discussion, there are two points we can take from this chapter's epigraph. Reflecting on the first part of Simpson's (1964:23) argument—that species "evolve exactly as if they [are] adapting as best they [can] to a changing world"—it is clear that the "changing world" to which humans adapt is not only physical but also hypersocial and hypercultural. Even selfishly motivated decisions individuals make to maximize some desired currency are affected by customs, institutions, and the behaviors of others; even currencies as basic as subsistence efficiency (cost-effective attainment of the food

one needs to survive) are culturally mediated (Chapter 3). Indeed, as we have seen, Patagonian social and cultural climates have to be considered important, along with the physical climate, in maintaining foraging where farming might otherwise have been profitable.

The fact that culture strongly influences our ability to extract energy from the environment, and even the amount of energy a body needs to survive, highlights the fact that we are not only adapting to a "changing world," we are changing the world to which we adapt (Chapters 3 and 7). It is only relatively recently, however, that social scientists have come to study the effects of culture on our biological selves. Our genes and culture do co-evolve, though, and it is becoming increasingly clear that we cannot accurately reconstruct the evolution of *Homo sapiens* without an explicit understanding of the ways in which culture shapes the adaptive environment.

Genetic studies have shown that the introduction of farming affected genes associated with human height and particular immunities, among other things (Mathieson et al. 2015). Recent research also has implications for subtler but perhaps equally profound effects of farming on human physiology and behavior that, if preliminary, are worth paying attention to. Strang and colleagues (2017) argue, for example, that the timing and amounts of particular macronutrients consumed can influence an individual's propensity to punish violators of social norms. In their study, a high carbohydrate-to-protein ratio in the morning meal induced metabolic changes coincident with higher rejection rates of unfair offers in the ultimatum game (increased willingness to punish). Conversely, subjects who ate a high protein-to-carbohydrate version of the same meal were more likely to tolerate unfair offers. While the proximal cause appears to be elevated levels of tyrosine in the blood with the high protein meal, the ultimate cause remains unclear (Raison and Raichlen 2018). Still, the idea that nutrition can affect social decision making is an intriguing proposition considering farmers' typically carbohydrate-rich diets compared to those of foragers. It is tempting to imagine a link between nutrients/

hormone synthesis and social norms like tolerated theft (passive sharing; Blurton Jones 1987) among protein-focused foragers and intolerance of freeloading (strong sense of private ownership) among carbohydrate-focused farmers. Clearly, each of these tendencies can be explained without reference to nutrient regulation of hormone synthesis, but if prosocial behaviors are less metabolically costly with the consumption of high-quality (meat-based) diets (Raison and Raichlen 2018), perhaps there is a role for the biological and behavioral effects of subsistence in our study of emergent sociopolitical complexity and the formalization (enforcement) of prosocial behaviors among fully agrarian societies.

Reflecting on the second clause in this chapter's epigraph—as they adapt to a changing world, species do *not* evolve "as if they were moving toward a set goal"—we see that the progressivism to which Simpson (1964:23) was responding continues to color our perception of groups that remained (or became) foragers in(to) the ethnographic present. In his essay, Simpson was responding to continued resistance—even within the scientific community—to natural selection as an important mechanism of evolutionary change, largely because of the theory's anti-progressivism. Recall from earlier chapters (especially 1 and 3) that well into the twentieth century some anthropologists clung to the notion that human (cultural) evolution is progressive, each next stage of development (e.g., savagery, barbarism; sensu Morgan 1877) bringing us closer to perfection. Simpson was primarily addressing an audience of paleontologists, but his commitment to demonstrating that evolution is not goal oriented is certainly relevant to our study of cultural evolution. One means by which he and other New Synthesists (e.g., Fisher, Haldane, Wright; Chapter 3) demonstrated this was through application of Darwinian "population thinking," which sees the variation within a population as the raw material on which selection acts. Tracking the effects of evolutionary forces on internally varied groups (rather than idealized, homogeneous ones) provides a radically different perspective

on developmental trajectories, as we saw in this chapter's analysis of Patagonian subsistence.

In Patagonia, it seems to have been the case that people were aware of farming and the fitness advantages it conferred on their northern neighbors (they could "see" the adjacent fitness peak and its relative height). People were at least trading for, and perhaps a small number of them even growing, domesticated plants. Variation in people's isotopic signatures suggests, at the very least, differential access to these products. This is clearly not a case where "the (homogenous) Patagonians" had a collective inability to farm; there was variation in interest, opportunity, success, and perseverance. This interpretation sees the persistence of foraging in Patagonia as the product of complex interactions between environment, culture, and demography rather than a matter of straightforward economics.

Final Thoughts

As with other topics covered in this book, as many questions as answers are generated by this exploration of farming potential, potential farming, and the influence of farming despite the persistence of foraging in Patagonia. This is a sign of the region's importance on the world stage of hunter-gatherer research, and of the vibrancy of ongoing work in southernmost South America. And while much remains to be done, one conclusion we draw from the evidence at hand is that cultural and social factors were as important as environmental ones in parts of Patagonia where farming would otherwise have been possible and economically beneficial. As significant is our recognition that the initial reason(s) for remaining a forager may have differed from the reason(s) people remained foragers at other times. In a similar vein to resisting Inca expansion, an alternative ripe for future exploration is the cultural evolutionary prediction that boundaries (ecological and social) can promote ethnic differentiation (Boyd and Richerson 1987; Boyd et al. 2005; McElreath et al. 2003) and favor traits irrespective of their effects on biological fitness: social relations between Patagonians and their farming neighbors might have been such that farming was avoided simply because it is what *They* do.

Also worth exploring is the possibility that farming was not an all-or-nothing prospect in southern South America. Some groups, including the Fremont of North America's eastern Great Basin and northern Colorado Plateau, appear to have moved nimbly between foraging and maize farming as circumstances dictated (Barlow 2006; Janetski and Talbot 2014). The Fremont cultivated maize between roughly 600 and 1300 CE but relied heavily on foraged foods as well, and the record indicates extreme variability in the relative importance of maize versus wild plants and animals through time and across space. This phenomenon is typically described in terms of spatiotemporal variability in environmental suitability for farming. Barlow (2006) explores an optimal foraging alternative that considers individuals' moment-to-moment decision making, specifically the relative profitability of investing each next unit of energy in foraging- versus farming-related activities. By her model, such short-term decision making can produce patterns consistent with the archaeological evidence while also accounting for the Fremont people's ability to preserve technologies and knowledge related to each subsistence system.

Beyond energy optimization, a wide variety of social, cultural, demographic, and environmental factors can influence subsistence decisions, as we have seen in this chapter. But because subsistence is so closely tied to economics, both in theory and, often, in practice, a clear view of prehistoric supply and demand will help us better understand how some of these other factors influenced decision making. This is precisely the subject of the next chapter: What was carrying capacity in prehistoric Patagonia and how did it change through time? As we will see, these questions are deceptive in their simplicity.

The "K" in Patagonia?

Numbers depend primarily on the means of subsistence, and this
depends partly on the physical nature of the country, but in a
much higher degree on the arts which are there practised.

—Charles Darwin (1871)

Previous chapters' conclusions build to the realization that prehistoric Patagonia's carrying capacity (K)—the number of individuals an environment can sustain (Krebs 2001; Ricklefs 2008; but see below)—was likely higher than suggested by the region's outward severity and sparse archaeological record. How much higher, and how K might have changed through time are decidedly less clear. Neither do we have a good sense of whether Patagonian populations hovered near carrying capacity—whatever it might have been at any given time—for much of prehistory, or whether they remained smaller than could have been supported by available resources. It would be unusual if Patagonian populations were in fact below K for appreciable stretches of prehistory; most populations are at or near carrying capacity most of the time (Richerson et al. 2009). Populations with unrealized growth potential would be epistemologically significant, too, because a group's proximity to local K is commonly thought to be a driver of cultural change. A reliable estimate of Patagonia's carrying capacity, and its variation across space and through time, will clarify our understanding of the region's archaeological record and guide future research agendas.

This concluding chapter (1) reviews evidence from preceding chapters that suggests Patagonia's population remained relatively small—perhaps below K, in an "expansion phase" (Lee et al. 2009)—until late prehistory,

(2) provides a correspondingly positive perspective on Patagonia's environmental quality relative to prehistoric people, and (3) offers an alternative hypothesis that sees Patagonia's relatively small, slow-growing population as a product of reciprocal relationships between demography and technology rather than a symptom of poor environmental quality per se. First, though, the ecological concept central to this chapter—carrying capacity—and archaeological approaches to K warrant some discussion.

Conceptions of Carrying Capacity

Despite its centrality to population ecology, sustainability science, and related fields (Dhondt 1988), there is some uncertainty around the concept of *carrying capacity*. Confusion stems, in part, from the fact that the term is not always explicitly defined and differences in its implied meaning create a theoretical gray area in which a population could simultaneously be both at and not at carrying capacity (Marshall 2020). Marshall (2020) has identified two main conceptions of K in the ecological literature, one that sees it as a property of the environment and the other, as a property of the population itself. In the first sense, an environment's carrying capacity relative to a particular population is defined in terms of environmental quality: it is the maximum number of individuals that *could be* supported in the long term given available resources. Conversely, carrying capacity in the second sense is the observed population size at equilibrium—the number of individuals that *is* supported by an environment (Marshall 2020). As such, a stable population (one that is neither growing nor shrinking) would be at carrying capacity in the second (property-of-the-population) sense, but could be below carrying capacity in the environmental-quality sense if some external force (e.g., predation) were holding population size below that which could theoretically be supported. This becomes problematic when the force(s) holding a population below property-of-the-environment carrying capacity go unrecognized and observed population size is taken to be an accurate reflection of environmental quality. The resulting environmental mischaracterization can easily color interpretations of new data and influence subsequent research agendas, leading to cyclical perception bias, which causes us to favor information that supports an existing belief and to overlook or dismiss valuable information that could, if acknowledged, change our initial beliefs or hypotheses (Garvey 2020; Risen and Gilovich 2007; Weiten 2008). The scientific implications of perception bias are far-reaching, so it is critical that we correctly identify the things that constrain the populations we study.

Humans Bend the (Ecological) Rules

Among humans, forces that hold populations below property-of-the-environment carrying capacity are as likely to be intrinsic as extrinsic; attitudes towards family size and technologies that affect survivorship can impact group size just as profoundly as, say, disease or warfare (things akin to predation). However, aside from their demographic effect (i.e., smaller-than-possible populations), many of these forces are archaeologically invisible. Still, archaeological approaches to carrying capacity frequently equate population size with environmental-quality: human groups grow large where resources are abundant (high-quality environment = high K = large population) and remain small where they are not (low-quality environment = low

K = small population). These are reasonable assumptions but, as Marshall (2020) cautions, neither small populations in low-quality environments nor large ones where resources are abundant are necessarily at carrying capacity. Freely equating human population size with environmental quality (and a particular K) is risky since largely-invisible, intrinsic forces can easily create disjunctions between size and quality (K), leading to exactly the kind of environmental mischaracterization and perception bias I just described.

Human hunter-gatherers typically live(d) at lower population densities than other animals of similar size (Burger et al. 2017), and both empirical data and formal simulations (e.g., Winterhalder et al. 1988) indicate that hunter-gatherer populations in fact stabilize(d) at levels far below property-of-environment carrying capacity. This may be a form of insurance against short-term fluctuations in resource availability (Bettinger et al. 2015:156–157), or as Cashdan (1983:63) puts it, "if populations are 'regulated' to environmental resources they are presumably regulated to the lean times, and consequently populations in varying environments would be below carrying capacity much of the time." Arguably, this is just down-regulation of "actual" carrying capacity, which would make insurance-adjusted population size the functional equivalent of property-of-environment carrying capacity. However, the relationship between population size/density and standard measures of resource availability among ethnographic hunter-gatherers suggests that such a simple calibration is unwarranted.

Recall from Chapter 3's discussion of macroecological models that, while biogeographical studies of nonhuman animals show strong correlations between environmental variables (e.g., temperature, precipitation) and population size and density, these relationships generally do not hold for people (Figure 3.1). For example, plant biomass (a proxy for food availability) is a poor predictor of human population density ($R^2 = 0.27$) among a large sample of ethnographic groups (n = 339; Binford 2001). If risk aversion reliably leads to down-regulation of "actual" carrying capacity, we would in fact

FIGURE 7.1. Oblique aerial photo of Black Rock City in 2010. The tent city rises out of northwestern Nevada's Black Rock Desert one week each year and the festival's policy is to leave no trace. While some trace is inevitably left, it is astonishingly little for the number of attendees, now upwards of 70,000 per year. Image in the public domain, obtained on January 5, 2019 from Wikimedia Commons: https://commons.wikimedia.org/wiki/File:Burning_Man_aerial.jpg.

expect a strong relationship between population density and primary productivity since, as Cashdan's comment suggests, groups in relatively low-quality environments should downregulate by a greater margin as a function of variance compensation. The fact that resource availability is such a poor predictor of human population density suggests that other—likely cultural—factors are in play.

People might avoid high-quality habitats or aggregate in low-quality ones for any number of reasons. For instance, resource-rich foothills environments could hypothetically be avoided for a long time following a major landslide. Conversely, people might be drawn to an area for its *human* resources regardless of subsistence resource availability, leading to a larger population than would be predicted by environmental quality alone. Social events drawing large groups of people might be deliberately held in resource-poor areas, to avoid scaring off game or damaging habitats important for subsistence. The annual Burning Man festival in northwestern Nevada's Black Rock Desert provides food for archaeological thought: On the one hand, this contemporary event—during which a tent city of over 70,000 people rises out of the desert for one week each year (Figure 7.1)—leaves astonishingly little trace. This is not by chance, but by mandate. Still, it is entirely possible that similar things happened in the prehistoric past, if on a smaller scale. It is contrarily conceivable that such a festival could, instead, leave a dispropor-tionality large record for its duration. We would hope the event's brevity would be obvious in such a record, but it would not necessarily be so. In these ways and countless others, beliefs, attitudes, customs, and happenstance can all create disjunctions between population size and environmental quality. Culture can also change the very quality of environments, as described in the next section.

Culture Sets Human Carrying Capacity

Population ecologists distinguish between fac-tors that *regulate* population size relative to K, and those that *limit* population by setting K in the first place (e.g., Krebs 2002). Contrary to most other species, among humans, culture is a primary factor in both regulation, as discussed in the previous section, and limitation: culture effectively sets carrying capacity in many in-stances. While not often described in these terms, the link between culture and population size has been a major theme in anthropology since the earliest days of the discipline.

Anthropologists have always known that culture determines the edible subset of all available resources in an environment. Rules, belief, and preferences define what is appropri-ate (and palatable) for consumption. Access to the culturally-defined edible set is then deter-mined by a variety of other cultural manifesta-tions—ecological knowledge and organization of work, to name a few—but technology in par-ticular has been central to our understanding of the ways culture interacts with environment to determine local carrying capacity. Our ap-proach to the relationship between technology and group size has certainly changed over the discipline's history (Chapters 2 and 3; see also Bettinger et al. 2015; Garvey and Bettinger 2014). Initially, the focus was near-exclusively on large-scale, "stage-defining" advances like agriculture (e.g., Morgan 1877), which increases produc-tivity per unit land area and, thus, the number of people the land can support. Increasingly, however, archaeologists explore smaller-scale and subtler effects of technology (and other

aspects of culture) on carrying capacity. The Darwinian principles applied in this book are well-equipped to do precisely this.

As described in the Preface, *Darwinian* refers here to theories that explain large-scale phenomena (e.g., a transition to agriculture) in terms of explicitly defined processes (e.g., natural selection, biased transmission) acting at a small scale, that of the individual (Bettinger et al. 2015:187). The (Darwinian) models pre-sented in Chapter 3 show that two otherwise identical individuals can have very different optimal diets when equipped with different technologies (Winterhalder and Bettinger 2010). Chapters 3 and 4 describe how two individuals equipped with identical technologies might, in-stead, have very different caloric needs (energy budgets) which could result in very different foraging strategies. Both sum to differences in the amount of energy extracted from an envi-ronment and, therefore, how many individu-als with the specified technologies and basal metabolic rates (and/or toolmaking and hunt-ing skills, access to and retention of ecological knowledge, etc.) an environment can support. Chapter 4 shows, further, that as individuals move into new habitats, initial habitat quality (with respect to food) depends at least as much on available knowledge and technologies as on inherent properties of the habitats themselves. As seen in Chapter 5, culture can also buffer the strain of resource scarcity: when local condi-tions deteriorate (a hypothetical decline in K), individuals can make settlement, subsistence, and technological adjustments, exploiting dif-ferent resources or using previously targeted ones differently, rather than their populations simply contracting. And as demonstrated in Chapter 6, adoption of a technology (in this case, farming) can be thwarted by existing cus-toms and social infrastructure despite the tech-nology's obvious K-enhancing potential. The Darwinian principles applied throughout this book are a powerful means of identifying and measuring culture's effects on carrying capacity because they track both short-term, individual-level decisions, survivorship, and fitness, and their long-term, group-level outcomes.

Population Size and Density Affect Cultural Developments

The effects of culture on human population size are undeniable, if sometimes underappreciated and still incompletely understood. The same is true when we reverse the causal arrow: population size clearly affects culture, but we still have much to learn about the mechanics of the involved processes despite a long history of study. There is a general recognition among anthropologists that, under population pressure, selection tends to favor adaptation (innovation) in the direction of increased carrying capacity. Or, to paraphrase Plato's more eloquent aphorism, necessity is often the mother of invention. However, population pressure is clearly not the *only* path to cultural change and not all change is adaptive. Moreover, even if we somehow determined that, on balance, most change is adaptive and population-induced resource stress is its most common cause, our understanding of cultural change would be incomplete. That is, "necessity" provides a motivation for change/innovation, but not an explanation for the development and spread of novelties—the mechanisms of change. For this, we need other tools.

As described in Chapter 3, evolutionary models predict (and empirical evidence supports) a positive relationship between group size/connectivity and cultural complexity (Collard et al. 2005, 2013; Henrich 2004; Kline and Boyd 2010). This is because (1) people tend to preferentially copy skilled individuals, (2) innovators and highly skilled individuals are (statistically) more common in larger groups, and (3) well-networked groups are effectively made larger (the number of potential innovators increased further still) by their connections with other groups. Larger groups are also less vulnerable to random losses of innovators and skilled individuals (Henrich 2004). So, when population growth is unchecked by external forces, positive feedback between population and technology can result: growing populations innovate in ways that raise carrying capacity, leading to further growth, and further innovations, and further growth, and so on (Richerson et al. 2009).

Identifying ultimate causation in a feedback loop (the circumstance that set it in motion) can present a bit of a chicken and egg problem, particularly when archaeological evidence is sparse. In rare instances, such as initial colonization of a previously unoccupied landscape, another ecological principle—ecological succession—can provide insights. Recall from Chapter 3 that ecological succession is gradual change in plant and animal communities that results from species' modifications of their own environments. Change is typically in the direction of increasing complexity. Rates and trajectories of successional change are influenced by both predictable and stochastic factors, as in the example I provided in Chapter 3: Following a fire, forest development depends in part on (predictable) characteristics of colonizing species and their (broadly predictable) subsequent effects on soil chemistry, and in part on (stochastic) events such as particular weather patterns and where seed-dispersing animals happen to have fed the day before. Whether a mature forest ever develops is contingent on both starting state and subsequent conditions and developments. This is a reasonable metaphor for cultural evolution following human colonization of previously unoccupied spaces (Richerson and Boyd 2005), and this concluding section draws together evidence from throughout the book to present a hypothesis regarding carrying capacity, habitat quality, population density, and cultural development in prehistoric Patagonia in light of ecological succession and feedback between population and innovation.

The "K" in Patagonia

Patagonia's outward severity and relatively sparse archaeological record suggest poor habitat quality and a correspondingly low carrying capacity through most of the Holocene. Much of the region is characterized by low precipitation, high winds (exacerbating evaporation), and low primary productivity. Patagonia's population appears to have remained small following initial colonization while many other New World populations grew rapidly. Population decline or regional abandonment are hypothesized for parts of the region as aridity increased during the middle Holocene. Farming never took hold—the original badge of environmental marginality—and even the insatiable Inca avoided Patagonia during latest prehistory.

Nevertheless, I hypothesize that fewer people lived in Patagonia than could have been supported by available resources—that the regional population was below property-of-environment *K*. Evidence presented in previous chapters supports alternative explanations for the archaeological patterns that otherwise suggest poor habitat quality and low carrying capacity. Next, I review and recontextualize this evidence in terms of population size-environmental quality mismatch.

Prehistoric Population Size in Patagonia

Scientists studying carrying capacity among nonhuman species in present-day environments can empirically establish (count or estimate) the number of individuals present and observe firsthand which of all available food resources they target, variation in feeding habits within a population at a given time, and changes in both population size and feeding habits through time. Archaeologists, of course, must instead reverse-engineer population size, "feeding habits" (i.e., subsistence patterns), and change through time to the best of our ability, which we do with variable success.

Assessing prehistoric population dynamics increasingly involves interpretation of radiocarbon summed probability distributions corrected for taphonomic loss (e.g., Freeman et al. 2018; Surovell et al. 2009). Where the effects of sample size, intrasite sampling, and other complicating factors can be estimated and controlled for, loss-corrected summed probability distributions can provide reliable estimates of population size and change through time (cf. Contreras and Meadows 2014; Crombé and Robinson 2014; Rhode et al. 2014). In Patagonia, however, several issues make this approach impracticable, namely the region's departures from underlying assumptions of the loss-correction model and sampling effects that are difficult to isolate and manage.

Taphonomic Loss Correction

Previous chapters describe regional-scale landscape remodeling and local-scale dynamics that alter(ed) the region's archaeological record, indicating that far more sites were created than are now discoverable due to taphonomic loss. As glaciers shrank following the Last Glacial Maximum, sea levels rose and erosion intensified, causing rapid downcutting of river channels and changing patterns of sediment deposition (Chapters 2 and 4). Sea levels continued to rise well into the middle Holocene, a period that also saw increased volcanism, seismicity, landslides, and glacial readvances that likewise changed the landscape dramatically and negatively affected archaeological records (Chapter 5). "Routine" local-scale dynamics, including annual melting of the snowpack—which contributes to downcutting and overbank deposition—aeolian redistribution of sediments, and lake-level changes at various timescales, also affect what is now available for archaeologists to study and date.

These processes are not unique to Patagonia and Surovell and colleagues (2009) have derived a model of taphonomic bias for estimating the effect of site attrition on archaeological radiocarbon distributions, provided they meet certain criteria. Their model assumes that long-term trends in a global record of radiocarbon-dated volcanic events "are entirely governed by the operation of taphonomic processes through time," and can, therefore, be used to "correct" archaeological radiocarbon frequencies for time-dependent loss (Surovell et al. 2009:1716). The authors argue that, by comparing the ratio of archaeological to geological radiocarbon dates, we should be able to produce summed probability distributions that more accurately reflect regional population histories. Since we know taphonomic processes to have affected the Patagonian record, a reliable estimate of these effects could substantially improve our understanding of the region's prehistoric population dynamics.

Leaving aside the possibility that geological records are also subject to sampling biases—exposed cutbanks (biased towards relatively recent geology) are routinely sampled more frequently than cores extracted for the express purpose of identifying and dating volcanic events, which would complicate the model's assumption that patterns reflect only taphonomic loss—it is likewise the case that Patagonia's dates database does not meet the criteria for confident application of Surovell and colleagues' model. The authors argue, for instance, that "the severity of taphonomic processes declines with site age," meaning a given site's chance of survival improves with time (Surovell et al. 2009:1718). It is logical and may well be true that, once sites are buried, their chances of survival improve. However, on erosional landscapes, as characterize large portions of Patagonia, sites are subject to very different dynamics. Where sites are buried very slowly or not at all, or are repeatedly buried and exposed as can happen where wind is a dominant meteorological phenomenon (Chapter 2), taphonomic effects do scale with time as Surovell and colleagues argue, but in the opposite direction: sites' chances of survival *decrease* with site age (Garvey and Bettinger 2018). Moreover, even if we were to alter the taphonomic model to account for local dynamics, the distribution of Patagonia's radiocarbon dates is unlikely to accurately reflect true demographic patterns, largely because of sampling effects.

Sampling Effects

Patagonia is a big place with limited infrastructure, and large portions of the landscape remain archaeologically unknown (Figure 2.19). What's more, because there is not currently a mechanism for routinely reporting negative results in archaeology, it is unclear the extent to which the voids evident in Figure 2.19 reflect sampling gaps versus actual site clustering (i.e., some places were avoided prehistorically). As currently unknown areas are systematically tested—and we archaeologists embrace the power of negative results—our estimates of Patagonia's prehistoric population dynamics will improve.

Even so, interpretations of radiocarbon frequencies are complicated by other factors, particularly within-site sampling strategies. The Patagonian radiocarbon database shows considerable variation in the number of dates per site. If we rank sites according to the number of radiocarbon dates each has, the top 5% (n = 32) account for a third of all dates in the database; the top 25% (n = 161) account for two-thirds (67%; Figure 7.2). This is partly an artifact of an economical and quite logical means of assessing the range of a site's occupation, used the world over, which is to date only the uppermost and lowermost strata. While it is true that sites' occupation ranges vary and that this variation should, theoretically, correct some of the skew created by bracket dating, the cumulative effect is still oversampling of early and late components. As we saw in Chapter 5, this can create radiocarbon troughs and the appearance of middle Holocene population decline. More generally, the fact that most Patagonian sites (56%) are represented by a single radiocarbon date contributes to the impression that the region's population was exceedingly small. This was well-illustrated in the previous chapter's comparison of Patagonia's dates database to that of the ecologically-similar U.S. states of Wyoming and Colorado (Zahid et al. 2016), an area half the size of Patagonia with a radiocarbon record four times as large (Table 6.2). Incidentally, patterns observed in the Wyoming-Colorado database are more likely to reflect true population trends than are patterns in the current Patagonian database, simply as a function of its larger size.

Effects of Prehistoric Behavior and Technology

Granting the logic of Rick's (1987:54) original "dates as data" proposition—that "the number of [radiocarbon] dates is related to the magnitude of occupation, or to the total number of person-years of human existence in a given area"—Freeman and colleagues (2018) recently argued that radiocarbon time series reflect trends in energy consumption rather than population size per se, and that consumption is a function of economic complexity. Their consumption model highlights the fact that most recent attempts to improve radiocarbon-based population

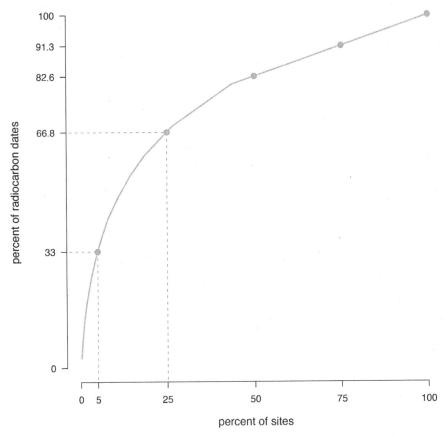

FIGURE 7.2. Accumulation curve of number of radiocarbon dates as a function of the number of sites. Sites are ordered in decreasing numbers of radiocarbon dates along the x-axis (N_{total} = 642 sites). The top 5% (best-sampled sites; n = 32) accounts for a third of all radiocarbon dates; the top 25% (n = 161) accounts for two thirds of all dates (67%). Note that the curve is, in fact, linear above (to the right of) 44% of sites. This reflects the fact that over 50% of sites (n = 362) are represented by a single radiocarbon date.

estimates center on external biasing factors (e.g., taphonomic loss), to the near exclusion of factors internal to prehistoric populations. In similar fashion, I argue that the relative visibility of prehistoric behaviors and technologies affects our ability to reliably estimate prehistoric population size from radiocarbon time series.

Chapter 5 describes a situation in which changed behaviors (e.g., reduced residential mobility) during the middle Holocene may have contributed to the appearance of a radiocarbon gap. Similarly, in Chapter 4, I argued that the relative speed of colonization can influence the size and character of the archaeological record: holding population size constant, fleet colonizers will create fewer and more ephemeral sites than slow-moving colonizers and will, correspondingly, produce a weaker radiocarbon signal.

The relative visibility of prehistoric toolkits can likewise generate discrepancies between population size and radiocarbon signal strength. Poor visibility leads to under-identification of sites and, therefore, underestimates of population size. An example from Chapter 5 illustrates the point: In Patagonia, bolas were sometimes made with readily-identifiable pecked stones, but at other times with unmodified stones placed in skin bags. Where unmodified bolas stones are indistinguishable from the noncultural lithic "background" and organic materials are poorly preserved, sites may go identified. Of course, the magnitude of this problem is very difficult to estimate, but simply acknowledging it makes us more likely to scrutinize radiocarbon frequency distributions in light of other archaeological data to identify potential biasing effects of prehistoric behaviors and technologies.

Preservation, sampling, and visibility complicate our estimates Patagonia's prehistoric population dynamics. Still, the very complications just summarized (and elaborated in previous chapters) indicate clearly that Patagonia's prehistoric population was larger than implied by the current radiocarbon database. That is, taphonomic loss and archaeological knowledge gaps as well as cryptic technologies, variable mobility, and other behavioral and technological characteristics all contribute to the appearance of a very small regional population through most of prehistory. Nonhuman population ecology indicates a positive relationship between environmental quality and population size, and the next section considers whether we can improve our estimates of prehistoric population dynamics through paleoenvironmental reconstruction.

Assessing Prehistoric Environmental Quality in Patagonia

Estimating the number of people Patagonia could have supported requires detailed information related to the abundance and distribution of resources. Archaeologists rely on proxy measures of environmental quality, including lake varves, pollen sequences, glacial records, and other paleoenvironmental data. From these, past environments and their effects on resource availability can be inferred, often relative to modern or historic resource availability. These data and inferences provide environmental context for radiocarbon trends and, when the goal is to interpret long archaeological time series, the fact that paleoenvironmental records obscure variation important on human timescales is generally unproblematic. However,

paleoenvironmental data are location-specific and may be of limited relevance across space, especially in a place like Patagonia where microclimates can have profound effects on habitat quality (Chapter 2). Local radiocarbon distributions should, whenever possible, be assessed relative to local paleoenvironmental records.

Whether in conjunction with paleoenvironmental data or independently, archaeologists quite rightly couple archaeological data and ecological/economic theory to interpret local resource availability. As discussed, the diet breadth model distills to the assumption that optimizing individuals should specialize in productive environments, taking only high-ranking resources, and be generalists with broad diets in relatively unproductive ones. Accordingly, the relative frequencies of high- and low-ranking resources—as indicated in archaeological sites' faunal, macrobotanical, and palynological records, as well as isotopic signatures in human skeletal remains—can be used to infer local habitat quality. These and other archaeological data provide the spatial and temporal resolution that is often blurred in paleoenvironmental records, which are better suited to descriptions of prevailing conditions and long-term trends. Importantly, though, archaeological measures of resource availability reflect a *ratio* of resources to people, and scarcity due to poor environmental quality is very different from scarcity due to an abundance of people. In fact, their respective implications for carrying capacity are at odds.

Neither paleoenvironmental nor archaeological records provide a straightforward account of past environmental quality and, in the Patagonian case, both records indicate considerable variation across space and through time. For a general assessment of Patagonia's environmental quality relative to prehistoric humans, we turn next to ecological measures of habitat suitability.

Ecological Evidence of Relative Abundance

Patagonia's coasts teem with fish, sea mammals, mollusks, shorebirds, and other resources. The bounty there is unquestionable. Elsewhere, resources may be sparser. Nonetheless, and despite extremes of temperature and rainfall, Patagonian vegetation is remarkably diverse. As Coronato and colleagues note (2008:38), "more than 65% of all families present in the south of South America are found in [Patagonia]." Even if much of the time foragers target only a subset of all available resources, "biodiversity decreases subsistence-related risk, which can positively affect hunter-gatherer population densities" (Tallavaara et al. 2018:1232). Likewise, the region's highest-ranked animal species, guanaco, makes (and likely made) good use of this diversity, readily feeding on a wide range of forage types and flexibly changing diets seasonally, annually, and situationally. Guanaco numbered between 30 and 50 million head at initial contact with Europeans (ca. 1500 CE; Sarno et al. 2015) despite the practice of killing calves and heavily pregnant females for the production of cloaks for trade, common among the Aónikenk (southern Tehuelche) (Prieto 1997). It is not clear how far back this practice goes, but motifs on pottery and stone plaques suggest that the cloak style of the historic period may date back to at least 500 BP. Guanaco were clearly thriving despite significant offtake. In fact, guanaco numbers at contact were comparable to those of bison in the North American "great bison belt." Prior to their near extirpation through overhunting, American bison (*Bos bison* spp.) may have numbered 60 million head or more (CABI 2019). Guanaco density in precontact Patagonia was considerably higher than bison density in late eighteenth-century North America, since the "great bison belt" covered a large portion of that continent (a landmass much larger than Patagonia's). This difference is offset to some extent by the fact that the average bison weighs about a ton—up to nine times the weight of the average guanaco. Still, the comparison serves to highlight the fact that food may have been ample in prehistoric Patagonia.

Of course, "ampleness" is relative, and, as our discipline has acknowledged for over half a century now (Lee and Devore 1968 and authors therein; Gowdy 1997 and authors therein), limited wants make for unlimited means. Even sparse resources can seem ample to small populations. In light of this, anecdotal evidence that Patagonians were not, in fact, struggling to wrest a living from a difficult landscape may not be so surprising. I refer here to one of the inspirations for the title of this book: the fabled Patagones, who were giants in the eyes of Magellan's men. The Aónikenk men thus described may have been six feet tall (182.88 cm; Fondebrider 2003), well above the current global average (173.23 cm [5' 8.16"]; n = 130 countries) and equal to (or nearly so) average male height in the three tallest countries in the world: the Netherlands, Montenegro, and Denmark (Smith 2017). A fair fraction of adult height owes to childhood health and nutrition, and it can be hard to grow a big body if calories and nutrients are in short supply, even when one is genetically predisposed. Great stature is at odds with the perception that Patagonia is a windswept wasteland. However, if Patagonian population size was small and groups lived below carrying capacity (or at equilibrium in accordance with the ideal free distribution; Chapters 3 and 4), per capita resource availability could have been quite high regardless of relatively low primary productivity.

Archaeological Evidence of Relative Abundance

Estimating average quality of life among prehistoric Patagonians is challenging, particularly for times and places lacking direct evidence of human health. Ideally, we would assess environmental marginality—a habitat's proximity to the lower limit of key-resource availability (e.g., water, kcals)—as biologists do, using physiological signs of stress at the population level (Soulé 1973). However, archaeologists rarely have access to skeletal populations sufficient to determine group health (see also Wood et al. 1992), and we often must rely on archaeological proxy data. This brief review of previous chapters' conclusions, each based in part on archaeological proxy data, suggests that prehistoric Patagonia was not marginal for human habitation and that, in fact, fewer people lived in Patagonia than could have been supported by available resources.

Whether New World colonization was fast or slow, Patagonia's earliest record supports a hypothesis of relative resource abundance. Some archaeologists interpret similarities in the timing and technologies of the two hemispheres' earliest sites as evidence of rapid colonization (Chapter 4). If true, this implies a subsistence strategy so general (e.g., mapping on to megafauna) that most environmental difference across the two continents was irrelevant. By extension, the Patagonian environment was as good as any, a hypothesis supported by the region's early record, which is at least coeval with that of North America. Alternatively, I argue that an earlier, slower colonization scenario better accounts for the level of landscape familiarity evident at Monte Verde (see also Dillehay 2012), and for the apparent loss of tailored clothing (and other technologies) to the "tropical filter" as people moved south from Siberia. By this hypothesis, environmental differences mattered a great deal. According to the ideal free distribution (Chapters 3 and 4), habitats should be occupied in rank-order, people moving into lower-ranked ones only once higher-ranked ones are "full," their resources depleted to the level of the next highest-ranked patch. If late Pleistocene Patagonia was as desolate and difficult as has been suggested (e.g., Salemme and Miotti 2008), it should not have been colonized until other habitats were "full," relatively late in the sequence, we would expect. Existing data do not support either late colonization of Patagonia or a "fullness" of adjacent regions sufficient to push people into a low-ranking Patagonian landscape circa 15,000 cal BP. It seems more likely that the earliest inhabitants were drawn to the region (pulled in) by available resources, which is to say that at least some Patagonian habitats were as rich (high-ranking) as habitats elsewhere.

Likewise, new data suggest that arid northern Argentine Patagonia was not abandoned during the hot, dry middle Holocene. Traditionally, the sparse middle Holocene record has been interpreted in terms of population decline or regional abandonment under the assumption that arid lands are not only marginal to begin with but simply get worse with decreased

rainfall and increased temperatures. However, as we saw in Chapters 2 and 5, arid-land species and ecosystems may be equipped to survive even prolonged droughts. Granting that data are few—precisely the middle Holocene problem—archaeofaunal records from this period suggest guanaco remained a key resource, which is at odds with the notion of resource scarcity sufficient to decimate human populations. Access to water (rather than food) may have been the limiting factor during the middle Holocene, but population size among ethnographic foragers is not limited by the abundance or timing of rainfall (Chapter 3), and decreased precipitation does not always result in an effective water deficit (Chapter 5). Data from systematic archaeological survey and obsidian hydration analyses suggest that, instead, populations simply repositioned themselves on a changed, but not necessarily degraded, landscape.

Finally, contrary to traditional interpretations that see Patagonian farming as either impossible due to environmental marginality or unnecessary because wild foods were adequate to sustain the region's relatively small population, evidence suggests both farming-favorable conditions (including environmental suitability) and declining foraging efficiency (K-induced pressure) across parts of the region during late prehistory. When taken together with alternative interpretations of initial colonization and the middle Holocene, a quite different picture of Patagonia, and of Patagonian prehistory, emerges.

An Alternative Hypothesis: Cultural "Succession" and Density Dependence

More people lived in prehistoric Patagonia than is suggested by the region's radiocarbon record, but the region could have supported more people than it did, even holding technology constant. Under most circumstances, intrinsic human population growth rates are high; unchecked by density dependent forces, populations tend to grow exponentially and to experience relatively constant pressure. Under population pressure, "selection will favor slow improvements in the adaptation of the population, with each increment of adaptive improvement rapidly resulting in the re-equilibration of the population given the new adaptation" (Richerson et al. 2009:213). So, unchecked, growing Patagonian populations should have iteratively increased property-of-environment carrying capacity through cultural innovations, leading to further population growth, as in the positive feedback loop described above.

Had that happened, we would expect material evidence of relatively rapid increases in technological and perhaps social complexity through time in spite of current data gaps due to sampling and postdepositional destruction. That we do not see this suggests prehistoric Patagonians did not experience relatively constant population pressure, and that something regulated Patagonian populations, holding them below equilibrium density (*K*). It is worth brief repetition of the ecological notions of population limitation and regulation, since these are not commonly used in archaeology. Factors that limit population are ones that set carrying capacity. We will return to these in a moment. Factors that regulate population hold it near or below carrying capacity (Krebs 2002). In prehistoric Patagonia, population-regulating factors were of at least two kinds: negative density dependence, a force with which most archaeologists are familiar, if not by that name, and positive density dependence.

Population regulation through negative density dependence is common in nature and, in fact, the sort of thing that inspired Thomas Malthus's thinking (1803), which in turn inspired Darwin's (1859). Negative density dependence is, in essence, growth restriction due to overcrowding, competition, and similar forces. Competition, for example, results in fewer resources and, potentially, fewer offspring per capita, limiting population growth. Competition also results from decreased resource availability, so environmental fluctuations affecting key resources can result in negative density-dependent population regulation, in much the way archaeologists have long described. Humans can, of course, break the sort of "stable limit" cycle that sees population growth followed by decline due to resource

depletion (Figure 7.3; Winterhalder et al. 1988), but this requires innovations that allow people to efficiently procure previously ignored resources. This is where positive density dependence comes into play.

Under positive density dependence, population growth increases rather than decreases at higher densities. This is sometimes referred to as the Allee effect, a concept I introduced in the context of the ideal free distribution model in Chapter 3. According to the ideal free distribution, the addition of foragers typically reduces patch quality through negative density dependence (overcrowding, competition). When there is an Allee effect, however, the addition of foragers initially offsets these detrimental effects through positive density dependence: larger groups might enjoy higher overall foraging returns through resource pooling, and higher returns can result in better survivorship and fertility; more individuals provide additional mating opportunities and defense against predators and enemies, both of which likewise lead to larger groups. Positive density dependence is critical because, as we have seen, larger populations are also more likely to produce *K*-altering innovations.

To a point, all human populations are subject to these countervailing forces, particularly in the critical period following colonization of a previously unoccupied space. If a population is too big, it faces famine and infighting; if too small, it may be unable to innovate its way to a higher ecological carrying capacity. In prehistoric Patagonia, the perfect storm of starting state (*sensu* ecological succession), environmental variation and variability, and geography may have kept populations relatively small and poorly connected, creating a crisis of positive density dependence and inhibiting the population-technology-population positive feedback cycle that might otherwise have resulted.

General characteristics of Patagonia's colonizing population likely affected subsequent population growth and technological development. The founding population was probably small (Borrero 1999; de la Fuente et al. 2018; Salemme and Miotti 2008), and the toolkit with

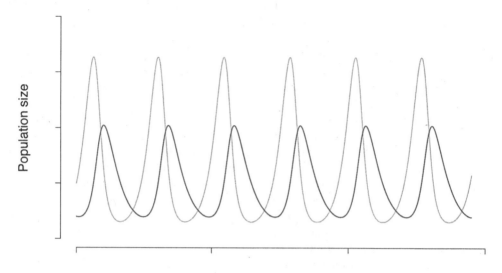

FIGURE 7.3. Basic predator–prey stable limit cycle based on standard Lotka-Volterra equations. The cycle describes population dynamics of two interacting species—a predator (blue) and its prey (gray)—whose numbers rise and fall asynchronously. When there are many prey, the predator population grows; increasing predation eventually causes the prey population to crash, which in turn causes predators to decline on a slight delay. When predation is relaxed (predators are fewer), prey populations rebound, leading to (lagged) growth in the predator population, and so forth. Figure by Andrew Marshall.

which it was equipped may have limited where, when, and how people hunted and gathered, particularly at higher latitudes. There are multiple ways in which this could be true, but here I refer specifically to the apparent lack of tailored clothing (Borrero 2012; Garvey 2018b). As I have argued (Chapters 3 and 4; Garvey 2018b), tailored clothing can improve foraging returns, survivorship, and fertility in cold environments, promoting population growth. Fitted clothing keeps the body covered while allowing a full range of limb motion, and the added warmth makes people less reliant on fires and shelters during the winter months, permitting longer and more distant winter foraging bouts. Well-clothed people require fewer calories for the maintenance of safe body temperatures in the cold, which can reduce resource competition and negative density dependence. Well-clothed women, in particular, may have higher fertility through the cold season, which is long at high latitudes. So, as with our "two identical foragers equipped with different technologies" (Chapter 3), colonizers

equipped with tailored clothing might have experienced an "effective environment" that was considerably more productive (higher initial carrying capacity) than was actually experienced by Patagonia's founding population. This "starting state"—a small population with limited cold-weather technologies—almost certainly influenced the rate and trajectory of subsequent cultural change in Patagonia.

Limitations imposed by the "starting state" were exacerbated by characteristics of Patagonian geography and environment, which conspired to keep populations low following colonization. For all the space I have devoted to arguments *against* Patagonia's ecological marginality, I concede that the region is marginal in one important sense: it is geographically isolated, the southern margin of the New World with a relatively narrow (W-E) contact plane between it and more northerly regions. Furthermore, the region is essentially *all* margin, a blade-like projection of land with limited direction-of-flow (of people and ideas) from most any location within Patagonia. The landform's longest axis, oriented north-south, spans nearly 20 degrees of latitude (Figure 2.3)—roughly equivalent to the distance between Las Vegas, Nevada, and Kodiak Island, Alaska. Along this axis, and across Patagonia more generally, climatic and geographic conditions change to such a degree and interact in such ways that the Patagonian landscape is best described as a mosaic of vastly different environment types. Prehistorically, this may have limited the relevance of particular experiences and adaptations from place to place, and resulted in relatively small numbers of people working towards common adaptive goals despite what might have been a healthy system of resource exchange (e.g., obsidian; Stern 2018). Such "geometric isolation" may be responsible for the regional genetic differentiation that occurred following initial colonization (de la Fuente et al. 2018), which would have compounded Patagonia's more general geographic isolation.

The effects of geography and environmental heterogeneity, which limited effective population size (i.e., the number of interacting social learners), were almost certainly exacerbated by stochastic events. Recall that small effective population size has been linked to relatively slower rates of cultural change, lower overall cultural complexity, and even maladaptive losses of culture (Chapters 3 and 4; Collard et al., 2013; Henrich 2004; Powell et al. 2009; Shennan 2001). This is partly because small populations are statistically more vulnerable to both extinction (Figure 7.4) and random losses of innovators/skilled individuals, who are primarily responsible for technological advances (see also Chapter 3). It is also true that the loss of entire small groups (or their relocation or dispersal) due to unpredictable events such as earthquakes, landslides, volcanic eruptions, and the like, would have broken or disrupted intergroup connections, further reducing effective population size.

In summary, culture can raise local carrying capacity, improve survivorship and fertility, and stimulate population growth, which can then feed back and effect subsequent technological change. This is a pattern we see frequently in archaeological records across the world.

In prehistoric Patagonia, however, a small colonizing population equipped with limited cold-weather technology remained relatively small, regulated by positive density dependence which, in turn, limited population by inhibiting K-increasing innovations. What resulted was a *negative* feedback cycle between population and technology rather than the positive one we might have expected otherwise. By this view, Patagonia is not an inherently difficult place to be a forager—the average prehistoric Patagonian may well have been healthy and well-fed. Patagonia is a place, like every other colonized by humans, where environmental, cultural, and demographic factors interacted in complex ways to produce complex cultural phenomena.

The View

How we view a place influences the questions we ask of it. The Patagonian landscape can certainly be challenging. It is, alternately, rugged, bewilderingly featureless, hot, bitterly cold, dry, torrentially wet ... And, paradoxically, the region's prehistoric record is at once relatively simple and exceedingly complex. That is, both material culture from archaeological contexts and objects and social structures observed ethnographically are comparatively simpler than, say, those of adjacent regions (e.g., Uruguay's late middle Holocene *Constuctores de Cerritos* culture, the Inca and their ancestors; "simpler" in the sense of fewer kinds of artifacts, fewer social divisions). However, as we have seen throughout this book, Patagonian prehistory is every bit as complex as other regions'. And it is as fantastically diverse as the landscape itself.

Focusing on the diversity that captivated a young Charles Darwin—the curious, if cryptic, abundance of life in Patagonia—affords a distinct view of the region's prehistory and generates hypotheses that warrant further exploration. Granting that the hypotheses explored in this book are limited in part by incomplete information, the fact that portions of the Patagonian landscape remain archaeologically unknown presents both challenges and opportunities. As every archaeologist knows, knowledge

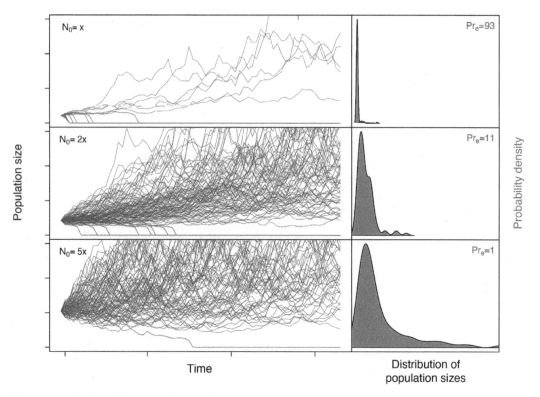

FIGURE 7.4. Simulated dynamics of populations with populations of different initial sizes. The left column depicts traces of 100 populations subject to the same amount of demographic stochasticity. Red traces indicate populations that go extinct. The right column depicts the distribution of population sizes at the end of the simulation run, with the percentage of runs that resulted in extinction given in red in the top right. The top row is a population of size x. In the middle row, the population size is doubled (2x), resulting in larger average population sizes and extinction probabilities that drop from 93% to 11%. The bottom row depicts a population with initial size of 5x, with a larger distribution of ending population sizes and an extinction probability of 1%. Figure by Andrew Marshall.

gaps are irresistibly enticing. They invite a closer look, a detailed exploration.

It is true that many important details are blurred when we zoom out to see the whole of Patagonia's million square kilometers and the entire sweep of its human occupation, however long we ultimately determine that to be. But such an exercise in perspective can sometimes change the way we see the details once we zoom back in. One thing this approach is likely to reveal is that microscale and macroscale explanations do not always align. Indeed, a key objective in the continued development of a unified science of cultural evolution (Mesoudi et al. 2006) is the expansion of empirical research that bridges microevolutionary and macroevolutionary models

of cultural evolution (Jordan et al. 2013:113). Archaeological data, which are often population-level data generated by individuals over long time spans, are essential to examining the multilevel dynamics of cultural evolution (Shennan 2013). Our role is central. And, as Simpson and Darwin themselves discovered nearly one and two hundred years ago, respectively, Patagonia is a place of unparalleled potential for the study of questions central to evolutionary theory. It is a land that inspired stories about giants, and that has since inspired scholarly giants in their work. Patagonia is an essential testing ground for pivotal hypotheses relating to hunter-gatherers, human ecology, and cultural evolution.

References

Abbott, Charles C.
1889   Evidences of the Antiquity of Man in East-
        ern North America. *Science* 12:103–105.

Adair, James
1775   *The History of the American Indian, Partic-*
        ularly Those Nations Adjoining to the Missis-
        sippi, East and West Florida, Georgia, South
        and North Carolina, and Virginia. Dilley,
        London.

Adovasio, James M., and Jake Page
2002   *The First Americans: In Pursuit of Archae-*
        ology's Greatest Mystery. Random House,
        New York.

Adovasio, James M., and David Pedler
1997   Monte Verde and the Antiquity of Human-
        kind in the Americas. *Antiquity* 71:573–580.

Aguirre, Luis
1985   The Southern Andes. In T*he Ocean Basins*
        and Margins, edited by Alan Nairn, William
        Kanes, and Francis Stehli, pp. 256–376. Ple-
        num, New York.

Aikens, C. Melvin, and David B. Madsen
1986   Prehistory of the Eastern Area. In *Hand-*
        book of North American Indians, Volume 11
        (Great Basin), edited by W. L. d'Azevedo,
        pp. 149–160. Smithsonian Institution Press,
        Washington, DC.

Albanese, John P., and George C. Frison
1995   Cultural and Landscape Change During the
        Middle Holocene, Rocky Mountain Area,
        Wyoming and Montana. In *Archaeologi-*
        cal Geology of the Archaic Period in North
        America, Special Papers #297, edited by
        E. Arthur Bettis, pp. 1–19. Geological Soci-
        ety of America, Boulder.

Alcamán, Eugenio
1997   Los Mapuche-Huilliche del Fatahuillimapu
        Septentroinal: Expansión Colonial, Guerras
        Internas y Alianzas Políticas (1750–1792).
        Revista de Historia Indígena 2:29–76.

Aldenderfer, Mark
1998   *Montane Foragers: Asana and the South-*
        Central Andean Archaic. University of Iowa,
        Iowa City.

Allan, William
1965   *The African Husbandman.* Oliver and Boyd,
        Edinburgh.

Allee, Warder C., and Edith Bowen
1932   Studies in Animal Aggregations: Mass
        Protection Against Colloidal Silver Among
        Goldfishes. *Journal of Experimental Zoology*
        61:185–207.

Allekotte, I., P. Baule, C. Bonifazi, et al.
2002   Site Survey for the Pierre Auger Observato-
        ry. *Journal of Physics G: Nuclear and Particle*
        Physics 28:1499–1509.

American Chemical Society
2015   Mosquito-Repelling Chemicals Identified
        in Traditional Sweetgrass. Press release
        August 14, 2015, accessed July 2018. https://
        www.acs.org/content/acs/en/pressroom
        /newsreleases/2015/august/sweetgrass.html.

Ames, Kenneth M., and Herbert D. G. Maschner
1999   *Peoples of the Northwest Coast: Their Ar-*
        chaeology and Prehistory. Thames and Hud-
        son, London.

Ancapichún, Santiago, and José Garcés-Vargas
2015   Variability of the Southeast Pacific Subtrop-
        ical Anticyclone and Its Impact on Sea Sur-
        face Temperature off North-Central Chile.
        Ciencias Marinas 41:1–20.

Anderson, David G., Daniel Sandweiss, and Kirk A.
Maasch (editors)
2007   *Climate Change and Cultural Dynamics:*
        A Global Perspective on Holocene Transi-
        tions. Academic Press, San Diego.

Andersson, Claes, and Petter Törnberg
2016   Fidelity and the Speed of the Treadmill:
        The Combined Impact of Population Size,
        Transmission Fidelity, and Selection on

the Accumulation of Cultural Complexity. *American Antiquity* 81:576–590.

Andrefsky Jr., William

1994   Raw Material Availability and the Organization of Technology. *American Antiquity* 59:21–35.

1998   *Lithics: Macroscopic Approaches to Analysis.* Cambridge University Press, Cambridge.

Angourakis, Andreas, José Ignacio Santos, José Manuel Galán, et al.

2014   Food For All: An Agent-Based Model to Explore the Emergence and Implications of Cooperation for Food Storage. *Environmental Archaeology* doi: 10.1179/1749631414Y .0000000041.

Anovitz, Lawrence, J. Michael Elam, Lee Riciputi, et al.

1999   The Failure of Obsidian Hydration Dating: Sources, Implications and New Directions. *Journal of Archaeological Science* 26:735–752.

Antevs, Ernst

1948   Climatic Changes and Pre-White Man. *University of Utah Bulletin* 38:167–191.

Aporta, Claudio, and Eric Higgs

2005   Global Positioning Systems, Inuit Wayfinding, and the Need for a New Account of Technology. *Current Anthropology* 46:729–753.

Aravena, Juan-Carlos

2007   Reconstructing Climate Variability Using Tree Rings and Glacier Fluctuations in the Southern Chilean Andes. PhD dissertation, University of Western Ontario. http://adsabs.harvard.edu/abs/2007PhDT ....168A.

Ariztegui, Daniel, Flavio S. Anselmetti, Adrian Gilli, et al.

2008   Late Pleistocene Environmental Change in Eastern Patagonia and Tierra Del Fuego: A Limnogeological Approach. *Developments in Quaternary Sciences* 1:241–53.

Arrigoni, Gloria I., Marcos Andrieu, and Cristina Bañados

2006   Arqueología de Cazadores-Recolectores Prehistóricos en la Costa Central del Golfo San Gorge. In *Arqueología de La Costa Patagónica: Perspectivas Para La Conservación,* edited by Isabel Cruz and María S. Caracotche, pp. 90–106. Río Gallegos, Universidad Nacional de la Patagonia Austral.

Aschero, Carlos, Rafael Goñi, María Teresa Civalero, et al.

2005   Holocenic Park: Arqueología del Parque Nacional Perito Moreno. *Anales de la Administración de Parques Nacionales* 17:71–119.

Austin, Amy T., and Osvaldo E. Sala

2002   Carbon and Nitrogen Dynamics across a Natural Precipitation Gradient in Patagonia, Argentina. *Journal of Vegetation Science* 13:351–360.

Bahamonde, Nora, Susana Martin, and Alicia Pelliza Sbriller

1986   Diet of Guanaco and Red Deer in Neuquén Province, Argentina. *Journal of Range Management* 39:22–23.

Bailey, Geoffrey C., and Nicholas C. Fleming

2008   Archaeology of the Continental Shelf: Marine Resources, Submerged Landscapes and Underwater Archaeology. *Quaternary Science Review* 27:2153–2165.

Bailey, Harry P.

1960   A Method of Determining the Warmth and Temperateness of Climate. *Geografiska Annaler* 43:1–16.

Baker, R. Robin

1978   *The Evolutionary Ecology of Animal Migration.* Holmes and Meier, New York.

Baldini, Ryan

2015   Revisiting the Effect of Population Size on Cumulative Cultural Evolution. *Journal of Cognition and Culture* 15:320–336.

Barberena, Ramiro, Karen Borrazzo, Agustina Rughini, et al.

2015   Perspectivas Arqueológicas para Patagonia Septentrional: Sitio Cueva Huenul 1 (Provincia del Neuquén, Argentina). *Magallania* 43: 137–163.

Barberena, Ramiro, M. Victoria Fernández, Agustina Rughini, et al.

2019   Deconstructing a Complex Obsidian 'Source-scape': A Geoarchaeological and Geochemical Approach in Northwestern Patagonia. *Geoarchaeology* 34:30–41.

Barberena, Ramiro, Adán Hajduk, Adolf Gil, et al.

2011   Obsidian in the South-Central Andes: Geological, Geochemical and Archaeological Assessment of North Patagonian Sources (Argentina). *Quaternary International* 245:25–36.

Barberena, Ramiro, César Méndez, and María Eugenia de Porras

2017   Zooming Out from Archaeological Discontinuities: The Meaning of Mid-Holocene

Temporal Troughs in South American Deserts. *Journal of Anthropological Archaeology* 46:68–81.

Barberena, Ramiro, Luciano Prates, and María Eugenia de Porras
2015   The Human Occupation of Northwestern Patagonia (Argentina): Paleoecological and Chronological Trends. *Quaternary International* 356:111–126.

Bárcena, Ramiro
2001   Prehistoria del Centro-Oeste Argentino. In *Historia Argentina Prehispánica*, tomo II, edited by Eduardo Berberián and Axel Nielsen, pp. 561–634. Editorial Brujas.

Barker, Graeme
2006   *The Agricultural Revolution in Prehistory: Why did Foragers become Farmers?* Oxford, Oxford, UK.

Barlow, K. Renee
2006   A Formal Model for Predicting Agriculture Among the Fremont. In *Behavioral Ecology and the Transition to Agriculture*, edited by Douglas Kennett and Bruce Winterhalder, pp. 87–102. University of California, Berkeley.

Barrientos, Gustavo
2001   Una Aproximación Bioarqueológica al Estudio del Poblamiento Prehispánico Tardío del Sudeste de la Región Pampeana. *Intersecciones en Antropología* 2:3–18.

Basgall, Mark E.
1987   Resource Intensification Among Hunter–Gatherers: Acorn Economies in Prehistoric California. *Research in Economic Anthropology* 9:21–52.

Bazzaz, Fakhri A.
1996   *Plants in Changing Environments*. Cambridge University Press, Cambridge.

Baumhoff, Martin, and Robert Heizer
1965   Postglacial Climate and Archaeology in the Desert West. In *The Quaternary of the United States: A Review Volume for the VII Congress of the International Association for Quaternary Research*, edited by Herbert E. Wright and David G. Frey, pp. 697–708. Princeton University Press, Princeton.

Bean, Lowell J., and Katherine S. Saubel
1972   *Temalpakh: Cahuilla Indian Knowledge and Usage of Plants*. Malki Museum Press, Banning, CA.

Beaudoin, Alwynne B., Milt Wright, and Brian Ronaghan
1996   Late Quaternary Landscape History and Archaeology in the 'Ice-Free Corridor':

Some Recent Results from Alberta. *Quaternary International* 32:113–126.

Belmar, Carolina A.
2019   *Los Cazadores-Recolectores y las Plantas en Patagonia: Perspectivas desde el Sitio Cueva Baño Nuevo 1, Aisén*. Social-Ediciones, Santiago.

Bender, Susan J., and Gary Wright
1988   High-Altitude Occupations, Cultural Process, and High Plains Prehistory: Retrospect and Prospect. *American Anthropologist* 90:619–639.

Benjamin, Jonathan
2010   Submerged Prehistoric Landscapes and Underwater Site Discovery: Reevaluating the 'Danish Model' for International Practice. *Journal of Island and Coastal Archaeology* 5:253–270.

Benson, Larry, Michaele Kashgarian, Robert Rye, et al.
2002   Holocene Multidecadal and Multicentennial Droughts Affecting Northern California and Nevada. *Quaternary Science Reviews* 21:659–682.

Bernal, Valeria, Paula González, Florencia Gordón, et al.
2016   Exploring Dietary Patterns in the Southernmost Limit of Prehispanic Agriculture in America by Using Bayesian Stable Isotope Mixing Models. *Current Anthropology* 57:230–239.

Bertrand, Sébastien, François Charlet, Bernard Charlier, et al.
2008   Climate Variability of Southern Chile since the Last Glacial Maximum: A Continuous Sedimentological Record from Lago Puyehue (40°S). *Journal of Paleolimnology* 39:179–195.

Betancourt, Julio, Claudio Latorre, Jason A. Rech, et al.
2000   A 22,000-yr Record of Monsoonal Precipitation from Northern Chile's Atacama Desert. *Science* 289:1542.

Bettinger, Robert L.
1980   Explanatory/Predictive Models of Hunter-Gatherer Adaptation. *Advances in Archaeological Method and Theory* 3:189–255.
2009a   *Hunter-Gatherer Foraging: Five Simple Models*. Eliot Werner Publications, New York.
2009b   Macroevolutionary Theory and Archaeology: Is There a Big Picture? In *Macroevolution in Human Prehistory*, edited by Anna Prentiss, Ian Kuijt, and James Chatters, pp. 275–295. Springer, New York.

2015   *Orderly Anarchy: Sociopolitical Evolution in Aboriginal California*. University of California Press, Oakland.

Bettinger, Robert L., and Jelmer W. Eerkens

1997   Evolutionary Implications of Metrical Variation in Great Basin Projectile Points. In *Rediscovering Darwin: Evolutionary Theory in Archaeological Explanation*, edited by C. Michael Barton and Geoffrey A. Clark, pp. 177–191. American Anthropological Association, Arlington, Virginia.

1999   Point Typologies, Cultural Transmission, and the Spread of Bow-And-Arrow Technology in the Prehistoric Great Basin. *American Antiquity* 64:231–242.

Bettinger, Robert L., Raven Garvey, and Shannon Tushingham

2015   *Hunter-Gatherers Archaeological and Evolutionary Theory*, 2nd ed. Springer, New York.

Bettinger, Robert L., and Mark Grote

2016   Marginal Value Theorem, Patch Choice, and Human Foraging Response in Varying Environments. *Journal of Anthropological Archaeology* 42:79–87.

Bettinger, Robert L., Ripan Malhi, and Helen McCarthy

1997   Central Place Models of Acorn and Mussel Processing. *Journal of Archaeological Science* 24:887–899.

Bettinger, Robert L., and Peter J. Richerson

1996   The State of Evolutionary Archaeology: Evolutionary Correctness, or the Search for the Common Ground. In *Darwinian Archaeologies*, edited by Herbert D. G. Maschner, pp. 221–231. Plenum, New York.

Bettinger, Robert L., Bruce Winterhalder, and Richard McElreath

2006   A Simple Model of Technological Intensification. *Journal of Archaeological Science* 33:538–545.

Bettinger, Robert L., and David A. Young

2004   Hunter-Gatherer Population Expansion in North Asia and the New World. In *Entering America: Northeast Asia and Beringia Before the Last Glacial Maximum*, edited by David B. Madsen, pp. 239–251. University of Utah Press, Salt Lake City.

Binford, Lewis R.

1968   Post-Pleistocene Adaptations. In *New Perspectives in Archeology*, edited by Sally R. Binford and Lewis R. Binford, pp. 313–341. Aldine, Chicago.

1980   Willow Smoke and Dogs' Tails: Hunter-Gatherer Settlement Systems and Archaeological Site Formation. *American Antiquity* 45:4–20.

2001   *Constructing Frames of Reference: An Analytical Method for Archaeological Theory Building Using Hunter-Gatherer and Environmental Data Sets*. University of California Press, Berkeley.

Bird, Douglas, and James O'Connell

2006   Behavioral Ecology and Archaeology. *Journal of Archaeological Research* 14:143–88.

Bird, Douglas, Rebecca Bliege Bird, and Brian F. Codding

2009   In Pursuit of Mobile Prey: Martu Hunting Strategies and Archaeofaunal Interpretations. *American Antiquity* 74:3–29.

Bird, Junius

1938   Antiquity and Migrations of the Early Inhabitants of Patagonia. *Geographical Review* 28:250–275.

1988   *Travels and Archaeology in South Chile*. University of Iowa Press, Iowa City.

Bird, Michael, Robin Beaman, Scott Condie, et al.

2018   Palaeogeography and Voyage Modeling Indicates Early Human Colonization of Australia Was Likely from Timor-Roti. *Quaternary Science Reviews* 191:431–439.

Bitocchi, Elena, Elisa Bellucci, Alessandro Giardini, et al.

2013   Molecular Analysis of the Parallel Domestication of the Common Bean (*Phaseolus vulgaris*) in Mesoamerica and the Andes. *New Phytologist* 197:300–313.

Bjerck, Hein, Heidi Mjelva Breivik, Ernesto Piana, et al.

2016   Exploring the Role of Pinnipeds in the Human Colonization of the Seascapes of Patagonia and Scandinavia. In *Marine Ventures: Archaeological Perspectives on Human-Sea Relations*, edited by Hein Bjerck, Heidi Mjelva Breivik, Silje Fretheim, Ernesto Piana, Birgitte Skar, Angélika Tivoki and A. Francisco Zangrando, pp. 53–74. Equinox, Sheffield.

Blackburn, Tim M., Kevin J. Gaston, and Natasha Loder

1999   Geographic Gradients and Body Size: A Clarification of Bergmann's Rule. *Diversity and Distributions* 5:165–174.

Bleed, Peter

1986   The Optimal Design of Hunting Weapons: Maintainability or Reliability. *American Antiquity* 51:737–747.

Bliege Bird, Rebecca, and Brian Codding
2015   The Sexual Division of Labor. In *Emerging Trends in the Social and Behavioral Sciences*, edited by Robert Scott and Marlis Buchmann, pp. 1–16. John Wiley & Sons, Hoboken, NJ.

Blitz, John
1988   Adoption of the Bow in Prehistoric North America. *North American Archaeologist* 9:123–145.

Blurton Jones, N.
1987   Tolerated Theft, Suggestions about the Ecology and Evolution of Sharing, Hoarding, and Scrounging. *Social Science Information* 26:31–54.

Boas, Franz
1896   The Limitations of the Comparative Method of Anthropology. *Science* 4:901–908.

Böcher, Tyge, Jens Hjerting, and Knud Rahn
1972   *Botanical Studies in the Atuel Valley Area, Mendoza Province, Argentina*, Parts I, II and III. Volume 22. Dansk Botansk Arkiv, Copenhagen.

Bogaard Amy, Michael Charles, Katheryn Twiss, and Andy Fairbairn
2009   Private Pantries and Celebrated Surplus: Storing and Sharing Food at Neolithic Catalhoyuk, Central Anatolia. *Antiquity* 83:649–668.

Boldurian, Anthony
2008   Clovis Type-Site, Blackwater Draw, New Mexico: A History, 1929–2009. *North American Archaeologist* 29:65–89.

Bonavia, Duccio, and Carlos Monge
2008   Notes on the Biology of the South American Camelids. In *The South American Camelids*, edited by Duccio Bonavia, pp. 11–56. Cotsen Institute, Los Angeles.

Borrazzo, Karen
2013   Tafonomía Lítica y Modelo de la Dinámica Eololacustre del Norte de la Bahía San Sebastián (Tierra del Fuego, Argentina). *Revista Comechingonia* 17:149–169.

2016   Lithic Taphonomy in Desert Environments: Contributions from Fuego-Patagonia (Southern South America). *Quaternary International* 422:19–28.

Borrero, Luis A.
1989   Spatial Heterogeneity in Fuego-Patagonia. In *Archaeological Approaches to Cultural Identity*, edited by Stephen Shennan, pp. 258–266. Routeledge, UK.

1990   Fuego-Patagonian Bone Assemblages and the Problem of Communal Guanaco Hunting. In *Hunters of the Recent Past*, edited by Leslie B. Davis and Brian O.K. Reeves, pp. 373–399. Unwin, Boston.

1997   The Origins of Ethnographic Subsistence Patterns in Fuego-Patagonia. In *Patagonia: Natural Prehistory, Prehistory and Ethnography at the Uttermost End of the Earth*, edited by Colin McEwan, Luis Borrero, Alfredo Prieto, pp. 32–45. British Museum Press, London.

1999   The Prehistoric Exploration and Colonization of Fuego-Patagonia. *Journal of World Prehistory* 13:321–55.

2003   Taphonomy of the Tres Arroyos 1 Rockshelter, Tierra Del Fuego, Chile. *Quaternary International* 110:87–93.

2004   The Archaeozoology of Andean 'Dead Ends' in Patagonia: Living Near the Continental Ice Cap. In *Colonisation, Migration and Marginal Areas: A Zooarchaeological Approach*, edited by Mariana Mondini, Sebastián Muñoz, and Stephen Wickler, pp. 55–61. Oxbow Books, Oakville.

2008   Early Occupations in the Southern Cone. In *The Handbook of South American Archaeology*, edited by Helaine Silverman and William H. Isbell, pp. 59–77. Springer, New York.

2009   The Elusive Evidence: The Archaeological Record of the South America Extinct Megafauna. In *American Megafaunal Extinctions at the End of the Pleistocene*, edited by Gary Haynes, pp.145–168. Springer, New York.

2012   The Human Colonization of the High Andes and Southern South America During the Cold Pulse of the Late Pleistocene. In *Hunter-Gatherer Behavior: Human Response During the Younger Dryas*, edited by Metin Eren, pp. 57–78. Left Coast Press, Walnut Creek.

2015   The Process of Human Colonization of Southern South America: Migration, Peopling and 'The Archaeology of Place. *Journal of Anthropological Archaeology* 38:46–51.

Borrero, Luis A., and Ramiro Barberena (editors)
2004   *Arqueología del Norte de la Isla Grande de Tierra del Fuego*. Editorial Dunken, Buenos Aires.

Borromei, Ana, and Mirta Quattrocchio
2008   Late and Postglacial Paleoenvironments of Tierra Del Fuego: Terrestrial and Marine

Palynological Evidence. *Developments in Quaternary Science* 11:369–382.

Bourgeon, Lauriane, Ariane Burke, and Thomas Higham

2017   Earliest Human Presence in North America Dated to the Last Glacial Maximum: New Radiocarbon Dates from Bluefish Caves, Canada. *PLOS ONE* 12:e0169486.

Bourlot, Tirso

2010   *Zooarqueología de Sitios a Cielo Abierto en el Lago Cardiel (Patagonia, Argentina): Fragmentación Ósea y Consumo de Grasa Animal en Grupos Cazadores-Recolectores Del Holoceno Tardío.* Archaeopress, Oxford.

Bowles, Samuel

2011   Cultivation of Cereals by the First Farmers Was not more Productive than Foraging. *Proceedings of the National Academy of Sciences* 108:4760–4765.

2015   Why Australia Remained a "Continent of Hunter-Gatherers." *Santa Fe Institute working paper 2015-06-016.* Accessed online June 2018 https://www.santafe.edu/research/results/working-papers/why-australia-remained-a-continent-of-hunter-gathe.

Bowles, Samuel, and Jung-Kyoo Choi

2013   Coevolution of Farming and Private Property during the Early Holocene. *Proceedings of the National Academy of Sciences* 110:8830–8835.

Boyd, Matthew, and Clarence Surette

2010   Northernmost Precontact Maize in North America. *American Antiquity* 75:117–133.

Boyd, Matthew, Tamara Varney, Clarence Surette, et al.

2008   Reassessing the Northern Limit of Maize Consumption in North America: Stable Isotope, Plant Macrofossil, and Trace Element Content of Carbonized Food Residue. *Journal of Archaeological Science* 35:2545–2556.

Boyd, Robert, and Peter J. Richerson

1985   *Culture and the Evolutionary Process.* University of Chicago Press, Chicago.

1987   The Evolution of Ethnic Markers. *Current Anthropology* 2:65–79.

Boyd, Robert, Peter J. Richerson, and Richard McElreath

2005   Shared Norms and the Evolution of Ethnic Markers. In *The Origin and Evolution of Cultures,* edited by Robert Boyd and Peter J. Richerson, pp. 118–131. Oxford University Press, Oxford, UK.

Bradley, Bruce, and Dennis Stanford

2004   The North Atlantic Ice-Edge Corridor: A Possible Paleolithic Route to the New World. *World Archaeology* 36:459–478.

Braje, Todd, Tom Dillehay, Jon Erlandson, et al.

2017   Finding the First Americans. *Science* 358:592–594.

Braje, Todd, Torben Rick, Tom Dillehay, et al.

2018   Arrival Routes of First Americans Uncertain—Response. *Science* 359:1225.

Bridges, E. Lucas

1951   *Uttermost Part of the Earth.* Hodder and Stoughton, London.

Broughton, Jack M.

1994   Late Holocene Resource Intensification in the Sacramento Valley, California: The Vertebrate Evidence. *Journal of Archaeological Science* 21:501–514.

Broughton, Jack M., Michael D. Cannon, and Eric J. Bartelink

2010   Evolutionary Ecology, Resource Depression, and Niche Construction Theory in Archaeology: Applications to Central California Hunter-Gatherers and Mimbres-Mogollon Agriculturalists. *Journal of Archaeological Method and Theory* 4:371–421.

Broughton, Jack M., Michael D. Cannon, Frank E. Bayham, and David A. Byers

2011   Prey Body Size and Ranking in Zooarchaeology: Theory, Empirical Evidence, and Applications from the Northern Great Basin. *American Antiquity* 76:403–428.

Broughton, Jack M., and James O'Connell

1999   On Evolutionary Ecology, Selectionist Archaeology, and Behavioral Archaeology. *American Antiquity* 64:153–165.

Brown, James A.

1985   Long-Term Trends to Sedentism and the Emergence of Complexity in the American Midwest. In *Prehistoric Hunter-Gatherers: The Emergence of Cultural Complexity,* edited by T. Douglas Price and James A. Brown, pp. 201–231. Academic Press, Orlando, Florida.

Brown, James A., and Robert K. Vierra

1983   What Happened in the Middle Archaic? Introduction to an Ecological Approach to Koster Site Archaeology. In *Archaic Hunters and Gatherers in the American Midwest,* edited by James L. Phillips and James A. Brown, pp. 165–195. Academic Press, New York.

Brücher, Heinz
1988   The Wild Ancestor of *Phaseolus vulgaris* in South America. In *Genetic Resources of* Phaseolus *Beans*, edited by Paul Gepts, pp. 185–214. Springer Netherlands, Dordrecht.

Bruinard, Enrique, and Lucila B. Osuna
1982   La Diagonal Árida Argentina: Un Límite Climático Real. *Revista Geográfica* 95:5–20.

Buchanan, Briggs, Michael O'Brien, and Mark Collard
2014   Continent-Wide or Region-Specific? A Geometric Morphometrics-Based Assessment of Variation in Clovis Point Shape. *Archaeological and Anthropological Sciences* 6:145–162.

Bujalesky, Gustavo
2012   Tsunami Overtopping Fan and Erosive Scarps at Atlantic Coast of Tierra del Fuego. *Journal of Coastal Research* 28:442–456.

Burger, Joseph, Vanessa Weinberger, and Pablo Marquet
2017   Extra-Metabolic Energy Use and the Rise in Human Hyper-Density. *Scientific Reports* 7:43869, accessed August 15, 2018. http://www.nature.com/articles/srep43869.

Burnside, William, James H. Brown, Oskar Burger, et al.
2012   Human Macroecology: Linking Pattern and Process in Big-Picture Human Ecology. *Biological Reviews* 87:194–208.

Butzer, Karl W.
1957   Late Glacial and Postglacial Climatic Variation. *Erkunde* 2:21–35.

CABI
2019   *Invasive Species Compendium*. CAB International, Wallingford, UK. www.cabi.org/isc.

Campagna, Claudio, Carlos Verona, and Valeria Falabella
2005   *Situación Ambiental en la Ecorregión del Mar Argentino*. https://web.archive.org/web/20131105114838/http://www.fvsa.org.ar/situacionambiental/Mar%20Argentino.pdf.

Canals Frau, Salvador
1963   The Huarpe. In *Handbook of the South American Indians, Volume 1: The Marginal Tribes*, edited by Julian H. Stewad, pp. 169–175. Cooper Square, New York.

Capitanelli, Ricardo
1972   Geomorfología y Clima de la Provincia de Mendoza. *Revista de la Sociedad Argentina de Botánica* 13:15–48.

Cardich, Augusto
1985   Una Fecha Radiocarbónica Más de la Cueva 3 de Los Toldos (Santa Cruz, Argentina. *Relaciones de la Sociedad Argentina de Antropología* 16:269–275.

Cardich, Augusto, Lucio Cardich, and Adán Hajduk
1973   Secuencia Arqueológica y Cronolólica Radiocarbónica de la Cueva 3 de Los Toldos. *Relaciones de la Sociedad Argentina de Antropología* 7:87–122.

Cardich, Augusto, and Laura Miotti
1983   Recursos Faunísticos en los Cazadores-Recolectores de Los Toldos (Prov. de Santa Cruz). *Relaciones de la Sociedad Argentina de Antropologia* 15:145–157.

Carré, Matthieu, Moufok Azzoug, Ilhem Bentaleb, et al.
2012   Mid-Holocene Mean Climate in the South Eastern Pacific and Its Influence on South America. *Quaternary International* 253:55–66.

Cashdan, Elizabeth
1983   Territoriality Among Human Foragers: Ecological Models and an Application to Four Bushman Groups. *Current Anthropology* 24:47–66.
1985   Coping with Risk: Reciprocity Among the Basarwa of Northern Botswana. *Man* 20:454–474.
1990   Introduction. In *Risk and Uncertainty in Tribal and Peasant Economies*, edited by Elizabeth Cashdan, pp. 1–16. Westview Press, Boulder, Colorado.

Cassiodoro, Gisela, Diego Rindel, Rafael Goñi, et al.
2013   Arqueología del Holoceno Medio y Tardío en Patagonia Meridional: Poblamiento Humano y Fluctuaciones Climáticas. *Diálogo Andino* 41:5–23.

Cattáneo, G. Roxana
2006   *Tecnología Lítica del Pleistoceno Final/Holoceno Medio: Un Estudio de los Cazadores Recolectores de la Patagonia Austral, Argentina*. BAR International Series, Vol. 1580. Archaeopress, Oxford.

Cavalli-Sforza, Luigi L., and Marcus W. Feldman
1981   *Cultural Transmission and Evolution: A Quantitative Approach,* Monographs in Population Biology 16. Princeton University Press, Princeton.

Ceballos, Rita
1982   El sitio Cuvín Manzano. *Series y Documentos* 9:1–66.

Chala-Aldana, Döbereiner, Hervé Bocherens, Christopher Miller, et al.

2018 Investigating Mobility and Highland Occupation Strategies During the Early Holocene at the Cuncaicha Rock Shelter Through Strontium and Oxygen Isotopes. *Journal of Archaeological Science: Reports* 19:811–827.

Charles, Michael, Hugues Pessin, and Mette Marie Hald

2010 Tolerating Change at Late Chalcolithic Tell Brak: Responses of an Early Urban Society to an Uncertain Climate. *Environmental Archaeology* 15:183–198.

Charlin, Judith E.

2009 *Estrategias de Aprovisionamiento y Utilización de las Materias Primas Líticas en el Campo Volcánico Pali Aike (Prov. Santa Cruz, Argentina).* British Archaeological Reports, International Series, Vol. 1901. Archaeopress, Oxford.

Charlin, Judith E., Karen Borrazzo, and Marcelo Cardillo

2013 Exploring Size and Shape Variations in Late Holocene Projectile Points from Northern and Southern Coasts of Magellan Strait (South America). In *Understanding Landscapes, from Land Discovery to Their Spatial Organization*, edited by François Djinjian and Sandrine Robert, pp. 39–50. British Archaeological Reports, International Series 2541, Archaeopress, Oxford.

Charnov, Eric L.

1976 Optimal Foraging: The Marginal Value Theorem. *Theoretical Population Biology* 9:129–136.

Chatwin, Bruce

1977 *In Patagonia.* Jonathan Cape, London.

Chavez, Francisco, Arnaud Bertrand, Renato Guevara-Carrasco, and Pierre Soler

2008 The Northern Humboldt Current System: Brief History, Present Status and a View Towards the Future. *Progress in Oceanography* 79:95–105.

Chiavazza, Horacio, and Valeria Cortegoso

2004 De la Cordillera a la Llanura: Disponibilidad Regional de Recursos Líticos y Organización de la Tecnología en el Norte de Mendoza, Argentina. *Chungará*, Volumen Especial, pp. 723–737.

Chichester, Francis

1966 *Along the Clipper Way.* Hodder & Stoughton, London.

Cibilis, Andrés, and Pablo Borrelli

2019 *Grasslands of Patagonia.* FAO.org, accessed January 2019. http://www.fao.org/3/y8344e/y8344e09.htm.

Clark, Peter U., Arthur S. Dyke, Jeremy D. Shakun, et al.

2009 The Last Glacial Maximum. *Science* 325:710–714.

Clarkson, Chris, Zenobia Jacobs, Ben Marwick, et al.

2017 Human Occupation of Northern Australia by 65,000 Years Ago. *Nature* 547:306–310.

Coan, Titus

1880 *Adventures in Patagonia: Missionary's Exploring Trip.* New York, Dodd, Mead & Company.

Codding, Brian, and Terry Jones

2013 Environmental Productivity Predicts Migration, Demographic, and Linguistic Patterns in Prehistoric California. *Proceedings of the National Academy of Sciences* 110:14569–14573.

Cohen, Jenny M.

2014 Paleoethnobotany of Kilgii Gwaay: A 10,700 Year Old Ancestral Haida Archaeological Wet Site. Master's thesis, Department of Anthropology, University of Victoria, Victoria, British Columbia.

Colinvaux, Paul

1996 Introduction: Reconstructing the Environment. In *American Beginnings: The Prehistory and Paleoecology of Beringia*, edited by Frederick H. West, pp. 13–19. University of Chicago Press, Chicago.

Collard, Ian F., and Robert A. Foley

2002 Latitudinal Patterns and Environmental Determinants of Recent Human Cultural Diversity: Do Humans Follow Biogeographical Rules? *Evolutionary Ecology Research* 4:371–383.

Collard, Mark, Briggs Buchanan, and Michael J. O'Brien

2014 Population Size as an Explanation for Patters in the Paleothic Archaeological Record: More Caution is Needed. *Current Anthropology* 54:S388–S396.

Collard, Mark, Briggs Buchanan, Michael J. O'Brien, and Jonathan Scholnick

2013 Risk, Mobility or Population Size? Drivers of Technological Richness Among

Contact-Period Western North American Hunter-Gatherers. *Philosophical Transactions of the Royal Society London B: Biological Sciences* 368:20120412.

Collard, Mark, Michael Kemery, and Samantha Banks

2005 Causes of Tool Kit Variation Among Hunter-Gatherers: A Test of Four Competing Hypotheses. *Canadian Journal of Archaeology* 29:1–19.

Collins, Michael B.

1997 The Lithics from Monte Verde, A Descriptive-Morphological Analysis. In *Monte Verde: A Late Pleistocene Settlement in Chile*, Vol. II, pp. 383–506. Smithsonian Institute Press, Washington.

Collins, Michael B., and Bruce A. Bradley

2008 Evidence for Pre-Clovis Occupation at the Gault Site (41BL323), Central Texas. *Current Research in the Pleistocene* 25:70–72.

Collins, Michael B., Dennis J. Stanford, D.L. Lowery, and Bruce A. Bradley

2013 North America Before Clovis: Variance in Temporal/Spatial Cultural Patterns, 27,000 to 13,000 Cal Yr BP. In *Paleoamerican Odyssey*, edited by Kelly Graf, Caroline V. Ketron, and Michael R. Waters, pp. 521–540. Center for the Study of the First Americans, College Station, Texas.

Contreras, Daniel, and John Meadows

2014 Summed Radiocarbon Calibrations as a Population Proxy: A Critical Evaluation Using a Realistic Simulation Approach. *Journal of Archaeological Science* 52:591–608.

Cooper, John M.

1946 The Yahgan. In *Handbook of South American Indians, Volume 1: The Marginal Tribes*, edited by Julian Steward, pp. 81–106. Smithsonian Institution, Washington, DC.

1963 The Patagonian and Pampean Hunters. In *Handbook of South American Indians, Volume 1: The Marginal Tribes*, edited by Julian Steward, pp. 127–168. Cooper Square, New York.

Coronato, Andrea, Fernando R. Coronato, Elizabeth Mazzoni, and Mirian Vázquez

2008 The Physical Geography of Patagonia and Tierra Del Fuego. *Developments in Quaternary Sciences* 11:13–55.

Coronato, Andrea, Patricia Fanning, Mónica Salemme, et al.

2011 Aeolian Sequence and the Archaeological Record in the Fuegian Steppe, Argentina. *Quaternary International* 245:122–135.

Coronato, Andrea, Mónica Salemme, and Jorge Rabassa

1999 Paleoenvironmental Conditions During the Early Peopling of Southernmost South America (Late Glacial-Early Holocene, 14–8 ka B.P.). *Quaternary International* 53:77–92.

Coronato, Fernando R.

1993 Wind Chill Factor Applied to Patagonian Climatology. *International Journal of Biometeorology* 37:1–6.

Cortegoso, Valeria

2006 Comunidades Agrícolas en el Valle de Potrerillos (NO de Mendoza) Durante el Holoceno Tardío: Organización de la Tecnología y Vivienda. *Intersecciones en Antropología* 7:77–94.

Cortegoso, Valeria, Ramiro Barberena, Víctor Durán, and Gustavo Lucero

2016 Geographic Vectors of Human Mobility in the Andes (34–36°S): Comparative Analysis of 'Minor' Obsidian Sources. *Quaternary International* 422:81–92.

Cortegoso, Valeria, Michael Glascock, Anna María De Francesco, et al.

2014 Chemical Characterization of Obsidian in Central Western Argentina and Central Chile: Archaeological Problems and Perspectives. In *Physical, Chemical and Biological Markers in Argentine Archaeology: Theory, Methods and Applications*, edited by Débora Kligmann and Marcelo Morales, pp. 17–26. British Archeological Reports, International Series 2678. Oxford.

Cortegoso, Valeria, Gustavo Neme, Martín Giesso, et al.

2012 El Uso de la Obsidiana en el Sur de Mendoza. In *Paleoecología Humana en el Sur de Mendoza*, edited by Gustavo Neme and Adolfo Gil, pp. 181–211. Sociedad Argentina de Antropología, Buenos Aires.

Cotter, John L.

1937 The Occurrence of Flints and Extinct Animals in Pluvial Deposits near Clovis, New Mexico. Report on the Excavations at the Gravel Pit in 1936. *Proceedings of the Philadelphia Academy of Natural Sciences* 89(4):2–16.

1938 The Occurrence of Flints and Extinct Animals in Pluvial Deposits near Clovis, New Mexico. Report on the Field Season of 1937. *Proceedings of the Philadelphia Academy of Natural Sciences* 90(6):113–117.

Courchamp, Franck, Ludek Berec, and Joanne Gascoigne

2008 *Allee Effects in Ecology and Conservation.* Oxford University Press, Oxford, New York.

Cox, Guillermo E.

1963 Viajes a las Regiones Septentroinales de Patagonia 1862–1863. *Anales de La Universidad de Chile* 23:3–239.

Crivelli Montero, Eduardo, Damiana Curzio, and Mario J. Silveira

1993 La Estratigrafía de la Cueva Traful 1 (Provincia De Neuquén). *Praehistoria* 1:9–160.

Crombé, Philippe, and Erick Robinson

2014 ^{14}C Dates as Demographic Proxies in Neolithisation Models of Northwestern Europe: A Critical Assessment Using Belgium and Northeast France as a Case-Study. *Journal of Archaeological Science* 52:558–566.

Cruz, Isabel, and María Soledad Caracotche (editors)

2008 *Arqueología de La Costa Patagónica: Perspectivas Para La Conservación.* Universidad Nacional de la Patagonia Austral, Río Gallegos.

Cueto, Manuel, Areil Frank, and Alicia Castro

2017 A Technomorphological and Functional Study of Late Pleistocene and Middle Holocene Lithic Assemblages from Patagonia Argentina. *Quaternary International* 442:67–79.

D'Altroy, Terence N.

2003 *The Incas.* Blackwell Publishing, Malden, Massachusetts.

Damiani, Oscar, and Alejandro García

2011 El Manejo Indígena del Agua en San Juan (Argentina): Diseno y Funcionameiento del Sistema de Calales de Zonda. *Multequina* 20:27–42.

Danielson, Eric, James Levin, and Elliot Abrams

2003 *Meteorology.* McGraw-Hill, New York.

D'Antoni, Hector L.

1983 Pollen Analysis of Gruta del Indio. *Quaternary of South America and Antarctic Peninsula* 1:83–104.

Darwin, Charles

1839 *Voyages of the Adventure and Beagle, Volume III, Journal and Remarks, 1832–1836.* Henry Colburn, London.

1859 *On the Origin of Species By Means of Natural Selection, Or The Preservation Of Favoured Races In The Struggle For Life.* John Murray, London.

1871 *The Descent of Man, and Selection in Relation to Sex.* John Murray, London.

Dawe, Robert J., and Marcel Kornfeld

2017 Nunataks and Valley Glaciers: Over the Mountains and through the Ice. *Quaternary International* 444:56–71.

Deacon, Janette

1974 Patterning in the Radiocarbon Dates for the Wilton/Smithfield Complex in Southern Africa. *South African Archaeological Bulletin* 29:3–18.

De Francesco, Anna Maria, Donatella Barca, Marco Bocci, et al.

2017 Provenance of Obsidian Artifacts from the Natural Protected Area Laguna del Diamante (Mendoza, Argentina) and Upper Maipo Valley (Chile) by LA-ICP-MS Method. *Quaternary International* 468:134–140.

De Francesco, Anna Maria, Víctor Durán, A. Bloise, et al.

2006 Caracterización y Procedencia de Obsidianas de Sitios Arqueológicos del Área Natural Protegida Laguna del Diamante (Mendoza, Argentina) con Metodología no Destructive por Fluorescencia de Rayos (XRF). *Annales Arqueología y Etnología* 61:53–67.

de Groot, Rudolf S., Matthew Wilson, and Roelof M. J. Boumans

2002 A Typology for the Classification, Description and Valuation of Ecosystem Functions, Goods and Services. *Ecological Economics* 41:393–408.

de la Fuente, Constanza, María C. Ávila-Arcos, Jacqueline Galimany, et al.

2018 Genomic Insights into the Origin and Diversification of Late Maritime Hunter-Gatherers from the Chilean Patagonia. *Proceedings of the National Academy of Sciences* 115(17):E4006–E4012.

de la Vega, Garcilaso

1609 *Comentarios Reales.* Pedro Crasbeeck, Lisbon, Portugal.

De Nigris, Mariana

2004 Guanaco and Huemul in Patagonian Hunter-Gatherers Diet. In *Zooarchaeology of South America*, edited by Guillermo L. Mengoni Goñalons, pp. 11–37. British Archaeological Reports,

International Series 1298. Archaeopress, Oxford.

De Nigris, Mariana, and Guillermo L. Mengoni Goñalons

2002 The Guanaco as a Source of Meat and Fat in the Southern Andes. In *The Zooarchaeology of Fats, Oils, Milk and Dairying*, edited by Jacqui Mulville and Alan Outram, pp. 160–166. Oxbow, Durham.

de Onis, Mercedes, and Monika Blössner

2003 The World Health Organization Global Database on Chid Growth and Malnutrition: Methodology and Applications. *International Journal of Epidemiology* 32:518–526.

De Pol-Holz, Ricardo, Osvaldo Ulloa, Laurent Dezileau, et al.

2006 Melting of the Patagonian Ice Sheet and Deglacial Perturbations of the Nitrogen Cycle in the Eastern South Pacific. *Geophysical Research Letters* 33:1–4.

de Porras, Maria Eugenia, Antonio Maldonado, Flavia Quintana, et al.

2014 Environmental and Climatic Changes at Central Chilean Patagonia since Late Glacial (Mallín El Embudo, 44°S). *Climate of the Past* 10:1063–1078.

Dhondt, André

1988 Carrying Capacity: A Confusing Concept. *Acta Oecolo* 9:337–346.

Diamond, Jared

1997 *Guns, Germs, and Steel: The Fates of Human Societies*. Norton, New York.

Diamond, Jared, and Peter Bellwood

2003 Farmers and Their Languages: The First Expansions. *Science* 300:597–603.

Díaz, Emilio, Fernando Gonzalez, and Kempton E. Webb

2020 Patagonia. *Encyclopedia Britannica*, https://www.britannica.com/place/Patagonia-region-Argentina.

Diéguez, Sergio, and Gustavo Neme

2003 Geochronology of the Arryo Malo 3 Site and the First Human Occupations in North Patagonia in the Early Holocene. In *Where the South Wind Blows: Ancient Evidence of Paleo South Americans*, edited by Laura Miotti, Mónica Salemme and Nora Flegenheimer, pp. 87–92. Texas A&M University Press, College Station, Texas.

Dillehay, Tom D.

1989 *Monte Verde: A Late Pleistocene Settlement in Chile*, Vol. I. Smithsonian Institute Press, Washington, DC.

1997 *Monte Verde: A Late Pleistocene Settlement in Chile*, Vol. II. Smithsonian Institute Press, Washington.

2000 *The Settlement of the Americas: A New Prehistory*. Basic Books, New York.

2012 Climate, Technology, and Society During the Terminal Pleistocene Period in South America. In *Hunter-Gatherer Behavior: Human Response During the Younger Dryas*, edited by M. Eren, pp. 25–56. Left Coast Press, Walnut Creek.

Dillehay, Tom D., Carlos Ocampo, José Saavedra, et al.

2015 New Archaeological Evidence for an Early Human Presence at Monte Verde, Chile. *PLOS ONE* 10:e0141923.

Dillehay, Tom D., C. Ramirez, Mario Pino, et al.

2008 Monte Verde: Seaweed, Food, Medicine, and the Peopling of South America. *Science* 320:784–786.

Dixon, E. James

1993 *Quest for the Origins of the First Americans*. University of New Mexico Press, Albuquerque.

1999 *Bones, Boats, & Bison: Archeology and the First Colonization of Western North America*. University of New Mexico Press, Albuquerque.

Dobzhansky, Theodosius

1947 *Genetics and the Origin of Species*. Columbia University Press, New York.

1950 Evolution in the Tropics. *American Scientist* 38:209–221.

1973 Nothing in Biology Makes Sense except in the Light of Evolution. *American Biology Teacher* 35:125–129.

D'Orazio, Massimo, Samuele Agostini, Francesco Mazzarini, et al.

2000 The Pali Aike Volcanic Field, Patagonia: Slab-Window Magmatism Near the Tip of South America. *Tectonophysics* 321:407–427.

D'Orbigny, Alcide

1835–1847 *Voyage dans L'Amérique Méridonale*, 9 volumes. Paris.

Doura, Miguel Armando

2011 Acerca del Topónimo "Patagonia," una Nueva Hipótesis de su Génesis. *Nueva Revista de Filología Hispánica* 59:37–78.

Dowdeswell, Julian A., and M. Vásquez

2013 Submarine Landforms in the Fjords of Southern Chile: Implications for Glacimarine Processes and Sedimentation in a Mild Glacier-Influenced Environment. *Quaternary Science Reviews* 64:1–19.

Durán, Víctor, Anna Maria De Francesco, Valeria Cortegoso, et al.

2012   Caracterización y Procedencia de Obsidianas de Sitios Arqueológicos del Centro Oeste de Argentina y Centro de Chile con Metodología No Destructiva Por Fluorescencia De Rayos X (XRF). *Intersecciones en Antropología* 13:423–437.

Durán, Víctor, Martín Giesso, Michael Glascock, et al.

2004   Estudio de Fuentes de Aprovisionamiento y Redes de Distribución de Obsidiana Durante el Holoceno Tardío en el Sur de Mendoza (Argentina). *Estudios Atacameños* 28:25–43.

Durán, Víctor, and Raúl Mikkan

2009   Impacto del Volcanismo Holocénico Sobre el Poblamiento Humano del Sur De Mendoza (Argentina). *Intersecciones en Antropología* 10:295–310.

Durán, Víctor, Diego Winocur, Charles Stern, et al.

2016   Volcanismo Holocénico y Poblamiento Humano en la Cordillera Sur de la Provincial de Mendoza (Argentina): Una Perspectiva Geoarqueológica. *Intersecciones en Antropología*, volumen especial 4:33–46.

Earle, Timothy

2000   Archaeology, Property and Prehistory. *Annual Reviews of Anthropology* 29:39–60.

Eerkens, Jelmer

1998   Reliable and Maintainable Technologies: Artifact Standardization and the Early to Later Mesolithic Transition in Northern England. *Lithic Technology* 23:42–53.

2003   Residential mobility and pottery use in the Western Great Basin. *Current Anthropology* 44:728–738.

2008   Nomadic Potters: Relationships Between Ceramic Technologies and Mobility Strategies. In *The Archaeology of Mobility: Old World and New World Nomadism*, edited by Hans Barnard and Willeke Wendrich, pp. 307–326. Cotsen Institute of Archaeology, Los Angeles.

Eerkens, Jelmer, and Robert L. Bettinger

2001   Techniques for Assessing Standardization in Artifact Assemblages: Can We Scale Material Variability? *American Antiquity* 66:493–504.

2008   Cultural Transmission and the Analysis of Stylistic and Functional Variation. In *Cultural Transmission and Archaeology: Issues and Case Studies*, edited by Michael J.

O'Brien, pp. 31–36. Society for American Archaeology, Washington, DC.

Eerkens, Jelmer, Robert L. Bettinger, and Peter J. Richerson

2014   Cultural Transmission Theory and Hunter-Gatherer Archaeology. In *Oxford Handbook of the Archaeology and Anthropology of Hunter-Gatherers*, edited by Vicki Cummings, Peter Jordan, and Marek Zvelebil, pp. 1127–1142. Oxford University Press, Oxford.

Eerkens, Jelmer, and Carl Lipo

2005   Cultural Transmission, Copying Errors, and the Generation of Variation in Material Culture and the Archaeological Record. *Journal of Anthropological Archaeology* 24:316–334.

Elias, Scott, and Barnaby Crocker

2008   The Bering Land Bridge: A Moisture Barrier to the Dispersal of Steppe–Tundra Biota? *Quaternary Science Reviews* 27:2473–2483.

Elkin, Dolores C.

1995   Volume Density of South American Camelid Skeletal Parts. *International Journal of Osteoarchaeology* 5:29–37.

Ellison, Peter T.

2001   *On Fertile Ground*. Harvard University Press, Harvard, MA.

2003   Energetics and Reproductive Effort. *American Journal of Human Biology* 15:342–351.

Ellison, Peter T., Claudia R. Valeggia, and Diana S. Sherry

2005   Human Birth Seasonality. In *Seasonality in Primates: Studies of Living and Extinct Human and Non-Human Primates*, edited by Diane Brockman and Carel P. van Schaik, pp. 379–399. Cambridge University Press, Cambridge.

Elston, Robert G., and P. Jeffrey Brantingham

2002   Microlithic Technology in Northeast Asia: A Risk Minimizing Strategy of the Late Pleistocene and Early Holocene. In *Thinking Small: Global Perspectives on Microlithization*, Archaeological Papers of the American Anthropological Association, Vol. 12., edited by Robert G. Elston and Steven L. Khun, pp. 103–116. American Anthropological Association, Washington, DC.

Erickson, Clark L.

1988   Raised Field Agriculture in the Lake Titicaca Basin: Putting Ancient Agriculture Back to Work. *Expedition* 30:8–16.

Erickson, Clark L., and Kay L. Candler
1989   Raised Fields and Sustainable Agriculture in the Lake Titicaca Basin of Peru. In *Fragile Lands of Latin America: Strategies for Sustainable Development*, edited by J. Browder, pp. 231–248. Westview Press, Boulder, Colorado.

Erlandson, Jon M.
2001   The Archaeology of Aquatic Adaptations: Paradigms for a New Millennium. *Journal of Archaeological Research* 9:287–350.

Erlandson, Jon M., Michael Graham, Bruce Bourque, et al.
2007   The Kelp Highway Hypothesis: Marine Ecology, the Coastal Migration Theory, and the Peopling of the Americas. *Journal of Island and Coastal Archaeology* 2: 161–174.

Erlandson, Jon M., Torben Rick, Todd Braje, et al.
2011   Paleoindian Seafaring, Maritime Technologies, and Coastal Foraging on California's Channel Islands. *Science* 331:1181–1185.

Eshleman, Jason, Ripan Malhi, and David G. Smith
2003   Mitochondrial DNA Studies of Native Americans: Conceptions and Misconceptions of the Population Prehistory of the Americas. *Evolutionary Anthropology: Issues, News, and Reviews* 12:7–18.

Espizúa, Lydia E.
2005   Holocene Glacier Chronology of Valenzuela Valley, Mendoza Andes, Argentina. *The Holocene* 17:1079–1085.

Espizúa, Lydia E., and Pierre Pitte
2009   The Little Ice Age Glacier Advance in the Central Andes (35°S), Argentina. *Palaeogeography, Palaeoclimatology, Palaeoecology* 281:345–350.

Fair, Susan W.
2006   *Alaska Native Art: Tradition, Innovation, Continuity.* University of Alaska Press, Fairbanks.

Favier Dubois, Cristián, Florencia Borella, Liliana Manzi, et al.
2006   Aproximación Regional al Registro Arqueológico de la Costa Rionegrina. In *Arqueología de la Costa Patagónica: Perspectivas Para la Conservación*, edited by Isabel Cruz and María Soledad Caracotche, pp. 50–69. Universidad Nacional de la Patagonia Austral, Río Gallegos.

Fernández, M. Victoria, Ramiro Barberena, Agustina Rughini, et al.
2017   Obsidian Geochemistry, Geoarchaeology, and Lithic Technology in Northwest Patagonia (Argentina). *Journal of Archaeological Science: Reports* 13:372–381.

Fiedel, Stuart
2017   The Anzick Genome Proves Clovis Is First, after All. *Quaternary International* 444:4–9.

Fladmark, Knut
1978   The Feasibility of the Northwest Coast as a Migration Route for Early Man. In *Early Man in America From a Circum-Pacific Perspective*, edited by Alan L. Bryan, pp. 119–128. Archaeological Researchers International, Edmonton, Alberta, Canada.
1979   Routes: Alternative Migration Corridors for Early Man in North America. *American Antiquity* 44:55–69.

Fletcher, Michael-Shawn, and Patricio Moreno
2012   Vegetation, Climate and Fire Regime Changes in the Andean Region of Southern Chile (38°S) Covaried with Centennial-Scale Climate Anomalies in the Tropical Pacific Over the Last 1500 Years. *Quaternary Science Reviews* 46:46–56.

Foley, Robert
1987   *Another Unique Species: Patterns in Human Evolutionary Ecology.* Longman Scientific & Technical, Harlow, Essex, England.

Fondebrider, Jorge
2003   *Versiones de la Patagonia.* Emecé Editores S.A., Buenos Aires.

Food and Agriculture Organization of the United Nations (FAO)
2018   http://www.fao.org/docrep/005/Y4351E /y4351e0i.htm.

Franklin, William L.
1982   Biology, Ecology, and Relationship to Man of the South American Camelids. In *Mammalian Biology in South America*, edited by Michael A. Mares and Hugh H. Genoways, pp. 457–489. University of Pittsburgh Press, Pittsburgh.

Freeman, Jacob, David Byers, Erick Robinson, and Robert Kelly
2018   Culture Process and the Interpretation of Radiocarbon Data. *Radiocarbon* 60:453–467.

Freeman, Milton M. R.
1971   A social and Ecologic Analysis of Systematic Female Infanticide Among the Netsilik Eskimo. *American Anthropologist* 73:1011–1078.

Fretwell, Stephen D.
1972   *Populations in a Seasonal Environment.* Princeton University Press, Princeton.

Fretwell, Stephen D., and Henry L. Lucas, Jr.
1970   On Territorial Behavior and Other Factors Influencing Habitat Distribution in Birds. *Acta Biotheoretica* 19:16–36.

Friedman, Irving, and William Long
1976   Hydration Rate of Obsidian. *Science* 191:347–352.

Friedman, Irving, and Robert Smith
1960   A New Dating Method Using Obsidian: Part I, The Development of the Method. *American Antiquity* 25:476–522.

Friedman, Milton
1953   *Essays in Positive Economics*. University of Chicago Press, Chicago.

Frisancho, A. Roberto, and Lawrence P. Greska
1989   Developmental Responses in the Acquisition of Functional Adaptation to High Altitude. In *Human Population Biology: A Transdisciplinary Science*, edited by Michael A. Little and Jere D. Haas, pp. 203–221. Oxford University, Oxford.

Frison, George C.
1975   Man's Interaction with Holocene Environments on the Plains. *Quaternary Research* 5:289–300.

Gallardo, Carlos R.
1910   *Tierra del Fuego: Los Onas*. CABAUT y Cia, Buenos Aires.

Galloway, Victoria, William R. Leonard, and Evgueni Ivakine
2000   Basal Metabolic Adaptation of the Evenki Reindeer Herders of Central Siberia. *American Journal of Human Biology* 12:75–87.

Gambier, Mariano
1985   *La Cultura de los Morillos*. Instituto de Investigaciones Arqueológicas y Museo, San Juan, Argentina.
2000   *Prehistoria de San Juan*. Ansilta Editora: San Juan, Argentina.

Garfinkel, Yosef, David Ben-Shlomo, and Tali Kuperman
2009   Large-Scale Storage of Grain Surplus in the Sixth Millennium BC: The Silos of Tel Tsaf. *Antiquity* 83:309–325.

Garreaud, Rene D.
2009   The Andes Climate and Weather. *Advances in Geosciences* 22:3.

Garrido, J. L., J. N. Amaya, and Z. Novacs
1981   Territorialidad, Comportamiento, Individual Diaria de Una Población de guanacos en la Reserva Faunística de Cabo Dos Bahía. *SECYT-CONICET-CNP Contribución* 42:26–27.

Garvey, Raven
2008   A Human Behavioral Ecological Approach to a Proposed Middle Holocene Occupational Gap. *Before Farming* 2008/2, article 2.
2012a   Human Behavioral Responses to Middle Holocene Climate Changes in Northern Argentine Patagonia. PhD dissertation, Department of Anthropology, University of California, Davis.
2012b   El uso de la hidratación de obsidianas en el sur de Mendoza, Argentina. In *Paleoecología Humana del Sur de Mendoza*, edited by Gustavo Neme and Adolfo Gil, pp. 213–227. Sociedad Argentina de Antropología, Buenos Aires.
2015a   A Model of Lithic Raw Material Procurement. In *Lithic Technological Systems and Evolutionary Theory*, edited by Nathan Goodale and William Andrefsky, Jr., pp. 156–171. Cambridge University Press, Cambridge.
2015b   Probabilistic Survey and Prehistoric Patterns of Land and Resource Use in Mendoza Province, Argentina. *Intersecciones en Antropología* 16:301–312.
2016   *Report of Findings, Río Ibáñez-6 West Site, Aysén, Chile*. Excavation report submitted to the Consejo Nacional de Monumentos Nacionales de Chile. On file with author.
2018a   Current and Potential Roles of Archaeology in the Development of Cultural Evolutionary Theory. *Philosophical Transactions of the Royal Society B* 373: 20170057.
2018b   Cultural Transmission and Sources of Diversity: A Comparison of Temperate Maritime Foragers of the Northern and Southern Hemispheres. In *Foraging in the Past: Archaeological Studies in Hunter-Gatherer Diversity*, edited by Ashley Lemke, pp. 19–48. University Press of Colorado, Boulder.
2019   Comment on "Forager Mobility in Constructed Environments" by Randall Haas and Steven Kuhn. *Current Anthropology* 60:517–519.
2020   Human Ecology, Perceptual Bias, and the Co-occurrence of Archaeolgical Gaps with Climate Change. In *Cowboy Ecologist: Essays in Honor of Robert L. Bettinger*, edited by Terry Jones, Michael Delacorte, and Roshanne Bakhtiary, pp. 1–22. Center for Archaeological Research at Davis.

Garvey, Raven, and Robert L. Bettinger
2014   Adaptive and Ecological Approaches to the Study of Hunter-Gatherers. In *Oxford*

Handbook of the Archaeology and Anthropology of Hunter-Gatherers, edited by Vicki Cummings, Peter Jordan, and Marek Zvelebil, pp. 69–91. Oxford University Press, Oxford.

2018 A Regional Approach to Prehistoric Landscape Use in West-Central Argentina. *Journal of Archaeological Science: Reports* 19:846–855.

Garvey, Raven, Tim Carpenter, Adolfo Gil, et al.

2016 Archaeological Age Estimation Based on Obsidian Hydration Data for Two Northern Patagonian Sources. *Chungara: Chilean Journal of Anthropology* 48:9–23.

Garvey, Raven, and Francisco Mena

2016 Confronting Complexities of Artifact-Geofact Debates: Re-Analysis of a Coarse Volcanic Rock Assemblage from Chilean Patagonia. *Lithic Technology* 41:114–129.

Gaston, Kevin, Tim M. Blackburn, and John I. Spicer

1998 Rapoport's Rule: Time for an Epitaph? *Trends in Ecology and Evolution* 13:70–74.

Gavrilets, Sergey

2010 High-Dimensional Fitness Landscapes and Speciation. In *Evolution: The Extended Synthesis*, edited by Massimo Pigliucci and Gerd Müller, pp. 45–79. MIT Press, Cambridge, Massachusetts.

Giardina, Miguel

2006 Preservación y Fragmentación de Restos de Aves en el Registro Zooarqueológico de Arroyo Malo 3, Alto Valle de Río Atuel, Mendoza, Argentina. In *Simposio de Zooarqueología y Tafonomía de Aves, Primer Taller de Zooarqueología*, Chile.

2010a Human Exploitation of Rheidae in Northern Patagonia, Argentina (South America). *Groningen Archaeological Studies* 10.

2010b El Aprovechamiento de la Avifauna entre las Sociedades Cazadoras-Recolectoras del Sur de Mendoza, un Enfoque Arqueozoológico. PhD dissertation, Facultad de Ciencias Naturales y Museo, Universidad Nacional de La Plata.

Giardina, Miguel, Mercedes Corbat, Eva Ailén Peralta, et al.

2015 El Registro Arqueológico en sitio La Olla (San Rafael, Mendoza): Implicaciones para las Ocupaciones Humanas en el Valle Medio del Río Atuel. *Revista del Museo de Antropología* 8:51–66.

Giesso, Martín, Víctor Durán, Gustavo Neme, et al.

2011 A Study of Obsidian Source Usage in the Central Andes of Argentina and Chile. *Archaeometry* 53:1–21.

Gil, Adolfo

2000 Arqueología de La Payunia: Sureste de Mendoza. PhD dissertation, Facultad de Ciencias Naturales y Museo, Universidad de La Plata, Benos Aires, Argentina.

Gil, Adolfo, Lumila Menéndez, Juan Atencio, et al.

2018 Estrategias Humanas, Estabilidad y Cambio en la Frontera Agrícola Sur Americana. *Latin American Antiquity* 29:6–26.

Gil, Adolfo, Gustavo Neme, and Robert Tykot

2011 Stable Isotopes and Human Diet in Central Western Argentina. *Journal of Archaeological Science* 38:1395–1404.

Gil, Adolfo, Gustavo Neme, Andrew Ugan, and Robert Tykot

2014 Oxygen Isotopes and Human Residential Mobility in Central Western Argentina: Oxygen Isotopes and Mobility in Western Argentina. *International Journal of Osteoarchaeology* 24:31–41.

Gil, Adolfo, Robert Tykot, Gustavo Neme, and Nicole Shelnut

2006 Maize on the Frontier: Isotopic and Macrobotanical Data from Central-Western Argentina. In *Histories of Maize*, edited by John Staller, Robert Tykot and Bruce Benz, pp. 199–214. Academic Press, New York.

Gil, Adolfo, Ricardo Villalba, Andrew Ugan, et al.

2014 Isotopic Evidence on Human Bone for Declining Maize Consumption During the Little Ice Aga in Central Western Argentina. *Journal of Archaeological Science* 49:213–227.

Gil, Adolfo, Marcelo Zárate, and Gustavo Neme

2005 Mid-Holocene Paleoenvironments and the Archaeological Record of Southern Mendoza, Argentina. *Quaternary International* 132:81–94.

Gilbert, M. Thomas P., Dennis Jenkins, Anders Götherstrom, et al.

2008 DNA from Pre-Clovis Human Coprolites in Oregon, North America. *Science* 320:786–789.

Gilligan, Ian

2007 Neanderthal Extinction and Modern Human Behaviour: The Role of Climate Change and Clothing. *World Archaeology* 39:499–514.

Goebel Jr., Julius
1971   *The Struggle for the Falkland Islands: A Study in Legal and Diplomatic History.* Kennikat Press, Port Washington, New York.

Goebel, Ted
2002   The "Microblade Adaptation" and Recolonization of Siberia During the Late Upper Pleistocene. In *Thinking Small: Global Perspectives on Microlithization*, Archeological Papers of the American Anthropological Association, Vol. 12, edited by R. G. Elston and S. Kuhn, pp. 117–131. American Anthropological Association, Arlington, Virginia.

Goebel, Ted, Michael Waters, and Dennis O'Rourke
2008   The Late Pleistocene Dispersal of Modern Humans in the Americas. *Science* 319:1497–1502.

Goldberg, Paul, Francesco Berna, and Richard I. Macphail
2009   Comment on 'DNA from Pre-Clovis Human Coprolites in Oregon, North America. *Science* 325:148–149.

Gómez Coutouly, Yan A.
2015   Anangula—A Major Pressure-Microblade Site in the Aleutian Islands, Alaska: Reevaluating Its Lithic Component. *Arctic Anthropology* 52:23–59.

Gómez-Otero, Julieta
2006   Arqueología de La Costa Centro-Septentroinal de Patagonia Argentina. In *Arqueología de La Costa Patagónica: Perspectivas Para La Conservación*, edited by I. Cruz and M.S. Caracotche, pp. 72–80. Universidad Nacional de la Patagonia Austral, Río Gallegos.

Gómez-Otero, Julieta, Hernán Marani, and Sergio Pérez
2002   Aprovechamiento Integral de Guanacos en Península Valdés, Provincia del Chubut. Estudio Arqueofaunístico Del Sitio La Armonía (Muestreo 2). *Intersecciones en Antropología* 3:17–28.

González, Mauro, Thomas Veblen, Claudio Donoso, and Luis Valeria
2002   Tree Regeneration Response in a Lowland Nothofagus-Dominated Forest after Bamboo Dieback in South-Central Chile. *Plant Ecology* 161:59–73.

González Díaz, E. F., A. Giaccardi, and Carlos Costa
2001   La Avalancha de Rocas del Río Barrancas (Cerro Pelán) Norte del Neuquén: su Relación con la Catástrofe del Río Colorado

(29/12/1914). *Asociación Geológica Argentina*, Revista 56:466–480.

González Díaz, E. F., Andres Folguera, Carlos H. Costa, and E. Wright
2005   Los Grandes Deslizamientos de la Cordillera Septentrional Neuquina Entre Los 36°–38°S: Una Propuesta de su Inducción por en Mecanismo Sísmico. *XVI Congreso Geológico Argentino, Actas* 3:625–626.

Gorban, Alexander, Lyudmila Pokidysheva, Elena Smirnova, and Tatiana Tyukina
2010   Law of the Minimum Paradoxes. *Bulletin of Mathematical Biology* 73:2013–2044.

Gosse, John C., and Edward B. Evenson
1994   Reinterpretation of the Evidence for a Significant Mid-Holocene Ice Advance in the Río Atuel Valley, Mendoza Province, Argentina. *Zeitschrift für Geomorphologie N.F.* 38:327–338.

Gowdy, John
1997   *Limited Wants, Unlimited Means: A Reader on Hunter-Gatherer Economics and the Environment.* Island Press, Washington, DC.

Gradín, Carlos, Carlos Aschero, and Ana Aguerre
1976   Investigaciones Arqueológicas en la Cueva de las Manos: Estancia Alto Río Pinturas. *Relaciones de la Sociedad Argentia de Antropología* 10:201–250.

Grayson, Donald K.
1993   *The Desert's Past: A Natural Prehistory of the Great Basin.* Smithsonian Institution Press, Washington, DC.

Grayson, Donald K., and Lisbeth Louderback
2008   Middle Holocene Human Behavioral Responses in the Great Basin of Western North America. Paper presented at the 73rd Annual Meeting of the Society for American Archaeology Vancouver, British Columbia.

Green, Lorraine, and Marcela Ferreyra
2011   *Flores de La Estepa Patagónica.* Vázquez Mazzini, Buenos Aires.

Greenberg, Joseph H., Christy G. Turner, Stephen L. Zegura
1986   The Settlement of the Americas: A Comparison of the Linguistic, Dental, and Genetic Evidence. *Current Anthropology* 27:477–497.

Grimm, Eric C., Socorro Lozano-García, Hermann Behling, and Vera Markgraf
2001   Holocene Vegetation and Climate Variability in the Americas. In *Interhemispheric*

Climate Linkages, edited by Vera Markgraf, pp. 325–370. Academic Press, San Diego.

Grosjean, Martin, and Lautaro Núñez
1994   Late Glacial, Early and Mid-Holocene Environments, Human Occupation, and Resource Use in the Atacama (Northern Chile). *Geoarchaeology* 9:271–286.

Grosjean, Martin, Lautaro Núñez, and Isabel Cartajena
2005   Cultural Response to Climate Change in the Atacama Desert. In *23°S: Archaeology and Environmental History of the Southern Deserts*, edited by M. Smith and P. Hesse, pp. 156–171. National Museum of Australia Press, Canberra.

Grosjean, Martin, Lautaro Núñez, Isabel Cartajena, and Bruno Messerli
1997   Mid-Holocene Climate and Culture Change in the Atacama Desert, Northern Chile. *Quaternary Research* 48:239–246.

Grosjean, Martin, Jay Quade, Jason Rech, et al.
2001   Mid-Holocene Climate in the South-Central Andes: Humid or Dry? *Science* 292:2391.

Grosjean, Martin, Calogero Santoro, Lonnie Thompson, et al.
2007   Mid-Holocene Climate and Culture Change in the South-Central Andes. In *Climate Change and Cultural Dynamics: A Global Perspective on Mid-Holocene Transitions*, edited by David G. Anderson, Kirk A. Maasch and Daniel H. Sandweiss, pp. 51–116. Academic Press, New York.

Grove, Matt, Eiluned Pearce, and Robin I. M. Dunbar
2012   Fission-Fusion and the Evolution of Hominin Social Systems. *Journal of Human Evolution* 62:191–200.

Gruhn, Ruth
1988   Linguistic Evidence in Support of the Coastal Route of Earliest Entry into the New World. *Man* 23:77–100.

Guillet, David
1987   Terracing and Irrigation in the Peruvian Highlands. *Current Anthropology* 28:409–418.

Guráieb, Ana Gabriela
2004   Before and After the Hiatus: Lithic Technology in Cerro de los Indios 1 Rockshelter, South Patagonia Argentina. *Before Farming* 2:1–19.

Gusinde, Martin
1982   [1937] *Los Indios de Tierra del Fuego: Los Selk'nam*. Centro Argentino de Etnología Americana, Buenos Aires.

Haas, Randall, and Steven L. Kuhn
2019   Forager Mobility in Constructed Environments. *Current Anthropology* 60(4):499–535.

Hajduk, Adán, Ana Albornoz, and Maximillano Lezcano
2004   El "Mylodon" en el Patio de Atrás. Informe Preliminar Sobre los Trabajos en el Sitio El Trébol, Ejido Urbano de San Carlos de Bariloche, Provincia de Río Negro. In *Contra Viento y Marea. Arqueología de Patagonia*, edited by M. Teresa Civalero, Pablo Marcelo Fernández, and Ana Gabriela Guráieb, pp. 715–731. INAPL-SAA, Buenos Aires.

Halligan, Jessi, Michael R. Waters, Angelina Perrotti, et al.
2016   Pre-Clovis Occupation 14,550 Years Ago at the Page-Ladson Site, Florida, and the Peopling of the Americas. *Science Advances* 2:e1600375–e1600375.

Hammel, Harold T.
1964   Terrestrial Animals in Cold: Recent Studies of Primitive Man. In *Adaptation to Environment*, Handbook of Physiology, Section 4, edited by D. Dill, pp. 413–434. American Physicians Society, Washington, DC.

Hammel, Harold T., R. Elsner, K. Andersen, et al.
1960   *Thermal and Metabolic Responses of the Alacaluf Indians to Moderate Cold Exposure*. WADD Technical Report 60-633.

Hammond, Heidi, and Leandro Zilio
2016   Cambios en el Tamaño de Exoesqueletos Calcáreos de Moluscos Durante el Holoceno Tardío: Arqueomalacología de Conceros en la Costa Norte de Santa Cruz, Patagonia Argentina. *Arqueología Iberoamericana* 32:17–24.

Harcourt, Alexander
2012   *Human Biogeography*. University of California Press, Berkeley.

Hassan, Fekri A.
1981   *Demographic Archaeology*. Academic Press, New York.

Hatcher, John B.
1903   *Reports of the Princeton University Expeditions to Patagonia (1896–1899, Volume I, Narrative and Geography*. Princeton University, Princeton.

Hawkes, Kristen
1996   Foraging Differences between Men and Women: Behavioral Ecology and the Sexual Division of Labor. In *Power, Sex*

and Tradition: The Archaeology of Human Ancestry, edited by Stephen Shennan and James Steele, pp. 283–305. Routledge, London.

Hawkes, Kristen, James O'Connell, and Nicholas Blurton Jones
2001   Hadza Meat Sharing. Evolution and Human Behavior 22:113–142.

Haynes, C. Vance
1966   Elephant-Hunting in North America. Scientific American 214:104–112.
1969   The Earliest Americans. Science 166:709–715.

Heintzman, Peter, Duane Froese, John W. Ives, et al.
2016   Bison Phylogeography Constrains Dispersal and Viability of the Ice Free Corridor in Western Canada. Proceedings of the National Academy of Sciences 113:8057–8063.

Henrich, Joseph
2004   Demography and Cultural Evolution: Why Adaptive Cultural Processes Produced Maladaptive Losses in Tasmania. American Antiquity 69:197–221.
2010   The Evolution of Innovation-Enhancing Institutions. In Innovation in Cultural Systems: Contributions from Evolutionary Anthropology, edited by Michael O'Brien and Stephen Shennan, pp. 99–120. MIT Press, Cambridge, Massachusetts.

Henrich, Joseph, and Francisco Gil-White
2001   The Evolution of Prestige: Freely Conferred Deference as a Mechanism for Enhancing the Benefits of Cultural Transmission. Evolution and Human Behavior 22:165–196.

Henrich, Joseph, and Richard McElreath
2003   The Evolution of Cultural Evolution. Evolutionary Anthropology 12:123–135.
2007   Dual Inheritance Theory: The Evolution of Human Cultural Capacities and Cultural Evolution. Oxford Handbook of Evolutionary Psychology, edited by Robin I. M. Dunbar and Louise Barrett, Ch. 38. Oxford University Press, Oxford.

Hermo, Darío
2008   Los Cambios en la Circulación de las Materias Primas Líticas en Ambientes Mesetarios de Patagonia. Una Aproximación Para la Construcción de los Paisajes Arqueológicos de las Sociedades Cazadoras-Recolectoras. PhD dissertation, Facultad de Ciencias Naturales y Museo, Universidad Nacional de La Plata, La Plata.

2009   Estructura de los Recursos Líticos y Paisajes Arqueológicos en el Nesocratónd del Deseado (Santa Cruz, Argentina). Arqueología Suramericana / Arqueologia Sul-americana 5:178–203.

Hermo, Darío, and Lucía Magnin
2012   Blade and Bifacial Technology in Mid-Holocene Occupations at Deseado Massif, Santa Cruz Province, Argentina. Quaternary International 256:71–77.

Hernández, Miquel, Carles Lalueza Fox, and Clara Garcia-Moro
1997   Fuegian Cranial Morphology: The Adaptation to a Cold, Harsh Environment. American Journal of Physical Anthropology 103:103–17.

Hershkovitz, Isreal, Gerhard W. Weber, Rolf Quam, et al.
2018   The Earliest Modern Humans Outside Africa. Science 359:456–459.

Heusser, Calvin
1989   Late Quaternary Vegetation and Climate of Southern Tierra Del Fuego. Quaternary Research 31:396–406.
1990   Ice Age Vegetation and Climate of Subtropical Chile. Palaeogeography, Palaeoclimatology, Palaeoecology 80:107–127.
2003   Ice Age Southern Andes: A Chronicle of Paleoecological Events. Elsevier, Amsterdam.

Hey, Jody
2011   Regarding the Confusion between the Population Concept and Mayr's 'Population Thinking.' The Quarterly Review of Biology 86:253–264.

Hijmans, Robert, and David Spooner
2001   Geographic Distribution of Wild Potato Species. American Journal of Botany 88:2101–2112.

Hiscock, Peter, and Val Attenbrow
2016   Dates and Demography? The Need for Caution in Using Radiometric Dates as a Robust Proxy for Prehistoric Population Change. Archaeology in Oceania: 51:218–219.

Hobbes, Thomas
1962   [1651] Leviathan. Collier, New York.

Hobson, Keith, and Henry Schwarcz
1986   The Variation in ^{13}C Values in Bone Collagen for Two Wild Herbivore Populations: Implications for Paleodiet Studies. Journal of Archaeological Science 13:101–106.

Hockett, Bryan
2016   Why Celebrate the Death of Primitive Economic Man?: Human Nutritional Ecology

in the 21st Century. *Journal of Archaeological Science: Reports* 5:617–621.

Hoffecker, John F.

2005a Innovation and Technological Knowledge in the Upper Paleolithic of Northern Eurasia. *Evolutionary Anthropology* 14:186–198.

2005b *A Prehistory of the North: Human Settlement of the Higher Latitudes.* Rutgers University Press, New Brunswick, New Jersey.

Hogan, C. Michael

2014a *Magellanic Subpolar Forests.* The Encyclopedia of Earth. https://editors.eol.org/eoearth/wiki/Magellanic_subpolar_forests.

2014b *Valdivian Temperate Forests.* The Encyclopedia of Earth. https://editors.eol.org/eoearth/wiki/Valdivian_temperate_forests.

Hogg, Alan G., Quan Hua, Paul G. Blackwell, et al.

2013 *Radiocarbon* 55:1889–1903.

Holen, Steven, Thomas Deméré, Daniel C. Fisher, et al.

2017 A 130,000-Year-Old Archaeological Site in Southern California, USA. *Nature* 544:479–83.

Holmes, Charles

2001 Tanana River Valley Archaeology circa 14,000 to 9000 BP. *American Anthropology* 38:154–170.

Holmes, William H.

1892 Modern Quarry Refuse and the Paleolithic Theory. *Science* 20:295–297.

Horta, Luis, and Carlos Aschero

2010 Evidencias de un Paleolago Pleistoceno Tardío Holoceno Temprano en el Área del Lago Pueyrredón, Noroeste de la Provincia de Santa Cruz. In *Arqueología Argentina en el Bicentenario de la Revolución de Mayo,* XVII Congreso Nacional De Arqueología Argentina, edited by Roberto Bárcena and Horacio Chiavazza, pp. 1929–1934. Uncuyo-CONICET, Mendoza.

Hubbell, Stephen

2001 *The Unified Neutral Theory of Biodiversity and Biogeography.* Princeton University Press, Princeton.

Huddleston, Lee E.

1967 *Origins of the American Indians: European Concepts, 1492–1729.* University of Texas Press, Austin.

Humphreys, J. B., and Anne Thackeray

1983 *Ghaap and Gariep: Later Stone Age Studies in the Northern Cape.* South African Archaeological Society Monograph Series, Volume 2.

Huxley, Julian

1942 *Evolution: The Modern Synthesis.* 2nd edition. Harper & Brothers.

Iglesias, Virginia, and Cathy Whitlock

2014 Fire Responses to Postglacial Climate Change and Human Impact in Northern Patagonia (41–43°S). *Proceedings of the National Academy of Sciences* 111:E5545–5554.

Iglesias, Virginia, Cathy Whitlock, Vera Markgraf, and María Martha Bianchi

2014 Postglacial History of the Patagonian Forest/Steppe Ecotone (41–43°S). *Quaternary Science Reviews* 94:120–135.

IIASA/FAO

2010 *Global Agro-ecological Zones (GAEZ v3.0).* IIASA, Laxenburg, Austria and FAO, Rome, Italy.

Ingold, Tim

2000 The Optimal Forager and Economic Man. In *The Perception of the Environment: Essays in Livelihood, Dwelling and Skill,* edited by Tim Ingold, pp. 27–39. Routledge, London.

Iriarte, José, Paulo DeBlasis, Jonas G. De Souza, and Rafael Corteletti

2017 Emergent Complexity, Changing Landscapes, and Spheres of Interaction in Southeastern South America During the Middle and Late Holocene. *Journal of Archaeological Research* 25:251–313.

Janetski, Joel

1997 Fremont Hunting and Resource Intensification in The Eastern Great Basin. *Journal of Archaeological Science* 24:1075–1088.

Janetski, Joel, and Richard Talbot

2014 Fremont Social Organization: A Southwestern Perspective. In *Archaeology in the Great Basin and Southwest: Papers in Honor of Don D. Fowler,* edited by Nancy Parezo and Joel Janetski, pp. 118–129. University of Utah, Salt Lake City.

Jefferies, Richard W.

2008 *Holocene Hunter-Gatherers of the Lower Ohio River Valley.* University of Alabama Press, Tuscaloosa.

Jenkins, Dennis, Loren Davis, Thomas Stafford, et al.

2012 Clovis Age Western Stemmed Projectile Points and Human Coprolites at the Paisley Caves. *Science* 337:223–228.

Jenny, Bettina, Blas Valero-Garcés, Rodrigo Villa-Martínez, et al.

2002 Early to Mid-Holocene Aridity in Central Chile and the Southern Westerlies:

The Laguna Aculeo Record (34°S). *Quaternary Research* 58:160–170.

Johnson, Amber, Adolfo Gil, Gustavo Neme, and Jacob Freeman

2015   Hierarchical Method Using Ethnographic Data Sets to Guide Archaeological Research: Testing Models of Plant Intensification and Maize Use in Central Western Argentina. *Journal of Anthropological Archaeology* 38:52–58.

Jones, George T., Charlotte Beck, and Richard E. Hughes

2003   Lithic Source Use and Paleoarchaic Foraging Territories in the Great Basin. *American Antiquity* 68:5–38.

Jones, George T., Donald K. Grayson, and Charlotte Beck

1983   Artifact Class Richness and Sample Size in Archaeological Surface Assemblages. In *Lulu Linear Punctate: Essays in Honor of George Irving Quimby*, edited by Robert C. Dunnell and Donald K. Grayson, pp. 55–73. University of Michigan Museum of Anthropology, Ann Arbor.

Jordan, Fiona, Carel van Schaik, Pieter Francois, et al.

2013   Cultural Evolution of the Structure of Human Groups. In *Cultural Evolution: Society, Technology, Language, and Religion*, edited by Peter J. Richerson and Morten Christiansen, pp. 86–116. MIT Press, Cambridge, Massachusetts.

Josenhans, Heiner, Daryl W. Fedje, Reinhard Pienitz, and John Southon

1997   Early Humans and Rapidly Changing Holocene Sea Levels in the Queen Charlotte Islands-Hecate Strait, British Columbia, Canada. *Science* 277:71–74.

Kahneman, Daniel

2005   Are You Happy Now? Interview with Daniel Kahneman, 10 February 2005. Gallop. https://news.gallup.com /businessjournal/14872/happy-now.aspx ?version=print.

Kaplan, Hillard, and Kim Hill

1985a   Food Sharing Among Ache Foragers: Tests of Explanatory Hypotheses. *Current Anthropology* 26:223–246.

1985b   Hunting Ability and Reproductive Success Among Male Ache Foragers: Preliminary Results. *Current Anthropology* 26:131–133.

Kaplan, Hillard, Kim Hill, Jane Lancaster, and A. Magdalena Hurtado

2000   A Theory of Human Life History Evolution: Diet, Intelligence, and Longevity. *Evolutionary Anthropology* 9:156–185.

Katz, Brigit

2017   Found: One of the Oldest North American Settlements. Smithsonian.com, April 5, 2017. https://www.smithsonianmag.com /smart-news/one-oldest-north-american -settlements-found-180962750/.

Kelly, Robert L.

1983   Hunter-Gatherer Mobility Strategies. *Journal of Anthropological Research* 39:277–306.

1988   The Three Sides of a Biface. *American Antiquity* 53:717–34.

1995   *The Foraging Spectrum: Diversity in Hunter-Gatherer Lifeways*. Smithsonian Institution Press, Washington, DC.

2013   *The Lifeways of Hunter-Gatherers: The Foraging Spectrum*. Cambridge University Press, Cambridge, UK.

Kelly, Robert L., and Lawrence C. Todd

1988   Coming into the Country: Early Paleoindian Hunting and Mobility. *American Antiquity* 53:231–244.

Kennett, Douglas, Atholl Anderson, and Bruce Winterhalder

2006   The Ideal Free Distribution, Food Production, and the Colonization of Oceania. In *Behavioral Ecology and the Transition to Agriculture*, edited by Douglas Kennett and Bruce Winterhalder, pp. 265–288. University of California Press, Berkeley.

Kim, Jung-Hyun, Ralph Schneider, Dierk Hebbeln, et al.

2002   Last Deglacial Seasurface Temperature Evolution in the Southeast Pacific Compared to Climate Changes on the South American Continent. *Quaternary Science Reviews* 21:2085–2097.

Kingsford, Richard T., and John L. Porter

1994   Waterbirds on an Adjacent Freshwater Lake and Salt Lake in Arid Australia. *Biological Conservation* 69:219–228.

Kintigh, Keith, and Scott Ingram

2018   Was the Drought Really Responsible? Assessing Statistical Relationships between Climate Extremes and Cultural Transitions. *Journal of Archaeological Science* 89:25–31.

Kitchen, Andres, Michael Miyamoto, and Connie Mulligan

2008   A Three-stage Colonization Model for the Peopling of the Americas. *PLOS One* 3: e1596:1–7.

Kline, Michelle, and Robert Boyd

2010   Population Size Predicts Technological Complexity in Oceania. *Proceedings of the Royal Society B* 277:2559–2564.

Kobayashi, Yutaka, and Kenichi Aoki

2012   Innovativeness, Population Size and Cumulative Cultural Evolution. *Theoretical Population Biology* 82:38–47.

Krebs, Charles J.

2001   *Ecology.* Benjamin Cummings, San Francisco.

2002   Beyond Population Regulation and Limitation. Wildlife Research 29:1–10.

Krieger, Alex D.

1964   Early Man in the New World. In *Prehistoric Man in the New World,* edited by Jesse D. Jennings and Edward Norbeck, pp. 23–81. University of Chicago Press, Chicago.

Kuhn, Steven L.

1991   "Unpacking" Reduction: Lithic Raw Material Economy in the Mousterian of West-Central Italy. *Journal of Anthropological Archaeology* 10:76–106.

Kuijt, Ian

2008   Demography and Storage Systems During the Southern Levantine Neolithic Demographic Transition. In *The Neolithic Demographic Transition and Its Consequences,* edited by Jean-Pierre Bocquet-Appel and Ofer Bar-Yosef O, pp. 287–313. Springer, Dordrecht.

Kuijt, Ian, and Bill Finlayson

2009   Evidence for Food Storage and Predomestication Granaries 11,000 Years Ago in the Jordan Valley. *Proceedings of the National Academy of Sciences* 106:10966–10970.

Kuzmin, Yaroslav, Susan G. Keates, and Chen Shen (editors)

2007   *Origin and Spread of Microblade Technology in Northern Asia and North America.* Archaeology Press, Simon Fraser University, Burnaby, BC.

Lagiglia, Humberto

1968   Secuencias Culturales del Centro Oeste Argentino: Valles del Atuel y del Diamante. *Revista Científica de Investigaciones del Museo de Historia Natural de San Rafael* 1:169–174.

1977   Arqueología Prehistórica del Atuel y del Diamante. *Revista del CINTER* 2:29–46.

1978   La Cultura de Viluco del Centro Oeste Argentino. *Revista del Museo de Historia Natural* 3:227–265.

1999   Nuevos Fechados Radiocarbónicos para los Agricultores Incipientes del Atuel. *Actas del XII Congreso Nacional de Arqueología Argentina,* edited by C. Marín, pp. 239–250. La Plata. Buenos Aires.

2001   El Paleoindio el Atuel en Sudamérica (Análisis de la Cronología Absoluta del Paleoindio del Atuel). *Notas del Museo* no. 48. Museo de Historia Natural de San Rafael, San Rafael, Mendoza.

2002   Arqueología Prehistórica del sur Mendocino y sus Relaciones con el Centro Oeste Argentino. In *Entre Montañas y Desiertos: Arqueología del Sur de Mendoza,* edited by Adolfo Gil and Gustavo Neme, pp. 43–64. Sociedad Argentina de Antropología, Buenos Aires.

Laland, Kevin N., and Michael J. O'Brien

2010   Niche Construction Theory and Anthropology. *Journal of Archaeolgoical Method and Theory* 14:303–322.

Lambeck, Kurt, Hélène Rouby, Anthony Purcell, et al.

2014   Sea Level and Global Ice Volumes from the Last Glacial Maximum to the Holocene. *Proceedings of the National Academy of Sciences* 111:15296–303.

Lamy, Frank, Dierk Hebbeln, and Gerold Wefer

1999   High-Resolution Marine Record of Climatic Change in Mid-Latitude Chile During the Last 28,000 Years Based on Terrigenous Sediment Parameters. *Quaternary Research* 51:83–93.

Lantis, Margaret

1984   Aleut. In *Handbook of North American Indians, Volume 5, Arctic,* edited by David Damas, pp. 161–184. Smithsonian Institution Press, Washington, DC.

Lara, Antonio, and Ricardo Villalba

1993   A 3,620-Year Temperature Reconstruction from *Fitzroya cupressides* Tree Rings in Southern South America. *Science* 260:1104–1106.

Larsen, Clark

2006   The Agricultural Revolution as Envi-
        ronmental Catastrophe: Implications for
        Health and Lifestyles in the Holocene. *Qua-
        ternary International* 150:12–20.

Larsen, Clark, Christopher Knüsel, Scott Haddow,
et al.

2019   Bioarchaeology of Neolithic Çatalhöyük
        Reveals Fundamental Transitions in Health,
        Mobility, and Lifestyle in Early Farmers.
        Proceedings of the National Academy of
        Sciences 116:12615–12623.

Larson, Peggy

1977   *Deserts of the Southwest*. Sierra Club, San
        Francisco.

Laue, Cheyenne, and Alden Wright

2019   Landscape Revolutions for Cultural Evolu-
        tion: Integrating Advanced Fitness Land-
        scapes into the Study of Cultural Change.
        In *Handbook of Evolutionary Research in
        Archaeology*, edited by Anna M. Pren-
        tiss, pp. 127–147. Springer Nature, Cham,
        Switzerland.

Layman, Craig, Marcio Araujo, Ross Boucek, et al.

2012   Applying Stable Isotopes to Examine Food-
        Web Structure: An Overview of Analytical
        Tools. *Biological Reviews* 87:545–562.

Lee, Charlotte, T., Cedric O. Puleston, and Shripad
Tuljapurkar

2009   Population and Prehistory III: Food-
        Dependent Demography in Variable Envi-
        ronments. *Theoretical Populaiton Biology*
        76:179–188.

Lee, Richard B.

1979   *The !Kung San: Men, Women, and Work in
        a Foraging Society*. Cambridge University
        Press, Cambridge.

Lee, Richard B., and Irven Devore (editors)

1968   *Man the Hunter*. Aldine, Chicago.

Lee, Richard B., and Irven Devore

1968   Problems in the Study of Hunters and
        Gatherers. In *Man the Hunter*, edited by
        Richard B. Lee and Irven Devore, pp. 3–12.
        Aldine, Chicago.

Legoupil, Dominique, and M. Fontugne

1997   El Poblamiento Marítimo de los Archipié-
        lagos de Patagonia: Núcleos Antiguos y
        Dispersión Reciente. *Anales del Instituto de
        la Patagonia* 25:75–87.

Lema, Verónica, Claudia Della Negra, and Valeria
Bernal

2012   Explotación de Recursos Vegetales Sil-
        vestres y Domesticados en Neuquén:
        Implicancias del Hallazgo de Restos de Maíz
        y Algarrobo en Artefactos de Molienda del
        Holoceno Tardío. *Magallania* 40:229–247.

Leonard, William, Stephanie Levy, Larissa Tarskaia,
et al.

2014   Seasonal Variation in Basal Metabolic Rates
        Among the Yakut (Sakha) of Northeastern
        Siberia. *American Journal of Human Biology*
        26:437–445.

Leonard, William, M. L. Robertson, and J. Josh
Snodgrass

2007   Energetic Models of Human Nutritional
        Evolution. In *Evolution of the Human Diet:
        The Known, the Unknown, and the Un-
        knowable*, edited by Peter Ungar, pp. 344–
        359. Oxford University Press, Oxford.

Leonard, William, Mark Sorensen, Victoria Galloway, et al.

2002   Climatic Influences on Basal Metabolic
        Rates Among Circumpolar Populations.
        American Journal of Human Biology
        14:609–620.

Lewontin, Richard

1983   Gene, Organism and Environment. In *Evo-
        lution from Molecules to Men*, edited by
        D. S. Bendall, pp. 273–286. Cambridge Uni-
        versity Press, Cambridge.

L'Heureux, Lorena, and Luis A. Borrero

2002   Pautas para el Reconocimiento de Con-
        juntos Óseos Antrópicos y No Antrópicos
        de Guanaco en Patagonia. *Intersecciones en
        Antropología* 3:29–40.

L'Heureux, Lorena, and J. Cornaglia Fernández

2015   *Lama guanicoe* (Müller, 1776) Body Size
        in Continental Patagonia and Tierra Del
        Fuego. *Geobios* 48:239–248.

Liritzis, Ioannis

2014   Obsidian Hydration Dating. In *Encyclo-
        pedia of Scientific Dating Methods*, edited
        by W. Jack Rink and Jeroen Thompson,
        pp. 1–23. Springer-Verlag, Berlin.

Llamas, Bastien, Lars Fehren-Schmitz, Guido
Valverde, et al.

2016   Ancient Mitochondrial DNA Provides
        High-Resolution Time Scale of the Peo-
        pling of the Americas. *Science Advances*
        2:e1501385–e1501385.

Llano, Carina

2011   Aprovechamiento de los Recursos Ve-
        getales Entre las Sociedades Cazadores-
        Recolectores del Sur de Mendoza. PhD
        dissertation, Universidad Nacional Del
        Comahue.

2014   La Exploratcion de los Recursos Vegetales en Sociedades Cazadores-Recolectora del Sur de Mendoza. *Darwiniana* 2:96–111.

Llano, Carina, and R. Barberena

2013   Explotación de Especies Vegetales en la Patagonia Septentrional: El Registro Arqueobotánico de Cueva Huenul 1 (Provincia De Neuquén, Argentina). *Darwiniana* 1:5–19.

Llano, Carina, Paula Sosa, Clara Sánchez Campos, and Ramiro Barberena

2019   Arqueobotánica de Cueva Huenul 1 (Neuquén, Argentina): selección y procesamiento de especies vegetales. *Intersecciones en Antropología* 20:211–223.

Llano, Carina, and Andrew Ugan

2014   Alternative Interpretations of Intermediate and Positive D^{13}C Isotope Signals in Prehistoric Human Remains from Southern Mendoza, Argentina: The Role of CAM Species Consumption. *Current Anthropology* 55:822–831.

Lodolo, Emanuele, Marco Menichetti, Roberto Bartole, et al.

2003   Magallanes-Fagnano Continental Transform Fault (Tierra del Fuego, Southernmost South America). *Tectonics* 22:1–17. https://doi.org/10.1029/2003TC001500.

Lof, Marie, Hanna Olausson, Karin Bostrom, et al.

2005   Changes in Basal Metabolic Rate During Pregnancy in Relation to Changes in Body Weight and Composition, Cardiac Output, Insulin-Like Growth Factor I, and Thyroid Hormones in Relation to Fetal Growth. *American Journal of Clinical Nutrition* 81:678–685.

Loud, Llewellyn, and M. R. Harrington

1929   *Lovelock Cave*. University of California Publications in American Archaeology and Ethnology 25.

Louderback, Lisbeth, Donald K. Grayson, and Marcos Llobera

2010   Middle-Holocene Climates and Human Population Densities in the Great Basin, Western USA. *The Holocene* 21:366–373.

Lourandos, Harry

1997   *Continent of Hunter-gatherers: New Perspectives in Australian Prehistory*. Cambridge University Press, Cambridge.

Lyell, Charles

1833   *Principles of Geology*. J. Murray, London.

Lyman, R. Lee

1994   *Vertebrate Taphonomy*. Cambridge University Press, Cambridge.

Lynch, Thomas F.

1990   Glacial-Age Man in South America?: A Critical Review. *American Antiquity* 55:12–36.

MacArthur, Robert H.

1972   *Geographical Ecology: Patterns in the Distribution of Species*. Princeton University Press, Princeton.

MacArthur, Robert H., and Eric R. Pianka

1966   On Optimal Use of a Patchy Environment. *American Naturalist* 100:603–609.

Mace, Ruth, and Mark Pagel

1995   A Latitudinal Gradient in the Density of Human Languages in North America. *Proceedings of the Royal Society B: Biological Science* 261:117–121.

MacNeish, Richard S.

1976   Early Man in the New World. *American Scientist* 63:316–327.

Madsen, David B., and David Schmitt

2003   Mass Collecting and the Diet Breadth Model: A Great Basin Example. *Journal of Archaeological Science* 25:445–455.

Magne, Martin, and Daryl Fedje

2007   The Spread of Microblade Technology in Northwestern North America. In *Origin and Spread of Microblade Technology in Northern Asia and North America,* edited by Yaroslov Kuzmin, Susan Keates and Chen Shen, pp. 171–188. Archaeology Press, Simon Fraser University, Burnaby, British Columbia.

Maldonado, Antonio, and Carolina Villagrán

2006   Climate Variability Over the Last 9900 Cal yr BP from a Swamp Forest Pollen Record Along the Semiarid Coast of Chile. *Quaternary Research* 66:246–258.

Malthus, Thomas R.

1803   *An Essay on the Principle of Population*. Johnson, London.

Mancini, María Virginia, Marta M. Paez, Alfredo Prieto, et al.

2005   Mid-Holocene Climatic Variability Reconstruction from Pollen Records (32-52 Argentina). *Quaternary International* 132:47–59.

Mann, Charles C.

2005   *1491: New Revelations of the Americas Before Columbus*. Vintage Books, New York.

Mardones, Vanessa

2007   *Sacred Plants: Green Allies Used in Ritual and Ceremony*. Presentation to the Olbrich Botanical Gardens, October 18, 2007.

Markgraf, Vera
1983   Late and Postglacial Vegetational and Pa-
         leoclimatic Changes in Subantartic, Tem-
         perate, and Arid Environments in Argenti-
         na. *Palynology* 7:43–70.
Marshall, Andrew J.
2020   (in press). Food and Primate Carrying
         Capacity. In *Primate Diet and Nutrition:
         Needing, Finding, and Using Food*, edited by
         Joanna E. Lambert and Jessica Rothman,
         University of Chicago Press, Chicago.
Martin, Fabiana, and Luis A. Borrero
2017   Climate Change, Availability of Territory,
         and Late Pleistocene Human Exploration of
         Ultima Esperanza, South Chile. *Quaternary
         International* 428:86–95.
Martin, Paul S.
1973   The Discovery of America. *Science*
         179:969–974.
Martin, Robert D.
1993   Primate Origins: Plugging the Gaps. *Nature*
         363:223–43.
Marx, Karl
1967   [1887] *Capital: A Critique of Political Econ-
         omy* (Vol. 1). International Publishers, New
         York.
1977   *Karl Marx: Selected writings*, edited by
         D. McLellan, Oxford University Press,
         Oxford.
Marx, Karl, and Friedrich Engels
1967   *The Communist Manifesto*. Penguin,
         Middlesex.
Masson, Valérie, François Vimeux, Jean Jouzel,
et al.
2000   Holocene Climate Variability in Antarctica
         Based on 11 Ice-Core Isotopic Records.
         Quaternary Research 54:348–358.
Massone, Mauricio
2004   *Los Cazadores Después Del Hielo*. Ediciones
         de La Dirección de Archivos y Museo, Co-
         lección En Antropología 7. Santiago, Chile:
         Museo de Historia Natural.
Massone, Mauricio, and Alfredo Prieto
2004   Evaluación de la Modalidad Cultural Fell
         1 en Magallanes. *Chungara*, Volumen
         Especial:303–315.
Massone, Mauricio, Alfredo Prieto, Donald Jackson,
et al.
1999   Los Cazadores Tempranos y sus Fogatas:
         Una Nueva Historia para la Cueva Tres
         Arroyos 1, Tierra del Fuego. *Boletín de la
         Sociedad Chilena de Arqueología* 26:11–18.

Mathieson, Iain, Iosif Lazaridis, Nadin Rohland,
et al.
2015   Genome-Wide Patterns of Selection in 230
         Ancient Eurasians. *Nature* 528:499–503.
Maxwell, Simon J., Philip Hopley, Paul Upchurch,
and Christophe Soligo
2018   Sporadic Sampling, Not Climatic Forcing,
         Drives Observed Early Hominin Diversity.
         *Proceedings of the National Academy of Sci-
         ences* 115:4891–4896.
Mayr, Christoph, Michael Wille, Torsten Haberzettl,
et al.
2007   Holocene Variability of the Southern
         Hemisphere Westerlies in Argentinean Pa-
         tagonia (52°S). *Quaternary Science Reviews*
         26:579–84.
Mayr, Ernst
1959   Darwin and the Evolutionary Theory in
         Biology. In *Evolution and Anthropology:
         A Centennial Appraisal*, edited by B. J. Meg-
         gars. Anthropological Society of Washing-
         ton, Washington, DC.
McCartney, Allen P.
1975   Maritime Adaptations in Cold Archipela-
         gos. In *Prehistoric Maritime Adaptations of
         the Circumpolar Zone*, edited by William
         Fitzhugh, pp. 281–338. Mouton, The Hague.
McCartney, Allen, and Douglas Veltre
1999   Aleutian Island Prehistory: Living in Insu-
         lar Extremes. *World Archaeology* 30:503–515.
McCorriston, Joy, and Frank Hole
1991   The Ecology of Seasonal Stress and the Ori-
         gins of Agriculture in the Near East. *Ameri-
         can Anthropologist* 93:46–69.
McCulloch, Robert, Michael J. Bentley, R.M. Point-
ping, and Chalmers Clapperton
2005   Evidence for Late-Glacial Ice Dammed
         Lakes in the Central Strait of Magellan and
         Bahía Inútil, Southernmost South America.
         Geografiska Annaler 87A:335–362.
McCulloch, Robert, and Sarah Davies
2001   Late-glacial and Holocene Palaeoenvi-
         ronmental Change in the Central Strait of
         Magellan, Southern Patagonia. *Palaeoge-
         ography, Palaeoclimatology, Palaeoecology*
         173:143–173.
McCulloch, Robert D., Christopher J. Fogwill,
D.E. Sugden, et al.
2005   Chronology of the Last Glaciation in Cen-
         tral Strait of Magellan and Bahía Inútil,
         Southernmost South America. *Geografiska
         Annaler* 87(A):289–312.

McElreath, Richard, Robert Boyd, and Peter J. Richerson
2003 Shared Norms and the Evolution of Ethnic Markers. *Current Anthropology* 44:122–129.

McEwan, Collin, Luis A. Borrero, and Alfredo Prieto
1997 *Patagonia: Natural History, Prehistory, and Ethnography at the Uttermost End of the Earth*. British Museum Press, London.

McEwan, Gordon
2006 *The Incas: New Perspectives*. W. W. Norton, New York.

Meltzer, David
1993 *Search for the First Americans*. Smithsonian Books, Washington, DC.
1995a Clocking the First Americans. *Annual Review of Anthropology* 24:21–45.
1995b Modeling the Prehistoric Response to Altithermal Climates on the Southern High Plains of Texas. In *Ancient Peoples and Landscapes*, edited by Eileen Johnson, pp. 349–368. Texas Tech University Press, Lubbock.
1999 Human Responses to Middle Holocene (Altithermal) Change on the North American Great Plains. *Quaternary Research* 52:404–416.
2009 *First Peoples in a New World: Colonizing Ice Age America*. University of California, Berkeley.

Meltzer, David, Donald Grayson, Gerardo Ardila, et al.
1997 On the Pleistocene Antiquity of Monte Verde, Southern Chile. *American Antiquity* 62:659–663.

Mena, Francisco
1983 Excavaciones arqueológicas en Cueva Las Guanacas (RI-16) XI Región de Aisén. *Anales del Instituto de la Patagonia, Serie Ciencias Sociales* 14:67–75.
1995 El Ser Humano y su Larga Relación con el Bosque. *Ambiente y Desarrollo* 11:63–69.
1997 Middle to Late Holocene Adaptations in Patagonia. In *Patagonia: Natural History, Prehistory and Ethnography at the Uttermost End of the Earth*, edited by Collin McEwan, Luis Borrero and Alfredo Prieto, pp. 46–60. British Museum Press, London.
2000 Un Panorama de la Prehistoria de Aisén Oriental: Estado de Conocimiento a Fines de Siglo. *Serie Antropología* 2:21–41.

Méndez, César, María Eugenia de Porras, Antonio Maldonado, et al.
2016 Human Effects in Holocene Fire Dynamics of Central Western Patagonia (~44° S, Chile). *Frontiers in Ecology and Evolution* 4: https://doi.org/10.3389/fevo.2016.00100.

Méndez, César, Adolfo Gil, Gustavo Neme, et al.
2015 Mid Holocene Radiocarbon Ages in the Subtropical Andes (~29°–35° S), Climatic Change and Implications for Human Space Organization. *Quaternary International* 356:15–26.

Méndez, César, and Omar Reyes
2008 Late Holocene Human Occupation of the Patagonian Forests: A Case Study in the Cisnes River Basin. *Antiquity* 82:560–70.

Méndez, César, Omar Reyes, Amalia Nuevo Delaunay, et al.
2016 Las Quemas Rockshelter: Understanding Human Occupations of Andean Forests of Central Patagonia (Aisén, Chile), Southern South America. *Latin American Antiquity* 27:207–26.

Menghin, Oswaldo
1952 Fundamentos Cronológicos de la Prehistoria de Patagonia. *Runa* 1:23–43.

Mengoni Goñalons, Guillermo L.
1996 La Domesticación de los Camélidos Sudamericanos y su Anatomía Económica. In *Zooarqueología de Camélidos* (Volume 2), edited by D. C. Elkin, C. Madero, Guillermo L. Mengoni Goñalons, Daniel E. Olivera, M. C. Reigadas, and Hugo D. Yacobaccio, pp. 33–45. Grupo Zooarqueología de Camélidos, Buenos Aires.
1999 *Cazadores de Guanacos de la Estepa Patagónica*. Sociedad Argentina de Antropología, Buenos Aires.

Merrill, William, Robert Hard, Jonathan Mabry, et al.
2009 The Diffusion of Maize to the Southwestern United States and Its Impact. *Proceedings of the National Academy of Sciences* 106:21019–21026.

Mesoudi, Alex, Andrew Whiten, and Kevin Laland
2006 Towards a Unified Science of Cultural Evolution. *Behavioral and Brain Sciences* 29: 329–347. doi:10.1017/S0140525X06009083.

Messerli, Bruno, Martin Grosjean, and Mathias Vuille
1997 Water Availability, Protected Areas, and Natural Resources in the Andean Desert

Altiplano. *Mountain Research and Development* 17:229–238.

Miller, Arthur
1976   The Climate of Chile. In *Climates of Central and South America*, World Survey of Climatology 12, edited by W. Schwerdtfeger, pp. 113–145. Elsevier Scientific Publishing, Amsterdam.

Milner, George
2019   Early Agriculture's Toll on Human Health. *Proceedings of the National Academy of Sciences* 116:13721–13723.

Miotti, Laura
1996   Piedra Museo (Santa Cruz): Nuevos Datos para la Ocupacion Pleistocenica en Patagonia. In *Arqueologia, Solo Patagonia*, edited by Julieta Gómez-Otero, pp. 27–38. CENPAT-CONICET, Puerto Madryn, Argentina.
1998   *Zooarqueología de la Meseta Central y Costa de Santa Cruz. Un Enfoque de las Estrategias Adaptativas Aborígenes y los Paleoambientes*. Museo de San Rafael, San Rafael.

Miotti, Laura, and Mónica Salemme
2004   Poblamiento, Movilidad y Territorios Entre las Sociedades Cazadoras-Recolectoras de Patagonia. *Complutum* 15:177–206.

Miotti, Laura, Mónica Salemme, and Jorge Rabassa
2003   Radiocarbon Chronology at Piedra Museo Locality. In *Where the South Winds Blow: Ancient Evidence of Paleo South Americans*, edited by Laura Miotti, Mónica Salemme, and Nora Flegenheimer, pp. 99–104. Center for the Studies of the First Americans—Texas A & M University Press, College Station, Texas.

Misarti, Nicole, Bruce Finney, James Jordan, et al.
2012   Early Retreat of the Alaska Peninsula Glacier Complex and the Implications for Coastal Migrations of First Americans. *Quaternary Science Reviews* 48:1–6.

Mitchell, Peter
2017   Disease: A Hitherto Unexplored Constraint on the Spread of Dogs (*Canis lupus familiaris*) in Pre-Columbian South America. *Journal of World Prehistory* 30:301–349.

Moreno, Patricio, Jean Pierre Francois, Christopher Moy, and Rodrigo Villa-Martínez
2010   Covariability of the Southern Westerlies and Atmospheric CO_2 during the Holocene. *Geology* 38:727–730.

Moreno-Mayar, J. Víctor, Ben Potter, Lasse Vinner, et al.
2018   Terminal Pleistocene Alaskan Genome Reveals First Founding Population of Native Americans. *Nature* 553:203–207.

Morgan, Christopher, Shannon Tushingham, Raven Garvey, et al.
2017   Hunter-Gatherer Economies in the Old World and New World. *Oxford Encyclopedia of Agriculture and Environment* DOI: 10.1093/acrefore/9780199389414.013 .164.

Morgan, Christopher, Dallin Webb, Kari Sprengeler, et al.
2018   Experimental Construction of Hunter-Gatherer Residential Features, Mobility, and the Costs of Occupying "Persistent Places." *Journal of Archaeological Science* 91:65–76.

Morgan, Lewis H.
1877   *Ancient Society*. World Publishing, New York.

Morlan, Richard
1988   Pre-Clovis People: Early Discoveries of America? In *Americans Before Columbus: Ice-Age Origins*, edited by Ronald C. Carlisle, pp. 31–43. Ethnological Monographs no. 12, Department of Anthropology, University of Pittsburgh.

Morrow, Juliet
2017   After Anzick: Reconciling New Genomic Data and Models with the Archaeological Evidence for Peopling of the Americas. *Quaternary International* 444:1–3.

Moseley, Michael E.
2001   *The Incas and Their Ancestors*. Thames and Hudson, New York.

Munday, Anthony
1619   The Famous and Renowned Historie of Primaleon of Greece, Sonne to the Great and Mighty Prince Palmerin d'Oliua, Emperour of Constantinople. In *The Second Booke of History of Primaleon of Greece*. Thomas Snodham, London.

Murdock, George, and Douglas White
1969   Standard Cross-Cultural Sample. *Ethnology* 9:329–369.

Musters, George
1871   *At Home with the Patagonians: A Year's Wanderings Over Untrodden Ground from the Straits of Magellan to the Río Negro*. Murray, London.

Nami, Hugo
1987 Cueva del Medio: Perspectivas Arqueológicas para la Patagonia Austral. *Anales del Instituto de la Patagonia* 17:73–106.

Nami, Hugo, and T. Nakamura
1995 Cronología Radiocarbónica con AMS Sobre Muestras de Huesos Procedentes del sitio Cueva del Medio (Ultima Esperanza, Chile). *Anales del Instituto de la Patagonia* 23:125–133.

Naranjo, J., and Charles Stern
1998 Holocene Explosive Activity of Hudson Volcano, Southern Andes. *Bulletin of Volcanology* 59:291–306.

Neme, Gustavo
2007 *Cazadores-Recolectores de Altura en los Andes Meridionales: El Alto Valle Del Río Atuel.* British Archaeological Reports, International Series 1591. Archaeopress, Oxford.

Neme, Gustavo, and Adolfo Gil
2001 El Patrón Cronológico el las Ocupaciones Humanas en el Holoceno Medio del Sur Mendocino: Implicancias para el Poblamiento Humano en Áreas Áridas-Semiáridas. *XIV Congreso Nacional de Arqueología Argentina, Rosario*, pp. 253–254.
2002 La Explotación Faunística y la Frecuencia de Partes Esqueletarias en el Registro Arqueológico del Sur Mendocino. In *Entre Montañas y Desiertos: Arqueología del Sur de Mendoza*, edited by A. Gil and G. Neme, pp. 141–156. Buenos Aires, Sociedad Argentina de Antropología.
2008a Biogeografía Humana en los Andes Meridionales: Tendencias Arqueológicas en el Sur de Mendoza. *Chungara* 40:5–18.
2008b Faunal Exploitation and Agricultural Transitions in the South American Agricultural Limit. *International Journal of Osteoarchaeology* 18:293–306.
2009 Human Occupation and Increasing Mid-Holocene Aridity. *Current Anthropology* 50:149–163.

Neme, Gustavo, Adolfo Gil, Raven Garvey, et al.
2011 El Registro Arqueológico de la Gruta de el Manzano y sus Implicancias para la Arqueología de Nordpatagonia. *Magallanía* 39:245–268.

Nettle, Daniel
1999 *Linguistic Diversity.* Oxford University Press, Oxford.

Nichols, Johanna
1990 Linguistic Diversity and the First Settlement of the New World. *Language* 66:475–521.

Noback, Marlijn, Katerina Harvati, and Fred Spoor
2011 Climate-Related Variation of the Human Nasal Cavity. *American Journal of Physical Anthropology* 145:599–614.

Novellino, Paula, Adolfo Gil, Gustavo Neme, and Víctor Durán
2004 El Consumo de Maíz en el Holoceno Tardío del Oeste Argentino: Isótopos Estables y Caries. *Revista Española de Antropología Americana* 34:85–110.

Núñez, Lautaro, Isabel Cartajena, and Martin Grosjean
2001 Human Dimensions of Late Pleistocene/Holocene Arid Events in Southern South America. In *Interhemispheric Climate Linkages*, edited by Vera Markgraff, pp. 105–117. Academic Press, San Diego.

Núñez, Lautaro, and Martin Grosjean
1994 Cambios Ambientales Pleistoceno-Holoceno: Ocupación Humana y Uso de Recorsos en la Puna de Atacama (Norte de Chile). *Estudios Atacameños* 11:11–24.

Núñez, Lautaro, Martin Grosjean, Bruno Miserli, and Hans Schrelier
1996 Cambios Ambientles Holocénicos en la Puna de Atacama y sus Implicancias Paleoclimáticas. *Estudios Atacameños* 12:31–40.

O'Brien, Michael, Matthew Boulanger, Briggs Buchanan, et al.
2014 Innovation and Cultural Transmission in the American Paleolithic: Phylogenetic Analysis of Eastern Paleoindian Projectile-Point Classes. *Journal of Anthropological Archaeology* 34:100–119.

Ocampo, Carlos, and Pilar Rivas
2004 Poblamiento Temprano de los Extremos Geográficos de los Canales Patagónicos: Chiloé e Isla Navarino 1. *Chungara* 36 Supplement:317–331.

O'Connell, James F., and Jim Allen
2012 The Restaurant at the End of the Universe: Modelling the Colonization of Sahul. *Australian Archaeology* 74:5–17.

O'Connell, James F., and Kristen Hawkes
1984 Food Choice and Foraging Sites Among the Alyawara. *Journal of Anthropological Research* 40:405–435.

O'Connell, James F., Kevin Jones, and Steven Simms
1982   Some Thoughts on Prehistoric Archaeology
        in the Great Basin. In *Man and Environ-
        ment in the Great Basin*, edited by David B.
        Madsen and James F. O'Connell, pp. 227–
        240. Society for American Archaeology,
        Washington, DC.

Odling-Smee, F. John
1988   Niche Constructing Phenotypes.
        In *The Role of Behavior in Evolution*, edited
        by Henry C. Plotkin, pp. 73–132. MIT Press,
        Cambridge, Massachusetts.

Odum, Eugene P.
1959   *Fundamentals of Ecology*. Saunders,
        London.

Olson, Everett
1991   *George Gaylord Simpson 1902–1984: A Bi-
        ographical Memoir*. National Academy of
        Sciences, Washington, D.C.

Orians, Gordon H., and N. P. Pearson
1979   On the Theory of Central Place Foraging.
        In *Analysis of Ecological Systems*, edited by
        David Horn, Gordon S. Stairs and Roger M.
        Mitchell, pp. 155–177. Ohio State University
        Press, Columbus.

Orquera, Luis A., and Ernesto Piana
2005   La Adaptación al Litoral Sudamericano
        Sudoccidental: Quiénes, Cuándo y Dónde
        se Adaptaron. *Relaciones de la Sociedad
        Argentina de Antropología* 30:11–32.
2006   El Poblamiento Inicial del Área Litoral
        Sudamericana Sudoccidental. *Magallanía*
        34:21–36.

Ortega, Isaac M., and William L. Franklin
1995   Social Organization, Distribution and
        Movements of a Migratory Guanaco Pop-
        ulation in the Chilean Patagonia. *Revista
        Chilena de Historia Natural* 68:489–500.

Ostfeld, Richard, and Felicia Keesing
2000   Pulsed Resources and Community Dynam-
        ics of Consumers in Terrestrial Ecosystems.
        Tree 15:232–237.

Oswalt, Wendel
1973   *Habitat and Ecology: The Evolution of
        Hunting*. Holt, Rinehart and Winston, New
        York.
1976   *An Anthropological Analysis of Food-Getting
        Technology*. Wiley-Interscience, New York.

Otaola, Clara, Miguel Giardina, and Fernando
Franchetti
2019   Human Biogeography and Faunal Exploita-
        tion in Diamante River Basin, Central

Western Argentina. *International Journal
        of Osteoarchaeology* 29:134–143.

Paredes, María Alejandra, Vivian Montecino, Vinka
Anic, et al.
2014   Diatoms and Dinoflagellates Macroscopic
        Regularities Shaped by Intrinsic Physical
        Forcing Variability in Patagonian and Fue-
        gian Fjords and Channels (48°–56°S). *Prog-
        ress in Oceanography* 129:85–97.

Parmesan, Camille, and Gary Yohe
2003   A Globally Coherent Fingerprint of Climate
        Change Impacts Across Natural Systems.
        Nature 421:37–42.

Paterek, Josephine
1994   *Encyclopedia of American Indian Costume*.
        ABC-CLIO, Santa Barbara, California.

Paunero, Rafael
1993–1994 El Sitio Cueva 1 de la Localidad Arqueo-
        lógica Cerro Tres Tetas (Estancia San Rafael,
        Provincia de Santa Cruz, Argentina). *Anales
        de Arqueología y Etnología* 48/49:73–90.

Pearce, Eiluned
2014   Modelling Mechanisms of Social Network
        Maintenance in Hunter-Gatherers. *Journal
        of Archaeological Sciences* 50:403–413.

Pearson, O.
1994   The Impact of an Eruption of Volcán
        Hudson on Small Mammals in Argentine
        Patagonia. *Mastozoología Neotropical*
        1:103–112.

Pedersen, Mikkel, Anthony Ruter, Charles Schwe-
ger, et al.
2016   Postglacial Viability and Colonization in
        North America's Ice-Free Corridor. *Nature*
        537:45–49.

Pedro, Joel, Helen Bostock, Cecilia Bitz, et al.
2015   The Spatial Extent and Dynamics of the
        Antarctic Cold Reversal. *Natural Geoscience*
        9:51–55.

Perucca, Laura, and Hugo Bastias
2008   Neotectonics, Seismology and Paleoseis-
        mology. *Developments in Quaternary Sci-
        ences* 11:73–94.

Piana, Ernesto, and Luis Orquera
2006   Shellmidden Formation at the Beagle
        Channel (Tierra del Fuego, Argentine).
        In *Actas of 15th Congress of the UISPP (Lis-
        boa)*, Session C 68 (D).

Piana, Ernesto, A. Francisco Zangrando, and Luis
Orquera
2012   Early Occupations in Tierra del Fuego and
        the Evidence from Layer S at the Imiwaia I

site (Beagle Cannel, Argentina). In *Southbound: Late Pleistocene Peopling of Latin America*, edited by Laura Miotti, Mónica Salemme, Nora Flegenheimer, and Ted Goebel, pp. 171–175. Center for the Study of the First Americans, College Station, Texas.

Piddocke, Stuart
1965 The Potlatch System of the Southern Kwakiutl: A New Perspective. *Southwestern Journal of Anthropology* 21:244–64.

Pigafetta, Antonio
1524 Relazione del Primo Viaggio Intorno al Mondo, 1524: "Il capitano generale nominò questi popoli Patagoni."

Piperno, Dolores, Anthony Ranere, Irene Holst, et al.
2009 Starch Grain and Phytolith Evidence for Early Ninth Millennium B.P. Maize from the Central Balsas River Valley, Mexico. *Proceedings of the National Academy of Sciences* 106:5019–5024.

Pitulko, Vladimir, and Elena Pavlova
2010 *Geoarchaeology and Radiocarbon Chronology of the Stone Age of North-East Asia.* Nauka, St. Petersburg.

Pitulko, Vladimir, Alexei Tikhonov, Elenea Pavlova, et al.
2016 Early Human Presence in the Arctic: Evidence from 45,000-Year-Old Mammoth Remains. *Science* 351:260–63.

Poinar, Hendrik, Stuart Fiedel, Christine King, et al.
2009 Comment on 'DNA from Pre-Clovis Human Coprolites in Oregon, North America.' *Science* 325:148.

Ponce, Juan, Jorge Rabassa, Andrea Coronato, and Ana María Borromei
2011 Palaeogeographical Evolution of the Atlantic Coast of Pampa and Patagonia from the Last Glacial Maximum to the Middle Holocene: Palaeogeography of Patagonia Since LGM. *Biological Journal of the Linnean Society* 103:363–79.

Ponte, Jorge Ricardo
2006 Historia del Regadío: Las Acequias de Mendoza, Argentina. *Revista Electrónica de Geografía y Ciencias Sociales*, Volume X, Number 218, 2006.08.01.

Porter, Claire, and Frank Marlowe
2007 How Marginal Are Forager Habitats? *Journal of Archaeological Science* 34:59–68.

Potter, Ben, Joshua Reuther, Vance Holliday, et al.
2017 Early Colonization of Beringia and Northern North America: Chronology, Routes,

and Adaptive Strategies. *Quaternary International* 444:36–55.

Potter, Brian, Alwynne Beaudoin, C. Vance Haynes, et al.
2018 Arrival routes of the First Americans Uncertain. *Science* 359:1224–1225.

Powell, Adam, Stephen Shennan, and Mark Thomas
2009 Late Pleistocene Demography and the Appearance of Modern Human Behavior. *Science* 324:1298–1301.

Powell, Joseph W.
1885 From Savagery to Barbarism. *Transactions of the Anthropological Society of Washington* 3:173–196.
1888 From barbarism to civilization. *American Anthropologist* 1:97–123.

Prates, Luciano, Gustavo Politis, and James Steele
2013 Radiocarbon Chronology of the Early Human Occupation of Argentina. *Quaternary International* 301:104–122.

Premo, Luke S., and Steven L. Kuhn
2010 Modeling Effects of Local Extinctions on Culture Change and Diversity in the Paleolithic. *PLOS ONE* 5:e15582. https://doi.org/10.1371/journal.pone.0015582.

Prieto, Alfredo
1991 Cazadores Tempranos y Tardíos en Cueva Lago Sofía 1. *Anales del Instituto de la Patagonia* 20:75–99.
1997 Patagonian Painted Cloaks: An Ancient Puzzle. In *Patagonia: Natural History, Prehistory, and Ethnography at the Uttermost End of the Earth*, edited by Collin McEwan, Luis Borrero, and Alfredo Prieto, pp. 173–185. Princeton University, Princeton.

Prieto, Alfredo, Charles Stern, and Jordi Estévez
2013 The Peopling of the Fuego-Patagonia Fjords by Littoral Hunter-Gatherers after the Mid-Holocene H1 Eruption of Hudson Volcano. *Quaternary International* 317:3–13.

Prohaska, Fritz
1976 The Climate of Argentina, Paraguay and Uruguay. In *Climates of Central and South America*, World Survey of Climatology 12, edited by W. Schwerdtfeger, pp. 13–112. Elsevier Scientific Publishing, Amsterdam.

Quammen, David
2009 Darwin's First Clues. *National Geographic* 215: 34–53.

Rabassa, Jorge, A. Coronato, Claudio Roig, et al.
2003 Un Bosque Sumergido en Bahía Sloggett, Tierra Del Fuego, Argentina: Evidencia

de Actividad Neotectónica Diferencial en el Holoceno Tardío. In *Procesos Geomorfológicos y Evolución Costera*, edited by Ramón Blanco Chao, Juan López Bedoya, and Augusto Pérez Alberti, pp. 333–345. Universidad De Santiago De Compostela, Santiago De Compostela.

Raedecke, Kenneth J.

1978   El guanaco de Magallanes, Chile: Su Distribución y su Biología. Corporación Nacional Forestal, Publicación Técnica n° 4, Santiago de Chile.

1982   Habitat Use by Guanacos (*Lama guanicoe*) and Sheeps on Common Range, Tierra del Fuego (Chile). *Turrialba* 32:309–314.

Raedeke, Kenneth J., and Javier Simonetti

1988   Food Habits of *Lama guanicoe* in the Atacama Desert of Northern Chile. *Journal of Mammology* 69:198–201.

Raghavan, Maanasa, Pontus Skoglund, Kelly Graf, et al.

2014   Upper Palaeolithic Siberian Genome Reveals Dual Ancestry of Native Americans. *Nature* 505:87–91.

Raison, Charles, and David Raichlen

2018   An Evolutionary Perspective on Nutrition and Social Decision Making. *Proceedings of the National Academy of Sciences* 115:E1331.

Ramos, Víctor, Alberto Riccardi, and Eduardo Rolleri

2004   Límites Naturales del Norte de la Patagonia. *Revista de La Asociación Geológica Argentina* 59:785–786.

RAMSAR

2002   *Misión Ramsar de Asesoramiento: Informe No. 48, Laguna de Llancaneo, Argentina* (2001). Ramsar Convention on Wetlands.

Rapoport, Eduardo

1982   *Areography: Geographical Strategies of Species*. Pergamon Press, New York.

Rappaport, Roy A.

1968   *Pigs for the Ancestors: Ritual in the Ecology of a New Guinea People*. Yale University Press, New Haven.

Read, Dwight

2008   An Interaction Model for Resource Implement Complexity Based on Risk and Number of Annual Moves. *American Antiquity* 73:599–625.

2012   Population Size Does Not Predict Artifact Complexity: Analysis of Data from Tasmania, Arctic Hunter-Gatherers, and Oceania Fishing Groups. UC Los Angeles: Human Complex Systems working papers. https://papers.ssrn.com/sol3/papers.cfm?abstract_id=2460379.

Reid, Kenneth

2017   Idaho Beginnings: A Review of the Evidence. *Quaternary International* 444:72–82.

Reimer, Paula J., Edouard Bard, Alex Bayliss, et al.

2013   IntCal13 and MARINE13 Radiocarbon Age Calibration Curves 0–50,000 Years cal BP. *Radiocarbon* 55:1869–1887.

Rey, Andrés, Pablo Carmanchahi, Silvia Puig, and M. Laura Guichón

2009   Densidad, Estructura Social, Actividad y Manejo de Guanacos Silvestres (*Lama guanicoe*) en el sur del Neuquén, Argentina. *Mastozoología Neotropical* 16:389–401.

Reyes, Omar, Mauricio Moraga, César Méndez, and Alexander Cherkinsky

2015   Maritime Hunter-Gatherers in the Chonos Archipelago (43°50'–46°50' S), Western Patagonian Channels. *The Journal of Island and Coastal Archaeology* 10:207–231.

Rhode, David, P. Jeffrey Brantingham, Charles Perreault, and David B. Madsen

2014   Mind the Gaps: Testing for Hiatuses in Regional Radiocarbon Date Sequences. *Journal of Archaeological Science* 52:567–577.

Richerson, Peter J., and Robert Boyd

2005   *Not by Genes Alone: How Culture Transformed Human Evolution*. University of Chicago Press, Chicago.

Richerson, Peter J., Robert Boyd, and Robert L. Bettinger

2001   Was Agriculture Impossible in the Pleistocene but Mandatory in the Holocene? *American Antiquity* 66:387–411.

2009   Cultural Innovations and Demographic Change. *Human Biology* 81:211–235.

Rick, John W.

1987   Dates as Data: An Examination of the Peruvian Preceramic Radiocarbon Record. *American Antiquity* 52:55–73.

Ricklefs, Robert E.

2008   *The Economy of Nature*. Macmillan, London.

Ridings, Rosanna

1996   Where in the World Does Obsidian Hydration Dating Work? *American Antiquity* 61:136–148.

Risen, Jane, and Thomas Gilovich
2007   Informal Logical Fallacies. In *Critical Thinking in Psychology*, edited by Robert J. Sternberg, Henry L. Roediger III, and Diane F. Halpern, pp. 110–130. Cambridge University Press, Cambridge.

Robertson, Eugene
1988   *Thermal Properties of Rocks*. United States Department of the Interior Open-File Report 88-441.

Rodríguez, Eduardo J., and Alberto C. Regairaz
1972   Resumen Geológico de la Provincia de Mendoza. *Revista de la Sociedad Argentina de Botánica* 13 (supplement):5–13.

Rogers, Alexander
2006   Induced Hydration of Obsidian: A Simulation Study of Accuracy Requirements. *Journal of Archaeological Science* 33:1696–1705.
2007   Effective Hydration Temperature of Obsidian: A Diffusion Theory Analysis of Time-Dependent Hydration Rates. *Journal of Archaeological Science* 34:656–665.

Roig, Fidel Antonio
1998   *La Vegetación de la Patagonia*. Flora Patagónica, INTA Colección Científica Tomo VIII (I).

Roig, Virgilio
1972   Esbozo General del Poblamiento Animal de la Provincia de Mendoza. In *Geología, Geomorfología, Climatología, Fitogeografía y Zoogeografía de la Provincia de Mendoza*, pp. 81–88, Vol. XIII. Socieded Argentina de Botánica, Mendoza, Argentina.

Rosetta, Lyliana
1993   Seasonality and Fertility. In *Seasonality and Human Ecology*, edited by Stanley J. Ulijaszek and S. S. Strickland, pp. 65–75. Cambridge University Press, Cambridge.

Rumold, Claudia, and Mark Aldenderfer
2016   Late Archaic–Early Formative Period Microbotanical Evidence for Potato at Jiskairumoko in the Titicaca Basin of Southern Peru. *Proceedings of the National Academy of Sciences* 113:13672–13677.

Salemme, Mónica, and Laura Miotti
2008   Archeological Hunter-Gatherer Landscapes Since the Latest Pleistocene in Fuego-Patagonia. *Developments in Quaternary Sciences* 11:437–483.

Salemme, Mónica, and Fernando Santiago
2017   Qué Sabemos y Qué No Sabemos de la Presencia Humana Durante el Holoceno Medio en la Estepa Fueguina. In *Patrimonio a Orillas Del Mar: Arqueología Del Litoral Atlántico de Tierra Del Fuego*, edited by Martín Vazquez, Dolores Elkin, and Jimena Oría, pp. 75–86. Editora Cultural Tierra del Fuego.

Salgán, Laura, Raven Garvey, Gustavo Neme, et al.
2015   Las Cargas: Characterization of a Southern Andean Obsidian Source and its Prehistoric Use. *Geoarchaeology* 30:139–150.

Sandweiss, Daniel H.
1998   Quebrada Jaguay: Early South American Maritime Adaptations. *Science* 281:1830–32.

Sandweiss, Daniel H., Kirk Maasch, and David G. Anderson
1999   Transition in the Mid-Holocene. *Science* 283:499–500.

Sandweiss, Daniel H., and Jeffrey Quilter
2012   Collation, Correlation, and Causation in the Prehistory of Coastal Peru. In *Surviving Sudden Environmental Change: Answers from Archaeology,* edited by Jago Cooper and Payson Sheets, pp. 117–141. University Press of Colorado, Boulder.

Santiago, Fernando, and Mónica Salemme
2016   Guanaco Hunting Strategies in the Northern Plains of Tierra del Fuego, Argentina. *Journal of Anthropological Archaeology* 43:110–127.

Sarno, Ronald, David Jennings, and William Franklin
2015   Estimating Effective Population Size of Guanacos in Patagonia: An Integrative Approach for Wildlife Conservation. *Conservation Genetics* 16:1167–1180.

Saxon, E. C.
1976   La Prehistoria de Fuego-Patagonia: Colonización de un Hábitat Marginal. *Anales del Instituto de La Patagonia* 7:63–73.

Scheinsohn, Vivian, Claudia Szumik, Sabrina Leonardt, and Florencia Rizzo
2009   Distribución Espacial del Arte Rupestre en el Bosque y la Estepa del Norte de Patagonia: Nuevos Resultados. In *Arqueología de Patagonia: Una Mirada Desde el Último Confín*, edited by Mónica Salemme, Fernando Santiago, Myrian Álvarez, Ernesto Piana, Martín Vázquez, María Estela Mansur, pp. 541–58. Editorial Utopías, Ushuaia, Argentina.

Schmidt-Neilsen, Knut
1964   *Desert Animals: Physiological Problems of Heat and Water*. Clarendon, Oxford.

Schroeder, Kari, Mattias Jakobsson, Michael Crawford, et al.

2009 Haplotypic Background of a Private Allele at High Frequency in the Americas. *Molecular Biology and Evolution* 26:995–1016.

Schwarcz, Henry

2006 Stable Carbon Isotope Analysis and Human Diet: A Synthesis. In *Histories of Maize Multidisciplinary: Approaches to the Prehistory, Biogeography, Domestication, and Evolution of Maize*, edited by John Staller, Robert Tykot, and Bruce Benz, pp. 315–321. Academic Press, New York.

Seelenfreund, Andrea, Charles Rees, Roger Bird, et al.

1996 Trace Element Analysis of Obsidian Sources and Artifacts of Central Chile (Maule River Basin) and Western Argentina (Colorado River). *Latin American Antiquity* 7:7–20.

Semper, Juan, and Humberto Lagiglia

1962–1968 Excavaciones Arqueológicas en el Rincón del Atuel (Gruta del Indio). *Revista Científica de Investigación, Mendoza* 1:89–158.

Shennan, Stephen

2001 Demography and Cultural Innovation: A Model and its Implications for the Emergence of Modern Human Culture. *Cambridge Archaeological Journal* 11. https://doi.org/10.1017/S0959774301000014.

2013 Long-Term Trajectories of Technological Change. In *Cultural Evolution: Society, Technology, Language, and Religion*, edited by Peter J. Richerson and Morten Christiansen, pp. 143–155. MIT Press, Cambridge, Massachusetts.

2015 Demography and Cultural Evolution. In *Emerging Trends in the Social and Behavioral Sciences: An Interdisciplinary, Searchable, and Linkable Resource*, edited by Robert Scott and Marlis Buchmann Kosslyn. John Wiley & Sons. DOI: 10.1002/9781118900772.etrds0073.

Sherratt, Andrew

1997 Climatic Cycles and Behavioural Revolutions: The Emergence of Modern Humans and the Beginning of Farming. *Antiquity* 71:271–287.

Shott, Michael

1986 Technological Organization and Settlement Mobility: An Ethnographic Examination. *Journal of Anthropological Research* 42:15–51.

Silberbaur, George

1981 *Hunter and Habitat in the Central Kalahari Desert*. Cambridge University Press, New York.

Silva, Nelson, and Cristian Vargas

2014 Hypoxia in Chilean Patagonian Fjords. *Progress in Oceanography* 129:62–74.

Silva Dias, Pedro, Bruno Turcq, M. Assunção, et al.

2009 Mid-Holocene Climate of Tropical South America: A Model-Data Approach. In *Past Climate Variability in South America and Surrounding Regions*, edited by Françoise Vimeux, Florence Sylvestre, and Myriam Khodri, pp. 259–281. Springer Netherlands, Dordrecht.

Simpson, George G.

1944 *Tempo and Mode in Evolution*. Columbia University Press, New York.

1964 *This View of Life: The World of an Evolutionist*. Harcourt, Brace and World, New York.

Smith, Eric A.

1983 Anthropological Applications of Optimal Foraging Theory: A Critical Review. *Current Anthropology* 24:625–651.

1988 Risk and Uncertainty in the "Original Affluent Society": Evolutionary Ecology of Resource Sharing and Land Tenure. In *Hunter-Gatherers 1. History Evolution, and Social Change*, edited by Tim Ingold, David Riches, and James Woodburn, pp. 222–252. Berg, Oxford.

Smith, Huron H.

1933 Ethnobotany of the Forest Potawatomi Indians. *Bulletin of the Public Museum of the City of Milwaukee* 7:42.

Smith, Oliver

2017 Mapped: The World's Tallest (and Shortest) Countries. *The Daily Telegraph*, London. https://www.telegraph.co.uk/travel/maps-and-graphics/the-tallest-and-shortest-countries-in-the-world/.

Snodgrass, Josh, William Leonard, Mark Sorensen, et al.

2008 The Influence of Basal Metabolic Rate on Blood Pressure Among Indigenous Siberians. *American Journal of Physical Anthropology* 137:145–155.

Soltis, Joseph, Robert Boyd, and Peter J. Richerson

1995 Can Group-Functional Behaviors Evolve by Cultural Group Selection? An Empirical Test. *Current Anthropology* 63:473–494.

Soto, J., and M. Vázquez
2000   Las Condiciones Climáticas de la Provincia de Santa Cruz. In *El Gran Libro De La Provincia De Santa Cruz*, edited by Godoy Manríquez. Milenio Ediciones e ALFA.

Soulé, Michael
1973   The Epistasis Cycle: A Theory f Marginal Populations. *Annual Review of Ecology and Systematics* 4:165–187.

Sowell, John
2001   *Desert Ecology: An Introduction to Live in the Arid Southwest*. University of Utah Press, Salt Lake City.

Spencer, Herbert
1864   *The Principles of Biology*. Williams and Norgate, Edinburgh.

Sperber, Dan, and Nicolas Claidière
2008   Defining and Explaining Culture (Comments on Richerson and Boyd, *Not by Genes Alone*). *Biology and Philosophy* 23:283–92.

Speth, John, and Katherine Spielmann
1983   Energy Source, Protein Metabolism, and Huner-Gahterer Subsistence Strategies. *Journal of Anthropological Archaeology* 2:1–31.

Spier, Leslie
1955   Mohave Culture Items. *Flagstaff Museum of Northern Arizona Bulletin* 28.

Stanford, Dennis J.
1983   Pre-Clovis Occupation South of the Ice Sheets. In *Early Man in the New World*, edited by Richard Shutler, pp. 65–72. Sage Publications, Beverly Hills.

Steager, Peter
1963   Yahgan and Alacaluf: An Ecological Description. *Kroeber Anthropological Society Papers* 32:69–76.

Steele, James
2010   Radiocarbon Dates as Data: Quantitative Strategies for Estimating Colonization Front Speeds and Event Densities. *Journal of Archaeological Science* 37:2017–2030.

Stern, Charles
2004   Obsidian Source and Distribution in Southernmost Patagonia: Review of the Current Information. In *Contra Viento y Marea: Arqueología de Patagonia*, edited by M. Teresa Civalero, Pablo Marcelo Fernández, and Ana Gabriela Guráieb, pp. 167–178. INAPL-SAA, Buenos Aires, Argentina.

2018   Obsidian Sources and Distribution in Patagonia, Southernmost South America. *Quaternary International* 468: 190–205.

Stevenson, Christopher M., Thegn Ladefoged, and Steven Novak
2013   Prehistoric Settlement Chronology on Rapa Nui, Chile: Obsidian Hydration Dating Using Infrared Photoacoustic Spectroscopy. *Journal of Archaeological Science* 40:3021–3030.

Stevenson, Christopher M., and Steven Novak
2011   Obsidian Hydration Dating by Infrared Spectroscopy: Method and Calibration. *Journal of Archaeological Science* 38:1716–1726.

Stevenson, Christopher M., Alexander Rogers, and Michael Glascock
2019   Variability in Obsidian Structural Water Content and Its Importance in the Hydration Dating of Cultural Artifacts. *Journal of Archaeological Science: Reports* 23:231–242.

Steward, Julian
1933   Ethnography of the Owens Valley Paiute. In *Publications in American Archaeology and Ethnology 33*, pp. 233–350. University of California Press, Berkeley.

1936   The Economic and Social Basis of Primitive Bands. In *Essays in Anthropology Presented to Alfred L. Kroeber*, edited by Robert Lowie, pp. 331–350. University of California Press, Berkeley.

1955   *Theory of Culture Change: The Methodology of Multilinear Evolution*. University of Illinois Press, Urbana.

Stewart, Norman, William Denevan, and M. Tulio Velásquez
2020   "Andes Mountains." *Encyclopedia Britannica*, https://www.britannica.com/place/Andes-Mountains.

Stine, Scott, and Mary Stine
1990   A Record from Lake Cardiel of Climate Change in Southern South America. *Nature* 345:705–708.

Stingl, H., and Karsten Garleff
1978   Gletscherschwankungen in den subtropisch-semiariden Hochanden Argentiniens. *Zeitschrift für geomorphologie N.F.*, Supplement 30:115–131.

1985   Glacier Variations and Climate of the Late Quaternary in the Subtropical and Mid-Latitude Andes of Argentina. *Zeitschrift für Gletscherkunde und Glazialgeologie* 21:225–228.

Stoessel, Luicana
2012   Evaluating Intensity in the Processing of
        Guanaco: Fragmentation Levels and Frac-
        ture Patterns Analysis. *International Journal
        of Osteoarchaeology* 24:51–67.
Strang, Sabrina, Christina Hoeber, Olaf Uhl, et al.
2017   Impact of Nutrition on Social Decision
        Making. *Proceedings of the National Acade-
        my of Sciences* 114:6510–6514.
Strong, William D.
1929   *Aboriginal Society in Southern California.*
        University of California Publications in
        American Archaeology and Ethnology.
        University of California Press, Berkeley.
Stuart, James
2009   "Eating Piñones." Eating Chilean. https://
        eatingchile.blogspot.com/2009/03/eating
        -pinones.html.
Stuiver, Minze, Paula J. Reimer, and R. W. Reimer
2020   CALIB 7.1 [WWW program] at http://calib
        .org, accessed 2020-2-6.
Surovell, Todd, Judson Byrd Finley, Geoffrey Smith,
et al.
2009   Correcting Temporal frequency Distribu-
        tions for Taphonomic Bias. *Journal of Ar-
        chaeological Science* 36:1715–1724.
Tallavaara, Miikka, Jussi Eronen, and Miska Luoto
2018   Productivity, Biodiversity, and Pathogens
        Influence the Global Hunter-Gatherer Pop-
        ulation Density. *Proceedings of the National
        Academy of Sciences* 115:1232–1237.
Tecklin, David, Dominick DellaSala, Federico Lueb-
bert, and Patricio Pliscoff
2011   Valdivian Temperate Rainforests of Chile
        and Argentina. In *Temperate and Boreal For-
        ests of the World*, edited by Dominick Della-
        Sala, pp. 132–153. Island, Washington, DC.
Thompson, L. G., Mary Davis, Ellen Mosley-
Thompson, et al.
1998   A 25,000-Year Tropical Climate His-
        tory from Bolivian Ice Cores. *Science*
        282:1858–1864.
Timpson, Adrian, Sue Colledge, Enrico Crema, et al.
2014   Reconstructing Regional Population Fluc-
        tuations in the European Neolithic Using
        Radiocarbon Dates: A New Case-Study
        Using an Improved Method. *Journal of Ar-
        chaeological Science* 52:459–557.
Tonni, Eduardo, Alberto Cione, and Aníbal Figini
1999   Predominance of Arid Climates Indicated
        by the Mammals in the Pampas of Ar-
        gentina During the Late Pleistocene and

Holocene. *Palaeogeography, Palaeoclimatol-
        ogy, Palaeoecology* 147:257–281.
Torrence, Robin
1983   Time Budgeting and Hunter-Gatherer
        Technology. In *Hunter-Gatherer Economy
        and Stone Tools*, edited by Robin Torrence,
        pp. 57–66. Cambridge University Press,
        Cambridge.
1989   Retooling: Towards a Behavioral Theory
        of Stone Tools. In *Time, Energy and Stone
        Tools*, edited by Robin Torrence, pp. 57–66.
        Cambridge University Press, Cambridge.
Tuhkanen, Sakari
1992   The Climate of Tierra del Fuego from a
        Vegetation Geographical Point of View and
        its Ecoclimatic Counterparts Elsewhere.
        Acta Botanica Fennica 145:1–64.
Turner, Lucien
2008   *An Aleutian Ethnography.* University of
        Alaska Press, Fairbanks.
Ugan, Andrew, Jason Bright, and Alan Rogers
2003   When Is Technology Worth the Trouble?
        Journal of Archaeological Science
        30:1315–1329.
UNESCO
2019   Cueva de las Manos, Río Pinturas.
        UNESCO World Heritage List, retrieved
        13 March 2019. http://whc.unesco.org/en
        /list/936.
Unkel, Ingmar, Svante Björck, and Barbara
Wohlfarth
2008   Deglacial Environmental Changes on Isla
        de los Estados (54.4°S), Southeastern Tier-
        ra del Fuego. *Quaternary Science Reviews*
        27:1541–1554.
Utrilla, Víctor R., Miguel A. Brizuela, and Andres F.
Cibils
2005   Riparian Habitats (Mallines) of Patagonia:
        A Key Grazing Resource for Sustainable
        Sheep-Farming Operations. *Outlook on
        Agriculture* 34:55–59.
2006   Structural and Nutritional Heterogeneity
        of Riparian Vegetation in Patagonia (Ar-
        gentina) in Relation to Seasonal Grazing
        by Sheep. *Journal of Arid Environments*
        67:661–670.
Valero-Garcés, Blas, Bettina Jenny, Mauricio Ron-
danelli, et al.
2005   Palaeohydrology of Laguna de Tagua Tagua
        (34°30'S) and Moisture Fluctuations in
        Central Chile for the Last 46,000 yr. *Jour-
        nal of Quaternary Science* 20:625–641.

Van Gijn, Annelou L.
2014   Science and Interpretation in Microwear
        Studies. *Journal of Archaeological Science*
        48:166–169.

Veit, Heinz
1996   Southern Westerlies During the Holocene
        Deduced from Geomorphological and
        Pedological Studies in the Norte Chico,
        Northern Chile(27–33ºS). *Palaeogeog-
        raphy, Palaeoclimatology, Palaeoecology*
        123:107–119.

Vich, Alberto, Patricia López, and Maria
Schumacher
2007   Trend Detection in the Water Regime of the
        Main Rivers of the Province of Mendoza,
        Argentina. *GeoJournal* 70:233–243.

Vilas, Federico, Alfredo Arche, Marcelo Ferrero,
and Federico Isla
1999   Subantarctic Macrotidal Flats, Cheniers
        and Beaches in San Sebastian Bay, Tierra
        Del Fuego, Argentina. *Marine Geology*
        160:301–326.

Villagrán, Carolina
1993   Una Interpretación Climática del Registro
        Palinológico del Ultimo Ciclo Glacial-
        Postglacial en Sudamérica. *Bulletin de l'Ins-
        titut Francais d'études Andines* 22:243–258.

Villagrán, Carolina, and Luis Filipe Hinojosa
1997   Historia de los Bosques del Sur de Sudamé-
        rica II: Análisis Biogeográfico. *Revista Chile-
        na de Historia Natural* 70:241–267.

Villa-Martínez, Rodrigo, and Carolina Villagrán
1997   Historia Vegetacional de Bosques Pantano-
        sos de la Costa de Chile Central Durante el
        Holoceno Medio y Tardío. *Revista Chilena
        de Historia Natural* 70:391–401.

Violante, Roberto, Ana María Osella, M. de la Vega,
et al.
2010   Paleoenvironmental Reconstruction in the
        Western Lacustrine Plain of Llancanelo
        Lake, Mendoza, Argentina. *Journal of South
        American Earth Sciences* 29:650–664.

Volkheimer, Wolfgang
1978   *Descripción Geológica de la Hoja 27b, Cerro
        Sosneado, Provincia de Mendoza.* Servicio
        Geológico Nacional, Buenos Aires.

Voorhies, Barbara, and Sarah Metcalfe
2007   Culture and Climate in Mesoamerica
        during the Middle Holocene. In *Climate
        Change and Cultural Dynamics: A Global
        Perspective on Mid-Holocene Transitions*,
        edited by David Anderson, Kirk Maasch,

and Daniel Sandweiss, pp. 157–187. Elsevier,
        Boston.

Wadley, Lyn
1986   Segments of Time: A Mid-Holocene Wilton
        Site in the Transvaal. *South African Archae-
        ological Bulletin* 41:54–62.

2000   The Wilton and Pre-Ceramic Post-Classic
        Wilton Industries at Rose Cottage Cave
        and Their Context in the South African
        Sequence. *South African Archaeological
        Bulletin* 55:90–106.

Wäger, P.
2009   Glaciar-Climate Modeling in Las Leñas, Cen-
        tral Andes of Argentina. Master's thesis, De-
        partment of Geography, University of Bern.

Waldmann, Nicolas, Daniel Ariztegui, Flavio Anselmetti, et al.
2010   Holocene Climatic Fluctuations and Posi-
        tioning of the Southern Hemisphere West-
        erlies in Tierra del Fuego (54° S), Patagonia.
        Journal of Quaternary Science 25:1063–1075.

Ward, Michael, James Milledge, and John West
1989   *High Altitude Medicine and Physiology.*
        Chapman and Hall Medical, London.

Waters, Michael R., and Thomas W. Stafford
2007   Redefining the Age of Clovis: Implications
        for the Peopling of the Americas. *Science*
        315:1122–1126.

Waters, Michael R., Thomas W. Stafford, H. Gregory
McDonald, et al.
2011   Pre-Clovis Mastodon Hunting 13,800 Years
        Ago at the Manis Site, Washington. *Science*
        334:351–353.

Weiten, Wayne
2008   *Psychology: Themes and Variations.* Cen-
        gage Learning.

West, Frederick H.
1996   Beringia and New World Origins. In *Amer-
        ican Beginnings: The Prehistory and Palaeo-
        ecology of Beringia*, edited by Frederick H.
        West, pp. 537–559. University of Chicago
        Press, Chicago.

Wheat, Amber
2012   Survey of Professional Opinions Regarding
        the Peopling of America. *SAA Archaeologi-
        cal Record* 12:10–14.

Whitley, David S., and Ronald I. Dorn
1993   New Perspectives on the Clovis vs. Pre-Clovis
        Controversy. *American Antiquity* 54:626–647.

Wiessner, Polly
1982   Risk, Reciprocity and Social Influences
        on !Kung San Economics. In *Politics and*

History in Band Societies, edited by Eleanor Leacock and Richard Lee, pp. 61–84. Cambridge University Press, Cambridge, UK.

Wilder, Edna
1976   *Secrets of Eskimo Skin Sewing*. University of Alaska Press, Fairbanks.

Willey, Gordon R., and Jeremy A. Sabloff
1993   *A History of American Archaeology*, 3rd edition. W. H. Freeman and Company, New York.

Wilmsen, Edwin M.
1965   An Outline of Early Man Studies in the United States. *American Antiquity* 31:172–192.

Winterhalder, Bruce P.
1977   Foraging Strategy Adaptations of the Boreal Forest Cree: An Evaluation of Theory and Models from Evolutionary Ecology. PhD dissertation, Department of Anthropology, Cornell University.
1981   Optimal Foraging Strategies and Hunter-Gatherer Research in Anthropology. In *Hunter-Gatherer Foraging Strategies: Ethnographic and Archaeological Analyses*, edited by Bruce Winterhalder and Eric A. Smith, pp. 13–35. University of Chicago Press, Chicago.
1986a   Diet Choice, Risk, and Food Sharing in a Stochastic Environment. *Journal of Anthropological Archaeology* 5:369–392.
1986b   Optimal Foraging: Simulation Studies of Diet Choice in a Stochastic Environment. *Journal of Ethnobiology* 6:205–223.
1990   Open Field, Common Pot: Harvest Variability and Risk Avoidance in Agriculture and Foraging Societies. In *Risk and Uncertainty in Tribal and Peasant Economies*, edited by Elizabeth Cashdan, pp. 67–87. Westview Press, Boulder, Colorado.
1997   Gifts Given, Gifts Taken: The Behavioral Ecology of Nonmarket, Intragroup Exchange. *Journal of Archaeological Research* 5:121–168.
2018   Archaeological and Ethnographic Applications of the Ideal Free and Ideal Despotic Distributions, or, the Anthropological Career of an HBE Model. Abstract, 12th Annual California Workshop on Evolutionary Social Science, University of California at Santa Barbara (4 May 2018).

Winterhalder, Bruce P., William Baillargeon, Frencesca Cappelletto, et al.
1988   The Population Ecology of Hunter-Gatherers and their Prey. *Journal of Anthropological Archaeology* 7:289–328.

Winterhalder, Bruce P., and Robert L. Bettinger
2010   Nutritional and Social Benefits of Foraging in California. *California Archaeology* 2:93–110.

Winterhalder, Bruce P., and Douglas Kennett
2006   Behavioral Ecology and the Transition from Hunting and Gathering to Agriculture. In *Behavioral Ecology and the Transition to Agriculture*, edited by Douglas Kennett and Bruce P. Winterhalder, pp. 1–21. University of California Press, Berkeley.
2020   Seven Behavioral Ecology Reasons for Persistence of Foragers with Cultivars. In *Cowboy Ecologist: Essays in Honor of Robert L. Bettinger*, edited by Michael Delacorte and Terry Jones, pp. 91–108. CARD (Center for Archaeological Research at Davis) Publication 19, Davis, California.

Winterhalder, Bruce P., Douglas Kennett, Mark Grote, and Jacob Bartruff
2010   Ideal Free Settlement of California's Northern Channel Islands. *Journal of Anthropological Archaeology* 29:469–490.

Winterhalder, Bruce P., Cedric Puleston, and Cody Ross
2015   Production Risk, Inter-Annual Food Storage by Households and Population-Level Consequences in Seasonal Prehistoric Agrarian Societies. *Environmental Archaeology* 20:337–348.

Wobst, H. Martin
1978   The Archaeo-Ethnology of Hunter-Gatherers or the Tyranny of the Ethnographic Record in Archaeology. *American Antiquity* 43:303–309.

Wohlgemuth, Eric
1996   Resource Intensification in Prehistoric Central California: Evidence from Archaeobotanical Data. *Journal of California and Great Basin Anthropology* 18:81–103.

Wolodarsky-Franke, Alexia, and Antonio Lara
2005   The Role of "Forensic" Dendrochronology in the Conservation of *Alerce* (*Fitzroya cupressoides* (Molina) Johnston) Forests in Chile. *Dendrochronologia* 22:235–240.

Wood, James W., George Milner, Henry Harpending, and Kenneth Weiss
1992   Osteological Paradox: Problems of Inferring Prehistoric Health from Skeletal Samples. *Current Anthropology* 33:343–370.

World Bird Database
2018   *Avibase.* http://avibase.bsc-eoc.org/checklist .jsp?region=arpg&list=howardmoore.

Wright, Sewall
1931   Evolution in Mendelian Populations. *Genetics* 16:97–159.

Yacobaccio, Hugo
1998   The Evolution of South Andean Hunter-Gatherers. *Proceedings of the XIII Meeting of the International Union of Prehistoric and Protohistoric Sciences* 5:389–394.

Yacobaccio, Hugo, and Marcelo Morales
2005   Mid-Holocene Environment and Human Occupatio of the Puna (Susques, Argentina). *Quaternary International* 132:5–14.

Yannielli, Joseph
2013   A Yahgan for the Killing: Murder, Memory and Charles Darwin. *The British Journal for the History of Science* 46:415–443.

Yesner, David
2004   Prehistoric Maritime Adaptations of the Subarctic and Subantarctic Zones: The Aleutian/Fuegian Connection Considered. *Arctic Anthropology* 41:76–97.

Yesner, David, Maria Jose Figuerero Torres, Ricardo Guichon, and Luis Borrero
2003   Stable Isotope Analysis of Human Bone and Ethnohisotric Subsistence Patterns in Tierra del Fuego. *Journal of Anthropological Archaeology* 22:279–291.

Yi, Mingjie, Loukas Barton, Christopher Morgan, et al.
2013   Microblade Technology and the Rise of Serial Specialists in North-Central China. *Journal of Anthropological Archaeology* 32:212–223.

Young, David, and Robert L. Bettinger
1992   The Numic Spread: A Computer Simulation. *American Antiquity* 57:85–99.

1995   Simulating the Global Human Population Expansion in the Late Pleistocene. *Journal of Archaeological Science* 22:89–92.

Young, Julie, and William Franklin
2004   Territorial Fidelity of Male Guanacos in the Patagonia of Southern Chile. *Journal of Mammalogy* 85:72–78.

Young, Steven
1972   Subantarctic Rain Forest of Magellanic Chile: Distribution, Composition, and Age and Growth Rate Studies of Common Forest Trees. *Antarctic Research Series* 20:307–322.

Zahid, H. Jabran, Erick Robinson, and Robert L. Kelly
2016   Agriculture, Population Growth, and Statistical Analysis of the Radiocarbon Record. *Proceedings of the National Academy of Sciences* 113:931–935.

Zárate, Marcelo, Gustavo Neme, and Adolfo Gil
2005   Mid-Holocene Paleoenvironments and Human Occupation in Southern South America. *Quaternary International* 132:1–3.

Zárate, Marcelo, and M. Paez
2002   Los Paleoambientes del Pleistoceno-Holoceno en la Cuenca del Arroyo La Estacada, Mendoza. In *30 Años de Investigación Básica y Aplicada en Ciencias Ambientales*, edited by Dario Trombotto and Ricardo Villalba, pp. 117–121. Instituto Argentino de Nivologia, Glaciologia y Ciencias Ambientales, Mendoza, Argentina.

Zeanah, David
2004   Sexual Division of Labor and Central Place Foraging: A Model for the Carson Desert of Western Nevada. *Journal of Anthropological Archaeology* 23:1–32.

Zeder, Melinda A.
2015   Core Questions in Domestication Research. *Proceedings of the National Academy of Sciences* 112:3191–3198.

Zhang, Jin-Tunn, and Cuihong Wang
2012   Biodiversity and Ecosystem Functioning: Exploring Large-Scale Patterns in Mainland China. *iForest* 5:230–234.

Index

Note: Arabic-numeral page numbers in *italics* refer to images or tables.